Hosea Williams

HOSEA Williams

A LIFETIME OF DEFIANCE AND PROTEST

Rolundus R. Rice

FOREWORD BY ANDREW YOUNG

THE UNIVERSITY OF SOUTH CAROLINA PRESS

Published by the University of South Carolina Press
Columbia, South Carolina 29208

www.uscpress.com

Manufactured in the United States of America

30 29 28 27 26 25 24 23 22 21
10 9 8 7 6 5 4 3 2 1

Library of Congress Cataloging-in-Publication Data
can be found at http://catalog.loc.gov/.

ISBN: 978-1-64336-256-4 (hardcover)
ISBN: 978-1-64336-257-1 (paperback)
ISBN: 978-1-64336-258-8 (ebook)

CONTENTS

ILLUSTRATIONS

FOREWORD

Hosea Williams and I had a love–hate relationship: I loved him, and he hated me.

That's a joke. I hope it is, at least. I don't believe Hosea actually hated me, but the two of us were at odds throughout the civil rights movement, and we often clashed—which is exactly as Martin Luther King Jr. wanted things to be. The roles he assigned to each of his top advisors suited our personalities and skills, but they guaranteed conflict among the upper ranks of the Southern Christian Leadership Conference (SCLC).

Hosea was militant, confrontational, and impatient, whereas I was calm, careful, and deliberate. He was an advocate of aggressive, often reckless "direct action," whereas I urged caution. Dr. King not only *wanted* me to be the voice of reason but he also *insisted* on it. Our leader, who was respected and loved by every one of us, wanted to be able to mediate our disputes and come down somewhere in the middle. It was only in this manner that Hosea's great passion for justice could be moderated, and everyone could be kept as safe as possible under whatever circumstances we faced.

Hosea at times seemed to have a death wish, but Martin most definitely did not—and he was the man with a target on his back.

Dr. King recognized a mad genius when he saw one, and he was wise enough to know we *needed* one. Or more than one. As it happened, the SCLC had a few. Hosea Williams was crazy like a fox, but James Bevel, another brilliant strategist, was probably clinically insane. Yet, he also had a role to play. That was the power of Dr. King and the nonviolent social movement that changed America in the 1960s—an unlikely team of misfits who came together under the direction of one of the greatest leaders of the twentieth century. Without Hosea Williams, some of the most important moments of the civil rights movement would never have happened. Without me, he'd have gotten us all killed many times over.

We were both on the front lines, but I was under orders *not* to get arrested or harmed, which caused me no small amount of embarrassment at the time. Dr. King wanted me to be the one to post bail for everyone else and work behind the scenes with white business leaders and elected officials to broker peaceful solutions. Hosea and some of the others frequently derided me as "pulling up the rear."

But I did get beaten once—savagely—and for that, I was always grateful. It made me "one of the guys." And guess who I had to thank for the experience?

▪ ▪ ▪ ▪

On June 9, 1964, Dr. King sent me to shut down a grassroots movement in St. Augustine, Florida, because he feared it could endanger passage of the Civil Rights Act, which was being filibustered in the US Senate. Hosea had gotten caught up with the locals, knew their cause to be righteous, and cared more about them than what happened in Washington, DC. As soon as I walked into the church where he had gathered demonstrators for a dangerous, nighttime march, he saw me from the pulpit and announced my arrival. "Ladies and gentlemen, here's the Rev. Andrew Young!" he shouted. "Martin Luther King Jr. has sent Rev. Young here tonight to lead this march!"

The reaction was so overwhelming, the enthusiasm was so great, I simply couldn't say no. I reasoned that if I led marchers to the edge of the downtown plaza, where they were able to see the angry mob that included hundreds of robed Klansmen, I could convince them to turn back.

But when we got there, nobody wanted to turn back.

Lives were at stake, and the Civil Rights Act hung in the balance, so I asked the marchers to wait where they were and let me cross the street and speak with a police officer. I was going to ask if we could walk as far as the old slave market, pray, and return immediately to the church.

I never got the chance.

Someone blindsided me—and that's all I remember. It would be decades before I ever saw film footage from news cameras and realized how severely I was kicked around the intersection of King Street and St. George Street. It's quite a sight. When everyone finally was out of harm's way, I slipped behind the church and wept, not in pain but with relief that no one else was hurt that night. I wasn't badly injured, but the responsibility for all those lives was as much stress as I could bear.

Hosea didn't realize what had happened until much later that night. Hotels and motels did not admit Blacks, and the brave folks who opened their small houses to the SCLC during the movement usually had only one bedroom, and only one bed, which they surrendered to as many of us as needed a place to sleep. At the time, nothing about it was funny, but imagine the comedic possibilities of a scene with two people so opposite, having to share the same bed at that particular moment. Hosea and I were the original "Odd Couple."

I still cussed him out.

I have no doubt Hosea felt bad, and I believe he worried that I carried a grudge, though that wasn't the case.

The following year, Hosea accused me of getting back at him in a big way.

He had organized a march in Selma, Alabama, to protest for the right to vote—but there was a great deal of confusion over the date it was supposed to take place. On March 7, 1965, both Martin Luther King and Ralph David Abernathy were committed to preach sermons in Atlanta, and they wanted to postpone the demonstration for a week. Hosea was adamant that it should proceed because so many people had turned out and were ready to march. After considerable discussion, Dr. King relented—but he told me not to risk getting into any trouble myself. We expected the participants to get arrested, and Dr. King said he wanted me free to do my job. But this was an SCLC march, and we needed a representative up front.

So, it came down to a coin toss—among me, Hosea, and James Bevel.

Hosea won—or lost, depending on how one looked at it. He would lead the march beside well-known student leader John Lewis, who was not an SCLC member but had shown up wearing a backpack, ready to go to jail. No one anticipated the violence that ensued that day on the Edmund Pettus Bridge.

I was at the rear of the line when people started running and stumbling back across the bridge, pursued by troopers on horseback as billows of tear gas filled the sky. It was a melee that changed the course of history and led directly to passage of the Voting Rights Act of 1965.

Many were seriously injured at the hands of Alabama troopers, and a few were singled out to be killed. John Lewis was beaten without mercy and left unconscious. Hosea was targeted, too, yet miraculously escaped. He avoided the troopers' batons and, uninjured, slipped out of the crowd and disappeared. For hours, none of us knew what had happened to him or where he was. It turned out he was able to take refuge in a nearby house and hide out until it was safe to resurface.

For days, Hosea accused me of rigging the coin toss to put him at the front of the line. He thought I was exacting revenge for the beating I took in St. Augustine, though nothing could have been farther from the truth, and no one could have foreseen or engineered the circumstances that made him the leader of our march on what came to be called "Bloody Sunday."

Then, the new edition of *Life* magazine hit the stands, with a color photograph on the cover of the Selma marchers—and Hosea Williams and John Lewis out in front.

Hosea could not have been happier. All was forgiven, at least for awhile.

■ ■ ■ ■

This personal sketch, written with affection and admiration, is just a thumbnail of the man I knew and the relationship we had. Hosea Williams was a brilliant, complex, flawed leader, and history owes him a great deal. Credit for his courage and heroism—not just during the movement but also from the cradle to the grave—is long overdue, and I am exceedingly grateful to Rolundus Rice for his determined work on this impressive book. A definitive biography of Hosea Williams is no small undertaking. Perhaps that is why there hasn't been one before now.

Most of us in the leadership of the SCLC had led relatively privileged lives for Blacks. None had endured as hardscrabble a life as Hosea. Born to blind parents in tiny Attapulgus, Georgia, he managed to overcome a violent childhood filled with deprivation, inadequate schooling, the rigors of working as a farmhand, and pursuit by a lynch mob bent on killing him for sharing a sandwich with a white girl. One of the few Black soldiers to see active combat in World War II—(he told me he joined the service so he could kill white people legally)—he was the sole survivor of a mortar attack that took out over a dozen other infantrymen in a foxhole. For months, he laid in a British hospital, wondering why he had been spared. Upon being discharged, he made his way back to South Georgia only to suffer another near-death experience. At a bus station in Americus, a gang of white hoodlums beat him senseless, and he spent more long months in a hospital. But after that, Hosea knew why he had been spared.

I happened to meet Rolundus Rice and his wife Dana in 2014 at an event at the King Center for Nonviolent Social Change, where he was working at the time. When he mentioned he was completing a doctoral dissertation on the life of Hosea Williams, I lauded the accomplishment—and encouraged him to consider expanding his research into a book. I even believe the story could be made into a movie because it reads like an action movie with a larger-than-life hero.

With the determination of an old-school detective and the objectivity of a scholar, Dr. Rice located and searched through obscure records and other source material to dig out clues to the identity and life story of Hosea Williams, and he looked far and wide to capture the nuance of a controversial, sometimes contradictory, central "character," who happened to have been my friend. As a result, the author delivers to his readers a rich analysis of who Williams was, the experiences and events that shaped him, and the forces that drove him to the lynchpin position of field general in a nonviolent war that shaped the second half of the twentieth century.

In this remarkable story, we embark on a tour of the last century with an expert guide. Through eight decades of one man's remarkable life, William's experiences are presented in the context of their times: the simultaneous struggles confronted by the American Black community. The story of Hosea Williams is Black History and American History. It is a lesson for the young and not so young—and a reminder that one's difficult life circumstances do not always deter him from destiny, but sometimes point him toward it.

Andrew Young
FORMER EXECUTIVE DIRECTOR, SCLC, AND
FORMER US AMBASSADOR TO THE UNITED NATIONS
ATLANTA 2021

ACKNOWLEDGMENTS

I have accumulated many debts during the writing of this book. Librarians and archivists at the Auburn Avenue Research Library on African American Culture; Emory University's Manuscript Archive and Rare Book Library; the Savannah State University Library and Special Collections; the Alabama Department of Archives and History; the King Library and Archives at the Martin Luther King Jr. Center, the Stanford University Libraries and Department of Special Collections, the Tulane University Special Collections and the Robert W. Woodruff Library of the Atlanta University Center were generous with sharing their time and expertise with me.

My family, chosen and kin, have sustained me. My wife, Dana, has sacrificed so much of herself to see me publish this book. She provided immeasurably helpful insight while proofreading many drafts of the manuscript. Her brilliance was always on full display throughout the writing of this book. Our four children, Madison (11), Marley (6), Rolundus II (2), and Remington (1), have also assisted me in ways that they will not understand until they are parents. Other family members, most notably my mother Felecia Clark, also merit mention. My mother drove me past Williams's house at 8 East Lake Drive in Southeast Atlanta each summer when I attended the Samuel L. Jones Boys Club as a child. She always pointed to Williams's house and said, "That's where ol' crazy Ho-say-uh lives." I was fascinated with his story ever since that time. Gloria Hill, my grandmother, has been my rock who kept me focused. I can still remember her wrapping pennies for me to buy gas for my 1979 Cadillac Fleetwood Brougham when I was an undergraduate student. I must also acknowledge my brother, Randall Rice, and aunt, Cherrica Swindle. My family through marriage has also made incalculable investments in me: William S. Lee I, Linda Lee, Neena Lee Weans, Andre Weans, William S. Lee II, and Sangima Lee have all played crucial roles in the six-year saga that culminated with the publication of this book.

I am also indebted to the professors, mentors, university administrators, friends, editors, and civil rights activists who encouraged me to complete this book: Dorothy Autrey, Willie Bolden, Tyrone Brooks, Doris D. Crenshaw, Marvin Crawford, Bertis English, George Flowers, Janice R. Franklin, Reagan Grimsley, C. B. Hackworth, Charles Israel, Adam Jortner, Bernice A. King, Mary Ann Lieser, Scott MacKenzie, Herman "Skip"

Mason Jr., Terrie Randolph, Clyde Robertson, Dawnelle Robinson, Howard O. Robinson II, Jack Thomas, Andrew Young, and Tara White. A special thanks is due to David Carter. Carter was my dissertation advisor during my doctoral studies at Auburn University. He believed in the project since our first conversation in his office in Thach Hall. These individuals freely tendered their thoughts to me. However, the interpretations expressed in this book are solely mine. Therefore, no one named should be held responsible for any opinions in this book.

The family of Hosea Williams was particularly helpful to me while I was writing this book. Family members invited me to attend exclusive special functions that allowed me to engage Williams's contemporaries. Williams's oldest daughter, Barbara Williams Emerson, went to great lengths in assisting me with securing documents and other materials necessary to explore and understand her father. Elisabeth Omilami, Williams's daughter who has assumed the responsibility of her late father's charity, Hosea Feed the Hungry and Homeless, was also instrumental.

Hosea Williams

Introduction

Around 9:00 AM on Sunday, March 7, 1965, the Southern Christian Leadership Conference (SCLC) president, Rev. Dr. Martin Luther King Jr., had a spirited conversation with his top advisors, including Ralph Abernathy, Andrew Young, Cordy Tindell "C. T." Vivian, Dorothy Cotton, Bayard Rustin, and his field lieutenant—Hosea Williams. King's brain trust, with the exception of Williams, had all supported King's decision to reschedule the fifty-four-mile march from Selma to Montgomery, Alabama, despite King's earlier agreement to participate in the march.

"No. Doc. I can't support you," said Williams. "We don't have the ability to stop the march. . . . They're gonna march without us."

"Call the march off today! Tell the people we're going to march tomorrow," said King. The SCLC president did not believe that Williams had adequately prepared to lead five hundred to seven hundred marchers on the fifty-four-mile trek to Montgomery. King estimated that Williams, the professional march planner and menace to segregationist southern city leaders, had not made provisions for food and lodging. The four cases of boiled eggs and twelve sleeping bags that he secured for the march were insufficient. King continued with a measured, diplomatic reason: Postponing the march until Monday "would give me a chance to help dad and march, too." King's father, the Rev. Martin Luther King Sr., was not feeling well enough to deliver the Men's Day Sunday morning sermon at Ebenezer Baptist Church in Atlanta, where his son had co-pastored since 1960. King's approach was not working; he had to develop a plan quickly to stop the march. Because Williams believed that there was no other alternative but to proceed to Montgomery, he was determined to pull from his arsenal of agitation every ingenious sophistry to proceed to Montgomery in defiance of King's explicit order.[1]

Martin Luther King Jr. deployed his chief diplomat, Andrew Young, to Alabama to meet with Williams and others to halt the march. Williams, the "bull in a china shop," often reached deep into what I refer to as his "arsenal of agitation" to wreak havoc in racist towns ahead of Young's peace offering with conditions. Young, who may have been eating breakfast with his family that morning, was directed to charter a plane from Atlanta to Montgomery shortly after the back-and-forth with King and SCLC staffers. Recalling the train of events of March 7, 1965, twenty years later, Young said, "It was also one of the things that not only did we not plan the way it happened, ah, we were trying to call it off right up to the last minute."

Young met Williams at the airport in Montgomery. "He got off the airplane and [was] acting crazy and everything," remembered Williams. Boisterously, Young claimed, "You know you weren't supposed to have this march. You have overstepped your boundaries! This is clear insubordination." Young drove to Selma with the objective of appealing to the march volunteers in or around Brown Chapel African Methodist Episcopal (AME) Church to march on the following day, Monday, March 8. He was not successful. "It was a bad meeting for Andy" said Stoney Cooks, an SCLC staffer who was not present in Selma on March 7.[2]

The march to Montgomery was not to be prevented. Despite his many strengths as one of King's most savvy lieutenants, Young was overwhelmed, in part, by Williams's obstinacy and, in other ways, his strategic leveraging of the marchers' pent-up passion that was on the verge of exploding after a series of rallies and speeches. The spirit in Selma, as well as the forces of fate, were too powerful for anyone, including Martin Luther King Jr., to quench. "I had people jumping all over the benches that morning," Williams bragged. Not yet an ordained minister, he preached to the people a fiery sermonette of liberation from the manacles of injustice that had for so long thwarted Black progress in Selma.[3]

The marchers' energy and tone changed as they left Brown Chapel lined up in twos in a double-column line. "No one said a word," recalled John Lewis. Lewis walked alongside Williams on the sidewalk as they marched across the bridge named for a Confederate general: Edmund Pettus. Marchers saw a gang of law enforcement officers wearing blue uniforms and gas masks and carrying guns and nightsticks by their sides. Some were on horseback. One unnamed male marcher, petrified with terror, abandoned the marchers and left his wife. "Hosea looked down at the Alabama River," said Lewis. "John, can you swim?" said Williams. Lewis responded with a barely audible "No."

The marchers continued walking, despite orders to disperse from Major John Cloud. Williams, the only marcher who spoke out loud to the police, responded with a question. "Major," Williams said, "may we have a word with you?" Within ninety seconds, an estimated one hundred troopers began moving closer to the unarmed marchers. The troopers proceeded to gas and beat Williams, Lewis, and other marchers. Pandemonium ensued. Additional law enforcement officers armed themselves with shotguns and chased marchers through the George Washington Carver low-income housing project and back to Brown Chapel. Ambulances soon arrived and transported the injured marchers to a Selma hospital that was operated by the Sisters of St. Joseph. Members of the blue posse began beating on the hoods of Blacks' automobiles and screeching at the drivers to leave. "Go on! We want all niggers off the streets!" shouted several troopers. Within thirty minutes, according to the *Selma Times Journal*, a "negro could not be seen walking the streets."[4]

"Bloody Sunday," the seminal event that gave President Lyndon B. Johnson the political capital to push a voting rights agenda through the 89th Congress, would not have occurred on March 7, 1965, if Williams had not defied Martin Luther King Jr. His insubordination was a serious organizational infraction. He rolled the proverbial dice on his career with the SCLC on the Edmund Pettus Bridge. The professional provocateur suspected that King would have fired him from the organization if the vicious attack on nonviolent marchers had not galvanized the nation. "They said they were going to get rid of me," Williams recalled. That his daring defiance, scrappiness, and unyielding self-serving quest for the spotlight were indivisible parts of his character were on full display for more than forty years as a bombastic civil rights activist helps to unravel the insoluble riddle that was Hosea Williams. There was not a civil rights campaign that better encapsulated these three traits than Bloody Sunday.[5]

Hosea Lorenzo Williams's life illuminates the entire landscape of the civil rights movement from a different vantage point, broadening the familiar geography and chronology of the Black freedom struggle even as it complicates our understanding of better chronicled events and civil rights campaigns. This book argues that, by any measure, Hosea Williams's activism was of central importance to the success of the movement, but for complicated reasons that might be boiled down to a question of historical "palatability," his role has for too long been eclipsed in historians' chronicles of the movement. Williams's role in pressuring municipal, state, and federal government officials to ensure that Blacks' social, political, and economic rights were fully guaranteed yielded notable victories in Savannah, St. Augustine, Selma, and elsewhere. His campaigns helped to create and maintain pressure on the White House, Congress, and the federal courts, and the resulting legislation and court rulings did more to topple the barriers of Jim Crow in a relatively brief period than anything in the century since emancipation and Reconstruction. Williams's grit and tactical genius, his motivational skills, and his ability to cultivate a reputation as one "unbossed and unbought" were critical to the success of the SCLC and the broader civil rights movement. He, too, is a founding father of the newer America. Understanding his activist trajectory enables us to view the long civil rights movement through the biographical prism of a subaltern who moved from the obscure periphery to the vital center of the most successful nonviolent revolution in human history.

Perhaps Williams was ignored because he was the defiant, rabble-rousing troublemaker who refused to replace the bullhorn with a lapel mic, despite his position as an elected member of the Georgia House of Representatives. Once when he was in an office on the fourth floor of the Georgia State Capitol, he noticed that marchers were protesting for a matter of which he was not aware. "I better go out and lead them," he told staff and fellow legislators. The marchers gave him a round of applause. They "gave me a bullhorn, too," claimed Williams. Even as a state legislator, more than twenty years after he last marched with Martin Luther King Jr., the thrill of marching feet still "energized" him. Williams was still rebelling.[6]

Williams's proclivity for rebelling against leadership and his hunger for full control were his modus operandi as an SCLC staffer, but they were also dually the essence of his tactical genius and effectiveness as a grassroots organizer. His hardnosed approach caused headaches for King, but his talents were indispensable. He was SCLC's competitive advantage. As Dorothy Cotton, the only woman on the SCLC's executive leadership team, maintained:

"Hosea's style could sometimes repel rather than draw to. Hosea turned every staff meeting into a fight. Martin needed Hosea at one level, in a way. . . . We were struggling once what to do with Hosea. Everybody wanted to take Hosea to staff for something he had done . . . there were constant confrontations in the family." However, despite his inability to conform as an ideal team player, Williams was invaluable, and King knew it. Cotton continued, "Martin said to me, who is going to get out there on the street and organize the way Hosea does?" Cotton gave a final appraisal of the root of Williams's inability, or his unwillingness at team building with SCLC leadership: "Hosea wanted total control. That is where the problems came—over budgets and staff."[7]

Williams's brashness and appreciation for his own imperfections created a cultlike following among the Black proletariat that is easy to detect throughout the pages of this book. He was the "Teflon Don" of Black Atlanta for the last thirty years of his life. There was not a jury comprising a majority of Black residents in Atlanta that would have convicted him of any crime, despite the overwhelming evidence stemming from his highly publicized incidents with law enforcement regarding the combustible mix of alcohol and automobiles. The white press, relentless in their coverage of every transgression, probably magnified his appeal through their vilification of the old movement warhorse. Williams aptly captured the sentiment of some Blacks in a 1996 interview: "Hell, I know he's no angel, but damn, he ain't that bad." According to Williams, even Martin Luther King Sr., who was no supporter because of his unwillingness to abandon the street protests of the 1960s for a more palatable approach to racial equity, allegedly told an unnamed white person to "Leave [Hosea] alone. You're going to mess around and make him mayor. Don't you see, the more you beat on him, the more these black folks come to his defense." There is no independent source that documents "Daddy King's" statement. Nonetheless, Black Atlantans are still coming to his "defense" at the time of this writing in 2021. Each year, volunteers and staffers who marched with Williams in campaigns in decades past still gather at his burial chamber at Lincoln Cemetery in Atlanta to sing songs, share stories, and light candles.[8]

Perhaps his magnetic connection with the poor was accentuated by his unrelenting attack on the establishment and his many contributions to the poor long after 1968, when he refused to abandon the streets for more mainstream approaches to systemic racism. He continued his visible, persistent lambasting of the "downtown power structure" that, in his view, consisted of prominent and affluent Blacks including Atlanta Life Insurance President Jesse Hill, construction magnate Herman Russell, and Atlanta Mayor Maynard Jackson. Williams referred to this wealthy trio as the chief "house niggers" because of their less invasive approach to race relations. His popularity with the Black working class was also strengthened by his widely heralded commitment to the dispossessed and disinherited. One unnamed columnist wrote in 1991 that "Williams was in the spirit of American populism, which has always included figures who combined, rascality, voter appeal and the guts to speak an uncomfortable truth."[9] Gary Pomerantz, another columnist for *The Atlanta Journal-Constitution*, showed considerable insight in arguing that Williams's "for-the-little man philosophy was a hybrid of Huey Long and Huey Newton." Williams began feeding Atlanta's hungry in 1971, and since that year when he started the Poor People's Chow House in the basement of the Wheat Street Baptist Church, the effort has fed an estimated one million Metro Atlantans, perhaps more than any non-state-affiliated entity in the State of Georgia since its founding.

Despite his standing as a folk hero in Atlanta, Williams has not been credited for his contributions to the civil rights movement and the modern Black freedom struggle.[10] Williams often claimed that John Lewis received more credit than he deserved for Bloody Sunday. To some extent, the lionization of Lewis began during the same time that Williams was being branded as a "useless mischief maker" by the Atlanta press while Lewis was in his fourth term representing Georgia's fifth district in the US House of Representatives. Lewis had greater cachet and leveraged his access in Washington, DC, while Williams was serving as a state representative in the Georgia House of Representatives. Lewis was the shining symbol of what the historian Evelyn Brooks Higginbotham coined as "respectability politics." He opted to extend the civil rights movement in a different way by "respectfully" representing the district that produced Martin Luther King Jr.; Auburn Avenue; and Morehouse, Spelman, Morris Brown, and Clark Colleges.[11]

The lionization of John Lewis came full circle when the seventeen-term congressman died of pancreatic cancer in 2020 at age eighty. On July 30, 2020, three of the four living former presidents of the United States—George W. Bush, Bill Clinton, and Barack Obama—were among the mourners who assembled at the historic Ebenezer Baptist Church in Atlanta to pay their final respects to the "Conscience of the Congress." The service at Ebenezer was the last of three nationally televised memorials that commemorated Lewis's lifetime of frontline activism for civil and voting rights, as well as his thirty-three years representing Georgia's Fifth Congressional District in the US House of Representatives. Two of the former presidents ascended to the pulpit from the pews to deliver their prepared remarks in the order in which they occupied the Oval Office. Bush referred to Lewis as an "American saint."[12] Clinton called Lewis a "legend."[13] The crowd interrupted the former presidents' tributes with occasional bursts of applause before giving them standing ovations at the end of their respective speeches. Barack Obama, now four years into his postpresidency, was the last dignitary to address the mourners.

President Obama took a deep breath, adjusted the microphone before beginning his remarks, and quoted a biblical passage from James 1:4—"Let perseverance finish its work so that you may be mature and complete, lacking nothing." After acknowledging Martin Luther King Jr. as the church's "greatest pastor," he immediately heralded Lewis as King's "finest disciple," likely because of Lewis's self-sacrificing spirit throughout the civil rights movement and more than three decades of service in Congress. (It is worth noting that Ebenezer's current pastor, the Rev. Dr. Raphael Warnock, was elected five months later as Georgia's first Black US senator.) Obama, who had awarded Lewis the Presidential Medal of Freedom in 2011, reserved his greatest compliment for Lewis near the end of his eulogy.[14]

Presidential utterances are consequential, especially in the social media age of Facebook and Twitter. Obama mentioned the names of other civil rights activists during his eulogy. The former president talked about C. T. Vivian, another civil rights activist and Presidential Medal of Freedom recipient. The appropriateness of acknowledging Vivian during Lewis's eulogy was fitting, especially considering that both timbers, he and the congressman, fell on the same day. Obama also highlighted the role of Joseph Lowery, whom he awarded the nation's highest civilian honor in 2009. The former president spoke the names of James Lawson, Robert "Bob" Moses, Diane Nash, and Bernard Lafayette—all familiar names in the historiography of the civil rights movement, all still living.

The president, when referring to Bloody Sunday, one of Lewis's most celebrated acts of bravery, quickly acknowledged Hosea Williams. Obama's recognition of "Hosea Williams and others" who played a role in the initial attempt to march from Selma to Montgomery in March 1965 was the first time that Obama, the first US president of African descent, publicly paid a mounting debt to Hosea Williams. Obama may not have awarded Williams the Presidential Medal of Freedom as he honored Lewis, Vivian, and Lowery, but he did bestow upon the controversial activist a posthumous gift that Williams never received during his lifetime—recognition from a statesman on the national stage. Unlike for Williams, however, Obama asserted that Lewis has a reservation in the pantheon of the nation's greatest heroes. When this country finally makes good on its founding promises to guarantee inalienable rights for all citizens, "John Lewis," said Obama, "will be a founding father of that fuller, fairer, better America."[15]

President Obama was not alone in relegating Williams to more of a footnote than a profound shaper of American history. Historians of the civil rights era have consistently downplayed the significance of Hosea Williams. Were it not for his presence at the front of the line on Bloody Sunday, he might have been virtually consigned to the dustbin of history altogether. It is difficult to overstate the significance of the events of Bloody Sunday. Eight days after the melee, President Johnson, a son of the South, addressed a joint session of Congress. Speaking in the House Chamber, Johnson, in his long southern drawl, poignantly captured the gravity of Bloody Sunday. "At times," Johnson said, "history and fate meet at a single time in a single place to shape a turning point in man's unending search for freedom. So it was at Lexington and Concord. So it was a century ago at Appomattox. So it was last week in Selma, Alabama." Bloody Sunday, Johnson believed, was as much a defining moment for the Republic as the first shots of the conflict that led to American independence from Great Britain. This memorable quote from the speech also elevates the significance of Bloody Sunday in American history to that of the assassination of Abraham Lincoln five days after Gen. Robert E. Lee surrendered to General Ulysses S. Grant to formally end the Civil War. Johnson did not acknowledge Williams in the speech that he used to galvanize Congress to take legislative action to address the disfranchisement of Black Americans. It took almost fifty-five years to the day that he signed the Voting Rights Act into law for his distant successor, Barack Obama, to credit Williams's leadership in the seminal event that led to the nation's most effective remedy to voter suppression.[16]

Hosea Williams is an anomalous figure, at once both known and unknown in the historiography of the civil rights movement. Historians have far too often relegated Hosea Williams to a peripheral figure seldom meriting more than a handful of sentences, a mere footnote in the pages of what have been otherwise solid treatments examining civil rights agitation in the United States in the years after the *Brown v. Board of Education* decision of 1954, what many scholars have referred to as the "classical phase" of the civil rights movement. Within the past forty years, academics from a variety of disciplines have been joined by journalists and historical participants themselves in generating a proliferation of monographs, memoirs, and biographies. Some of the most acclaimed historians of the period have afforded only scant and fragmentary attention to Williams's contributions to civil rights, and the historiographical silence is nearly absolute for the years preceding and following his fifteen-year career with the local Savannah affiliate and national SCLC from 1963 to 1979.

No author has attempted a biographical treatment of Williams's life, even though some scholars have recognized Williams's pivotal role in the 1960s. Moreover, only a few scholars recognized that Williams was actively engaged in civil and voting rights activism before meeting King and his subsequent full-time employment with the SCLC. Historians have been similarly silent regarding Williams's post-1968 contributions to the struggle for Black equality for the thirty-two years after King's assassination. His work clearly demonstrates that the civil rights movement did not end on a Memphis balcony in 1968.

Williams did receive some recognition for his life's work after his passing on November 16, 2000, at the age of seventy-four. In an interview in *The Atlanta Journal-Constitution* on the day after his death, David Garrow, author of the Pulitzer Prize-winning book *Bearing the Cross: Martin Luther King, Jr., and the Southern Christian Leadership Conference*, said: "In the 1964–1965 timeframe, Hosea was as valuable as anyone in SCLC to Dr. King because of his courage and willingness to lead dangerous demonstrations. . . . People may remember Andy Young and John Lewis, but . . . Hosea was just as important to the movement."[17] Williams has been universally portrayed as courageous, fearless, and integral to the modern civil rights movement by the activists who marched alongside and strategized with him during some of the most dangerous protests during the 1960s. Even the recently anointed "founding father" and canonized "American saint," John Lewis, believed that Williams, too, deserved a carving on the same slab of granite reserved for those responsible for America's rebirth. Lewis, who marched shoulder to shoulder with Williams on the Edmund Pettus Bridge in Selma, Alabama, on Bloody Sunday, called the fiery activist an authentic hero. "Hosea Williams must be looked upon as one of the founding fathers of the new America," he said. "Through his actions, he helped liberate all of us."[18] Joseph Lowery, a founder of the SCLC and Williams's former boss who fired him as executive director of the SCLC in 1979, portrayed the old warhorse of the movement as fearless. "Hosea wasn't afraid of Goliath," he said. "In fact, I was thinking about it, and I don't think there anything he was scared of." He remembered Williams as someone who tackled "the Goliaths of greed and indifference" that created a permanent underclass.[19] These more celebrated peers of Williams, both recipients of the nation's highest civilian honor, suggest that he shared some of the same characteristics that they embodied. Perhaps the lack of historiographical representation is one of the reasons Williams is not mentioned in the same vein as Ralph Abernathy, Andrew Young, John Lewis, Jesse Jackson, and Joseph Lowery.

Williams was an integral member of the brain trust of the SCLC who merits biographical treatment, especially during a period where state and federal legislators are attempting to roll back the gains of the civil rights movement. Overall, there remains a dearth of full-length biographies of civil rights activists who were at the epicenter of the classical—or what Peniel Joseph refers to as the "heroic"—phase of the modern civil rights movement, which began in 1954 with the banning of segregation in the public school system and culminated with the passage of the Voting Rights Act of 1965.[20] After the critical success of recent biographies written on Septima Poinsette Clark and Ella Baker, the literature is begging for scholarly portraits of other activists involved with SCLC and the Student Nonviolent Coordinating Committee (SNCC) during the high tide of the modern Black freedom struggle.[21]

This book explores how Williams's legacy and undeniable talent for organizing working-class Blacks as a civil rights activist and elected representative have been overshadowed by defects in his personal decision-making, not by deficiencies of courage or effectiveness as a member of the SCLC brain trust. This includes a thorough examination of Williams as a leader within the Savannah, Georgia, branch of the National Association for the Advancement of Colored People (NAACP); a political organizer with SCLC; and one of the four top lieutenants to the Rev. Dr. Martin Luther King Jr. during the peak years of the movement for equality in the middle of the twentieth century during the prime of his professional career. C. T. Vivian, an aide to Dr. King who was awarded the Presidential Medal of Freedom in 2013, maintained that "Hosea achieved status but it didn't satisfy him. He gave up more than any of us ever had." Williams, the only aide to Dr. King with a degree and graduate coursework in chemistry, turned his back on a lucrative career as a research chemist with the US Department of Agriculture to work full time for SCLC. Elizabeth Williams Omilami, Williams's second oldest daughter, claimed that her father, who had sacrificed so much for the cause of freedom, was simply a "prophet without honor."[22]

This book examines several important issues, seeking to explore through the lens of biography the magnetic leadership of Hosea Williams. What were the sources of his anxiety, and how did he manage to preserve his sense of humor at the core of his personality in very serious, life-threatening situations? What led him to cast his lot with the modern freedom struggle when he was enjoying a comfortable middle-class life in Savannah, Georgia, and had professional opportunities available to only a tiny minority of Blacks in the Deep South? He had secured a comfortable job with the US Department of Agriculture and was being steadily promoted when other Blacks could not even secure an interview. However, he knowingly drew the ire of his colleagues and supervisors by leading boycotts and voting rights initiatives against the local and federal governments.

Hosea Williams demonstrated a remarkable capacity to transcend class and educational divisions within Savannah's Black community, and that ability served him admirably throughout the remainder of his career as a proud "civil rights agitator" in a host of other cities in and beyond the South. One might reasonably expect that Williams's academic training as a chemist at Morris Brown College and Atlanta University would have hindered him in relating to the masses of undereducated Blacks, some of whom were still unable to read and write in the decades following World War II. However, like Martin Luther King Jr., Williams had an uncanny ability to connect with the poorest of the poor, many of whom had never traveled outside of their home states.

Williams's capacity to touch and transform the minds of the forgotten rank and file he mobilized in the South during and after the classical phase of the civil rights movement was attributed to his genius as an organizer, and his belief that movements involved the community, not the "well-educated intellectuals and theoreticians"—individuals he routinely lambasted. He endeared himself to the "crazies," people who were willing to go to jail or lose their lives for freedom. Williams believed that these "crazies" who were the "salt of the movement" had guts—the foundation of any sustaining campaign for a worthy cause. The "crazies" were drawn to him because, despite his middle-class status, he, too, was a "crazy" who dwelled amongst, and understood the aspirations of this vitally important movement demographic. At an informal graveside memorial service, which I attended in 2013, Willie Bolden, one of Williams's closest friends who was considered a son, said in his remarks that, after watching Williams during the Savannah desegregation campaign, he thought that "he was either crazy or one hell of a leader. He was both," Bolden said nostalgically. To make the point more clearly, Williams neatly fits the definition of what the Italian Marxist theorist Antonio Gramsci referred to as an "organic intellectual." In Gramsci's thinking, the organic intellectual is not formally recognized as an "intellectual" in the traditional sense. The conventional intellectual is detached from everyday life and learns through reading and writing essays while being supported by university endowments and other forms of academic patronage. By contrast, the organic intellectual learns about life and the world they ultimately change from appreciating and understanding the expressed needs and aspirations of the group to which they belong by choice or circumstance. Gramsci also suggests that organic intellectuals are so firmly committed to social action that it is inextricably woven into the fabric of their existence. Social action is all-consuming. It is indivisible from one's personhood.[23]

This book also situates Williams's organizational talents and background within the larger group of King's colleagues, including Ralph Abernathy, Andrew Young, James Bevel, and later, Jesse Jackson. It is widely known that Hosea Williams and the remainder of King's inner circle of lieutenants were constantly jockeying for favor and proximity to the president of the SCLC because of his influence and appeal to wider audiences. Examining Williams and his fellow SCLC lieutenants as they sought to advance the civil rights agenda despite these obstacles suggests that, ultimately, Dr. King was the glue that kept their egos in check. This book's exploration of these dynamics is modeled on Doris Kearns Goodwin's *Team of Rivals: The Political Genius of Abraham Lincoln*. Goodwin's prize-winning work focuses on Lincoln's ability to balance the conservative and radical factions in his cabinet by shrewdly and subtly manipulating his various secretaries to push his agenda. The following chapters demonstrate that King used a similar method with his own inner cabinet of advisers. Goodwin analyzed the lives of Salmon P. Chase, William Seward, Edward Bates, and Edward Stanton, dissecting their respective backgrounds, personality traits, and career ambitions in contrast to Lincoln's. A similar approach with King's five lieutenants—Ralph Abernathy, Andrew Young, James Bevel, Jesse Jackson, and Hosea Williams—can also bear analytical fruit. Observers often contend that Williams and, to a lesser degree, James Bevel were the most contentious lieutenants in King's inner circle.[24] This book sheds critical light on the question of how the internal politics of the SCLC shaped organizational strategy and tactics.

The pages that follow span Hosea Williams's life from his birth in 1926 until his death in 2000. The narrative attempts to weave many disparate events and psychological analysis into a concise chronological framework. These chapters enter into Williams's world and analyze how he moved through it, directly addressing his complex and, at times, conflicting personality traits. In addition to Williams's own self-examination, the chapters rely on the perspectives of family members, friends, enemies, and colleagues. Their written and oral testimonies, in combination with his own accounts, help to paint a rich portrait of an underappreciated civil rights activist.

ONE

"Little Turner," World War II, and Atlanta

Hosea Williams's early life in rural south Georgia and the circumstances surrounding his birth and rearing helped define his commitment to the poor and disinherited. His defiant nature as a child was evident when he disregarded the southern mores that almost led to him being lynched for having sex with a white girl. The first twenty years of his life are filled with overcoming remarkable circumstances. Williams was born to blind, unwed parents, Larcenia Williams and Willie "Blind Willie" Wiggins on January 5, 1926, in Attapulgus, Georgia. He was reared by his maternal grandmother and grandfather, Turner and Leila Williams. The younger Williams, known as "Little Turner," was never referred to as Hosea in this small city in the far southwest corner of the state, because he exhibited many of the characteristics of his strong and domineering grandfather, whom he affectionately referred to as "Papa." Although illiterate, Papa instilled a sense of toughness and courage into his grandson that enabled him to survive in hostile environments, including his tour of duty in the US Army during World War II and the many civil rights campaigns he led during the movement and post-1968.

Hosea Lorenzo Williams was born in an era when Georgia was a one-party state dominated politically by the Democratic Party and its elected officials who fought to preserve segregation through fear and intimidation, as well as through ingenious legal sophistry. During the first eighteen years of Williams's life, many citizens of Georgia routinely elected staunch defenders of states' rights and the status quo who wittingly appealed to white racial fears of Negro equality. Nearly every state and local officeholder, from governors to US senators, as well as mayors and sheriffs, knew from an instinct tempered by history and experience that espousing campaign rhetoric or advocating policies that granted a semblance of the rights to

Blacks already enjoyed by whites would be political suicide. Richard B. Russell—who, after a brief stint as the governor of Georgia from 1931 to 1933, served in the US Senate for thirty-eight years until his death in 1971—represents only one example of how an elected official's shrewd political pragmatism in Georgia was influenced by race. Russell's predecessor in the governor's mansion was Democrat Eugene Talmadge, who was elected four times to the state's highest office (he died shortly before being inaugurated for his fourth term). Talmadge's political success was rooted in his ability to appeal to poor whites by offering voters a hybrid version of populism and racism, even as his policies did very little for the "common man" and favored political and economic elites. Both Russell and Talmadge popularized a strategy that Williams as a top lieutenant to Martin Luther King Jr. during the modern civil rights movement and later as an elected representative in the State of Georgia would work tirelessly to topple.[1]

Eugene "Ol' Gene" Talmadge, referred to by Vernon Orlando (V. O.) Key as Georgia's "demagogue," was perhaps the most polarizing and controversial figure in the history of his state's politics. Talmadge was a candidate in nearly every statewide Democratic primary during the first eighteen years of Hosea Williams' life. The career politician sought the office of commissioner of agriculture three times, ran for the US Senate twice, and ran for the governorship six times, losing twice to Richard Russell. Talmadge was elected three times for Georgia's top agriculture post and four times as the state's chief executive (the governor-elect passed away before he could begin his fourth term in office. Even when the "Wild Man from Sugar Creek" was not seeking an elective office, particularly in 1936, he held enough cachet to transfer, literally, his vote to an ally of his choosing who, with blind loyalty, subscribed to the Talmadge platform. Key identified this phenomenon as "Talmadgeism," recognizing that the ideals exploited by Talmadge—chiefly, aid to the "poor dirt farmer" and the maintenance of white supremacy—transcended the man at the state level. His "loyalty" to the forgotten white man is illustrated here: "The poor dirt farmer ain't got but three friends on this earth: God Almighty, Sears Roebuck and Gene Talmadge." His perception of the Negro is equally clear. His biographer sums it up succinctly: "Talmadge's attitude toward blacks was that they were childlike, basically stupid, barely removed from savage ancestry, and should be closely controlled. He did not hate the race, but he had very little respect for blacks as human beings." Although Talmadge, a rabid racist and staunch opponent of the New Deal (though a vociferous ally of farmers) and integration, likely never entered the same circle as Williams, the governor's policies and ideals directly affected the conditions that Williams and his family confronted daily in southwest Georgia.[2]

Life and politics at the local level in Attapulgus, Georgia, where Hosea Williams was reared, were controlled by mayors and sheriffs who modeled their governing philosophy as after that of Talmadge and Russell. From 1929 through 1944, five mayors—J. L. Donalson, S. A. V. Christiphine, M. M. Robinson, O. B. Thomas, and Carl Welch—ran City Hall using the same political rhetoric and calculus as that of the state politicians. Low taxes and the subordination of the Blacks to membership in a permanent underclass were "safe" political strategies. These local chief executives keenly understood that with Blacks disfranchised in Attapulgus because of the white primary, poll taxes, and literacy tests, Black influence on political matters remained negligible because their voting interests did not have to be considered.[3]

Named after his mother's blind brother, Hosea Lorenzo Williams grappled with formidable odds from birth. Evidence suggests that predetermined circumstances and the penetrating pain and poverty he witnessed around him during his formative years invariably shaped his enduring commitment to the poor and the disinherited. He was the only child born to Larcenia Williams and Willie "Blind Willie" Wiggins, both of whom were students in Macon, Georgia, at the School for the Colored Blind in 1925 when he was conceived.[4] Larcenia Williams, without informing anyone of her pregnancy, including Hosea's father, wrapped her petite frame in sheets to avoid detection and abruptly fled the school in December a few weeks before delivering her first child. On Tuesday, January 5, 1926, only three years before the beginning of the Great Depression, Williams was born in Attapulgus, Georgia. He later recalled the first year of his life as it had been relayed to him:

> She left the baby with a family and told 'em she would be back to claim the baby in two weeks . . . was an old friend of her father's down in the turpentine stills. She didn't get back until three and a half weeks. The family would not give up the kid. She had to leave the kid. About a year later, the gentleman was killed and the kid ended up in an orphanage for the next year.[5]

Both Hosea and his mother returned to Georgia to reside with her parents in Attapulgus before he reached his second birthday.[6]

Life in the South before the New Deal, particularly during the late 1920s and early 1930s, did not present many opportunities for the Williams family and other similarly situated Negroes to climb the ladder of upward mobility, as the overwhelmingly rural region was still heavily reliant on agriculture for its subsistence. In 1930, the South was almost sixty-eight percent rural. Nearly forty-three percent of its workforce labored on farms, collectively earning a per-capita income of one hundred eighty-nine dollars vis-à-vis four hundred eighty-four dollars for jobs unrelated to the farming industry. Historian James C. Cobb, who has written extensively about the social and cultural conditions of Georgia, cites H. L. Mencken, the leading literary luminary of the first half of the twentieth century and his 1931 study to identify the "worst American state." According to Mencken's benchmarks, of the forty-eight states in the Union at the time, Georgia ranked forty-third in wealth and forty-eighth in education.[7]

The National Emergency Council, which included the cabinet secretaries of labor, commerce, and agriculture, published a more detailed study relative to the financial outlook of the South in 1938 at the request of President Franklin D. Roosevelt. The committee that prepared the report on the thirteen southern states comprised governors, university presidents, professors, and attorneys, all of whom lived and worked in the South. Submitted to Roosevelt on July 25, 1938, the report was titled "The Economic Conditions of the South." The document can be viewed as a political attack on one of Roosevelt's most vocal opponents, Senator Walter George of Georgia. Along with implicitly discrediting George, the report examined fifteen components that retarded the growth of the southern economy. The sections covered in the report, to cite a few, included education, health, economic resources, labor, purchasing power, industry, and women and children; these sections highlighted barriers that prevented the region from effectively exploiting its natural resources. The study concluded that the South's dismal economy was rooted in abysmally low wages and the planter elite's continued domination of politics and an outdated agricultural industry.[8]

Williams's desires and later pursuit of undergraduate and graduate degrees in chemistry, as well as a career with the US Department of Agriculture as a research chemist analyzing the chemical compounds of insecticides, had deep roots in the red soil of Attapulgus, Georgia. Attapulgus, located in the deep southwestern corner of the state in Decatur County, is named after a Creek Indian word meaning "dogwood grove." The city is about five miles north of the Georgia–Florida line. Incorporated in 1866, the area has always been known for its high concentration of attapulgite, a type of fuller's earth clay that can only be found in one additional county in the United States—Gadsden County, Florida. The mineral has various commercial uses as a pesticide, paint thickener, and purifier of hydrocarbons. Notwithstanding the potential for economic gain in the area because of its mineral wealth, life for the young Williams and his family appeared bleak as the prospect of being upwardly mobile was constrained by race, class, and a near-primitive educational system.[9]

Decatur County played a crucial role in the production of tobacco in the State of Georgia during the first thirty years of the twentieth century. In 1891, A. Cohn and Company purchased fourteen thousand of the nearly one million acres of arable land for the cultivation of tobacco. Naming the area Amsterdam, approximately two miles from where Williams was reared, Cohn owned the largest tobacco plantation in the world that was in the possession of an individual owner. In 1907, some of the other tobacco producers merged and created the American Sumatra Company, creating a division in Amsterdam. The company's central focus was the production of shade-grown tobacco, also recognized on the market at the time as cigar wrapper tobacco. By August 5, 1926, at one of the company's warehouse openings in Bainbridge, which was about twelve miles from Amsterdam, industrious businessmen were selling "high-quality" tobacco to major buyers. Some purchasers, including J. F. Hagerty, representing the R. J. Reynolds Company, purchased ten thousand pounds of tobacco from Sumatra. According to press reports, Hagerty and other buyers were "exceedingly well pleased . . . and expressed great satisfaction" with the product. At this particular sale, the company sold 42,174 pounds of tobacco at an average rate of $21.02 per pound.[10]

Evidence suggests that Williams was reared in a family in which grandfathers, in spite of any deficiencies with reading and writing, were instrumental in providing structure and stability and instilling into the male family members the importance of home ownership. Williams, affectionately referred to as "Little Turner" because of his "aggressive spirit . . . and ability to solve problems and make injustices right," came of age in the home of his maternal grandparents, Turner and Leila Williams. His "aggressiveness" was one of his defining personality traits. His aggressive, defiant image would only strengthen his reputation as a "bull in a china shop" during the civil rights movement and his post-1968 activism in metropolitan Atlanta.[11]

Turner Williams, whom Hosea always called "Papa," by appearance, was not an imposing figure. Visual inspection of an image gives credence to the assertions of family members that Hosea inherited some physical features from his maternal grandfather. He was about five feet, six inches in height. He could be described as relatively handsome, with smooth, sun-bronzed, blemishless skin and pretty white teeth. Papa had high cheekbones that had not sunk even under the weight of time. He had fairly round eyes that were light brown in color. His nose was rather large. His lips were full and did not indicate any usage of tobacco, although he worked in environments where the crop was plentiful. His ears were fairly small, with his right ear protruding from the face about three-quarters of an inch farther than his left ear. Overall, he maintained a low haircut and did not wear a beard or a goatee, further accentuating his facial features. Turner's wife and Hosea's grandmother, Leila, possessed equally attractive facial features.[12]

Leila Williams, whom Hosea affectionately referred to as "Mama," had a very soft and supple appearance. Born in Georgia on May 17, 1878, she was one year older than her husband, Turner, when the couple married in 1899. Census records suggest that Turner was her second husband and that she had given birth to nine children, only three of which were still living in 1910. By many standards of measurement, she was a beautiful woman whose exterior contradicted the effects of the physiological and psychological effects of burying six children before her thirty-second birthday. Her oldest living daughter, Hosea's mother, Larcenia, would die in 1936. Attempting to describe the most prominent physical features of members in his family, Williams stated that "most of my family was black and olive brown people with kind of long hair." He was likely thinking of his grandmother when giving this description. Leila was about five feet in height. Her hair was long and silky, worn mostly up and in a bun. Her skin was soft and flawless as a result of her probable use of petroleum jelly and cocoa butter to keep her body moisturized after working long days as a "dipper" in the turpentine industry. She had a petite frame, likely toned over the many years she performed laborious jobs on various plantations before her husband reached a point of relative financial security in the late 1930s.[13]

Turner and Leila Williams, Hosea Williams's maternal grandparents, were hard workers and had lived in northern Florida and Mississippi—both states known for their commercial production of turpentine—before settling down in Attapulgus, Georgia. Evidence suggests that before 1919, the couple had worked in the turpentine industry for nearly twenty years. Turner had worked as a "chopper," and Leila worked in the woods as a "dipper." It is likely that the Williams family chose to migrate to Attapulgus in the late 1920s because of their previous experience working in the turpentine industry during World War I. The area was emerging as a hub for the industry in southwest Georgia. The county was first introduced to turpentine as an economic engine in the late nineteenth and early twentieth centuries by E. R. and Mid Powell, likely the owners of the first turpentine still in Decatur. Turpentine in Decatur County, also referred to as "green gold," was used in the production of shingles, poles, boxes, and gum naval stores. By 1920, after the closing of the Stuart Lumber Company, Lindsay Ball and P. S. Cummings purchased nearly 40,000 acres for the value they saw in the longleaf pines. This large land acquisition, as well as a reliable supply of labor and an abundance of trees, created many jobs in the small town.[14]

Evidence suggests that Little Turner's industriousness as an entrepreneur and compassion for the less fortunate was inculcated in him by Papa. By 1930, four years after Little Turner's birth, Turner Williams had settled down in Attapulgus and accumulated property valued at four hundred dollars along State Highway No. 1 on Amsterdam Road, an area where large plantations were cultivated for tobacco farming. Papa was a self-sustaining man who provided for his ten-member household by raising hogs, cows, and peanuts. His seven surviving children—Hosea (Little Turner), Essie Mae, Azzie, Ethel, Turner Jr., John, and Bernice—saw that their father, although unable to read and write, was an intelligent man "who could never be cheated." The children also witnessed him assume the responsibilities of raising his grandchildren, Little Turner, Reasin Clarence, and Charlotte. Although Papa made an honest living by farming, he supplemented his income by cutting hair in his two-room structure in Attapulgus on the weekends, even on Sunday morning before church for neighbors and church members who worked extended hours on Saturday night. The elder Williams also owned and operated a café on US-27, five miles south of the street that currently bears his name. He sold snacks, sodas, beer, and prepackaged sandwiches that were likely made from the animals and produce that he raised on his own land. People in the community obviously realized that Turner was an ambitious man who lived in relative comfort, especially for an illiterate Black man in the Deep South who lacked any formal education. According to one informed family member, he was "very philanthropic" and willing to assist neighbors and visitors who approached him for money and food.[15]

Attapulgus in 1930 was, in many respects, a microcosm of the Deep South. According to the census for that year, nineteen hundred people lived in this section of Decatur County, Georgia: 1,276 were classified as "Negroes," and the remaining 624 people were identified as "White." As with many counties in the South and throughout the United States in the 1930s, Decatur County was sharply divided along racial and class lines. Hosea Williams later bitterly recalled how the white family of Walter "Bear" Chester would refuse to ride on a bus with Blacks or interact with Blacks in general, regardless of the fact that the Chester family was held in very low regard in white circles because of their educational level and lack of social refinement. Describing the family's attitude toward Blacks, Williams stated that the Chester family was not allowed to ride the bus. "Ever since I can remember the Chester family walked. But they had that white pride. Even though they were poorer than us, they had to walk to school, they walked on the opposite side or they walked ahead or behind us." The family's disdain for Blacks was inculcated into the younger children, Laura, Robert, and Maxwell Chester. Williams recalled how the three children were reprimanded for playing with Black children: "And when some of the little ones would try to play with us, the [older] ones would spank 'em, make 'em get back over there cause you white." Although this is an analysis of one particular poor, southern white family, this example is arguably symptomatic of the general racial mores among children that pervaded Attapulgus and other rural communities in the United States, especially in the Deep South.[16]

The Ku Klux Klan (KKK), because of its numerical strength and ability to maintain the status quo, played a prominent role on the religious, political, and social scenes in Decatur County during Little Turner's formative years. The hooded order influenced ministers, politicians, and educators. The Klan, for example, financed Baptist revivals in the county seat in Bainbridge. One attendee observed that nearly two hundred members of the terrorist group "gave a very touching testimonial" one particular Friday night. The Klan was so impressed with how the ministers conducted the revival that "right before the sermon . . . six Klansmen in robes marched down to the altar and gave the preacher $100 . . . and a most earnest letter assuring the preachers of their most hearty cooperation" in fulfilling their obligation to Christ and the church in the area, or what historian Nancy MacLean, in her examination of the Klan in Georgia, describes as "old time" religion. The night riders also held large meetings at the Decatur County courthouse, which leads one to infer that the group held influence over judges, juries, and police officers. One specific "educational" meeting in 1930 is worth mentioning. Men who were held in high esteem were all in attendance: for example, Dr. H. W. Evans, Imperial Wizard and head of the organization; Dr. Samuel Green, Grand Dragon of the State of Georgia;

and Georgia State Senator Eurith "Ed" Rivers (Rivers would be elected the 68th governor of Georgia three years later). The organization had expressed a "deep interest" in the education of the white students in the area and wanted to discuss "recent activities" of some organizations seeking to address years of inferior academic preparation of Black pupils. The Klan was likely referring to the fact that a small, one-room school had been recently erected to educate Black students just North of Attapulgus on US-27, a result of tax revenue that the organization thought should be utilized in support of the education of white students. Although verifiable accounts of the organization's violence toward "uppity" Blacks and "dishonorable" whites in the area are nonexistent for the period under examination, the records suggest that the Klan's presence was effective enough without violence in keeping Blacks "in their place": subordinate to local whites.[17]

School attendance in Decatur County was mandatory by the time Little Turner reached age six. The county administrators and educators took great pains to ensure that pupils regularly attended school, because appropriations were inextricably bound with student turnout. County officials placed a lengthy article on the front page of the local newspaper imploring fathers to allow their children to attend school, because "Men who keep their children out of school do not only hamper their own children but they hamstrung the children that do go." The contributors posited that three hundred fifty "colored" children and 250 white children were routinely kept home because of parental "indifference," or because parents "claimed" that they were unable to buy books, potentially resulting in an eight-thousand-dollar loss of tax-supported funding. The editorial continued: "It seems that pleading and begging men to do their duty by their children doesn't get anywhere. . . . The man that is guilty of this neglect better get busy and get his child in school. . . . We mean business." The author concluded the article with a final admonition: "This effort is by determined men and it means that every child in Decatur County must be in school or some folks will smell the patching." The irony inherent in the committee's desires to fill the desks should be viewed in contrast to the conditions under which the "colored" children learned.[18]

Little Turner's academic journey began in Decatur County, Georgia, during a period when white stakeholders wanted to ensure the success of its white pupils while county and city administrators neglected the educational needs of its Black students—in spite of the rhetoric that permeated the aforementioned news article. The historian James D. Anderson suggested, in *The Education of Blacks in the South, 1860–1935*, that there are "essential relationships between popular education and the politics of oppression." Little Turner, likely unaware of the oppressive nature of his schooling, enrolled in Attapulgus Colored School around 1932 at age six. The school burned down two years later in 1934 and was later renamed the Attapulgus Vocational School. Located north of Attapulgus on US-27, adjacent to the Second Morning Star Missionary Baptist Church, the new structure was still indicative of the city's and county's attitudes insofar as their "colored" children were concerned. The building suffered from primitive construction techniques, poor supplies, and overall disinterest in the welfare of Black pupils. In terms of its faculty, Attapulgus Vocational School would have likely been staffed by Black female teachers whose formal education was not equal to the training of the white teachers at neighboring all-white Bainbridge Elementary School, located less than five miles away. By 1934, presumably because of budgetary constraints, the terms of local white and "colored" schools were cut. White school administrators cut the terms of the "colored" schools to six months, but the white students, even in times of economic peril caused by the Great Depression, still attended school for eight months, ensuring that the latter were given a chance to be better prepared academically than their Black counterparts and simultaneously saving on overall school expenditures. Notwithstanding these challenges, Little Turner displayed a capacious intellect and keen interest in mathematics and science through his seventh-grade year. He would not complete his high school education until returning from fighting in Europe during the Second World War. Before leaving to fight tyranny abroad, Little Turner had to grapple with a family tragedy that devastated him and irrevocably changed his life.[19]

On October 17, 1941, less than two months before the Japanese sneak attack on the US Pacific fleet at Pearl Harbor, Little Turner, and the rest of the Williams family, was rocked by tragedy after the sudden death of the family's matriarch, Leila Williams. Evidence suggests that her passing was due to blood poisoning as the result of a decayed tooth. Her death was "devastating." "Mama" was a welcomed contrast to the stoic and stern patriarch of the family. She has been described as "warm, caring and fun-loving . . . she was the 'go-to' person" whom everyone in the family could approach in moments of trial and triumph. Her passing seemed to have had a spiritual impact on the entire family, including her normally reserved widower. According to Leila's daughter, Little Turner's aunt, Ethel, Leila had been persuading her husband for years to join the membership at the Second Morning Star Missionary Baptist Church in Attapulgus. Although he frequently attended church with his family, he always stopped shy of walking down the aisle during the "invitation to discipleship." After the eulogy, likely being faced with his own mortality, Turner finally joined the church. Accounts of the event reported that the church "went wild." Since that cool October day, Turner remained a devoted member as a church trustee and leader of the religious body's board of ushers. His unceasing devotion to the church obviously meant that an emphasis on church attendance and participation in various auxiliary ministries would be now be required for Little Turner.[20]

Religion and spiritual worship became an integral component of Little Turner's life after October 17, 1941. Church attendance was now required for him and the remainder of the Williams household. Evidence suggests that he may have joined the church shortly after Mama's funeral. One can also infer that he likely became a member of the board of ushers while Papa was the president of this particular church auxiliary. In church matters, Papa's stern demeanor was witnessed at the church. "Uncle Doc" ran a "tight ship," says nephew and fellow church member, Deacon Leopold Wise. He continued, "Your kids didn't go in the church chewing gum and crying. You and your kids had to go outside. . . . The church ran smooth, then." Although he was a religious man, he was also a "mean" man, said Wise. "If you mess wit' him, you had problems, didn't care if you was white or black . . . white folks respected him" around the church and local community. Little Turner invariably witnessed Papa's authoritative leadership style and would assume many of his characteristics as an adult. Although whites respected Papa to a limited degree, he, too, still had to "behave" within the societal parameters determined by race.[21]

Little Turner experienced the deep-seated racism and whites' false sense of superiority when witnessing the humiliation that Black adults routinely experienced when interacting with those of the dominant culture. Most Blacks, regardless of age, education, and cultural refinement, were only permitted to enter a white person's home through the back door. Eugene Talmadge, the controversial and colorful three-term governor of Georgia, held sentiments that were closely aligned with those of the majority of white Georgians: "I want to deal with the nigger this way; he must come to my back door, take off his hat, and say, 'yes, sir.'" Hosea witnessed how Talmadge's convictions played out in Attapulgus: "Back in those days black people were not allowed to go up to the front door of any white folk. Not even was 'leading niggers' like Papa was allowed to go up to the front door of even the home of 'red-neck' white trash." He continued, "All white people look upon this as just about the most disrespectful thing a black person could do. I mean any Black male, female, little child, or old senior citizen" were held in the lowest regard simply because of the hue of their skin color. Little Turner, although very young, was a perceptive observer of the backward racial mores of his hometown and understood early in his formative years that race, more than gender or class, was the pivot on which southern society turned. He would experience the racial societal rigidity on a very personal level in early 1942.[22]

Little Turner's knowledge of, but blatant defiance of, the rigid societal barriers that had been erected between Blacks and whites, especially Black males and white females, which would become a hallmark during his later career as a civil rights activist, nearly cost him his life before he reached adulthood. Little Turner was something of a dandy. He was handsome, charismatic, and witty—physical and personality traits that were bound to attract many women regardless of race. One such white girl was his neighbor and member of the "low-breed" white family who had what he referred to as "cracker pride." Laura Chester was the youngest daughter and fourth child of Walter "Bear" Chester. Evidence suggests that Laura was born in 1922, making her approximately four years younger than Little Turner. One can infer that Laura was the one responsible for first crossing the racial boundaries that had hitherto segregated Blacks and whites. Little Turner vividly recalled how the illicit association began as she frequented the Williams property: "So every year I could remember ole' Laura getting over our fence—her old daddy was so sorry, he didn't care—but 'Momma' let her come out there and pick blackberries, plums, and grapes for as long as I could remember." He continued, "We had a large orchard . . . about thirty feet long and about thirty feet wide. And Laura and I used to go, we used to climb—I used to get her ass up in them bushes." Laura, although younger than Little Turner, was also acutely aware of how the power dynamics, invariably strengthened by law and custom, extended to their sexual relationship. Although Laura engaged in and likely enjoyed Little Turner's company and sensuality, she degraded and dehumanized him. "Come over here, nigger—come here. Fuck me, nigger," stated Laura on several occasions. Little Turner obviously felt some affection for her. When describing the relationship, he stated that "It was really low," and hindsight allowed him to classify Laura as the "epitome of white trash."[23]

News of Little Turner's illicit relationship with Laura Chester spread quickly around the small South Georgia town one Sunday afternoon in 1942 after Clara Mae, a jealous suitor of Little Turner, revealed details of the relationship at Lavonia's Confectionary—a gathering hub where many of Attapulgus's youth gathered after church services to socialize and drink sodas. "Laura going with Hosea," said Clara Mae. Little Turner's male friends started to tease Laura. Ashamed, likely feeling used and taken advantage of, Laura began to cry. She ran home and relayed the day's events to her mother. Enraged, Sarah Chester relayed the information to her husband, "Bear" Chester. Hitherto described by Little Turner as "sorry" and disinterested in the everyday affairs of his own daughter Laura, Bear immediately devised a plan to defend his youngest daughter's honor. According to Little Turner, "He went out and organized crackers—organized a lynch mob." The gang of rag-tag, similarly situated whites first approached George Smith, Clara Mae's father. Described by Little Turner as being "a great big old man," stretching nearly six feet in height and weighing almost three hundred pounds, the mob forced Smith to beat his daughter until she was incoherent and unresponsive—presumably for publicly giving voice to the lynchable offense. "And George Smith beat that girl so. They let him rest, his arm would get tired, but he beat his own daughter until she was unconscious," recalled Little Turner.[24]

The lynch mob, regardless of the fulfillment it derived from forcing George Smith to nearly kill his daughter for uttering the taboo in public, would not be satisfied until Little Turner was hanging lifeless from a tree. Tipped off by a friend regarding the mob's plans for his grandson, the normally stoic yet always fearless patriarch prepared anxiously to defend Little Turner with an arsenal of weaponry that included twelve-gauge and pump automatic shotguns. At almost fifty years old, he had keen eyesight and had a reputation for his marksmanship. "Papa was supposed to be so good. He wouldn't shoot a squirrel on a limb—he'd make a noise, and when that squirrel would jump and head for another limb, they'd catch him in the air. . . . It was a disgrace to shoot a squirrel sitting." Apparently emboldened by his skill with a gun, and determined to prevent his grandson from being lynched, Papa's anxiety was subordinated to his parental instincts to protect his deceased daughter's only son. Little Turner's recollection of the morning of the incident merits extensive quotation:

> My granddaddy said, "Get up, here they come." . . . He got up and he had all those guns loaded. All those guns on the sofa—he had six or seven guns, including two or three pistols. "You get you a gun, and don't any of you shoot until I shoot. And when I shoot, you try to kill those son of a bitches." And they was coming up, and they all had

> guns. When they came about five feet, walking, kind of rushing . . . walking real fast. Papa yelled, "what you want?" And they said, "We want to see Little Turner." . . . My granddaddy said "NO, not today. Little Turner is a minor, and I'm his father, and whatever he's done, you hold me guilty of. . . . You can't get Little Turner. He's my son."[25]

Aware that Papa would not sit by idly and surrender his son, the mob eventually retreated, vowing to return: "We gonna get you nigger, goddammit, nigger. We gonna get you and your goddamn bastard son," screamed one member of the bloodthirsty gang.[26]

Papa, known for his wisdom and characteristic clearheadedness, was keenly aware that his and Little Turner's lives were in greater danger than before his initial confrontation with the gang. He knew that he had to seek the assistance of a revered white male who could provide an impregnable heat shield against subsequent attacks. Papa, Little Turner, and his sister Teresa fled to safety in the home of Warner Miller. Miller, a large white man weighing approximately two hundred seventy-five pounds, was the wealthy owner of three plantations. Referred to as "The Boss" by Little Turner, he lorded over Attapulgus in the 1930s as if the city was his personal fiefdom. "You see," said Little Turner, "Mr. Miller was not only the big white boss that all nigger people in our town looked up to, he was just as big a boss over the white crackers, if not a bigger boss over the crackers. . . . He was the undisputed big boss over that entire tobacco belt." He had amassed a relatively hefty fortune by exploiting Black sharecroppers. Describing Miller's exploitative techniques, Little Turner posited that:

> He [Miller] was a big tobacco grower. I seen that man in his office, in his safe one day—it looked like a million dollars—money he paid no taxes on, money he took in. And the way he had those Negroes was to give you a house. He'd give you and your wife a house, "mmmm, John, this your house, son mmmm. You can pay me later on, hear partner." . . . He worked them for a low salary but he looked out for them like people look out for cattle.[27]

After a hasty flight from the zealous mob, Papa and Little Turner arrived at the "Big House," Warner Miller's primary residence. Little Turner felt an overwhelming sense of safety once there: "safe at last, safe at last, thank God." After entering through the back door, Turner informed Miller of what had just occurred only a few minutes earlier: "Mr. Miller, I got to see you, something very bad has happened." Miller sat down in his big rocking chair, crossed his legs, and grabbed a jug of homemade moonshine. "Mr. Miller, a lot of whites came to kill Little Turner," the elder Turner said. Miller asked why Little Turner was in danger. The elder Turner responded, "Word's out that Little Turner has been messing with Bear Chester's gal [Laura]." After hearing the reasoning behind the mob's desire to kill Little Turner, Miller responded: "Don't worry, Turner, goddammit, they ain't going to mess with your boy. I ain't gonna let them, Turner." After seeing Miller's car, the mob "scattered," only to be chased down by "The Boss." Confronting the leader of the mob, Miller issued a warning: "You son of a bitch, don't you ever go to Turner's house again. . . . If another son of a bitch goes to Turner's house, I'm going to blow his muthafuckin brains out." Members of the mob obviously had no avenues of redress. According to Little Turner, "Miller was so powerful they hardly never had an election. He'd just say, mmmmm partner, 'I'm going to make you the police this year, and you'd be the police, too.'" After the incident, Little Turner decided that he should leave Attapulgus under the cover of darkness to spare his grandfather the burden of having to worry about him. He reasoned that he might be killed if he was sighted outside the presence of his grandfather or Miller. The fugitive from vigilante justice, likely in a panic, took sixty-nine dollars from a fund that had been entrusted to Papa—the treasurer of the trustee board at church. He, then enlisted the assistance of Leroy Wise, a cousin who was sympathetic to his circumstances. Wise transported him to Tallahassee, Florida. We may never know all of the details surrounding the backroom deal-making that preserved Little Turner's life. However, Big Turner's prominence as a landowner and industrious Black man defied, in some respects, the negative stereotypes levied against Blacks in the town—possibly endearing him to the rural white aristocracy.[28]

Little Turner's insistence on leaving town may have been the result of his recollection of, or his grandfather informing him of, a lynching a few years earlier. It is unlikely that neither would have known of the 1937 lynching that happened just a few miles from their home in Attapulgus, in the county seat of Bainbridge. Willie Reed, a twenty four-year-old-Black man, who had been in the employ of a turpentine firm, allegedly raped and stabbed to death two white Bainbridge women with a hack sharpener—a sharp object used to chip bark from trees. Reed fled to Dothan, Alabama, where he was apprehended by deputies from Decatur County. Once they returned, Reed, who was unarmed, handcuffed, and shackled, according to four white deputies, tried to escape confinement. He was shot by a deputy. Once he was pronounced dead, Reed's body was transported to the Tom

Bynes Funeral Home. F. C. Clements, a local cotton merchant observed that a mob of "several hundred men, women, and children" had forced their way inside the funeral home and stolen Reed's lifeless body. The mob dragged the body to a Black ballpark, where they tarred and feathered the remains before stringing it up over a bonfire. In a grisly manner typical of "spectacle lynchings" in the South, those in attendance gathered "relics" from the scene. This particular episode of extralegal violence shows that mere death was not an acceptable form of punishment for assaulting white women. In the eyes of some whites, only the desecration of a Black man's remains in the most brutal manner would satisfy the mob's twisted sense of "justice." More pointedly, the deputy who boasted of shooting Reed was subsequently elected county sheriff, with the popular support of Bainbridge locals.[29]

Many Blacks in the South were not as fortunate in fleeing from the lynch mob as Little Turner, especially in Georgia. W. Fitzhugh Brundage, the eminent historian who specializes in historical memory and lynching, argues that four hundred twenty-six Blacks were lynched in Georgia from 1880 to 1930; of this total, one hundred seventy-six were lynched in south Georgia. It is true that white men were also lynched, albeit at a rate far less than that of Blacks. During the same fifty-year period, only nineteen whites were killed at the hands of the mob, usually for spousal or child abuse, or for practicing what Brundage calls "unorthodox moral, social, or political beliefs." Brundage argues that Blacks were lynched for seemingly insignificant offenses: insulting a white, petty theft, or refusing to accept defeat in an argument with a white, regardless of the facts and circumstances supporting the Black's reasoning. Murder of, and sexual relations with whites, real or imagined, were reasons to incite mob violence where lynching was explicitly or tacitly accepted.[30]

The white mob's attempt to lynch Little Turner is telling for a variety of reasons. The near-tragedy showed the depths of love and affection that Turner, the normally stern and reserved grandfather, had for his only grandson. This threat of mob violence also displayed the relationship that Turner had with the white propertied elite, proving that the Williams family enjoyed the favor of whites when the majority of Blacks in Attapulgus had precious few allies among whites, especially relationships with whites on a level where they could be considered friends. Little Turner witnessed how having money and owning property, in a sense, gave him and his family special privileges that other Blacks simply did not enjoy. Little Turner did not always get along with his grandfather, because they shared many of the same personality traits: Both were boisterous, ambitious, industrious, and unwilling to conform. Although Little Turner and his grandfather had what was at times a problematic relationship, the grandson had a high degree of respect and admiration for his grandfather.

Turner Williams, described by his grandson as one of three "leading niggers" in Attapulgus, along with the Black doctor and Black superintendent who lived in Bainbridge, was one of the most respected Black men to ever live in the small city. Referring to his grandfather and the power he wielded, Little Turner glowingly reflected: "That Turner Williams was something, brother." Hosea Williams often cited various civic and residential advantages that his grandfather routinely enjoyed that were primarily reserved for whites and that almost always eluded Blacks. For example, the elder Turner was "completely illiterate," unable to read and write but was voting during a time when many Blacks and poor whites were disfranchised because of a cumulative poll tax, literacy tests, and blatant and vicious intimidation. Little Turner suggested that his grandfather's privileges were rooted in the fact that the Williams family was viewed differently than other Blacks in the area: "I bet if you go down there right now . . . they really looked at us different from niggers, now that's the truth. . . . My grandfather was registered to vote while hardly nobody else in that county [Decatur] was hardly registered to vote" if they were not one of the aforementioned three "leading niggers." Not only was Turner voting in local elections, the Williams family's patriarch also curried favor with state highway department officials, as evidenced by the Division's willingness to circumvent bureaucratic and budgetary constraints to pave his driveway. Reflecting as an adult on his grandfather's clout in the community, Hosea Williams suggested that the state highway department had constructed the "half of block" driveway "as a favor to my granddaddy." This assertion is particularly interesting because the historian Gilbert Fite suggests that the 1930 gubernatorial campaign, which pitted lawyer and Speaker of the Georgia General Assembly Richard Russell against John N. Holder, identified paved roads along with tax reform; fiscal responsibility; and improved education at the elementary, high school, and collegiate levels as Georgia's most urgent needs.[31]

Little Turner grew up in relative privilege and invariably benefited from the fact that his grandfather was a hard worker who believed in one's economic independence. When referring to his grandfather's financial security, Little Turner posited that "Papa was the wealthiest black person in that part of the county when it came to land and finance." It is difficult to gauge whether a doting grandson's recollection of his grandfather's assets can be verified. What can be authenticated, however, is that by 1940, the elder Turner had accumulated nearly one hundred acres of land. According to the 1940 US Census, Little Turner's grandfather was "working on his own account," which allowed him and his family to enjoy a level of independence that proved elusive to so many southerners and Georgians, especially illiterate Blacks. According to the same census data, Turner's property along State Highway No. 1 on Amsterdam Road was valued at one thousand five hundred dollars when many Blacks and whites in the area were manacled by the shackles of sharecropping, which prevented them from earning enough disposable income to purchase land for themselves. Little Turner inherited his industrious grandfather's ability to generate revenue streams to ensure a degree of economic independence by working hard. In a moment of reflection, Little Turner recalled that "He'd work me like hell all day, keep me out of school to work me. . . . I always had money; I never was broke. I ain't never been broke in my life. . . . I always was wise, wise with money."[32]

The conditions for Blacks in Tallahassee before the civil rights movement did not differ much from those in cities in the former Confederacy. Blacks had, indeed, attacked some of the vestiges of the Civil War in the 1930s through the NAACP, specifically by filing lawsuits against the city that led to higher pay for Black teachers. By the late 1940s, Black residents constituted approximately 34% of the city's population but possessed little to no political power. Tallahassee was dominated by its three-member city commission, which routinely voted in the interests of what the historian Glenda Alice Rabby referred to as a "close-knit group of white men—attorneys, landowners, bankers and businessmen." Moreover, this powerful business bloc reinforced the social norms and mores that subordinated Blacks to the bottom of society. Tallahassee Blacks would later stage and sustain a boycott of the city's segregated public transportation system that changed the tone and tenor of race relations.[33]

The independence that accompanied financial security was a major motivational factor for Little Turner after he fled to Tallahassee in 1942. He had witnessed how his grandfather had prospered and managed to exercise some rights that were generally restricted to whites in Attapulgus. While in Florida over the next eight weeks, Hosea Williams held a series of jobs until the circumstances calmed down at home, including the pimping of prostitutes and working in a coal mine where he was on the clock five and one-half days per week, earning twenty dollars weekly for loading coal.

Little Turner also worked in the kitchen at a train station washing dishes. Reflecting on the wages that he earned, he stated that he washed "dishes from 6:00 AM in the morning 'til 6:00 in the evening, at $12.00 each week." He also saw the dark side of life while on the road.[34]

Little Turner and two of his friends, "Buddy" and "Rooster," lived in what Little Turner identified as a "whore house." He was the one most prepared to adapt to changing circumstances. He recalled how "the other boys used to get paid off on Saturday and by the time I's get there at 7:00 PM, them niggers would be broke . . . the whores done beat them out of their money. . . . They just couldn't make it; they wasn't smart enough to adapt." His friends did not have the hustler instincts that would be so critical to Little Turner's survival as a soldier in the US Army; a community leader in Savannah, Georgia, with the NAACP; and, ultimately, as a lieutenant to Rev. Martin Luther King Jr., activist, and politician in the State of Georgia.

Little Turner decided to return home in 1943. However, he faced a stern Papa, who told him one Saturday night, "If you're going to stay, face it [the lynch mob], you ought to stay. And if you're going to leave, you ought to go ahead and leave. They're going to hear about you coming back here, and they're going to catch you." After this conversation, Little Turner thought to himself, "If I leave this time, it would be a long time before I could come back. . . . But I thought it was best." He again went to Tallahassee—this time on his own. He found a job working at Superior Dry Cleaners in Florida's capital city. Although the money was less than what he was used to earning, he was able to survive for the next few years, because he kept his daily and monthly expenses low. Little Turner was only paying $2.50 per week for rent. While on the road and away from home, he constantly worked to improve his lot, trying his hand as an electrician with the National Youth Administration (NYA), a trade association housed at historically Black Florida Agricultural and Mechanical College for Negroes (now Florida A&M University). He changed his mind when he was almost fatally electrocuted after touching a rail that had been wired with electricity. "It knocked me out cold. I was unconscious," he remembered. His life would be quite unremarkable until he left Tallahassee to serve in the US Army in World War II.[35]

The United States officially entered World War II on December 8, 1941, when President Franklin D. Roosevelt requested that Congress declare war on Japan after the latter bombed the US naval fleet at Pearl Harbor. The historian David Kennedy maintains that Japan's desire to control China, strengthen its hold on Southeast Asia, and secure the preeminent status of its navy were three of the principal reasons for the empire's surprise attack on the United States. Japanese air forces killed 2,403 servicemen, 1,103 of whom were permanently entombed within the USS *Arizona* when the battleship sank after being hit at least four times by bombs dropped from Japanese aircraft. The loss of American ships and planes was also devastating. Eighteen of the American vessels, including eight battleships, were either sunk or required extensive repairs to ensure seaworthiness. At least three hundred aircraft suffered severe damage. Of three hundred planes, approximately one hundred eighty were completely destroyed. However, Isokoru Yamamoto, the esteemed Japanese admiral and primary architect of the attack on Pearl Harbor, was right when he stressed his fear that all the Japanese did was "awaken the sleeping giant and fill him with a terrible resolve."[36]

Anticipating a war in Europe long before the attack on Pearl Harbor, US leaders sought to increase America's military prowess through numeri cal strength and industrial capacity by selecting, recruiting, and training Blacks for service in the military and defense industries. First, the Selective Service and Training Act, enacted on September 16, 1940, provided that all men between the ages of 18 and 36, regardless of color, were allowed to serve in the armed forces. Another clause in the Act declared that discrimination based on race and color was prohibited in the training of soldiers. However, there was one caveat: The War Department was still given the discretion to admit or reject prospective volunteers for service if evaluators desired.

Whether from a sense of a higher purpose or, in some instances, a desire to leave the United States, where many Blacks were still relegated to the status of second-class citizenship, Blacks rallied to the Allied cause. As part of the "Double V" campaign, which represented victory over racism at home and victory over fascism abroad, Blacks joined the military effort and fought in defense of rights and freedoms abroad that they were denied at home. Ten months after the enactment of the Selective Service and Training Act, President Franklin Roosevelt, facing pressure from Black labor leader A. Philip Randolph of the Brotherhood of Sleeping Car Porters—who was threatening to lead a march of tens of thousands of Blacks on the nation's capital—issued Executive Order 8802. The Order prohibited employment discrimination based on race, color, creed, or national origin in the defense industries and within the government and created the Fair Employment Practices Committee (FEPC). Although the creation of the FEPC was criticized both at the time and by historians in the years since as relatively "toothless"—it let enforcement of nondiscrimination in federal contracts take a backseat to the imperative of winning the war—it nevertheless represented an important symbolic victory and was a sign of an increasingly restive Black population in the United States.[37]

The Selective Service Act and Executive Order 8802 were crucial factors that led to increased Black participation in the overall war effort. Under the 1940 Act, more than three million Blacks registered to serve in the US Armed Forces. Draft boards, however, rejected Black applicants at a rate of 18.2 percent, compared with 8.5 percent of whites. Although illiteracy and other deficiencies that resulted from a lack of both a quality formal education and access to health care influenced some of the board's decisions to reject potential draftees, many of the Black applicants were prevented from joining the military because of their skin color. Because of the growing threat of Adolf Hitler and the Axis powers, draft boards received pressure from the federal government to induct more Blacks. Only 2,069 Blacks were selected for service in the military in 1940, but the next year saw explosive growth. In 1941, more than 100,000 Blacks qualified and were accepted into the armed services. Three years later, approximately 701,678 Blacks were serving in some capacity in the US Army alone.[38]

Hosea Williams watched most of the war unfold as a teenager. By the spring of 1945, he was nineteen years old and professed to have been eager, at least initially, to join the war effort. He took a physical as a prerequisite for service in the US Army in April 1945. "It meant all in the world for me to pass that exam," he said, and its importance in his mind led him to choose not to inform the evaluating physician that he had been diagnosed with rheumatic fever three years earlier. His condition prevented him from riding a bike, swimming, or enjoying other recreational activities. Because he failed to disclose his past medical history, he passed the physical without much difficulty. "I whipped through, and I passed the exam and entered the Army," said Williams.[39]

Even in his own recollection, however, his induction into the military was a more complicated affair. After a brief period, he evidently had second thoughts about joining the Army and wanted to change his mind. Williams recalled that one of the last officials he needed to see before formal induction into the service was a medical official. He witnessed others offer excuses and fabricate life circumstances in futile attempts to avoid service in the Army. The man in front of him, Williams said, told Army personnel that his father was a carpenter and that the house fell on him—requiring the war dodger to stay home and care for the family's immobile patriarch. Williams referred to this story as a "fairy tale." "So when I finally confessed that I had rheumatic fever, it also sounded like a fairy tale," he recalled. Medical personnel were obviously skeptical about Williams's reported health condition. "If you are telling the truth," the Army official stated, "you go back home, and you get a letter from a licensed physician verifying the stuff you have told us, because if you are telling the truth, we don't want you in the Army." Williams went home to Attapulgus on a furlough to obtain the necessary paperwork and returned to Fort Benning in Columbus, Georgia, on the day he was to be sworn in. He submitted his medical records to someone he referred to as the "top man." The gentleman, whose rank and title are unknown, asked Williams what was the result of rheumatic fever. "It gives you a bad heart," he responded. The Army official then preceded to tear up the medical recommendation. "Goddamn, boy," said the officer in Williams's recollection. "You're in the right place. This place will get your heart right. Get your ass in that line." Williams, expecting sympathy for his medical condition, was shocked at this response. "Lord, have mercy," he said as he promptly assumed his place in the drill line.[40]

Hosea Williams was officially inducted into the US Army with the rank of private at Fort Benning, Georgia, on May 16, 1945. His enlistment papers listed his race as "Negro." His height was measured at sixty-nine inches, and his weight topped off at one hundred forty-seven pounds. His eye color and hair color were identified as "brown," and "back," respectively. Williams listed his civilian occupation as "farm hand." Because his service records indicate that his education level did not exceed high school, he was unable to qualify for a military occupational specialty classification beyond "cargo checker." Private Williams and his company left Fort Benning for Fort Leavenworth, Kansas. Once he arrived and settled into his barracks, one of his first responsibilities was to learn how to drill and march in accord with the instructor's commands. He acknowledged that he had some difficulty in following orders—a defining characteristic trait that was inseparable from his later life as an activist and politician. During one drill, Private Williams recalled that his failure to follow a command had dire consequences. "I made a wrong turn . . . and the sergeant made me run around with two big boxes of rocks five times. The next morning, that stuff [rheumatic fever] came down on me," he said. After a thorough examination, a nonplussed physician asked Private Williams pointedly: "How in the hell did you ever get in the Army?" Williams required around-the-clock medical attention. Hospitalized for approximately four months, the ailing soldier was soon taking eighteen pills per day as part of his daily dosage of medication. He credited the Army with saving his life. "That's why I'm here today," he recalled in an interview nearly a half century later. "I tell you the truth. That's the best thing that ever happened to me."[41]

Private Williams ultimately recovered from the flare-up of his rheumatic fever and was scheduled to be honorably discharged because of the recurring medical condition that had intensified because of the physical demands of military service. However, in a mysterious turn of events, he was inexplicably ordered to go through basic training again at Fort Leavenworth, Kansas, because his recent convalescence kept him from the learning the rudiments of military life with the soldiers with whom he had enlisted several months earlier. After Private Williams completed basic training without serious incident, he was transported to Camp Plauche, once an Army staging area in Harahan, Louisiana, for his technical training. After successfully completing this course, he was transferred to Fort Jackson, South Carolina, for infantry training that would prepare him for service in the European Theater of Operations.[42]

In later years, Hosea Williams would vividly relate stories of his service during his deployment in Germany. The actual details of his months in Europe are far cloudier, and the documentary record of his service record is regrettably incomplete. Hosea was closely connected with twelve Black soldiers in his segregated Army unit. "We were just like blood brothers . . . no way anybody could have been closer," Williams said. He would later recount in a compelling narrative how his life was forever changed when he was faced with the imminent threat of death in Europe. Williams asserted in a 1991 interview with historian Taylor Branch that his company had been given an assignment to rescue a group of British prisoners of war who had been captured earlier. During his company's attempt to liberate the soldiers in Einbeck, Germany, a small town not far from Hanover, all twelve of the soldiers he had bonded with as "brothers" were killed in action, he said. Williams indicated that he had been wounded by flying shrapnel in the upper and lower torso, survived, and was discovered by other allied soldiers. As he was being carried away, Private Williams would later assert that a German grenade had exploded under his stretcher, killing two emergency medical personnel. He was soon found and admitted into what he described as a "little Army hospital . . . a British hospital. Underground." He was struck by the fact that it was the first time he had encountered female physicians; there was "nothing but women doctors," he noted. He remained in Europe for several months recovering and receiving misinformation from his platoon and battalion commanders regarding his return to the United States. "I spent three or four months before I got everything straight" and "found out my company had de-evacuated and returned home," he said many years later. Recalling his return to civilian life late in 1946, an even forty-five years later, Williams told interviewer Taylor Branch in 1991 that he had left the Army with extensive dental bridgework, a leg damaged by many scars, and "a chest full of medals."[43]

Williams's accounts of the attack on his company are impossible to authenticate. That he served in the Army and was part of the occupation forces deployed to Europe late in 1945 is beyond dispute, but beyond that, the evidence grows murky. In an interview in 1991, he appears to have misidentified his infantry unit and initially told historian Taylor Branch that the alleged attack had occurred in April 1945, then backtracked and supplied the specific date of February 5, 1945. However, his enlistment records show that he was not inducted into the Army until May 16, 1945, just over a week *after* the German forces had unconditionally surrendered to the Allied forces in the aftermath of Hitler's April 30 suicide. Compounding the problems with the timeline of his enlistment and deployment in the written record as opposed to his oral reminiscences, he was stricken with rheumatic fever shortly after he was sworn in and was forced to spend several months recovering in a stateside Army hospital. This prevented him from deploying to Europe until November of 1945.[44]

Williams later claimed that he had been awarded a Purple Heart medal for being wounded, and various sources, some perhaps based on the civil rights veteran's own claims, reference this decoration. His official Enlisted Record and Report of Separation documenting his honorable discharge on October 30, 1946, however, only indicates that he was awarded a World War II Victory Medal and an Occupation Ribbon for his service in Germany.[45] Moreover, both Box 32 "Battles and Campaigns" and Box 34 "Wounds Received in Action" on his discharge report read "None."

Thus, the chronology of Hosea Williams's deployment and available evidence strongly suggest that his recollection of his wartime service was adversely affected by time. Having noted these many caveats, it is important to note that his Standard Form (SF-50), Notice of Personnel Action Form, dated July 21, 1960, shows that he was given a ten-point veteran disability preference. Other primary source evidence reaffirms that he suffered some form of injury or incurred a disability while serving his country in World War II. Also, he later received disability compensation for "service-connected disability" while in the US Army. If, in fact, Williams's accounts of the military action and injuries he described in later interviews in the 1980s and early 1990s did not occur as he claimed to remember them, one could reasonably infer that the disability might have been related to flare-ups of his rheumatic fever.[46]

Black soldiers in the segregated Army had fewer opportunities to showcase their competency and valor during World War II. Thousands of Black soldiers were remanded to menial, degrading jobs that did not fully capitalize on some of their abilities. Worse, the Office of War Information (OWI), the unit responsible for propagandizing the war abroad to a suspicious citizenry, took great pains to avoid publishing images of Black servicemen in uniform and were especially committed to suppressing most news and pictures of Black soldiers in combat to satisfy white readers. Black soldiers were routinely reminded of their "place"; at the same time, many whites believed that the war effort had made Black servicemen "unruly and unmanageable." Many Black soldiers were heralded as heroes among family and friends and may have been reluctant to share the painful reality: that service to their country was relegated to areas that were not as glamorous as the battlefield. As a result, some soldiers may have been compelled to exaggerate their wartime service to those closest them as well as prospective employers, the latter especially after assessing the employment opportunities in the post-war period.[47]

The recently promoted Sergeant Williams was honorably discharged from the US Army on October 30, 1946, only to return home to the same racially charged environment that had defined his existence when he donned a US Army uniform a year and a half earlier. He flew into Fort Bragg, South Carolina, from Europe in early November. His travel arrangements called for him to catch a bus from the military installation to Atlanta and then to Americus, Georgia, before riding the final leg of the trip to Bainbridge. While waiting to change buses in Americus, Williams was again reminded of his second-class status as a Black man in the South. One of countless exemplars of the "Double V" campaign, he had joined the Army to risk his life fighting against fascist tyranny abroad, but on returning to the United States, he could not enjoy the basic liberties undergirding a democratic society.

Williams had been advised to drink copious amounts of water as a prophylactic measure to thwart any subsequent bouts with rheumatic fever. He realized that the segregated Black section of the bus station where he was waiting contained an area for dispensing coffee but lacked a water fountain. He did not consume the caffeinated beverage because of a long-held folk belief: "They used to tell us little children, when we went to the white folks' house, that drinking coffee will make you black," recalled Williams. Thirsty, he pleaded with the white female attendant to grant him access to the "whites only" water fountain. Hewing to southern customs, she flatly refused. He bought some coffee and disposed of the beverage so that he could use the cup to drink some water. "I hobbled around to the front door; I didn't try to go in. I just leaned in and put the cup up to the dispenser to get me some water." When a group of whites present at a nearby gas station realized that Williams was disregarding southern norms and mores, they attacked him, punching and kicking the uniformed Army veteran until he lay motionless. In Williams's vivid recollection, "They beat me up and left me on the sidewalk. They thought I was dead."[48]

The injuries that Williams sustained at the hands of the white mob were so serious that many white onlookers believed that they had witnessed a brutal—yet, in their minds, justifiable—homicide. Someone called Mama's Funeral Home to retrieve Williams's body, which appeared lifeless. Reflecting many years later, he referred to the Black-owned and operated mortuary as "one of the finest, largest, and most beautiful funeral homes in any little rural county in America." As the driver was placing Williams's body in the ambulance, he felt a very faint pulse and noticed his chest slowly moving. The funeral parlor employee transported the badly wounded veteran to an Army hospital almost ninety miles away in Thomasville, Georgia. He spent approximately two months recovering from injuries unrelated to wartime combat. Immobile and mentally broken, Williams spent hours reflecting on the previous two years of his life. In one moment of sobering reflection, he reached the despairing conclusion: "Goddamn it. I fought on the wrong side."[49]

Williams finally arrived home in Attapulgus after his eight-week convalescence. His homecoming was another bitter reminder for Blacks in the Deep South that their skin color was a badge of inferiority. One evening in January 1947, Williams, now twenty-one years old, was longing for one of his favorite dishes: pork chops with a lot of black pepper. His aunt, Azzie Mae, volunteered to fry the pork chops if he picked the meat up from the store. "I drove her car up the store," Williams said. He went into the only supermarket in town and encountered Mr. Boyd, the white proprietor. Williams, in his Army uniform, told Boyd that he wanted two pounds of pork chops. As he was reaching for the pork chops, Boyd recognized Williams and asked if he was "Little Turner."

"Yes," Williams said.

"Nigger," said Boyd, "don't you say yes to me. You say, yes sir to me, goddamn it." Boyd continued on his racist rant: "All the other nigger boys come back from the Army and come in this store and say, 'How you doing, Mr. Boyd?'"

Williams, likely still upset and grappling with the injuries from his shellacking in Americus, told Boyd: "I don't give a damn how you doin'!" Boyd reached for his shotgun, with undoubtedly lethal intent. Fortunately, Boyd's wife intervened, and Williams fled unscathed. Papa and Aunt Azzie Mae encouraged him to leave home again, as many whites in the town were eager to finally carry out the lynching that had almost occurred a few years earlier, after his relationship with Laura Chester had been made public. For the second time, Williams was forced to abandon his family and home to avoid imminent death at the hands of vigilante whites.[50]

Hosea Williams left Attapulgus for Bainbridge in February 1947. "My granddaddy told me to go away and get some learnin,'" he remembered. At some point in early 1947, he decided to resume the education he had abandoned after he left school in either his eighth- or ninth-grade year. "I realized the need for education so I went and convinced the principal in Bainbridge to let me into school," said Williams. She agreed to let him register for school if he would make a concerted commitment to his schoolwork. The twenty-one-year-old Williams was obviously uneasy about the prospect of sitting in class with younger classmates. "It was embarrassing to sit up in class with kids who were sixteen year olds," he lamented. Nevertheless, he enrolled in Hutto High School. Hutto was originally known as the Whittier School and Tabernacle for Colored Children, the first school organized by former slaves in 1869 Decatur County. Named for longtime principal George Hutto, the school had a long tradition of educating the community's Black pupils despite its meager resources, leaky roofs, and cramped quarters—hallmarks of Black schools at the time. Hutto would have likely been staffed at that time by Black female teachers whose formal education was not equal to the training of the white teachers at neighboring all-white Bainbridge High School less than five miles away. In spite of these deficiencies, Williams graduated at the end of the academic school year.[51]

Although Williams had been steadfastly committed to graduating from high school, he still found time for involvement with the ladies. He was particularly fond of Carrie Mae Pugh. Pugh, three years his junior, was a native of Bainbridge and the daughter of Gordie Pugh Sr. and Virgilene C. Beard. Carrie was extraordinarily beautiful; Hosea recalled having practically "melted" after seeing her for the first time. Carrie, for her part, found Hosea to be handsome and charismatic. The two began dating during their senior year at Hutto High. Carrie became pregnant around May 1947, shortly after she and Hosea graduated. They were married four months later in a quiet ceremony performed by the Rev. J. C. Hamilton on September 15 of that same year. After the nuptial exchange, Carrie left Bainbridge to begin college at Fort Valley College, an historically Black institution in Fort Valley, Georgia.[52]

During this period of his life, Hosea Williams entered into an unlikely friendship with Cheney Griffin, the younger brother of Marvin Griffin, who, in 1955, would succeed Herman Talmadge as Georgia governor, running on a staunchly segregationist platform. Williams's relationship with Cheney Griffin played a critical role in the young veteran's and father-to-be's decision to attend college. Although the origins of the relationship are somewhat unclear, Williams forged a strong, nearly fraternal relationship with Cheney Griffin, who was about a decade older. Marvin Griffin would go on to serve as a rabidly segregationist Georgia governor, but Williams thought that his younger brother was cut from a different cloth: "There was never two brothers more different," Williams said. "Marvin Griffin was a racist to the core. White superiority was an obsession with him. . . . Cheney was more like Lester Maddox and George Wallace. Cheney was much more willing to accept a person for who he was." Whatever their underlying motivations, the two white brothers embraced segregationist positions out of political expediency. The Griffin family owned the *Bainbridge Searchlight*, the city's conservative newspaper. By age twenty-six, Cheney Griffin had been elected mayor of Bainbridge. At the same time, Marvin Griffin was making a name for himself in the Georgia General Assembly as a state representative and establishing statewide political credentials. In Williams's recollection, whatever segregationist views Cheney espoused publicly, they did little to deter him from befriending Williams. "We were doing everything that two men could do other than have a sexual relationship," he jovially remembered. The two of them did have sexual relationships with white women and Black women and shared moonshine-fueled drunken escapades together. According to Williams, they even scammed white patrons at a venue where Williams served as the head Black waiter. "We would beat them rednecks out of their money. . . . When time come to pay the bill . . . Cheney would start rantin' and ravin' to bring attention when the bill was due. . . . The whites would say, 'What's the bill, boy?'" Williams and Griffin would collude to pad the bill and thus have the whites pay an inflated cost, with the ill-gained overage then split between the two unlikely friends.

Ultimately, the friendship took an unexpected turn. "Cheney was red as beet when he walked up to me [one day] and said very angrily, 'I'm WHITE and you're BLACK. . . . I can make it in this town because I'm white. . . . You'll never make it here because you're black.'" Griffin pleaded with his friend to leave Decatur County to seek a college education. "You know I'm broke, don't have no money," said Williams. Griffin smiled and made a deal with Williams. He promised, "You go to college and I'll pay the bill." The two shook hands. "He gave me seventy-five dollars" toward tuition, said Williams. This unexpected donation, along with his GI Bill benefits, would defray some of his collegiate expenses. However, he still had to be admitted into an institution.[53]

Hosea Williams initially wanted to study at Morehouse College in Atlanta after a friend from Bainbridge had convinced him that he could get Williams admitted into the Atlanta University Center's flagship institution in spite of his lack of high school credit hours. Unfortunately, but not unexpectedly, Morehouse rejected Williams's application for admission. Undeterred, Williams's friend continued to search for colleges for him to attend. "I know damned well I can get you in at Clark [College]," said the buddy from Bainbridge, in Williams's recollection, but Clark also rejected the aspiring collegian. Williams's friend and advocate had another trump card that he was willing to use as a last resort: His father was an officer in the African Methodist Episcopal (AME) Church. "His father called an AME Bishop at Morris Brown College for me . . . the bishop was willing to give me a chance because he knew the boy's father," said Williams. The bishop agreed to admit Williams under two conditions: if he agreed to "keep his nose clean and get his lessons," remembered the anxious student. Williams had gained admission, and he knew that his financial assistance from his veteran's GI Bill would help to cover many of the expenses associated with tuition, books, and room and board.[54]

Williams began his studies at Morris Brown College in September 1947 and soon selected a major in chemistry and a minor in biology. During his second semester, his and Carrie's first and only child, Barbara Jean Williams, was born in Bainbridge on March 7. He was unable to be present for the birth because he was in school and did not have a car. More pointedly, he was likely too afraid to miss classes, fearing that he might fall behind in his coursework—an attitude that was invariably tempered by his age and maturity. He even dressed the part. Williams was a sharp dresser, claimed fellow chemistry major Emmogene Williams. "He wore bowties to class all the time," she said. Victoria Jenkins, a cheerleader and Williams's classmate, claimed that he was a "very serious student." Jenkins continued, "We took a religion course together from Dean Edward C. Mitchell during our freshman year and he spent a lot of time in the library" doing schoolwork. He was a "serious" pupil who apparently possessed the ability to navigate through a course of study that required him to be analytical and deliberate.[55]

Evidence suggests that he was not particularly fond of the humanities or other subjects that required a lot of writing, which was reflected in his performance in these areas. "I got all the good grades in the classes that I enjoyed," he said. "I was a hell of a chemist at Morris Brown. I flunked English and history, but math and calculus, oh, man, I made some grades." Emmogene Williams recalled Williams as "a very gifted student." Her observations were shaped during the science classes they both took from brothers and West Virginia natives, Drs. Artis and Linwood Grays. She asserted that her former classmate was "one of the best chemistry students who came out of Morris Brown." Williams remembered that his abilities as a budding chemist enabled him to work in a student program in the Emory University science lab, a segregated white institution in Atlanta, while immersed in the science program at Morris Brown College.

Hosea Williams's formative experiences in South Georgia and Florida, and in Europe as soldier in a segregated unit in the US Army during World War II, made him a socially conscious student while at Morris Brown College. Like many Black college students in the late 1940s, he was frustrated with race-based discrimination and wanted to join organizations that addressed issues relative to Blacks' attainment of full citizenship rights.[56] Seeking affiliations with groups that had as their mission bringing about meaningful change, Williams joined the Atlanta chapter of the NAACP in the late 1940s, during a time when the state organization was headed by John Wesley Dobbs. (Dobbs's grandson was Maynard Jackson, who would go on to become the first Black elected mayor of any major city in the Deep South almost thirty years later when he won office in Atlanta.) Although Dobbs was a visionary and a leader in the Black community as Grand Master of the Prince Hall Masons of Georgia and the founder of the Atlanta Civic and Political League, Williams remembered that Dobbs and other influential Black activists did not have a lot of contact with students in the capital. Williams remained abreast of the social issues affecting Blacks in Atlanta and in the country by attending some of the state chapter meetings. He contended that some of the students at Morris Brown College were not yet heavily engaged in protests. "Basically, during that time," Williams remembered, "we were only having meetings in our community since the only major resistance to racism was through the courts." Nevertheless, Williams's budding curiosity relative to how he could strategically address the inequities that he and other Blacks had to grapple with was heightened during the NAACP meetings he attended while working toward his bachelor of science degree.[57]

Williams's relationship with his wife Carrie had suffered because of the distance and his inability, or unwillingness, to travel home to south Georgia. They divorced after only a few years of marriage, and despite his garrulous nature, Williams subsequently would never reference his first wife. While in Atlanta in 1950, he met Juanita "Nit" Terry. Juanita, born in Atlanta on January 3, 1925, was the only child of Elizabeth Virginia Terry and Jesse Brown. She was raised by her grandmother, Elizabeth Golden Terry. Juanita described her grandmother as a "very proud Black woman, determined to give me the very best" out of life. Juanita graduated from Atlanta's Booker T. Washington High School and, subsequently, from Reid's Business College. She moved to Washington, DC, during World War II to work as a civilian clerk typist with the US Department of the Army, but she resigned from this position after the job became emotionally overwhelming. "It broke my heart to send out letters to parents telling them about the death of their children in the war. I could not take it anymore," she said. After leaving the nation's capital, she found a job in Atlanta as a stenographer at one of the city's leading Black financial institutions, Citizen's Trust Bank. She recalled meeting Williams while working one day in 1950. "He came into the bank just being his own self," she remembered. "Just flirtin' and carrying on. . . . I thought [he] was something since he was going to college." After a courtship that lasted a little more than a year, Hosea Williams married Juanita Terry shortly after he graduated with his bachelor of science degree in chemistry from Morris Brown College on June 6, 1951.[58]

Williams's responsibilities and ambition for upward mobility convinced him that an advanced degree would strengthen his chances to provide a life of luxury for his family. In the summer of 1951, he was admitted into the graduate school at Atlanta University to pursue a master's degree in chemistry. To make ends meet, he withdrew from his degree program to take a job teaching high school science in the Douglas County, Georgia, school system for the 1951–1952 academic year for an annual salary of one thousand nine hundred dollars. "We needed the money," said Juanita. "It wasn't just that. He had all this energy that had to be put in some direction. He never could just relax. At that time of his life, he just put it into work." He ultimately resigned from the school after a heated dispute with the county superintendent over the limited budget that he was given to purchase supplies for his students. Williams then resumed his coursework toward the master's degree at Atlanta University during the summer of 1952. His life revolved around schoolwork, studying between classes during the day and work at night and over the weekends sorting parcels with the Railway Mail Service, a division of the US Post Office. He constantly sought a more secure standard of living and the prestige of a white-collar position. In September 1952, he returned to public school work as a science teacher at the all-Black J. P. Carr High School in Rockdale County, Georgia, at an annual salary of two thousand four hundred dollars—five hundred dollars more than his previous teaching job in Douglassville, Georgia. Although he enjoyed the increase in salary, he was not content with the way that he and other Black teachers were treated by the local school system, and he encouraged his colleagues to express their disdain with the county's Jim Crow policies collectively through meetings and protests at the county headquarters. "The white folks basically ran Hosea away from that place," recalled Tyrone Brooks, a mentee who viewed Williams as a father figure. Left with few options in the school system because of his growing reputation as one who disturbs the status quo, he left J. P. Carr High School on December 1, 1952, after he was granted a transfer from his federal job as a mail sorter with the US Post Office to the US Department of Agriculture's Marketing Research Division within the Biological Sciences Branch in Savannah, Georgia. This job transfer and change of scenery placed Williams on a trajectory that would change the course of his and Juanita's life.[59]

TWO

"The Defiant Head House Nigger"

"Every day at 12—you could set your watch by it. Hosea would lead 200 or 300 people downtown to the Johnson Park right across the street from the Manger Hotel. In that park there is a statue of an Indian chief by the name of Tomochichi. Hosea would climb up on that statue, and he would talk about white folks like you had never heard! I mean he did it every, single solitary day!" These are the words that Willie Bolden used to describe Hosea Williams's method of marshaling and appealing to Savannah Blacks on his lunch breaks during the desegregation campaign of the early 1960s. Williams did not begin his tenure in Savannah as a rabble-rousing troublemaker who railed against the white establishment. His mounting frustration started on his job as a chemist with the US Department of Agriculture's Bureau of Anemology and Plant Quarantine, within the Chemical Division. According to Williams, he was one of the first persons of African descent to be employed as a research chemist with the federal government south of the Mason-Dixon Line. His secretary was a white woman. He believed that he finally landed on the path to upward mobility. He soon realized that he was a "token" employee to satisfy calls for equality within the agency at a time when the Department of Agriculture was not hiring other Black chemists. He reached the conclusion that he was falsely secure in his position because he was being used as the "head house nigger." He was using this charged phrase to compare his position with that of the slave in an antebellum plantation household who held the highest rank and did not perform grueling physical labor in the fields but worked instead in the relative comfort of the master's house.[1]

In January 1952, shortly after his twenty-sixth birthday, Hosea Williams moved to Savannah, Georgia, to accept a job as one of the first Black research chemists with the US Department of Agriculture in the Deep South.

His transition from graduate student at Atlanta University in the state's largest metropolis to middle-class professional in the small Atlantic port city of Savannah during the Cold War occurred only two years before the beginning of the classical phase of the modern Black freedom struggle in 1954. His new posting reminded him that the reality of his status as a decorated World War II veteran and holder of a college degree in chemistry with additional graduate-level work did not shield him from the racism and bigotry in a city known for its "moderate" race relations. This revelation thrust Williams to the forefront of the city's civil rights leadership as chief apprentice to Westley Wallace "W. W." Law, the domineering president of the Savannah branch of the NAACP. Williams's talent at organizing Black students and working-class adults to unite in one common cause was cultivated and refined while occupying various positions of leadership within the Savannah branch of the NAACP, which had been functioning, although not always continuously, since 1917. Williams did not make the local NAACP chapter in Savannah: The local branch, which had organized over several decades, made him.[2]

Between 1954 and 1963, Williams chaired the branch's Membership, Education, Legal Redress, and Negotiating Committees, respectively. Although he was effective in each of these demanding capacities, his role as president of the NAACP's political arm, the Chatham County Crusade for Voters (CCCV), would later capture the attention of Rev. Martin Luther King Jr., the SCLC president and, arguably, the most celebrated figure of the modern civil rights movement. The NAACP's pressure on moderate politicians and white business leaders and religious leaders brought about the collapse of segregation in public accommodations in Savannah in October 1963—almost a full year ahead of President Lyndon B. Johnson's signing of the landmark Civil Rights Act into law in the summer of 1964. By January 1964, in large measure because of the diligent labor of Williams and Law, Martin Luther King Jr. proclaimed Savannah "as the most desegregated city south of the Mason-Dixon Line." Williams's growing commitment to the cause of civil and human rights was, in no small part, the result of the race-based discrimination he experienced on the job as an employee of the US government.[3]

Savannah, named for the neighboring Savannah River, is Georgia's oldest city and was settled in May 1733 by James Edward Oglethorpe. An Englishman by birth, Oglethorpe came from an affluent family in England and was elected to the British Parliament in 1722. As a Member of Parliament, he chaired a committee that investigated the conditions of English jails and the inmates who had been imprisoned for being unable to discharge their debts. His findings led to the release of a number of prisoners who would constitute the population of a new American colony that could protect British land and interests from France and Spain. Upon an initial survey of the land in close proximity to the colony of South Carolina, Oglethorpe chose an area that was easy to defend and had an adequate supply of fresh water. Comfortable with the land advantages, he built a positive working relationship with Tomochichi, a "man of unalterable fidelity" and chief of the Yamacraw Indians. Nearly two hundred thirty-three years later, Williams would hold mass rallies in the square named for Tomochichi, who had commanded a small tribe near Yamacraw Bluff.[4]

Williams's visual inspection of Savannah in 1952 would have revealed the city's genteel southern character. Parts of Savannah were picturesque and charming. The urban landscape was defined by long stretches of green space and numerous parklike public squares, reminiscent of Oglethorpe's vision to foster in each neighborhood a sense of individual community. Suburban Savannah included monuments and quaint nineteenth- and early twentieth-century homes. The city's downtown streets were lined with centuries-old live oaks. Their branches stretched out in all directions to provide pedestrians shade from the subtropical climate of Savannah's sweltering summers. Spanish moss draped the telephone lines and trees alike, drifting and swaying in the damp air, adding to the ambiance of the city. The Savannah landscape was also sprinkled with palmetto trees and azalea bushes. In spite of its undeniable beauty, Savannah had a dark and ugly side. Its wealth and beauty were inextricably tied to the Peculiar Institution, and despite the efforts of Blacks to assert themselves, the shadow of slavery endured in the form of Jim Crow.[5]

The system of discrimination that Hosea Williams would tirelessly fight to destroy had been inextricably tied to southern law and custom for many decades by the time he arrived in Savannah. At the end of the Civil War in 1865, Blacks, by custom, had already been excluded from schools, many hospitals, insane asylums, and public accommodations. Historian Howard Rabinowitz notes that "before the resort to widespread de jure segregation—de facto segregation had replaced exclusion as the norm in southern race relations." Even before voter disfranchisement began in earnest in 1890, however, states in the former Confederacy had begun to codify laws that systematically segregated the races. Southern historian C. Vann Woodward documents that Florida was the first state to adopt such a law in 1887. Mississippi, Texas, and Louisiana followed suit in 1888, 1889, and

1890, respectively. The following year, Alabama, Arkansas, Kentucky, and Georgia enacted versions of the discriminatory statutes in their respective states. Georgia became the first state to adopt a law requiring segregation on streetcars in 1891. Georgia's segregation ordinance was passed with the disclaimer that it be enforced "as much as practicable." By 1899, the state expanded race-based discrimination to cover railroad sleeping cars. Blacks in Georgia, particularly Savannah, vigorously protested the passage of the 1899 statue, but to no avail.[6]

Although various protests broke out in other cities in Georgia during the flurry of segregation legislation, the historians, August Meier and Elliot Rudwick, suggest that "the most sustained protest occurred in Savannah" after a fight between Black and white commuters led the Georgia General Assembly to pass an ordinance in 1906 requiring streetcar companies to enforce segregation between the races. Meier and Rudwick, conclude that that, in many cities throughout the South, streetcar companies opposed such legislation because the policy was both problematic and expensive to enforce. Moreover, the companies were reluctant to implement race-based discrimination out of fear of losing Black patronage. Blacks in Savannah proved that the streetcar companies' reservations about segregation were prophetic, as they initiated a boycott almost immediately after the passage of the discriminatory legislation. With this protest, Blacks, under the banner of the Chatham County Emancipation Association, began a tradition of boycotting Savannah businesses that endorsed segregation by withholding their patronage from the streetcars operated by the Savannah Electric and Power Company. The boycott continued through 1907, ultimately costing the company fifty thousand dollars in revenue (approximately $1,250,000 adjusted for inflation). Internal dissension within the Black professional community, including among the instructors at Georgia State Industrial College, a Black institution, caused the protesting spirit to weaken before the Black community could negotiate a favorable compromise. However, the protest showed that Savannah Blacks would not sit by idly when discriminated against—a tradition that Hosea Williams would continue as a member of the Savannah branch of the NAACP.[7]

The Savannah branch of the NAACP was one of the strongest and most powerful chapters in the Deep South at the time Williams joined its ranks upon moving to the city. The chapter had long benefitted from politically astute and dynamic branch presidents who worked well within the conservative national organization. The history of the Savannah branch of the NAACP can be traced back as early as 1915, six years after the national organization was founded in New York in 1909. Georgia State College (later Savannah State University) professor Miken L. Pope wrote to then-director of publications and research and co-founder of the organization, William Edward Burkhardt (W. E. B.) Du Bois, inquiring about the necessary steps required to form a branch in Georgia's oldest city. The initial inquiry within itself was a bold—some would argue, imprudent—move, as less than five of the national organization's seventy branches existed in the former Confederacy, a region that Archibald Grimke aptly identified as "enemy territory." Professor Pope, motivated by the plight of Blacks and their woeful ignorance of the implications of racial segregation in Savannah, had already established a club of activist-minded men and women who were eager to tackle the ills of racism and discrimination in Savannah. Pope, the catalyst, hoped to transform this already functioning unit into a local branch of the NAACP. Although a branch was not founded in Savannah as a result of Pope's efforts, Blacks' sensitivity to the significance of the race problem was heightened. Within two years, a branch would be chartered in the city.[8]

On March 7, 1917, James Weldon Johnson, the NAACP's new national field secretary, addressed a modest crowd at the St. Paul Christian Methodist Episcopal Church. Included among the one hundred twenty attendees were leaders of the Black business community in Savannah. From the pulpit, Johnson proclaimed, "Our race is moving forward and leaving the leaders in the rear." For him, the Savannah event demonstrated that, with strong and effective leadership from an influential core group, local organizers would be able to create and sustain a vigorous branch in the port city. Four months later, the NAACP chartered a Savannah branch with seventy-nine members. The branch's inaugural officers represented the elite tier of Black society. The new branch elected as president Fannin S. Belcher, one of Savannah's few Black physicians. His friend, James Garfield Lemon, a local attorney and insurance salesman for the Pilgrim Life Insurance Company, was chosen to serve as the branch's first secretary. Equally respected in the area was the branch's first-elected treasurer, Albert B. Singfield. This core group of officers would remain in place for the next two years.[9]

The Savannah branch of the NAACP actively waged the fight against racism in and around the city. During this period, the branch championed various cases in which Blacks had been unduly administered harsh southern injustice in the courts. For example, the national office asked the branch to investigate the circumstances surrounding the arrest and conviction of James Harvey and Joe Jordan after both Black men were found guilty of assaulting and raping a white woman in September 1921. With nearly one thousand dollars in financial assistance from the national office and the Atlanta branch, the Savannah branch concluded that the defendants had been denied their basic constitutional privileges. They had not been permitted to call any witnesses, nor were they allowed to participate in procedures insofar as jury selection was concerned. Harvey and Jordan were also denied competent counsel. The two were sentenced to die on three separate occasions after a series of Georgia Supreme Court rulings and execution stays from Governor Thomas Hardwick. Although the trial had been held in Jessup, Georgia, less than fifty miles southwest of Savannah, the court ordered that both defendants be transported to the coastal city for "safekeeping." On July 1, 1922, while en route to Savannah in the custody of the sheriff's deputies, Harvey and Jordan were kidnapped and hanged by a mob of angry whites. The Savannah NAACP collected evidence against five perpetrators, but no one was ever convicted of the crime.[10]

The acquittal of the defendants accused of participating in the lynching of Harvey and Jordan dampened the enthusiasm of the local NAACP and the Black community in Savannah. The branch was inactive from 1925 to 1930. After a brief revival in 1930, the national office sent a duplicate charter to a newly reactivated branch with two hundred sixty-six members, but the local chapter proved unable to sustain the necessary momentum to keep Blacks in the city motivated enough to stand with and actively support an organization that was perceived by most whites to be a threat to maintaining traditional white dominance. The branch was once again classified as "inactive" from 1938 to 1942. On March 7, 1942, Rev. Dr. Mark Gilbert, pastor of the First African Baptist Church, one of the oldest Black churches in the United States, wrote a letter to E. Frederick Morrow, national branch coordinator for the NAACP. Gilbert informed him that he had "secured the fifty members necessary to start a branch" and that a "committee on permanent organization" had been formed to avoid the branch's earlier tendencies to lapse into inactivity and ensure that the branch would survive in perpetuity. On April 13, only five weeks later, the branch was rechartered with three hundred members.[11]

By January 1943, nine years before Hosea Williams arrived in Savannah, the local branch had emerged as the operational nucleus for the NAACP in Georgia. Gilbert and the Savannah branch "took the initiative" and formed a statewide NAACP Conference "for the purposes of more effectively making the NAACP articulate on matters affecting the Negroes in the state of Georgia." Of the state's eleven branches, seven sent delegates to the three-day meeting held at Gilbert's church. Gilbert, the organizer of the meeting, was elected president, a position he would hold until 1950. His fellow member in the Savannah branch, Stella J. Reeves, was elected chairman of the youth council. He championed a platform mutually agreed upon by the delegates that included attacking the poll tax, supporting a retirement fund for Negro teachers, and agreeing to embark on a rigorous program to get members registered and voting in elections. By the time the meetings concluded on January 17 over a turkey dinner at First African Baptist Church, the Savannah branch had emerged as the only branch with two members occupying leadership positions. The delegates elected Professor C. L. Harper of the Atlanta branch vice president, N. M. Tomas of Columbus as secretary, and Rev. M. F. Adams of Albany as treasurer. The state and local branches would enjoy relative success in registering Blacks to vote during the next five years. By 1949, the Savannah branch, however, was one again on the precipice of dissolution, until the emergence of W. W. Law.[12]

W. W. Law, Hosea Williams's mentor in the NAACP, became branch president in 1950. Law told National Director of Branches Ruby Hurly that "Dr. Ralph Mark Gilbert and just about all of his crew ran out on me . . . it was like seeing the rats leaving a sinking ship . . . they willed the branch presidency to me." Law was twenty-seven years old at the time and was to be employed as a postal worker with the US Post Office. He worked with previous and current members to rebuild the branch but was forced to grapple with the same issues that had previously plagued the local NAACP. In a letter to National Membership Secretary Lucille Black, Law outlined an ambitious campaign to meet and exceed the seven-hundred-fifty-member quota prearranged by the national organization. However, he also lamented that "many of the preachers, teachers, and professional people (like the doctors and whatnots) have a million excuses for not working in the membership drive." Although he referred to this situation as "disgusting," he optimistically concluded that, "If we can get enough help in the membership drive we can and will do well." It was this attitude and commitment to civil rights activism that enabled him to be elected as the youngest member of the NAACP National Board of Directors at age thirty-two.[13]

Hosea Williams's service in the US Army and satisfactory performance rating on the General Service exam earned him a job with the US Department of Agriculture's Bureau of Anemology and Plant Quarantine, Chemical Division. His score on the civil service exam ranked in the ninetieth percentile, which was augmented by a ten-point bonus because of the disabled veteran's status.[14] Getting this job "was like going to heaven," he later said. However, Williams's initial enthusiasm over the appointment was dampened after Ciprian Cueto, the Cuban-American head chemist, gave him an initial tour of the chemistry lab.

Feeling an overwhelming sense of inadequacy, the new hire began to tear up after seeing certain pieces of scientific equipment for the first time. "I was about to bust out and start crying," he recalled. Startled by Williams's reaction, Cueto began to question why his new employee's demeanor had changed from happiness to dread. "What's the matter? You don't want the job?" Williams replied: "Mister, I have to be honest with you. I ain't never seen nothing like this on Earth. . . . You know all those instruments you just showed me. . . . I ain't even seen them in a book." The meager resources available to the students at Morris Brown College and Atlanta University were in stark comparison to the equipment at the disposal of the students and some of Williams's colleagues who had attended the state's flagship institution. According to Williams, "The white boys from a school like the University of Georgia had not only seen the instrument and worked with it in college, they'd had a course called echelon maintenance . . . where they learned to take the damn thing apart and put it back together again." Cueto, whom Williams remembered as "a chemical nut," offered his colleague a proposition: "I'll make a deal with you. I'll teach you if you are willing to learn."[15]

Williams formally accepted the job and began a rigorous routine that acclimated him to the complexities of his new position as a research chemist. Cueto, who often felt marginalized in the United States because of his own ethnic heritage, did not have many friends and, according to Williams, "just wanted some company." Through the middle of 1953, both men went to their offices in the stored-product insects section at the Savannah station each morning around 8:00 and worked until 10:00 each night. During these thirteen-hour days, according to Williams's job description, he assisted in the conducting and planning of experiments to "correlate with the entomological research" of the section. He was also tasked with "modifying existing chemical analytical methods and laboratory techniques for the determination of various insecticide concentrates and residues," which required "independent judgment and skill in several phases of chemistry." By the end of 1953 and under the expert tutelage of Cueto, Williams was "developing special insecticide formulations prescribed by entomologists . . . while also conducting complicated analyses involving volumetric, gravimetric and spectrophotometric methods for insecticide determinations." In laymen's terms, Williams became proficient in examining volume and applying the techniques and procedures pioneered by Theodore R. Richards, a professor of chemistry at Harvard University and the first American to win the Nobel Prize in chemistry, to determine various formulas for insecticides.[16]

By the end of 1954, Hosea's development as a professional analytical research chemist was being noticed by his peers, all of whom were non-Blacks. "I was finally matching brains with the boys from Yale, Princeton and Harvard," he claimed. Williams, in his characteristic brashness, continued: "I kicked their ass and called names." His bold declarations have some merit. That year, he co-wrote an article titled "Insect Control on Feathers" with Hamilton Laudani, P. H. Clark, and W. E. Dale. The article appeared in *Soap and Chemical Specialties*, a professional journal that circulated among chemists and physicists. His first academic publication would not appear until August 1956, when his article titled "A New Colorimetric Method for Pyrethrins" was published in the *Journal of the Association of Official Agricultural Chemists*. However, he was a chemist on the rise within the Department of Agriculture. "I worked and studied hard so I went right up the ladder. . . . I'd go top of the GS grade five and top of grade seven," Williams said. In another recollection of his rapid rise within the government's ranks, he stated, "I was really treated like a king. . . . I even had a white secretary, which was the epitome of success," for a Black man in the State of Georgia.

In spite of his "success," Williams was routinely reminded that his intellect and expertise as a chemist did not shield him from the racism and segregation that plagued the South and its institutions.[17] He was unable to receive just recognition from the wider scientific community, because he was prevented from presenting his research at the meetings and conferences of the American Chemical Society. He recalled that he was barred from attending many of the regional meetings because they were held at land-grant colleges in the South. He was prohibited from going to one particular meeting at the University of Mississippi, thwarting his attempt to share his "greatest work," which was a "quantitative chemical analysis for pyrethrum." Pyrethrum was one of the most effective insecticides in the world. However, the chemical's instability forced the US government to spend "at the time, millions of dollars" buying the insecticide from India and Africa. Williams suggested that his new method specifically analyzed the chemical's parent compound, which allowed a scientist to use only seven to fifteen micrograms, which are equivalent in the metric system to one millionth of a gram. The method that Williams devised as a result of his pioneering research made his procedure yield results that were "thousands of times more sensitive and specific," ultimately saving the federal government money while conferring prestige and professional respectability on the chemist who would have been given credit for the research. According to Williams, "this was the finest pieces of research I'd ever done." However, Dr. John F. Sweeney, a white chemist with the Department of Agriculture, presented the paper at the University of Mississippi in 1954 and was credited with being the chief author. Sweeney "got one of the finest jobs in his life . . . and left the Department of Agriculture with my work," lamented Hosea.[18]

Williams was an advocate of the self-help advice prescribed by Booker T. Washington to impoverished and uneducated Blacks in the early 1900s. Washington, born into slavery, went on to found Tuskegee Institute in Alabama and to serve as an advisor to several US presidents. He challenged Negroes to "pull themselves up by their bootstraps" if they desired to improve their respective lots. Williams echoed this Washingtonian adage to Blacks in Savannah. The middle-class Williams remembered telling other Negroes: "You can make it because I made it. . . . You are not trying to make it. . . . You want someone to give it to you. . . . But if you work like I work," other Blacks, too, can be upwardly mobile and will be accepted by well-meaning whites.

For a brief period while he was living comfortably within the social parameters controlled by whites in Savannah, Williams was slowly becoming culturally isolated and unable to relate with the masses of Negroes. E. Franklin Frazier, the eminent Black sociologist and professor, would, in his seminal study, *Black Bourgeoisie*, assert that middle-class Blacks, such as Williams, who embraced similar admonishments unknowingly "lived in a world of make-believe," which divorced them from the painful reality that racism and all of its vestiges influenced nearly every aspect of southern society.

An avid reader, Hosea Williams likely read *Black Bourgeoisie* while working for the Department of Agriculture. He soon realized that Blacks, regardless of intellect and the necessary scientific aptitude, were not being considered for white-collar positions. A recent graduate with honors from Savannah State University, who eventually became a medical doctor, applied for a position as a biological aide, an entry-level position in the Bureau of Anemology and Plant Quarantine, but was not hired because of his color. Upon further investigation, Williams discovered that "Blacks used to come out there downtown where they [Department of Agriculture] had employment offices. The employment office was segregated. Blacks would go upstairs and the whites downstairs. So when a job was out there they would never register it upstairs." The jobs were only posted where they would be available to the "white boys," Williams said. These same "white boys" would come out there for interviews and were frequently hired. He reached the conclusion that the Department was using him as a "token Negro" in an effort to systematically bar additional Blacks from gaining federal employment. Williams ruefully concluded that, just as Booker T. Washington had been tokenized a generation earlier, he now was being used as the "head house nigger." With this reality check, and the recollection of his having been prevented from sharing his research at the meetings of the American Chemical Society, the young chemist's interest in the local NAACP increased markedly.[19]

Williams's introduction to the Savannah branch of the NAACP was the direct result of his relationship with local dentist, Dr. John William Jamerson Jr. Upon moving to Savannah, Williams was introduced to Jamerson by Anna Spikes, a young lady who had previously worked in Jamerson's dental office as a dentistry aide. Jamerson was a tall man of mixed ancestry; his mother was Black, and his father was white. According to Williams, Dr. Jamerson "looked like a white man." Because he lived alone, the new chemist moved in with the dentist, who, at this time, was estimated by Williams to be near seventy years of age. Both men had a passion for science, as evidenced by their professional backgrounds, and often engaged in intellectual sparring at Jamerson's home on 458 West Broad Street. Jamerson had been affiliated with the local NAACP as early as 1924, spearheading many membership drives as chairman of the branch's membership committee for several years—a position that Williams later assumed.[20]

His landlord's religious affiliation was also decisive in getting Williams involved with the NAACP. Jamerson attended the Butler Presbyterian Church and was responsible for encouraging Williams to join the church where the Rev. Pickens A. Patterson served as pastor. Rev. Patterson moved to the city in 1948 and "was the most outspoken minister in the town," according to Williams. He continued, "All the ministers used to meet and would do all their griping and militarizing in the black community, but always when they wanted someone to get on radio or go downtown, they always chose P. A. Patterson." Patterson also chaired the Legal Redress Committee of the Savannah branch of the NAACP. "He won my admiration," Williams declared. "I started going to the NAACP meetings, really because of Dr. Jamerson and Reverend Patterson's influence."[21]

However, it was the influence of W. W. Law, president of the NAACP branch in Savannah, and the senseless killing of a Black man in town that proved to be the most important factors in driving Williams to take a proactive role in civil rights agitation. Law and Williams started working together in 1953 after white Chatham County policeman murdered an unarmed Black man named "Party Arty" after he physically evaded a few of the armed officers outside of a Savannah nightclub. He fled from the officers into the nightclub. Once the policemen cornered him, he followed their orders and placed both of his hands in the air. The officers then fired two bullets into the man's chest, killing him instantly. The NAACP hastily called a meeting. "We went to the NAACP meeting, and that night," Williams said, "I was very disgusted that this man had been murdered." He was also perturbed by other members' ambivalence and seeming willingness to make excuses when Law challenged them to protest this senseless killing. Williams stood upright and made a firm commitment before everyone in attendance: "I work in the chemistry lab from 8:00 AM in the morning til 5:00 PM in the evening, so I'm free from 5:00 in the evening til 8:00 the next morning to do whatever you want me to do." Law, seeing Williams's desire to set an example by taking a decisive stance, began assigning him tasks, including fundraising for the decedent's funeral and serving as a liaison between the branch and the Chatham County Board of Commissioners and the Savannah Police Department. "This was my first venture out into civil rights," Williams recalled. Although the police officers did not face any criminal charges, Law, the veteran activist, and Williams, the willing apprentice, forged a bond so strong that they became identified by their contemporaries as the "civil rights twins," because of their symmetrical philosophies regarding Black oppression and the means by which Blacks in Savannah could defeat hatred and injustice.[22]

Described by Williams as "astute, scholarly, and well-read," Law had an indelible impact on the budding activist's views toward race-based injustices. "I learned a lot from Westley," said Williams. "Westley taught me a hell of a lot about dignity and about human rights, about self-respect and about repression." Although Law was three years older than Hosea, they shared much in common. Both were born in the 1920s; Law in Savannah in 1923 and Williams in 1926. Both served in the Army during World War II and attended Black colleges with the financial benefits provided through the GI Bill. Both men graduated with bachelor's degrees in science-related disciplines; Williams completed some graduate coursework in chemistry at Atlanta University, and Law graduated with a baccalaureate degree in biology from Savannah State College. After college, both men were eventually hired as civil servants with the US Federal Government; Law was hired in 1950 as a letter carrier with the US Postal Service, and Williams was hired as a chemist with the US Department of Agriculture. Both men were fired from their government jobs after assuming leadership roles in the civil rights protests in Savannah only to successfully appeal their terminations and win reinstatement to their former positions. Both Law and Williams also came of age without their fathers. West Law died of congestive heart failure in 1933 when his son was only nine years old. Williams, on the other hand, did not meet his father, Willie Wiggins, until he was twenty-eight years old.[23]

Hosea Williams met his father for the first time in October 1954. Their initial face-to-face meeting was a matter of happenstance. Williams; his wife, Juanita, who was six months pregnant; and his two daughters, six-year-old Barbara Jean and two-year-old Elizabeth, traveled to Jacksonville, Florida, in his Cadillac to watch a football game between his alma mater, Morris Brown College, and one of the school's biggest rivals, Bethune-Cookman College. While en route, he decided to stop to grab a snack. "I saw this beautiful fruit right in front of the little black college there . . . so I parked my car . . . and I went in the store," Williams later remembered. Already suspecting that his father lived in Jacksonville, Florida, he asked the female cashier if she knew Willie Wiggins. She responded, "you mean 'Blind Willie?'" "Yes, I mean 'Blind Willie,'" said Williams. The cashier knew where Wiggins lived, and she gave Williams directions to his father's home. "I got the fruit and I got all nervous," said an anxious Williams. Refusing to answer an inquiry from Juanita, he directed his family to wait in the car until he returned from the residence. "I just stood in front of that house . . . and I finally knocked on the door," he recalled.

Florence Wiggins, "a heavy black woman," came to the door. Although she had never seen her husband's firstborn son, she said, "You got to be Hosea." After he responded in the affirmative, in shock, his stepmother "turned white," Williams said. He shared a striking resemblance with his father. "I looked so much like him. I looked more like him [his father] than any child she'd birthed," recalled Williams. His father, obviously unable to see, walked in the room and started to touch Williams's face. Blind Willie, likely experiencing joy and anxiety, started to cry. Although there is no documentary record of the pair's relationship after this meeting, it appears that Williams never harbored any ill feelings toward his father for being absent, as his mother did not reveal his existence for several years. This visit to Jacksonville, Florida, in the fall of 1954 would be one of the last respites Williams could enjoy with his family. Within a fourteen-day period the following January, his first son, Hosea Lorenzo Williams II, would be born, followed by the elder Hosea Williams's election to an influential position with the Savannah Branch of the NAACP.[24]

Williams assumed his first leadership position in the Savannah branch of the NAACP when he was elected chairman of its membership committee in January 1955. The branch president, W. W. Law, obviously had high expectations for his new recruiting chief. Law wrote to National Membership Secretary Lucille Black, requesting that one thousand membership receipt envelopes, buttons, and posters be mailed to Williams as quickly as possible. Two months later, Williams began a membership campaign on Tuesday, March 28, at the West Broad Street YMCA to reach the quota of one thousand new members set by the local branch. Williams invited Dr. L. A. Pinkston to deliver the keynote address at the kickoff program. Dr. Pinkston was the former president of the State Baptist Convention of Georgia and, coincidentally, served with Morehouse College President Dr. Benjamin E. Mays on the ministerial council that had ordained the young Martin Luther King Jr. for the Baptist ministry eight years earlier. Pinkston, using the recent US Supreme Court ruling in *Brown v. Board of Education* as a recruiting tool, told the attendees that the ruling on May 17, 1954, "gave the United States its proper place in the world, bringing vindication for the wrong so long imposed on a large segment of its citizens" and that a continued fight against racial oppression would be costly, requiring many "dimes and dollars" to win. Evidently, the speech resonated with the Black community in Savannah. By May 1955, Williams had reported to the national membership secretary that his branch had produced four hundred seventy-eight new memberships; he had remitted $587.75 to the national office to cover its share of the membership fees. He was able to recruit three hundred seventy-seven more members during the next seven months, adding a total of eight hundred fifty-five new members for the year. Although he was unsuccessful in reaching his first-year goal of one thousand new members, he had come within striking distance. Law recognized that Williams was driven by a dogged determination to expand the reach of the Savannah branch. Williams's sensitivity to the need for a strong local branch was likely heightened by the killing of Emmett Till, a fourteen-year-old Black boy near Money, Mississippi.[25]

Williams and other Blacks in Savannah, Georgia, and throughout the United States, were horrified by the brutal murder of Emmett Till in August 1955 for allegedly whistling at Carolyn Bryant, a twenty-one-year-old white woman. The *Savannah Tribune*, a Black newspaper, included a vivid synopsis of the killing and description of Till's mutilated body that confirmed to Williams and the NAACP the need for increased civil rights reform in the South. According to the *Tribune*, the "entire right side of his face had been caved in . . . almost all of his teeth had been knocked out," and he had a small bullet hole through the temple. Capturing Mamie Till's first look at her deceased son after his body had been transported to the Rayner & Sons Funeral Home in Chicago, Illinois, the *Tribune* reported to Black Savannahians the heart-wrenching comments that a broken mother made to her son's unembalmed and badly decomposed remains: "My darling, my darling, I would have gone through a world of fire to get to you." Till then informed the funeral directors to plan for an open-casket service: "Let the people see what they did to my boy," she said. An estimated ten thousand mourners crowded into and around the St. Paul's Church of God in Christ in Chicago to hear Bishop Louis H. Ford deliver the eulogy. Till's senseless murder for violating the southern taboo of showing interest to a white woman reminded Williams that he had almost suffered a similar fate almost eleven years earlier, after a mob attempted to murder him for having an intimate relationship with Laura Chester, a white girl who lived near his grandfather's home in Attapaulgus, Georgia. This reality and a nonviolent protest in Montgomery, Alabama, were two major episodes in the 1950s that hardened his resolve to agitate for civil rights.[26]

An arrest nearly four hundred miles away from Williams's middle-class neighborhood in Savannah would unalterably change his life and solidify his commitment to civil and human rights. On December 1, 1955, Montgomery police arrested Rosa Parks, a forty-two-year-old seamstress and longtime civil rights activist with the Montgomery branch of the NAACP, after she refused to surrender her seat to a white man on a city bus. Parks's dignified act of defiance as a protest to segregation on a bus owned and operated by the Montgomery City Lines outraged the Black community in the state's capital. Shortly after the arrest, Jo Ann Gibson Robinson, an English professor at the all-Black Alabama State College, along with two reliable students, duplicated fifty thousand leaflets on the college's mimeograph machine announcing Parks's arrest and calling for a one-day boycott of the buses on December 5—the day of Parks's trial. After Parks was found guilty of violating the city's segregation ordinance, Rev. Martin Luther

King Jr., a freshly minted PhD and the pastor of Dexter Avenue Baptist Church, was asked to lead a new organization, the Montgomery Improvement Association (MIA).

The MIA would spearhead a prolonged boycott of the buses until the city and the bus company came to the negotiating table; King and other local leaders initially merely wanted to ensure that Blacks would be treated fairly on the buses, including being allowed to ride the coaches on a first-come, first-serve basis, but when Montgomery's white powerbrokers refused any compromise, the MIA sought the outright abolition of segregated seating practices. Boycott participants developed a sophisticated carpooling service, requiring the wealthy to loan their cars to the boycott in what was, according to one author, "a radical act of togetherness." Almost two hundred sedans shuttled between thirty thousand and forty thousand protesting Blacks to work, to school, and on shopping trips for over a year. The nonviolent protest, lasting three hundred eighty-one days, ended on December 20, 1956, nearly one month after the US Supreme Court upheld Alabama's Middle District Court ruling in *Browder v. Gayle* that segregation on the city buses was unconstitutional. The successful protest placed Martin Luther King Jr. on a path toward immortality, but it also provided a template for other cities and local leaders throughout the South, including Savannah, Georgia, to incorporate, with appropriate modifications, to their respective locales in opposition to Jim Crow.[27]

Acutely aware of the significance of the boycott in Montgomery and the mounting racial anxiety in Savannah, Hosea Williams traveled with three members of the NAACP Youth Council to Montgomery, Alabama, in December 1955 for a three-day trip. They heard Martin Luther King Jr. speak at one of the weekly mass meetings that was held to communicate the goals and objectives of the boycott to the city's nearly fifty thousand protesting Blacks. Evidence suggests that the encounter had a profound impact on Williams, compelling him to rethink his approach to, and appraisal of, race-centered discrimination. In a sense, hearing King preach to a packed, standing-room-only audience transformed Williams's flickering fire for activism into a full-scale firestorm that would not be extinguished for the next forty-five years. "I had never met God until I met Martin Luther King Jr. . . . King was not my God, but I saw God within King," Williams said. He continued, "I watched him teach. I watched him inspire. And I said to myself, if he can do it in Montgomery, Alabama, I can do it in Savannah." Although he did not have the opportunity to formally introduce himself to King during this visit to the capital known as "the cradle of the

Confederacy," he felt as if he and King had somehow connected through King's passionate rhetoric about freedom and equality. Anxious to assume a more "militant" role as an activist with the NAACP, an organization he had first joined while studying for his baccalaureate degree in chemistry at Morris Brown College, Williams sped away from Montgomery in his new Cadillac at one hundred miles per hour, headed for Savannah. He was determined to be the Kinglike figure in the city within the civil rights leadership structure that was firmly under the control of Savannah NAACP branch president, W. W. Law.[28]

By 1956, Williams had assumed the vice-chairmanship of the Savannah NAACP branch's Arrangement Committee. The office, on its face, seemed undistinguished and limited in scope. However, this position within the branch allowed him to interact with other Black power brokers within the Georgia State Conference of NAACP Branches. His first opportunity to meet with influential Black leaders from the state and throughout the country occurred during the Arrangement Committee's planning for the Fourteenth Annual Convention for the Georgia NAACP Conference, held at Savannah's Bryant Baptist Church. Fifteen of the state's thirty-one branches were in attendance. The business meetings were delineated into five sections: "Branch Administration and Membership Campaigns;" "Desegregation and Integration;" "Registration, Voting and Political Action;" "Role of the Church in Desegregating the Community," and "How to Get Youth on the Team". Williams's later chairmanship of committees that incorporated each of these objectives with the respective agendas within the NAACP and SCLC can be traced back to this meeting on December 1, 1956. He discussed strategy with various luminaries who attended the conference, including: Gloster Current, NAACP national director of branches; Constance Baker Motley, assistant special counsel to Thurgood Marshall; A. T. Walden, the attorney who later argued the case that desegregated the University of Georgia; and keynote speaker John Wesley Dobbs, grand master of the Prince Hall Masons of Georgia and co-founder of the Atlanta Civic and Political League and the Atlanta Negro Voter's League.[29]

The Fourteenth Annual Convention of the Georgia State Conference of the NAACP in 1956 was also important to Williams's grooming for large roles as a civil rights activist, because his mentor, W. W. Law, at age thirty-three, was elected president of the organization. Law succeeded an ailing Dr. William Madison Boyd in the very organization that had coalesced around fellow Savannah activist Dr. Ralph Mark Gilbert's leadership thirteen years earlier. With Law's ascendancy to the presidency over the conference encompassing thirty-one branches, the Savannah branch of the NAACP was again at the epicenter of civil rights activism in the State of Georgia. With his election, Law's "civil rights twin" stood poised to learn strategy, logistics, and mass organizing from the activists, attorneys, and other professionals who had been fighting southern racism for several decades. Williams was finally finding his niche within the civil rights struggle in Savannah. A family tragedy the summer of the following year, however, would briefly slow him down.[30]

Hosea Williams's maternal grandfather, Turner "Papa" Williams, died on July 4, 1957. Papa had raised Williams and played a pivotal role in rearing him to be tough, bold, ambitious, and outspoken. The personality traits between the two were so similar that young Williams was known as "Little Turner" in Attapulgus, Georgia, even though his grandfather had a son also named Turner. Papa suffered from the "dropsies," a colloquial name for edema, the swelling of soft tissues, probably caused by congestive heart failure. The long-term illness caused Papa unbearable discomfort. "His feet would swell up and his legs [would get] real large. . . . We would have to lay him down and kind of raise his feet above his heart" to minimize his pain, said Williams. The disease had impaired his grandfather's mobility to the point that Williams compared him to an "invalid"; death represented an escape from that suffering. Williams later admitted, "I was kind of glad when he died. I remember the day; I smiled." His grandfather's death unquestionably strengthened his resolve to stand with the NAACP in its fight for equality for the oppressed and disinherited. He recalled the many instances as a child when Papa defended himself and his family against whites and the systemic racism that plagued Blacks in southwest Georgia. He was committed now, more than ever, to combat racism and segregation in Savannah as a tribute to Papa.[31]

Williams returned from the funeral in Attapulgus with Juanita, Elizabeth, and Hosea Jr. and turned his attention to the Savannah NAACP branch's campaign to integrate public housing in that city. The branch had been involved with securing fair and equitable treatment for Blacks in low-rent housing with the Savannah Housing Authority since 1942. Then-branch president, Dr. Ralph Mark Gilbert, wrote to W. H. Stillwell, executive director of the Savannah Housing Authority, complaining that the Garden Homes Estate and Yamacraw Village Housing Projects had systematically excluded Blacks from working within these all-Black public developments. Gilbert maintained that "we have men adequate to the task if they are given a chance to perform in the only place they can perform, in projects set aside for our race." Gilbert continued, "As the project now stands, Negroes are given a right to live in them but they are barred the right to draw a salary in connection with them." Stillwell failed to respond to this letter and subsequently received correspondence from Gilbert regarding the number of units designated for Negroes. Gilbert petitioned Stillwell and the Housing Authority to designate a number of houses for Blacks in proportion to the Black population in Savannah. According to Gilbert, seven hundred fourteen family units had been completed for whites, whereas only six hundred fifty-six houses had been completed for Black occupancy. Even worse, the Housing Authority was in the process of constructing two thousand eight hundred ninety-five units, but no additional units were being designated for Blacks. Stillwell responded with a letter saying that the properties were being "efficiently and effectively managed" and that record did not "warrant any changes." The allotment for spaces and employment opportunities for Blacks remained relatively unchanged by the time Williams and the Savannah branch of the NAACP resumed their protests and petitioning in 1958.[32]

The Savannah branch of the NAACP brought a federal suit against the Savannah Public Housing Administration in 1958. Constance Baker Motley, A. T. Walden (both of whom Williams knew as early as 1956), and Thurgood Marshall represented Queen Cohen against the Public Housing Administration in Savannah, which was still administered, sixteen years later, by the same H. W. Stillwell. Cohen argued that she had been denied admission to the all-white Fred Wessels Homes because of her race. Attempting to avoid federal intervention, the Authority had offered to build the Robert Hitch Homes as a suitable, yet still segregated, all-Black substitute. During the oral argument before the Fifth Circuit of the US Court of Appeals, Stillwell posited that "segregation is essential to the success of public housing" so that the program could avoid the phenomena of "white flight."[33]

Cohen, after several hearings before the district and federal courts, eventually became the sole plaintiff after seventeen of her co-plaintiffs voluntarily removed themselves from the court case that became known as *Cohen v. Public Housing Administration.* "They got it where those people got in court and would withdraw their petition; every single client we had," recalled Williams. Plaintiffs were afraid of losing their jobs for participating in the case. "But we had to go out and get other clients," he said, "and I went and guaranteed jokers their salaries. . . . I did some of everything that was possible, ethical, or unethical to get folks to sign that thing [petition]."

Determined to integrate the low-income housing, Williams even attempted to move into the projects himself, only to be denied consideration because, as a research chemist with the US Department of Agriculture, his annual salary of eight thousand dollars exceeded the maximum income requirements. The NAACP took the suit to the US Supreme Court, ultimately winning the right to integrate public housing in Savannah in 1959. The victory, however, increased the already simmering tension between Williams and the Department of Agriculture.[34]

Williams's visibility during the Savannah NAACP branch's successful lawsuit against the public housing administration led to the Department of Agriculture's sustained and unrelenting efforts to fire him from his job as a research chemist. "They wanted to run me away from there out of my job," he said. In a letter to Williams from G. V. Wells, an arbitrator with the Biological Services Branch, dated November 1, 1958, Wells responded to a set of complaints submitted by Williams in May of that same year. Williams had accused Dr. Randall Latta, branch chief, and Dr. C. V. Bowen, his laboratory head, for failing to treat him fairly in comparison to his white colleagues. He grouped grievances into two categories: "Dissatisfaction with the disposition of manuscripts which [he] submitted for possible publication; and dissatisfaction with the selection for promotion over [him] for another employee in the laboratory who [he] considered to be less qualified for the promotion than him." Williams had submitted manuscripts relating to a "colormetric method for determination of P-Dichlorobenzene," as well as an improved procedure for the "separation of pyrethrins and piperonyl butoxide." Wells admitted in this correspondence that he viewed neither submission in an "unfavorable" manner insofar as possible publications were concerned. However, the arbitrator mysteriously concluded, "the primary purpose of the Savannah laboratory was not to conduct methodical research seeking to develop new or improved chemical techniques." Rather, Williams's role in the laboratory should be that of "working with known techniques." It is clear from this communication that Williams, in spite of his ability to pioneer new methods for chemical analysis, was not expected to improve the efficiency of the branch.[35]

Wells's memo also addressed accusations leveled by Williams's direct supervisor, Dr. C. V. Bowen. Bowen, whom Williams referred to with handwritten notes in the margins of the memo as a "lying man," indicated that, on "several" occasions, Williams had failed to follow the proper procedures in using annual and sick leave. Wells's investigation concluded that "the facts did not produce the existence of substantive facts to support a statement that [he] had failed 'on several occasions' to use both types of leave" in accordance with governmental policy. One can conclude with a reasonable degree of certainty that the sick and annual leave days that Williams requested facilitated his participation in the well-publicized protests against the Savannah Public Housing Administration when he was guaranteeing the salaries of potential plaintiffs to encourage them to participate in the NAACP-sponsored lawsuit. The Department of Agriculture attempted to intimidate Williams in the same manner that other white employers in Savannah used to discourage other Blacks from protesting the city's discriminatory practices. Unsuccessful, the Department used another method.[36]

The Department of Agriculture in Savannah was committed to firing Williams for his participation in civil rights demonstrations in the city. The laboratory supervisors started assigning Williams nearly three times as many samples to analyze as his white colleagues. "They'd be like fifteen or twenty samples behind. I would be like eighty or ninety behind. And I knew a batch would come in, they'd assign them to me. Many days, I worked, and those other boys were sitting down, reading books at the desk," Williams said. After the strategy to overwork him failed, the supervisors, according to Williams, stopped assigning any samples so that they could make a case to fire him for not producing. Dr. Bowen, Williams's immediate supervisor, was eventually able to remove him from his job in early 1959. However, Williams appealed the firing, which led to a hearing in Washington, DC. Clarence Mitchell, an NAACP attorney, defended Williams against what appeared to be trumped-up charges of insubordination and lack of productivity. Williams, prepared for the charges, presented a certificate of appreciation that he was awarded from his supervisor only twelve months before the beginning of the NAACP's lawsuit against the Savannah Public Housing Authority, effectively showing his ability and willingness to produce six hundred samples, whereas his white colleagues were only producing one hundred samples. The hearing officer cited nearly twenty infractions that Dr. Bowen alleged Williams had committed. "Not a single item on the bill had been able to stand challenges," said Williams after the hearing. "Unbossed," and refusing to be bullied by his employer's unspoken warning for participating in the desegregation protests in Savannah, Williams assumed an even larger role in organizing Blacks to register to vote.[37]

The year 1959 signaled the beginning of Hosea Williams's involvement in encouraging and preparing Blacks to participate in the political process.

Williams, along with his pastor and fellow NAACP member, Rev. P. A. Patterson, formed the First Congressional District's Council on Registration and Voting to "double the Negro vote" in the district's eighteen counties. Williams was elected by the council's delegates to serve as the First Congressional District chairman. Patterson was elected county chairman. As part of the statewide effort lead by John Wesley Dobbs, the council adopted two objectives that would govern their operation: "Registering all unregistered eligible voters, and seeing that all registered voters vote." The nonpartisan council's long-term mission was to exert Black political influence from the state level down to the highway levels of every district, county, city and town. This strategy was especially important, because the number of registered Black voters was so volatile as a result of the pernicious practices exercised by county registrars to keep Blacks off the voter rolls. Three years before the council's founding, nine thousand seven hundred twenty Blacks were registered to vote in Chatham County. By 1957, the number of registered voters had escalated to ten thousand ninety. The next year, the Commission on Civil Rights concluded that Blacks in Chatham County only accounted for 12.5 percent of all registered voters—not enough to make a significant shift in state electoral power. Because the council was not formed in an election year, the organization had ample time to sway the votes in the First Congressional District's election the following year as a result of sustained registration efforts in the wake of spontaneous student protests.[38]

On February 1, 1960, Ezell Blair Jr., Joseph McNeil, Franklin McCain, and David Richmond, four freshmen at the North Carolina Agricultural and Technical College, sat immovably at an L-shaped, "whites-only" lunch counter at Woolworth's in protest of the Jim Crow practices that had long governed that city's social relationship between its Black and white residents. The historian William Chafe agreed with one observer that the "Greensboro Coffee Party" was the twentieth-century equivalent to the Boston Tea Party as a "harbinger of revolutionary shifts in the social order." The Greensboro demonstration gave rise to a new era in which Blacks throughout the United States, especially in its southern region where segregation and race-based discrimination were more pronounced, would no longer allow whites, regardless of their moderate or liberal leanings, to determine the scope or scale of what it meant to be a first-class citizen. The Greensboro sit-ins spurred a wave of student-led protests, first throughout the State of North Carolina, and within days, throughout the nation, that proved to be nothing less than a full-frontal assault on segregation. More pointedly, as argued by sociologist Aldon Morris, the sit-ins provided the tactical template and strategy that would be emulated by various organizations during the 1960s; most notably, SNCC. Savannah, Georgia, home of Savannah State College, joined other colleges, Black and white, in over one hundred cities voicing in unison their festering frustration with the grip of segregation in their respective locales.[39]

Students affiliated with the NAACP Youth Council in Savannah launched the first wave of student-led protests in that city on Wednesday, March 16, 1960, when Ernest Robinson, a twenty-year-old social science major at Savannah State College; Joan Tyson, a seventeen-year-old senior at Alfred E. Beach High School; and Carolyn Quilloin, also seventeen years of age and a senior at Beach High, sat down at the "whites-only" downtown lunch counter in Levy's department store. The trio was told by the manager that they had two minutes to leave before he called the police. Robinson, Tyson, and Quilloin remained seated, unfazed by the manager's threat. They were arrested around 4:00 PM for violating the recently passed law requiring potential patrons to vacate the premises of an establishment when asked to do so by the owner or any employee. Mayor W. Lee Mingledorff Jr. echoed other white mayors of cities whose power structures were committed to maintaining the status quo: "I regret that such an incident had to take place in Savannah where our race relations had been so excellent." County Commissioner Chairman H. Lee Fulton Jr. referred in very simple terms to the sit-in as a "bad situation." Two days later, a contributor to the *Savannah Evening Press*, the city's conservative newspaper, called the protest "irresponsible" and "ill advised" and asserted that Blacks in the city did not have legal standing to dine at "whites-only" restaurants. Although this initial protest had not at the time been sanctioned by the local NAACP, Williams, now the vice chairman of the branch's Legal Redress Committee, said that "We are proud that Negroes in general, with or without the support of the NAACP, are ready to do something within the bounds of the US Constitution to bring about full equality and full citizenship." Although the branch had not prepared the students for this demonstration, Williams and the remainder of the leadership within the organization saw the protest as a vehicle by which to incorporate Savannah's youth into the NAACP's larger mission of ensuring first-class citizenship for Blacks in Chatham County, despite the National NAACP's stance toward the sit-in movement in general.[40]

The 1960 student movement in Savannah gave Williams an opportunity to expand his role within the local NAACP and to cultivate a following among the students who were drawn to his rebellious, charismatic personality. Within ten days after the initial sit-down protest at Levy's department store on Broughton Street, the city's main thoroughfare, twenty-five students were arrested for sitting down at the Greyhound and Trailways bus stations and at the Savannah train station, Union Station. On March 27, 1960, twenty-five hundred people gathered for a two-hour mass meeting at the Greater St. James AME Church to endorse a multipronged boycott of Levy's, Woolworth's, Kress, McCrory's, and Silver's—department stores in Savannah that discriminated against Blacks. The attendees demanded nothing less than total desegregation of all lunch counters and better jobs for Blacks, specifically in the stores' clerical and supervisory ranks. The crowd also agreed that establishment owners and employees must use appropriate and courteous titles when addressing Blacks instead of nicknames like "preacha," "boy," "girl," and "auntie." Protesters unanimously agreed not to cross the picket lines at the targeted stores, and at the urging of Williams, those in attendance pledged to withhold their patronage when shopping for the Easter holiday that was one week away. The group later identified the holiday as "Black Easter." Blacks were discouraged from buying new clothes as was the tradition. Instead, kids would wear overalls and dungarees. Williams, in his characteristically combative voice, told the "gregarious" crowd: "We have two great allies in our fight for equal rights. These are our money and our vote." Within one month, downtown businessmen would lose over one million dollars in revenue. Because of the response Williams received at this meeting, he was assigned to work with the six-hundred-fifty-member NAACP Youth Council to train the students for future demonstrations.[41]

Mayor Mingledorff and the city administrators acted swiftly after the initial sit-ins in a futile attempt to halt the student demonstrators. The mayor formed a biracial committee with an objective to divide the Black community. He declined to consider anyone from the Committee for Withholding Retail Patronage, the official NAACP steering team that organized the boycott. Mingledorff also neglected to include Williams, P. A. Patterson, and Dr. J. W. Jamerson as part of the committee to resolve the racial discord in the city. W. W. Law, the branch and state NAACP president, warned Blacks to not be fooled by the mayor's halfhearted efforts. He told them, "Don't hitch your wagon to a star that will never go into orbit." William B. Hartsfield, in his sixth term as mayor of Atlanta, denounced the idea of the biracial committee for a different reason. Hartsfield, an old hand at dealing with the race issue in Georgia's largest city, argued that the committee was just "a face-saving gesture by people new to the subject. The people who would be listened to will not serve. The people who will serve are resented by most of the people," said Hartsfield. Williams did not idly sit by after realizing that the idea of a biracial committee was untenable. He instead channeled his attention to the segment of people who ultimately become his most fervent disciples—college and high school students—even if it meant risking the loss of his job and middle-class status and income.[42]

By May 1960, two months into the boycott, Williams still failed to heed the coded warnings that he received from the Department of Agriculture. The hard-headed chemist continued to take a very visible role in the civil and voting rights demonstrations in the city. Tensions remained high between him and his laboratory head, Dr. C. V. Bowen, whom Williams referred to as a "squirt." According to Andrew Young, Williams's future SCLC colleague, the Department of Agriculture "viewed his militancy and activism with extreme disfavor." On May 1, 1960, he was transferred from the Marketing Research Division of the Biological Sciences branch, within the stored-product insect section, to the Market Quality Research Division. At the time of the reassignment, Williams was classified as GS-9 on the civil service pay scale, grossing six thousand eight hundred eighty-five dollars per year as an analytical chemist at a time when the median family income in Savannah was four thousand seven hundred sixty-one dollars. He was keenly aware that the Department of Agriculture would continue in its effort to terminate his employment with the federal government. However, he remained steadfast in his commitment to train and prepare students for subsequent protests.[43]

Although Williams had forged a strong relationship with the students, he may not have initially been the best choice to train pupils in nonviolent techniques. He had no training in nonviolence. Evidence does not reveal that he met or knew of Bayard Rustin or Glen Smiley, both of whom were experts in the philosophy. Moreover, Williams readily admitted that "[He] knew very little about Gandhi." He researched the Indian independence leader and the impact of his philosophy on Martin Luther King Jr. in the Montgomery bus boycott. After many hours of self-reflection and meditation, Williams recalled that "I formulated my own nonviolent strategy and technique . . . my method was a means of escape; it was an instrument; it was a means to an end." He admitted that his philosophy had nothing to do with love as was taught by Martin Luther King Jr. In a candid revelation, Williams posited that "I probably learned to hate more" while exposing the students to a preparatory course in nonviolent civil disobedience. He held the training sessions upstairs in the West Broad Street YMCA. The sessions simulated a live sit-in protest, complete with a counter and stools. Williams even replicated scenarios in which a white girl would stand behind the counter and encourage other whites to participate in the verbal and physical abuse of the demonstrators. "We actually spit in those kids faces. We'd go along and say, you god damn Nigger, . . . and slapping the shit out of them" in the process. By the time the students staged the next protest, they were prepared for almost any assault they would likely encounter, even death. The psychological bond that was born in what Williams called "horrible sessions" had an unintended effect: The students had shifted their loyalties. "These kids now looked at me as their leader, not Westley any longer, but me, because I trained them" in a technique that could be used as the battering ram to destroy the system that had oppressed them and their families. In a sense, he gave them power in a community where their voices had hitherto been muted.[44]

Being completely stripped of his defense mechanisms and the ability to defend himself against angry white men and women placed Williams in a state of psychological nakedness. The protests exposed him and the students to what appeared to be whites' innate animosity toward Blacks. He was unable to comprehend the notion of loving one's enemies as articulated by Martin Luther King Jr. "I didn't find the love that Dr. King talked about. I found more distrust for white men," Williams said. He was studying nonviolence daily and was drawn to an approach that did not embrace hurting or killing his enemy. However, Williams found himself somewhat of a hybrid in the middle between the polar-opposite philosophies advocated by Martin Luther King Jr. and Malcolm X, the charismatic minister of the Nation of Islam. However, the 1960 demonstrations were, according to Williams, "the first time I became revolutionary-minded." For a revolution to be successful, he understood now, more than any time in his life, that the oppressed must demand to be free and this freedom would always be a hollow concept without unrestricted access to the ballot—the pivot upon which society turned.[45]

THREE

Savannah's Rebellious "Negro Chieftain"

Hosea Williams was described in the local newspaper as Savannah's "Negro Chieftain." His pioneering use of the tactic of "night marches" in the city resulted in consternation on the part of whites and Blacks alike, and the activist's willingness to use the tactic throughout his career helped him earn the nickname of "King's kamikaze." Williams's positions of leadership in the Savannah branch of the NAACP and the CCCV brought about meaningful change with white-owned businesses and within the local political establishment. Because of Williams's efforts, Savannah was one of the first cities in the South to integrate public accommodations before the passage of the Civil Rights Act of 1964.

Williams continuously admonished the students and the community that boycotting the stores and withstanding brutal beatings while sitting in at lunch counters were important, but sit-ins needed to be paired with an emphasis on winning the right to vote. On April 3, 1960, three weeks after the first sit-in demonstration at Levy's department store, the NAACP launched the CCCV, with Williams as its founding president. According to the *Savannah Morning News*, Williams gave his usual "spirited" report of the progress of the demonstrations to the twenty-five hundred "hymn-singing Negroes" in attendance at the First Tabernacle Baptist Church on 310 Alice Street. Many of the attendees were students from nearby Savannah State College and the all-black Alfred Beech High School. The stated goal of the organization was to ensure that every qualified Negro in the county was registered to vote. Rev. L. S. Stell, pastor of the Bethlehem Baptist Church, and Cody Thomas, chairman of the CCCV, also appealed to the audience for their continued support of the three-week-old boycott against all establishments in the city that discriminated against Blacks in any way. J. L. Hightower, pastor of the St. Paul Christian Methodist Episcopal (CME)

Church, followed Stell and gave remarks, which, on their face, appeared to take a shot at W. W. Law while subtly giving an endorsement of Williams. "The children of Israel took 40 years to make a 40-day trip. What they lacked was leadership," said Hightower. The appeals yielded one thousand thirty dollars in donations that would be used to finance continued picketing activities. Portions of the donations would also be placed in the start-up treasury of the CCCV.[1]

Williams and the CCCV obviously lacked start-up capital and did not have a facility to house the operation. However, Sidney Jones, a local mortician and businessman, donated the old Monroe Funeral Home building on 611 West Broad Street to the CCCV. Jones told the Crusade for Voters that, "You hold the keys to more than just a building, but to the freedom of Negroes now and generations unborn, the almighty vote." Williams responded to the donation as the "answer to our largest prayer yet." The Crusade's headquarters were "open all day, six days a week," reported the *Herald*. Williams, now with a building and a secretary, was poised to upset the political balance in Savannah.[2]

Williams's role as president of the CCCV gave him a powerful platform as a voting rights activist in a general election year in a city still in the midst of the boycott of the downtown stores. "It was the transition from the NAACP to the Crusade for Voters when I became the real leader of our outfit," he said. Williams referred to the CCCV as the "undercover political arm of the NAACP" because the brass in New York, where the organization was headquartered, did not want to engage in political activities beyond voter registration. Law, a member of the NAACP's National Board of Directors, was cautiously receptive of his apprentice's new role within the organization. Within one month of the CCCV's founding, the local branch's executive committee granted Williams's request for aid to assist in defraying the CCCV's operational expenses for the next three months. The money was granted under the condition that funds not be used for salaries but for expenses directly associated with voter registration, such as transportation, night classes, advertisements and block workers. The CCCV, under Williams's leadership, evolved into a well-oiled political machine in a short period of time.[3]

The CCCV invariably benefited from what the historian Adam Fairclough calls Williams's "marked organizational talent." The internally circulated "Get-Out-The-Vote" Guideline" diagram called for local leaders and ministers to "accept some responsibility" to inform and organize the "ineligibles." As for geography, each county was dissected into districts. For example, in 1960, Rev. Oliver W. Holmes, the uncle of Hamilton E. Holmes, the first Black to be admitted to the University of Georgia and pastor of the one-thousand-member First Congregational Church on Habersham Street, chaired the first district. Pastors were chosen as leaders, because they were only accountable to their members and could not be subjected to the harassment of a hostile employer. Their churches served as available venues to house events associated with voter registration. Within each district, precincts were established in the northern, southern, eastern, and western precincts of each city. Each precinct was organized down to the block level. The CCCV required each candidate to meet with the organization in person before they would issue a public endorsement of that candidate. The voting rights group also furnished copies of questions voters would likely encounter at the county registrar's office. Questions on the thirty-question exam included "What is the definition of a felony in Georgia?" and "What are the names of the three branches of government?" Another question was "What is the seat of your county?" If a person could not read or write, they had to correctly answer at least twenty of the thirty questions when registering to vote.[4]

The effectiveness of the CCCV could be gauged as early as June 23, three months before the next election. Within the previous week, twenty-nine Negroes were added to the county voting rolls as CCCV workers transported potential voters to from the organization's headquarters at 611 West Broad Street to the county courthouse. Four months later and twenty-seven weeks into the boycott of the city's stores that discriminated against Blacks, Savannah held its first election since the organization's founding. At the time of the election, Savannah was estimated to have just shy of one hundred fifty thousand persons, fifty-four thousand of whom were Blacks. Nearly seven thousand of the nine thousand registered Blacks voted in a referendum against the city fathers. Of the nineteen candidates endorsed by the CCCV, eleven of them won their respective offices. Specifically, of the seven county commissioners endorsed by the CCCV's Political Guidance Committee, six were elected. The seven thousand Blacks also sent another message by defeating the city's conservative chief executive, W. Lee Mingledorff Jr. The incumbent mayor lost his bid for reelection in large measure because of the way he had managed the sit-ins and his appointment of a token biracial committee that failed to include key leaders of the local NAACP to negotiate the end of desegregation in Savannah. A change in law enforcement in Savannah was also at hand. Sheriff William C. Harris, an advocate of segregation, was defeated. "These White people would have preferred losing rather than seeing the Negro united politically," Williams said to a reporter of the *Pittsburgh Courier*. He continued, "We are united in our efforts to destroy segregation."[5]

The CCCV's power and ability to harness the Black vote was evidenced in the defeat of four-term US Representative for Georgia's eighteen-county First Congressional District, Prince H. Preston Jr. A staunch segregationist, an avid supporter of Georgia Governor Marvin Griffin, and an advocate of the innate inferiority of Blacks, Preston was barely defeated by Elliot Hagan, a moderate, in his bid for reelection. After the September 14 primary, Preston demanded a recount on the grounds that voting irregularities might have occurred in Chatham County—the heartbeat and headquarters of the Crusade for Voters. The recount proved that Hagan had won by four hundred popular votes, allowing him to claim twenty-six county unit votes to eighteen county unit votes for Preston. Georgia's county unit system, in itself a discriminatory device to limit the voice of minority voters, gave two unit votes for each elected representative of the lower house of the Georgia General Assembly. Each of Georgia's six most populated counties had three representatives. The next twenty-six most populous counties had two representatives. The smallest one hundred twenty-seven counties received one representative each in the county unit system. Hence, the CCCV's ability to organize effectively in spite of the inherent disadvantages of this system was a testament to the unyielding dedication of the organization's leadership. Andrew Young, Williams's future colleague in the SCLC, soon informed his colleagues in the civil rights organization that the "SCLC should be identified with it [the CCCV] . . . it is the best in the South."[6]

Williams and the CCCV had shown the white community in Savannah that the Black community could organize with effective and charismatic leadership on a mass scale to sway the local elections. Williams intuitively grasped that continued success in subsequent elections depended on adding qualified voters to the registration rolls. Illiteracy was one of the biggest problems the CCCV had to grapple with while trying to register people to vote. Williams appealed to Septima Poinsette Clark of Highlander Folk School in Monteagle, Tennessee; he and Juanita had visited the school in early 1961 during the boycott to observe the school's pedagogical approach to teaching illiterates. Clark and the school were known for the citizenship-schooling program that incorporated what the historian Barbara Ransby referred to as "practical literacy with political and economic literacy." Katherine Mellen Charron, Septima Poinsette Clark's biographer, posits that the renowned citizenship teacher knew that "grassroots civil rights activism remained inseparable from grassroots education" and that this theory undergirded her teaching methods. After Williams's observation of Clark in the classroom, he later admitted that she had taught him a lot insofar as teaching adults was concerned. He subsequently wrote her: "I want you to know my wife was over inspired. She has not stopped talking about the things we have been doing wrong yet."[7]

Williams returned to Savannah and incorporated what he had obtained from Septima Clark into his citizenship program. One lesson that he learned from Clark was to make white people feel at ease with the programs. "We were telling the white people we were just teaching the people how to read and write" so they could "drive the trucks better, so they could send them to town, you know, so they could read the signs going to town . . . so they could buy stuff for them like groceries or fertilizer or plow lines," Williams said. He witnessed how an older man in Charleston, South Carolina, went through a crash course in Clark's adult citizenship school that enabled him to read the King James Version of the Bible. However, the man could not read anything else, including a newspaper. With the help of Juanita, who was an educator and former instructor at Savannah State College, he figured out a way to teach people how to read any type of literature through directly appealing to one's interest. This technique fostered a healthy environment that was conducive to teaching an illiterate how to read and to increasing the number of eligible voters in Chatham County.[8]

"The adult citizenship schools turned out to be the real thing that built the Crusade for Voters," Williams said. He personally worked with a man in Savannah who attended a small church that perfunctorily passed the Bible around during Sunday School so that everyone could read a verse. One individual was passed over every Sunday because he could not read. After a few months of working with this senior citizen, the man supposedly "stopped the book in church and said: 'I'm reading today.'" To teach women, Williams used grocery advertisements, because many of the women wanted to shop like other ladies. This method yielded the same results. Williams suggested that Clark would have been more effective if she had not used educated teachers, because they were less able to keep the attention of the class. He used the same people his school had taught to read to instruct others. He said, "The best teachers were always the uneducated teachers . . . because they had a better understanding." This was just another example of how Williams's ingenuity and ability to adapt to the circumstances allowed him to reach and teach those who were willing to follow him.[9]

On March 17, 1961, the local NAACP and the Black community celebrated the one-year anniversary of the boycott of the Broughton Street stores at the St. James Baptist Church. Although the economic embargo of the stores was the crux of the campaign, the Black community was also effective in using the boycott as leverage to force concessions from Malcolm Maclean, the moderate mayor whom the Williams-led CCCV helped to elect six months earlier. Daisy Bates, a leading NAACP activist in Little Rock, Arkansas, who was crucial to the challenge to school desegregation in that embattled city, was the guest speaker at the 53rd consecutive weekly mass meeting that commemorated the withholding campaign. The success of the campaign had resulted in the removal of "Whites Only" signs on buses; the NAACP had launched a campaign to have Blacks hired as bus drivers; Rev. William Oliver Holmes, the uncle of the first Black person to enroll at the University of Georgia, was named by the all-white city council to a five-man commission; city parks had been opened on a nonsegregated basis; and two store owners had been forced to relocate their businesses from the Broughton Street shopping district. NAACP National Secretary Roy Wilkins sent a wire to the mass meeting that read: "You have noticed to the South that the Negro [dollars] can be a force of dignity." Williams was at the vital center of both the Savannah branch of the NAACP and the Chatham County Crusade for Voters, the two organizations responsible for organizing and spearheading the boycott and harnessing the Black voting bloc that elected the officials at the city level who were taking a proactive posture in eliminating segregation in Savannah.[10]

Five days after the NAACP marked the one-year anniversary of its boycott of the stores, sixteen hundred students under the direction of Williams boycotted their local area schools after the abrupt firing of Sol C. Johnson High School principal Alflorence Cheatham. The Black principal was relieved of his duty for allegedly supporting a drive to register Blacks as voters. One thousand students from Johnson High and one hundred three of the one thousand students enrolled at Beech High refrained from attending the all-Black high schools. The protest even extended to Beach Junior High, where two hundred thirty-nine of the nearly seven-hundred-member student body boycotted classes. Within forty-eight hours, Williams, now the second vice president of the NAACP, spoke up at a meeting, requesting that the state allocate additional funds to establish private schools for Blacks. E. H. Gadsden, a Black attorney who had defended almost eighty Blacks over the past year in integration lawsuits and a vociferous opponent of the school boycott, informed Williams that the plan was legally untenable. Gadsden and fellow attorney, B. Clarence Mayfield, were both a part of Hub, a civic organization of Black businessmen and other professionals. The coterie issued a statement calling the boycott "ill-advised and irresponsible" when it was learned that Cheatham had resigned in anger after he was told that his contract would not be renewed the following year.[11]

The local newspaper joined the chorus of dissent. An article in the *Morning News* called the protest "shameful," because it impeded the progress for the students who "so desperately" needed a firm education. The conservative elements in the community claimed to support Black education but rallied against an administrator who supported the right of Blacks to vote. The article also stated that the NAACP "feeds on agitation" and uses it as a means to "create further disunity with whites and Negroes in Savannah." Undeterred, Williams addressed a crowd of about two thousand students and adults at a mass meeting at the St. James Baptist Church. Although the principal had resigned, the fact still remained that his contract was not renewable because of his support of the voter registration drive. Williams rallied the crowd and called for the firing of the school superintendent, D. Leon McCormack. "We should make McCormack realize that we fired Mayor Mingledorff, and we can fire McCormack, too," Williams said. Although the boycott ended on March 29, six days after the initial protest began against the school system—and notably without Cheatham's contract being renewed—Williams's hold over his near cultlike following was unquestioned, and his reputation as the most militant member of the local NAACP was now secure.[12]

The white community in Savannah had begun slowly but steadily to capitulate to the NAACP's demands. By June, 1961, sixty-six weeks into the boycott, Hadley B. Cammack, a manager at the Savannah Transit Authority, informed the city that the company had begun a program to train Blacks as bus drivers on certain routes. By June 15, Roger Shank, a former student at Savannah State College, had been hired as the first Black bus driver in the city and would be driving the 52nd Street Extension route. Joining the Transit Authority, the Savannah Public Library Board also gave up its fight to preserve segregation in its facilities; eight Blacks had filed suit a year earlier. Williams, who was then the NAACP education chair, and seven other plaintiffs were represented by attorneys A. T. Walden, D. L. Hollowell, and Constance Baker Motley, who argued that their clients' rights had been deprived under the Fourteenth Amendment. Mayor Maclean, in need of the CCCV's endorsement in the next election, was eager to avoid another public relations nightmare, and quietly issued a statement on June 20 declaring that the public library was "now open for use by both the Negro and White races." Savannah may have followed Atlanta and Macon in integrating its public libraries, but the local NAACP and the Black community had shown the coastal city and the country that Williams's statement, which had ignited the boycott over a year earlier, still resonated: "We have two great allies in our fight for equal rights. These are our money and our vote."[13]

After fifteen months and seventy-one mass meetings in local Black churches, the NAACP voted to end the Broughton Street Boycott. Savannah had become the first city in Georgia to desegregate its lunch counters. W. W. Law told the one thousand Blacks who had assembled for the 4:00 PM meeting at the St. Phillip Church AME Church that, "in the spirit of goodwill and cooperation," the Blacks who tirelessly negotiated with the citizen's committee "recommend that the fifteen-month-old boycott" be lifted, because Black patrons could now "shop with dignity and self-respect." Those who had gathered at the historic house of worship gave a voice vote by saying "thank God" in unison. Shortly after the announcement was made, Broughton Street stores began to remove "whites only" and "Colored" signs from water fountains, rest rooms, and powder rooms. Law also stated that store owners and operators were beginning to address Black patrons as "Mr.," Mrs.," and "Miss." The results of this boycott had proven to the NAACP and the community that Blacks could organize in Savannah to spearhead meaningful change. The NAACP had even been accused by the *Savannah Morning News* of using tactics that were "indefensible" after the local branch began a one-day boycott of Alex's Super Duper Market to pressure the owner, Alex Kaplan, to hire Blacks as cashiers, even though store needs did not merit additional personnel. After Kaplan gave in to the NAACP's demands, the *Morning News* unwittingly complemented Williams's and the organization's effectiveness: "Local NAACP leaders are apparently interested more in showing their power . . . and flexing their muscle" to strong-arm the white community.[14]

The boycott of the downtown stores also affected Williams in ways unrelated to civil rights and equitable treatment for Blacks. Since 1952, he had wrestled with his inability to wisely manage his finances. "It's amazing how much money I was making and I was really living to rob Peter to pay Paul," said Williams. His unyielding compulsion to shop had thrust him and his family into a considerable amount of debt. By all accounts, he was a sharp dresser, but to maintain that reputation, he had to spend a lot of money. Shopping "was like a disease," he said. "I could not pass those stores downtown unless I bought something. I was always buying scarves, ties, jackets and shirts." By the beginning of 1960, he was in debt to the bank, his doctor, his dentist, several clothing stores, and a jewelry store. Once the boycott commenced, he restrained his desire to shop. "I didn't even buy a pocket handkerchief," said Williams. He was a "free man," he recalled. "I didn't owe any of those white folks downtown. It was really like being liberated. I was getting my freedom like white folks get. And ever since then, I vowed that as long as I live, that's one damn trick bag I will never fall into again," said the debtless Williams. Besides saving money, the boycott also demanded an inner strength to abstain from a behavior that Williams had thought was beyond his control. More pointedly, the boycott showed how committed he was to the cause that he helped to lead. This was Williams's first of many subsequent lessons and tests of leadership.[15]

After the boycott ended in July, 1961, Williams's proven leadership within the administrative hierarchy of the local NAACP lent him a relative degree of credibility with the community insofar as his organizational skills were concerned. Refusing to rest on his laurels, he led a lawsuit in June 1962, with thirty-five other parents who sought legal remedy on their children's behalf to desegregate the Chatham County School System. Eight years after the *Brown v. Board of Education* decision, schools in the South had yet to completely desegregate its school systems. *Brown* became a campaign platform in every southern state. The historian Numan Bartley asserted that the landmark US Supreme Court directive was "the issue" in Georgia, "inundating all others, as politicians maneuvered frantically to occupy the extreme segregationist position." The Chatham County School System at the time of the suit was operating thirty-five white schools and twenty schools for Blacks. The suit against the Chatham County School System mentioned county superintendent, D. Leon McCormack, and twelve Board of Education members as defendants. Williams and his co-plaintiffs asked that the defendants be enjoined from perpetuating a segregated school system that assigned teachers and pupils to certain schools based solely on race. The trial and deliberation lasted for nearly one year before the Fifth Circuit of the US Court of Appeals ordered the desegregation of the school system. As part of the decree, Chatham County was ordered to "completely" desegregate at least one grade during the 1963 school year and to desegregate, at the very least, one grade every year after 1963 until all segregation no longer existed in the county schools. The plan by which the school would implement the decision had to be submitted by July 5, 1963. The quick implementation of a proposed plan was the result of Chatham County's strategy to ignore the decision in *Brown*. Freeman Levert, an attorney for the State of Georgia, had claimed that a plan of this magnitude could only be produced after many months of preparation. Chief Judge of the Court of Appeals Elbert Tuttle informed Levert that the schools had "nine years to cogitate and think about this thing. . . . Your board has done nothing in the nature of providing a plan." Williams and his co-plaintiffs were now able to claim another sweet victory in their pursuit to end segregation in Savannah. However, Williams would suffer a bitter defeat at the hands of the local NAACP, as he sought election to the organization's National Board of Directors.[16]

Williams's failure to be elected to the NAACP's Executive Board was the result of Roy Wilkins's jealousy of, and ideological differences with, Martin Luther King Jr. Williams's calculated decision to work concurrently with the NAACP and the SCLC, led by King, placed him in a precarious predicament with Wilkins. Wilkins's frustration with King and the latter's direct-action strategies had its origin in the Montgomery bus boycott. The boycott of the city buses in Montgomery, which began seventeen months after the 1954 *Brown* decision, represented an "ocean shift in black attitudes toward segregation and racism. As a consequence of this shift, King became the best known Negro in the United States," said Nashville activist and nonviolent trainer James Lawson. The Montgomery branch of the NAACP, particularly E. D. Nixon and Rosa Parks, were "deeply involved" in that protest during a time when NAACP National Executive Secretary Roy Wilkins "operating in the North, did not understand the new direct-action phase of the movement and did not want to catch up with it," Lawson said. Yvonne Ryan, Wilkins's biographer, posited that he had a "discomfort with direct action . . . and boycotts in particular" because they "were at best pointless and at worst dangerous." His beliefs came as a result of his feeling that Blacks did not have the numerical, economic, or political leverage to apply the required pressure to the system they despised. Williams's philosophy was diametrically opposed to that of Wilkins's, as evidenced by the former's visible and vocal support of direct-action tactics in Savannah.[17]

Williams was also responsible for contributing to one of Wilkins's greatest fears: that the NAACP might lose its prominence as the eminent civil rights organization in the United States. Wilkins and other NAACP national leaders felt threatened by King and the SCLC because of the

Baptist minister's appeal to the youth movement before 1961. Compounding Wilkins's disdain for the more militant SCLC was his belief that King and his organization were gaining an operational and financial advantage in southern states where the older organization had been banned from operating. The SCLC, in the NAACP's absence, set up local affiliates in these states, which prevented the NAACP from rebuilding its brand and presence after the federal courts enjoined the states—for example, Alabama and Louisiana—from outlawing the organization. Although King was adamant that the SCLC had no intentions of interfering with NAACP activities and objectives, both organizations courted the support of the same group of local community organizers and member pool. Williams's successful work with the SCLC's Citizenship Education Program (CEP) spoke to Wilkins's fears.[18]

The SCLC established the CEP in 1962 to train adults in literacy, voting rights, community organization, and economic development. Andrew Young suggested that the goal of the CEP was to find the "natural leaders" with "Ph.D. minds [and] third-grade educations" to train for service in their respective communities. Williams worked at CEP's Dorchester Center, located approximately thirty miles south of his home and headquarters in Savannah. Speaking of his workload with the program, Williams said, "I had a third of the classes nationally. I had one or two classes in eleven counties" throughout Georgia and South Carolina. He "brought many of the Savannah youth into the Dorchester Citizenship Program," said Andrew Young. Williams was diverting the same youth that Roy Wilkins coveted for the NAACP programs to the SCLC. W. W. Law was also unhappy with Williams working with the SCLC. "We [Roy Wilkins] don't want King nowhere down here. We don't want him in this territory," fumed Law. Williams asserted later that it was after his refusal to cease his work with CEP that Wilkins and Law "turned their backs on me." In exchange for Williams's commitment to recruit the youth in Savannah, the SCLC assisted him in his ongoing legal fight with the Department of Agriculture to keep his job after Law, according to Williams, "tried to get Clarence Mitchell," an NAACP attorney, from "representing me." The relationship between Williams and the local and national branches of the NAACP would be irretrievably broken in 1962.[19]

During July 1962, Williams ran for a position on the NAACP's National Board of Directors at the organization's national convention at the Atlanta Municipal Auditorium. At the time of the convention, he was serving as the vice president for both the Georgia State Conference of Branches and the

Savannah branch of the NAACP. He had convinced various states within the southern region of the NAACP to vote for him, including the delegations from South Carolina and Alabama. Williams felt confident that he would be elected until a member of the Mississippi delegation told him that he would not receive their vote because W. W. Law had persuaded them to vote for Father T. Gibson of Miami, Florida.

Williams found and confronted Law: "Westley, what is this about the Georgia delegation not going to vote for me?"

Law responded, "That's right. We can't support you . . . because of Mr. Wilkins." Stunned, his adrenaline pumping, Williams walked directly into Wilkins's office and asked why was he campaigning to keep him off the board. Wilkins told Williams, "You are too militant and that your loyalty to this organization is in question."

"My loyalty?" Williams asked.

"Yes," said Wilkins, "What program were you involved with in SCLC?"

Williams asked to him to reconsider. Wilkins said that he had made a "definite decision." After the votes were counted, Georgia had cast fourteen votes against Williams. Williams was at an all-time low after this perceived betrayal. "I don't know anything that hurt me worse. The way I laid my job on the line, my life on the line. . . . I was a big ass fool for the NAACP," he bitterly recalled. Williams soon found out that Wilkins and the NAACP had treated other civil rights activists the same way.[20]

The Georgia branch's failure to support Williams was a watershed moment in his life. His confusion was surpassed only by his sense of betrayal by the organization and the people whom he cared for on a very personal basis. He began searching for guidance. He looked in the Georgia Yellow Pages and found the telephone number to the SCLC's headquarters and called the office of Martin Luther King Jr., the president of the SCLC. He then walked to King's office at 41 Exchange Place in Atlanta, only a few blocks from where the convention was held. Never having met King face to face, Williams hastily arranged a meeting through the leader's secretary, Dora McDonald. After sitting down in King's office with teary eyes, Williams explained to him what had occurred less than sixty minutes earlier. Ralph Abernathy, treasurer of the SCLC and King's best friend and confidant since the Montgomery bus boycott, walked into the office while King and Williams were talking. Williams, casting his lot fully with the Black freedom struggle, asked King if he could work for the SCLC on a full-time basis. He pledged to King that, if hired, he would bring "all of his loyalties" to him and the SCLC. After informing Williams that he would hire him,

King offered some words of consolation: "You ought not to feel bad, Mr. Williams, because you've gotten further than I've ever gotten—at least you had a chance to run for the Board; they blocked me before I ever had a chance to run."[21]

Williams returned to Savannah after the convention, knowing that he had reached his proverbial fork in the road with the NAACP. He took solace knowing that he would soon be working out of Atlanta with King and the SCLC once he established a timeline to move to the state's capital city. Although his prospects as an activist were brighter after the convention, he was still embittered by the state conference's betrayal. According to Adam Fairclough, the defiant Williams "turned the crusade (CCCV) into his own, autonomous power base." By March 1963, nearly thirteen thousand Blacks were registered to vote in Chatham County in large measure because of the CCCV's efforts. John Calhoun, a member of a voter's league in Dorchester County, called the CCCV "the most effective political action group in the state." On March 7, Williams announced that the CCCV would start raising its own finances after the Savannah NAACP informed him that the Crusade would no longer receive financial assistance from the local branch because of a "shortage of funds," according to the *Savannah Evening Press*. Williams's limitless ego and his determination to succeed in the face of yet another slight by the NAACP immediately stirred him to expand the CCCV's activities to include fifteen citizenship classes that aimed to teach Blacks how to read and write so that they could register to vote. Williams also began a program to conduct sophisticated surveys to determine the problematic areas where the number of Black registered voters was low. Although the voting rights group could no longer rely on the NAACP to defray operating expenses, Williams was confident that the CCCV could still thrive. "We have now become of age and have won the respect of Chatham County. . . . We have become productive enough to become financially separate," Williams said. Within three months, Williams and the CCCV would initiate an ultramilitant protest that ultimately led to the wholesale desegregation of Savannah.[22]

Williams's plans for the protest began on a warm Sunday night in May 1963, during a conversation with his youth lieutenant, Benjamin Van Clark. Clark, about nineteen years old, was about five feet, six inches tall and was known in Savannah as the "Little General." Williams and Van Clark left the office after a long evening at the CCCV's office on West Broad Street and stopped at the same drug store where one year earlier, Williams had shopped with Williams Jr. and Andre, his youngest son, to buy an extension hose to water his Zoysia lawn. The two children, ages six and seven, respectively, asked Williams to buy them a hot dog and a cold Coke, but the lunch counter was, by custom, for "whites only." After he told them "no," they began crying controllably. "And I remember stoopin' down and I started crying because I realized I couldn't' tell 'em the truth," Williams said. The recollection of this incident, as well as continuing competition with the local NAACP and W. W. Law to remain the most visible and powerful civil rights organization in Savannah, fueled Williams's determination to turn Savannah upside down.[23]

The spark that ignited the two-month protest occurred in the middle of the afternoon on Wednesday, June 5, 1963, when nine teenagers, under the guidance of Williams and the CCCV, were arrested after they attempted to dine at Anton's Restaurant on Broughton Street in downtown Savannah. By 5:30 PM, Williams's wife, Juanita, and Carolyn Roberts, a leader with the CCCV, were mimeographing thousands of leaflets announcing the arrest and inviting Blacks in the community to a mass meeting at the First African Baptist Church, where a large crowd agreed to continue the demonstrations protesting race-based segregation in the city's restaurants, hotels, and movie theatres. Two days later, nearly forty black youth marched from the all-Black west side of the city to Anton's Restaurant and Morrison's Cafeteria. After they refused to leave, the demonstrators, including Williams and Van Clark, were arrested on trespassing charges. In the hallmark defiance that characterized his personality and approach to the white power structure, Williams loudly shouted: "We'll fill up the jails," a strategy that had been implemented in several civil rights demonstrations, including the recent SCLC-led protests in Birmingham, Alabama, which centered on direct-action protests in the city's downtown stores, which invariably led to mass arrests.[24]

Williams, in many respects, followed the template used by the SCLC in the famous "Project C" 1963 spring protests in Birmingham in terms of staging rallies and marches resulting in confrontations with the city's law enforcement under "Bull" Connor and mass arrests. Williams held mass rallies during the day while he was on lunch break from the Department of Agriculture. According to Willie Bolden, an employee at the plush, five-star Manger Hotel, "Everyday, around 12:00 . . . you could set your clock by it, Williams would lead 200 or 300 people" to Johnson Park, which was across the street from his job and "would climb on the rock named for Chief Tomochichi" and talk about "white folk so bad" with such passion that listeners felt motivated to follow him. Additionally, Williams introduced a new protest strategy in Savannah: night marches. The new strategy presented challenges and rewards. "People thought the marches was too dangerous because you can't see who is about to attack you, but his thinking was that at night people are off from work and can participate," said Barbara Williams—Hosea Williams's eldest daughter. W. W. Law and the NAACP, losing its primacy and already at odds with Williams and the CCCV, publicly opposed the new type of protest. "We believe that night protest marches . . . will not serve the best interests at this time in reaching our goals," said a statement signed by Law and other branch leaders. Williams was not swayed by the NAACP's suggestion that he refrain from leading protests at night. "Certain other Negro groups feel that the night marches are not in the best interest of the community. The only reason they feel that is they are not leading them," said Williams. Although Williams and Law displayed a united front in public, Mercedes Wright, a longtime NAACP member, said she was "soundly convinced that Law and Williams had a personal feud, that both have psychiatric problems and that the wounds will never be healed."[25]

Protests in Savannah continued, requiring state troopers. Thirteen days after the initial arrest of nine young men at Anton's Restaurant, the local police had arrested nearly six hundred protesters, and there was no sign of relief from the daytime and nighttime protests. On June 17, an estimated five hundred Blacks marched to the Savannah Chamber of Commerce offices after merchants were adamant in their opposition to a resolution sponsored by the Chamber of Commerce asking them to desegregate their facilities. "We have information that certain restaurants refused to integrate due to the refusal of their competitors. The hotels blamed their refusal on the restaurants, and the theaters said they couldn't go at it alone," said Williams to the gathering crowd at the Chamber. In response to the march, Governor Carl Sanders dispatched fifty-two state patrol officers to Savannah to assist the local police force in maintaining law and order. Frustrated by the negative publicity, Mayor Malcolm Maclean scheduled a meeting to negotiate a truce.[26]

Malcolm Maclean was under enormous pressure to restore order to the city after two hundred seventy-four out of an estimated one thousand demonstrators were arrested outside of police headquarters on June 19. Police fired tear gas after Blacks in the crowd threw bricks and bottles at the assembled officers; the melee resulted when the crowd of protesters refused to leave the new, segregated Holiday Inn motel. Some of the demonstrators had broken windows at the H&W Sales Company, Davis Furniture, the Reils Seed Company, and the Savannah Saw Company—all en route to the police department. Andrew Young, who was present and jailed after the march, recalled the tone and tenor of the protest in this way: "As we marched along, I was distressed by the lack of discipline shown by the marchers. The mood was disorderly, there were no marshals, and no one to lead freedom songs." Williams placed the blame on the mayor and the police chief. "They tried to arrest too many of them niggers in one night and damn near tore Savannah up." Mayor Maclean issued a statement saying that he would attempt to meet with "responsible Negro leadership" to request that the night marches be halted. In the interim, however, he scheduled a special city council meeting to investigate the feasibility of passing an ordinance under an emergency circumstance banning the night protests.[27]

Williams and some of his most loyal followers observed Independence Day by hosting an 11:00 PM rally, the first since June 24, against segregation on the corners of Habersham and McDonough Streets near the Chatham County Jail. Almost three hundred fifty followers gathered at a building that was once a symbol of fear but had now become an edifice of empowerment and assertion. Instead of participating in the routine activities usually associated with the Fourth of July holiday, demonstrators, according to the Savannah Morning News, "sang, chanted, and listened" to speeches for nearly an hour in the presence of policemen as the officers held their riot guns and tear gas. Williams reminded the crowd and the attending officers that night marches would not cease and that the city should expect "thousands of demonstrators" to converge on the streets of Savannah in the days and weeks ahead until the city complied with the CCCV's demands for complete desegregation. Williams, referred to as Savannah's "Negro Chieftain," had called off marches during negotiations with the city. Whites in southern cities typically called for such cooling-off periods before they would agree to negotiate with Black civil rights leaders. However, he was not pleased with the progress between the two sides. Mayor Maclean and other city officials were convinced that Williams was the impediment to solving the tense race situation, so they had him arrested by Deputies Fred DerBaum and John Hughes at his home at 3:00 AM on July 8 on a "good behavior warrant." Inell Lubeck, a middle-aged white woman, was coerced into complaining that Williams had been disturbing the peace and complained that she was unable to sleep because of the loud singing. His bond was set at two thousand five hundred dollars, an absurdly high amount that Municipal Court Judge Victor Mulling stated was the result of the integrationist leader's multiple infractions. Seven additional good behavior warrants were brought against Williams before he could be bonded out of jail, escalating his bail to thirty thousand dollars. When B. Clarence Mayfield protested the amount as unreasonable, the judge stated that Titles 76–101 and 76–102 of the Georgia Code had been on the books since 1863, the year of Abraham Lincoln's Emancipation Proclamation.[28]

The city of Savannah's plan to derail the demonstrations by jailing Williams on questionable charges backfired. Blacks, young and old alike, now joined the protests that had been largely dominated by high school and college-aged students. On the night after Williams's arrest, Ben Van Clark led a crowd of nine hundred protesters to a half-hour mass meeting around 12:30 AM in front of City Hall. Van Clark, Williams's trusted lieutenant, rallied the large crowd while standing on an empty casket which symbolized the dying system of segregation in Georgia's oldest city. Protesters had reconvened after an earlier rally at the Flamingo Recreation Center on Gwinnet Street, a short distance from City Hall, where C. T. Vivian, an aide to Martin Luther King in the SCLC, spoke of the Savannah movement in the same vein as the United States's liberation of Europe during World War II. Vivian's personal words about Williams underscore the reputation he had built outside of Savannah with King and other SCLC brass. "If Williams is in jail," Vivian said, "every Negro in the nation should know about it." To further motivate the crowd, Juanita, Williams's wife, who was not new to the fight for civil and voting rights—she had run unsuccessfully for the clerk of city court in 1961—also spoke to the large crowd.[29]

Williams's incarceration in the county jail and the threat of a visit from Martin Luther King Jr. to Savannah to lead mass demonstrations were arguably the deciding factors that pushed white city leaders and a biracial committee to hammer out a compromise to end segregation in Savannah and stop the night marches led by the CCCV. During the time Williams was still imprisoned on a good behavior warrant, James Bevel, another aide of Martin Luther King Jr., had been ordered to Savannah to assist with the marches and maintain an SCLC presence. At a CCCV rally on August 1, Bevel threatened to resume the night marches in Williams's stead if ongoing negotiations did not yield fruitful results. He told the crowd of an estimated two hundred fifty attendees that Martin Luther King Jr. "had already bought his ticket" and was preparing to make the four-hour drive from Atlanta. Before Bevel's meeting, members from the "Committee of 100" met at 10:30 AM at the DeSoto Hotel. Representatives from the five hotels, two bowling lanes, the Weis and Savannah Theaters, Town Motel,

Towne and Country Motel, and the Alamo Plaza met in concert with W. W. Law and other Black leaders. The minutes from the meeting suggest that businesses were willing to integrate as long as their competitors did so, because they feared losing white customers. For example, the Lucas and Avon Theaters would only agree to desegregate their respective facilities if the other white theaters and the four hotels and three downtown motels responded in kind. October 1 was designated as the date of desegregation. However, the stipulations were firm. For example, "there should only be two customers a day during the off hours for the first few days and none on the weekends." Other provisions required that "Negroes agree to keep any future demonstrations away from any of the facilities in the package [deal]" and that "hotels would not serve more than four at one time in the dining room for three months."[30]

By August 3, a relative peace between the CCCV and the city of Savannah appeared to be on the horizon, as word leaked that a compromise was being seriously contemplated between a committee of one hundred business owners and Black leaders who had been working for the previous three weeks. Martin Luther King Jr. decided to cancel his trip and issued a statement saying that he had received "authoritative information that good faith negotiations have taken place and the announcement of a just and reasonable situation is imminent." Exactly one week later, Williams's bond was reduced to fifteen thousand dollars, and he was released after spending exactly one month in jail. Bond was secured by eleven pieces of property valued at nineteen thousand dollars, ten of which were put up by Russell Lavender, a Black preacher in the city. Although critics would argue that Williams's absence from the biracial committee meetings led to the favorable compromise between the white businesses and the Black leadership, the settlement would have been impossible without the direct-action protests. The night marches had applied extraordinary pressure on the city of Savannah.[31]

The civil rights movement in Savannah from 1960 to 1963 largely owes its success to Williams and his ability to organize the Black population to press for meaningful change. The irreducible common denominator of the success of the civil rights struggles during these three years proved to be the high number of registered voters. Fifty-seven percent of the black population in Savannah was registered to vote. Because of this high margin, Blacks were able to form a large voting bloc, which allowed them to elect a moderate municipal government. White politicians could not completely ignore Black voters. Savannah did not have to grapple with the same violence as other cities in the Deep South—in particular, Little Rock, Arkansas; Birmingham, Alabama, and Jackson, Mississippi, where demagoguery in city halls was mirrored by often brutal police responses. The high number of registered voters resulted initially from the NAACP, but after April 1960, Williams and the CCCV held an ironclad grip on the Black vote. White candidates knew the effectiveness of the CCCV and knew that they needed that organization's endorsement. "We had developed enough political savvy in Savannah to get every single politician in office to speak at the Crusade meetings," Williams said. For example, Charles Debele, a candidate seeking reelection as the chairman of the Chatham County Board of Registrars, appeared before the CCCV and agreed to grant their requests to ensure that Blacks would continue to be treated with dignity and respect when they attempted to register. Debele had learned from the mistakes of former Mayor Lee Mingledorff, who also appeared before the CCCV and asked for its members' endorsement but was eventually defeated. Williams was right when he brazenly boasted, "It used to be said 'so the first (district) goes so the election goes.' Now they are saying 'so go the Negroes, so the election goes.'"[32]

Perhaps what was most critical to the success of the Savannah movement was Williams's ability to control and motivate the large youth population in the city. The students, following the model of protesters in Greensboro, North Carolina, began a new phase of the Black freedom struggle of the 1960s. The students, naively idealistic, participated in civil rights demonstrations in Savannah because they believed they could end segregation and did not have to suffer financial reprisal from an employer. Williams was especially successful in cultivating a relationship with young Blacks aged seventeen to twenty-five, a demographic that the NAACP had hitherto struggled to reach and incorporate in civil rights activities. Williams, twenty years senior to those he motivated, was viewed by the young activists as the cool uncle, whereas Law was perceived as an old-timer grandfather, although he was only three years older than Williams. Williams, an educated member of Savannah's middle-class, did not have the same reputation for appearing stuffy and aristocratic, traits that undercut W. W. Law and other members of the NAACP, which consisted of medical doctors, dentists, and formally educated ministers.[33]

Williams may have related so well with the youth because he was a self-proclaimed "thug" and "hustler," who was at ease when entering bars, pool halls, and other areas where youth frequented—places that middle-class, ultrareligious, and conservative blacks refused to go. One could argue that he honed what would become his competitive organizing advantage when marshaling the dispossessed and disinherited in the looming civil rights campaigns in St. Augustine, Selma, and Grenada. He recruited figures such as "Big" Lester Hankerson, the six-foot, four-inch "thug" of the waterfront, to participate in demonstrations. Williams, keenly aware of the optics associated with civil rights activism, knew that many whites in Savannah were cowards who loved to attack defenseless Blacks. He responded by recruiting young men like "Trash" and "Old Mama," whom Williams described as "big niggers" who had no problem threatening whites and calling them "motherfuckers" during civil rights protests. Willie Bolden, who met Williams when he was twenty-two years old and was one of Williams's captains, succinctly summed up his mentor: "The way he talked about white people in general and segregation. . . . this guy was either crazy or he is one helluva leader; I found out that he was both."[34]

Williams and the CCCV had made a lasting impact on the city of Savannah after the 1963 summer campaign to end segregation. Williams was well aware that tensions with the Department of Agriculture were beyond repair. He also wanted to play a more meaningful role in getting people registered to vote in states throughout the South. He knew that the time was right to move from Chatham County, and he again approached Martin Luther King Jr. about joining the SCLC on a full-time basis. King had taken note of Williams's tireless commitment in recruiting and organizing Blacks to vote in Savannah and knew that his contentious temperament would provide a balance within the SCLC's inner circle. King told Andrew Young, "We need people who are confrontational. . . . Some of us have the tendency to become too comfortable with injustice. Not Williams. He's going to go out there and start something, and though we don't know what it might lead to, we need people like that." On the basis of this vote of confidence, Williams was hired as the SCLC's coordinator of political action at a salary of twelve thousand dollars—the highest paid associate within the organization—which was subsidized by the Presbyterian Church at the request of Young. Williams's salary was a testament to his talents and proven record in civil and voting rights activism. Keenly aware that his salary would be resented by staff members whose work in the SCLC predated his, he knew he had to deliver once he moved to Atlanta in 1964.[35]

FOUR

"King's Kamikaze"

ST. AUGUSTINE AND THE CIVIL RIGHTS ACT OF 1964

"St. Augustine was a generally a very bad situation. It was more Hosea Williams' project than anything else. None of us really wanted to be bothered with St. Augustine—certainly not Martin." This is how Andrew Young summarized feelings within SCLC that accurately portrayed Williams as the chief protagonist in the last major civil rights campaign before the passage of the Civil Rights Act of 1964. Hosea Williams had proven in the Savannah campaign that he had refined his organizational skills with young Black students and working-class adults. St. Augustine, the oldest city in the United States, proved that he also appealed, when necessary, to elite white women. He had convinced Mrs. Mary Peabody, the mother of Massachusetts Governor Endicott Peabody, to get arrested after a trip to a drugstore as a way to raise awareness of Blacks' struggle in St. Augustine. The Rev. Fred Shuttlesworth worked with Williams in the Ancient City and saw the efficacy of his SCLC colleagues' nonviolent scorched-earth tactics, particularly Williams's pioneering marches at night. "The daytime marches, said Shuttlesworth, "had special value, but to do it at night would create more attention." The night marches, the fearless Shuttlesworth maintained, would keep the community "in a state of unrest," especially the "police even though they had guns and dogs" for protection.[1]

1964 ushered in an era of uncertainty for the Black freedom movement. President John F. Kennedy, a northeastern liberal who was seen by Hosea Williams and a great many Blacks as an ally of the movement, had been assassinated by Lee Harvey Oswald on November 22, 1963, in Dallas, Texas. President Kennedy, though prodded, had taken some politically dangerous stances against racism. As early as 1957, then-Senator Kennedy told a vitriolic and venomous crowd in Jackson, Mississippi, that he supported the controversial decision in *Brown v. Board of Education*. "I accept the

Supreme Court decision as the law of the land. . . . We must all agree on the necessity to uphold law and order in every part of the land." As a candidate for the presidency three years later, he was once again faced with the opportunity to show that he was sympathetic to the interests of Blacks after Martin Luther King Jr. was sentenced to four months in a Georgia state penitentiary for violating the terms of his probation after he was convicted on a technicality for driving with an Alabama driver's license. Kennedy, a shrewd political pragmatist, called King's wife, Coretta, after what Ted Sorensen, Kennedy's speechwriter referred to as an "intensive hotel room debate," to offer words of support and consolation a few weeks before the winning election which had pitted him against Republican and Vice President Richard Nixon. After Alabama Governor George C. Wallace prevented a Black person from entering the University of Alabama by standing at the entrance to the state's flagship university, Kennedy went on national television to denounce racism and discrimination. Eight days later on June 19, 1963, he submitted to Congress what Sorensen called "the most comprehensive civil rights bill in history," with a message that "race has no place in American life or law." The tone and tenor of the president's speech and actions had given some Blacks a sense of confidence in feeling that their president was, in the words of Godfrey Hodgson, "a magnificent lion slaying their enemies for them" while spearheading meaningful change in the area of civil rights legislation. This optimism faded quickly after the tragedy in Dallas for Williams and many activists who had been agitating for equality in the South.[2]

Williams had personally benefitted from the Kennedy administration's calculated benevolence. The US Department of Agriculture had determined to fire Williams, the only Black research chemist in the Deep South, after his release from a Savannah jail on August 10, 1963, for leading civil rights demonstrations in the city. As Williams later recalled, he was lambasted by his department head in Washington after he called to preempt his firing. "Hosea, who do you think you are. You don't qualify no longer to be a part of this agency. You're a disgrace," said the administrator. Williams asked Martin Luther King Jr. to contact Robert Kennedy, the US attorney general and the president's brother, on his behalf to influence Orville Freeman, the US Secretary of Agriculture. The attorney general agreed to intercede. Williams traveled to visit the same administrator in Washington who had recently ridiculed his role as the chieftain of the Savannah civil rights protests. He entered the department head's office and was greeted cordially. He told his superior that he wanted to work with the

SCLC without losing his tenure and benefits with the federal government. After dinner, he was told that the department would grant him a leave of absence for one year to engage in educational activity to help him perform his job as a scientist at a higher level. Williams used his role as an instructor in the SCLCs adult citizenship school program to justify the leave. "Those people just wanted to get me outta there without firing me," said Williams. "They knew damn well that these citizenship schools were teaching adults how to read." The autobiographical scenario may be a mixture of fact and fable, but it is plausible that Robert Kennedy used the weight of his office to work clandestinely with King to decrease the probability of incendiary racial conflicts evolving into national issues that would force him and the president to intervene in a way that would be a political liability for the Administration. Although Williams was granted his leave of absence, he did not fulfill his end of the bargain with the Department of Agriculture to work exclusively with SCLC's adult citizenship schools.[3]

Williams and the Southeastern Crusade For Voters (SCFV), one of the SCLC's most productive affiliates, met at Savannah's previously segregated Manger Hotel on January 1, 1964, to launch an ambitious drive to register six thousand Black voters. By 1964, Georgia ranked second behind Texas among the former eleven Confederate States with two hundred sixty-eight thousand Black registered voters. Fifteen thousand Blacks from a total population of fifty-five thousand registered voters were already qualified to vote in Chatham County when the campaign was initiated. The SCFV still believed that twenty-two thousand Blacks of voting age remained untapped. Herman Pride, a real estate company executive and recently elected chairman of the organization, maintained that the campaign was "expected to be one of the most extensive voter registration drives staged in the Coastal Empire." Two weeks after the campaign was launched, Williams had convinced Martin Luther King Jr., recently named *Time*'s "Man of the Year," to address a crowd of eighteen hundred at Savannah's Municipal Auditorium to encourage community participation in the drive. King told Williams at the mass meeting that the SCLC would continue to pledge its resources and manpower to ensure that the voter registration drive was a success. King also told the crowd that, although "Savannah has not reached the promised land," Williams's leadership had "possibly pushed the city ahead of Atlanta" in the area of race relations, because Atlanta had "fallen back." Its leaders no longer seemed so receptive to rapid racial progress. King's praise invariably made a lasting impact on the Black community in Savannah.[4]

Williams, now the SCLC's special projects director and on a one-year leave of absence from the US Department of Agriculture, was devoted full time to securing six thousand new Black registered voters. He and the SCFV got off to a fast start, registering between thirty and forty voters daily. Within the first month of the four-month voter registration drive, the Crusade had successfully registered one thousand four hundred thirty-five new voters. The registration campaign's mission was to reach the "hard core" of ineligible Black voters in Chatham County who had not been participants in the political process. Williams believed that the thirty percent who were registered to vote were primarily of the "middle class." He decided that the SCFV would concentrate on registering working-class and unemployed Blacks in hopes of increasing the power of what already constituted into a formidable voting bloc. Although Williams was no longer working what, in essence, had been two full-time jobs as a civil rights activist and research chemist, the demands on his time were still very heavy. His attention was often divided, causing him to sleep very little at night, making him irritable and sometimes erratic in behavior.[5]

This tendency was most obvious while driving one of his powerful and expensive cars. Status-conscious Williams's luxury automobile of choice was usually a Cadillac convertible with a strong V8 engine. The Cadillac, built for speed and plush comfort, garnered attention from many drivers—especially the white police officers who staffed many police agencies in the Deep South during the 1960s and 1970s. Williams, a boisterous Black man who was unapologetic for the material manifestations of his hard work and hustling mentality, only exacerbated whites' seething envy of a seemingly successful Black person. Charged on March 18, 1964, for several traffic violations, including passing on a yellow line, improper lane usage, and forcing a witness off of a highway, he blamed local authorities for attempting to punish him for his civil rights activism. The registration was traced back to Juanita, but Williams claimed that while he was, indeed, driving the car, he was in another area of Savannah at the time that John B. Brooks, the victim, claimed that he had been run off the road near the Ogeechee Wrecking Company, located off of Ogeechee Road, approximately sixteen miles from Williams's home at 3115 Gilbert Street. Racially motivated incidents in St. Augustine, Florida, required him to divert his attention from his legal problems in Savannah and channel his energies to the Ancient City in dire need of his justly celebrated organizational skills.[6] Pedro Menendez, a Spanish naval officer, founded the city in 1565 as a fortified town to protect Florida against future French invasions. Although the city had been named for a man of color, the theologian, St. Augustine of Hippo, the ancient town in northeast Florida, had an inglorious reputation for its treatment of non-whites. "Historically, age and time designate wisdom. This is not true in St. Augustine, Florida, a city 399 years old. St. Augustine has trapped, preserved, and perpetuated all of the prejudice, Jim Crowism and bigotry and hate to every non-white American that ever resided, even temporarily, within her boundaries," Williams said. In 1964, Blacks made up just under a quarter of the city's population. Blacks had been barred from all four of the city's hotels and its twenty-four motels, as well as from all twenty-four restaurants. Recreational facilities, including the YMCA, also prohibited Blacks from enjoying its services. Only a few whites employed Blacks in positions where they had contact with patrons. Although no overt pattern of segregation in the area of housing existed, the US Commission on Civil Rights found that Blacks were only allowed to buy homes from other Blacks. St. Augustine's Blacks, however, did not passively accept these conditions and anticipated working with the NAACP and the SCLC to highlight inequality during a time when the city would be celebrating its founding.[7]

By 1962, representatives of the local chapters of the NAACP and SCLC had led sustained efforts to encourage the federal government to end racial discrimination. On April 6 of that year, Black residents in the city filed suit in the federal court to end desegregation in the public school system. On February 23, 1963, the St. Augustine branch of the NAACP sent a letter to Vice President Johnson asking him to cancel his proposed speaking engagement at some restored buildings on St. George Street on March 11, 1963, for two reasons: The city government incorporated segregation in all of its affairs, and Blacks had not been selected to serve on the official welcoming and planning committees. Vice President Johnson refused to renege on his promise to speak but promised to bring city officials and the Black community together to work on civil rights issues if Blacks did not picket the event. Blacks upheld their promise, but no elected officials or city administrators showed up for the meeting. The local NAACP continued to appeal to the executive branch. The St. Augustine branch sent a letter in May asking President John F. Kennedy to prevent any earmarked federal funds from being used by the city in celebration of its four-hundredth anniversary in 1965. The local branch of the Congress of Racial Equality (CORE) also lobbied President Kennedy to use the might of his office to block federal funding for the city's quadricentennial commemoration if Blacks were not permitted to participate in a substantive way in the planning of anniversary events. CORE members sent a telegram to the nation's chief executive on June 18, asking him to deny the city's request of three hundred fifty thousand dollars to assist in defraying expenses associated with festivities, as the funding will be used to "celebrate 400 years of slavery and segregation in the nation's oldest city." Because neither of the requests was granted to their satisfaction, Blacks resorted to direct action.[8]

Local Blacks, displeased with the executive branch's indifference to the simmering racial powder keg on the verge of igniting in the Ancient City, staged continuous protests beginning in July 1963. On July 22, eight Black high students were arrested for sitting at a downtown Woolworth's lunch counter. Willie Carl Singleton, Samuel White, Audrey Nell Edwards, and JoAnn Anderson, known as the "St. Augustine Four," begged their parents to refuse to sign a conditional document that stated that the minors' release was predicated on their pledge to refrain from protesting at local businesses. Singleton and White were remanded to the Florida International School for Boys in Marianna, Florida, and their two fellow female demonstrators were transferred to the girls' reform school in Ocala, Florida. Protests continued throughout the month of August. On August 9, nine protesters were arrested for demonstrating on private property and charged with trespassing. Three weeks later, twelve Blacks were arrested for disturbing the peace at a segregated restaurant in the downtown district.[9]

The racial animus and unrest that continued to plague St. Augustine during the next month were eerily reminiscent of the events that Williams had experienced in Savannah. On September 3, protests throughout the city resulted in the arrest of thirty-nine Blacks for demonstrating against discriminatory practices. Twenty-seven were detained on charges of holding a meeting in a public park without a city-issued permit. Another twelve Blacks were arrested for sitting in at lunch counters in downtown St. Augustine. Less than one week later, the city commission passed emergency measures allowing City Manager Charles Barrier to prohibit indefinitely all marches, demonstrations, and open meetings in the city in an attempt to achieve a cooling-off period. However, the city's white residents, particularly those involved and interested in the local KKK, avoided the measure by planning a meeting three miles outside the city limits of St. Augustine. On September 18, while trying to observe the planned gathering of racists committed to maintaining the status quo through violence, Dr. Robert Hayling, a Black dentist and member of the local NAACP and SCLC chapters, was severely beaten, along with three additional Black observers. The next day, the Klan held a rally with an estimated 2,500 Klan members in attendance. Violence in the old city worsened over the next month.[10]

The racial discord that had plagued the city especially after 1962 finally climaxed in murder. On October 25, William David Kinnard, a twenty-four-year-old white male, died after he was shot in the head while he and three white associates were riding in a sedan on Central Avenue. Central Avenue was located in a predominately Black neighborhood. When Kinnard was killed, policemen who arrived on the scene discovered a loaded shotgun in his vehicle. Although no shots were reported to have been fired from the car, it is plausible that the four white males, because of the ongoing racial strife, were either simply trying to protect themselves or planning to harm Blacks. The former scenario is probably closer to the truth, as the victim and his companions were driving through a Black neighborhood under cover of darkness. Three days later, likely as a retaliatory response to Kinnard's murder, individuals in moving vehicles fired into two nightclubs owned by Blacks and two homes owned and occupied by Blacks. One week after the shootings, St. Augustine police arrested Goldie Eubanks Sr., an active member in the St. Augustine branch of the NAACP, and his son. They were charged with the murder of Kinnard. However, no arrests were made as a result of the shooting incidents associated with the two Black nightclubs or two Black-owned homes. There were no additional racially charged episodes in St. Augustine until someone fired shotgun shells into the home of Dr. Hayling on February 8, 1964. Although neither he nor any of his family members was injured, the shotgun blasts killed his dog.[11]

The SCLC entered the St. Augustine movement in March 1964. Dr. Hayling wrote a letter on March 11 to Virgil Wood, president of the Massachusetts chapter of the SCLC, requesting that Black and white college students who were planning to travel to Florida for spring break festivities consider joining protests in the city before going on to their destinations in Destin and Daytona Beach. The next day, nearly one hundred seventy-five newsmen and journalists converged on St. Augustine, expecting a newsworthy story. By March 23, close to thirty students, clergymen, and faculty members from northeastern colleges had arrived in the Ancient City with plans to stage antisegregation protests. Among the northerners who were planning to visit St. Augustine and engage in unlawful protests was Mrs. Mary Peabody, the mother of Endicott Peabody, the governor of Massachusetts. The US Commission on Civil Rights presented a report to President Johnson on May 18, 1964, which declared that "St. Augustine represents a potential source of continued racial unrest and agitation and of embarrassment to the federal government." The Commission's report proved to be prophetic. Williams and fellow SCLC Board member Bernard Lee suggested that the organization stage a frontal assault in the city in protest of its discriminatory tactics. The Board, forever searching for opportunities to garner media attention for civil rights protests, agreed.[12]

Williams, serving as the SCLC's coordinator for the campaign in St. Augustine, arrived in the city for his first out-of-state civil rights crusade as a full-time staff member of the SCLC on March 26, 1964, one week after he was issued driving citations for improperly driving in Savannah. Reflecting on the previous struggles in St. Augustine and his decision to send Williams into the city, Dr. King stated that "Dr. Hayling had waged a courageous year-long battle against the evil forces in St. Augustine." However, Hayling and the local chapter of the NAACP and the city's SCLC affiliate had been unable to claim any substantive gains against the city fathers or create traction in the media outside of Florida. King maintained that the crusade against injustice, no matter how noble, had. Once Williams entered St. Augustine, "from then on we had a movement," as King recalled in September at SCLC's Eighth Annual Convention, which met in Williams's home turf in Savannah. According to the June 1964 edition of the *SCLC Newsletter*, mass meeting attendance jumped from sixty to six hundred attendees in a few days. Williams was ready to prove his worth as SCLC's highest paid staff member and, at the same time, relieve his forever mounting frustration with southern cities' insistence on relegating Blacks to the status of second-class citizenship. "I was angry. I was impatient. I was militant. I wanted to go get with it," Wiliams said. He remembered that the SCLC was not wholly excited about devoting manpower and resources to St. Augustine, because the staff was mentally and physically exhausted after the campaigns in Birmingham, Alabama, and Albany, Georgia. "They really didn't want a movement at that time," Williams said. Andrew Young, who had just been appointed SCLC's executive director, opposed turning St. Augustine into a major SCLC initiative. "I thought all of our efforts should be concentrated on pressuring the President and Congress to pass the civil rights bill," said Young. However, Williams was determined to draw the SCLC and its top leadership into the St. Augustine struggle.[13]

Williams's first task after arriving in Florida was to assess the situation and provide some guidance to Dr. Hayling. Hayling was to the St. Augustine NAACP what Williams was to the Savannah branch of the organization. Neither embraced the approach of the notoriously conservative NAACP. "Roy Wilkins, the Executive Secretary, called me and wanted to get us in line with the practices, philosophies and procedures with the national organization," Hayling recalled. Williams and Hayling were both employed in positions outside of the civil rights struggle. Hayling earned approximately six thousand dollars of his nine-thousand-dollar annual salary from his white clientele. Williams's salary stood around nine thousand dollars while he was employed full-time with the US Department of Agriculture. Although both men were equally committed, they fought injustice very differently. Williams chose militant nonviolent direct action; Hayling's militancy permitted the use of weapons, which ultimately turned out to be counterproductive. The dentist had maintained that "passive resistance is no good in the face of violence." He continued, "I and others of the NAACP have armed ourselves and we will shoot first and ask questions later." In Williams's analysis, Hayling "had just messed up their movement" in St. Augustine with his tactical error. "He had gone out to confront them white folks with violence and had nothing but a few pistols. . . . So he got everybody beat up and put in jail," Williams said. He eventually confronted Hayling and bluntly informed him that he had erred while leading the movement. He was losing the moral high ground and public sympathy by resorting to violence. Hayling "didn't understand the weakness of violence," said Williams. Hayling, who was just as egotistical and defiant as Williams, did not receive this chiding in a positive manner. However, "we eventually came to terms, we battled and battled. I drove that sucker crazy," said Williams. King's lieutenant told the dentist that if they had any chance of forcing meaningful concessions from the city fathers, they would have to wholeheartedly embrace nonviolence and face jail time. He advised Hayling that "we've got to prove that we can take a beating. Let them beat us. We've got to take that away from them." Nonviolent direct action was not only a prudent approach in St. Augustine, it was also critical to the passage of the Civil Rights Act that was currently being filibustered in the US Senate. Williams and the SCLC understood intuitively that the southern congressmen would use any ammunition to derail the passage of the landmark act that was being pushed through the halls of Congress by President Lyndon B. Johnson.[14]

The ascension of Kennedy's vice president and successor, southerner Lyndon "LBJ" Johnson, to the Oval Office, gave new urgency to the mounting concern of Blacks who were sensitive to the need for substantive civil and voting rights legislation at the federal level. Kennedy had advocated a gradual strategy in dealing with the civil rights question that was simultaneously simple and complex: dependence on an expanding Black electorate to outmaneuver and depose resistant federal lawmakers, which would eventually enable Blacks to secure what they believed to be first-class citizenship. Johnson quickly embraced a strategy emphasizing immediate redress of Blacks' complaints with the state and federal governments. Although Johnson was ambitious, sometimes dishonest, and coarse, he sincerely believed that racism and poverty should be eradicated in the United States, if not for moral purposes, then certainly to appear favorable in the court of world opinion during the height of the Cold War. Johnson's actions before Kennedy's assassination had already provided a window into his thinking on the civil rights question. As early as 1957, as Senate majority leader, he had steered the first Civil Rights Act through Congress since 1875. Six years later, he spoke at a commemoration service as vice president in Gettysburg on May 20, 1963, and told those who had gathered on that symbolically sacred ground that "We do not answer those who lie beneath this soil—when we reply to the Negro by asking, patience." These bold stances at the expense of valuable political capital with southerners led Martin Luther King Jr. to assert shortly before the SCLC's entrance into the St. Augustine movement that Johnson "might do more than any other president before him" in using political adeptness to counter all opposition in ensuring a civil rights bill. Hence, King and other executives in the SCLC did not want to risk passage of the bill by exposing Johnson to unnecessary obstacles while he was making deals and accumulating additional political debts to shepherd the bill to signing. Although King had pressed the president for federal intervention in St. Augustine, Lee White, an aide to Johnson, advised the nation's chief executive to avoid King's request, because "the situation could be used in showing the need for a civil rights bill."[15]

Hosea sensed that the stakes were high at the beginning of the crusade in St. Augustine and knew how deep racism penetrated the culture of the oldest city in the United States. Williams, King, and the Johnson White House received a much-needed proverbial shot in the arm when journalists reported that Mary Peabody, the mother of Endicott Peabody, the governor of Massachusetts, and two of her companions, Mrs. Esther Burgess, a fair-skinned Black woman and wife of Episcopal Bishop John Burgess, and Mrs. Hester Campbell, wife of Bishop Donald Campbell, had traveled to Florida and wished to participate in the "Florida Spring Project." Williams became the bridge to usher these prominent women into the demonstrations. He met the trio of northerners in Jacksonville on Sunday, March 29, and drove them forty-two miles to St. Augustine. On arriving in the oldest segregated city in the South, the three women, all over sixty years old, attended a mass meeting and remained until eleven o'clock that night. They retired into two separate homes, both owned and occupied by Blacks. Their first night in the city was uneventful. However, their protests over the next two days and Hosea's insistence that they go to jail would elevate the nation's interest in demonstrations in St. Augustine.[16]

Williams's nonviolent teaching techniques and lectures on the severity of the civil rights crusade in St. Augustine impressed each member of the northern trio but had a different resonance with Burgess. Reflecting on Williams's ability and passionate teaching approach, Hester Campbell maintained that "The teaching is remarkable. . . . Mr. Hosea Williams is a person of extraordinary spiritual quality." On March 30, Peabody, Campbell, and Burgess entered the plush, twenty-two-dollar per-day Ponce de Leon Motor Lodge to have lunch. The manager asked them to leave. Peabody asked, "Why must we leave?" The manager responded, "You have Negroes in your company. We will be happy to serve them in the kitchen and we will serve you here." Burgess, the lone Black person, remained seated and was adamant about being arrested, according to Peabody, to "show her people what she was doing for them." She was arrested for "trespassing and being an undesirable guest" and placed in a police cruiser next to a big police dog. Burgess was not disturbed by a tactic clearly intended to intimidate her; she loved dogs.[17]

Williams's raw gifts and passionate powers of persuasion were in evidence the next day when he convinced the seventy-two year-old Peabody, referred to as the "indomitable grand dame of an old New England dynasty," and sixty-five-year-old Campbell to risk arrest and incarceration overnight in jail. Peabody and Campbell had insisted that their plans in St. Augustine did not include being arrested, because the implications could have dire consequences for their families' reputations. However, Williams knew that their arrest was of paramount importance. Their detention would invariably spark outrage across the country and ratchet up pressure on the legislators, including Senators Richard Russell and Robert Byrd, who were holding firm in their opposition to the pending Civil Rights Act in Congress. Williams approached Campbell on the morning of March 31 and told her, "You know, our Negro community is very distressed that of your three ladies that came down from Massachusetts, the Negro woman has gone to jail willingly and none of you have." Campbell and Peabody discussed the possible consequences with their husbands, both Episcopal bishops and respected in and beyond ecclesiastical circles. Peabody also conferred with her son, Endicott, the sitting governor of Massachusetts, as she did not want to harm his political future. The ladies received unmistakable assurance from their family members that they would be supported regardless of the consequences. After deciding to go to jail, Campbell said, “Hosea was absolutely delighted. In fact, he was quite overcome when we told him we were going to do it.”[18]

Peabody and Campbell, along with Dr. J. Lawrence Burkholder of the Harvard Divinity School, as well as five black females—Nellie Mitchell, Lillian Robinson, Georgia Ann Reed, Kuter Ubanks, and Rosalee Phelps—were arrested around 2:00 PM on March 31 after the biracial group attempted to dine together in the Ponce de Leon Motor Lodge’s segregated dining facility. Each individual was subsequently fingerprinted and booked on a one-hundred-dollar bond in the St. John’s County Jail and charged with trespassing. Peabody, dressed in a pink suit, told a reporter in a jailhouse interview that she wanted to fight for a “better deal” for Negroes. She was disturbed that only young people were committing themselves to the struggle for civil rights in St. Augustine. “We need some old people in this thing. . . . We are what they say we are, do-gooders,” Peabody said. She continued, “I want the experience of staying in jail.” Her change of heart was the direct result of Williams’s urging that that they needed to “make their witness.” Peabody and Campbell remained in the county jail until posting bond on April 2. They boarded a plane in Jacksonville and returned to Boston later that evening. “I think what we have done has brought the community’s attention to the situation here,” said Peabody before she left. The governor’s mother was correct. The arrests of three elderly and prominent women—two of them white—for peacefully agitating for the fundamental rights guaranteed under the Fourteenth Amendment to the US Constitution had, indeed, garnered the needed publicity that Williams and King had hoped for. However, the incident only stiffened white resolve in St. Augustine to maintain the social status quo.[19]

March 31 was a very busy day for Hosea Williams. He had convinced three women of high New England society to go to jail, a tactic identified in the “Report of the Legislative Committee on the Racial and Civil Disorder in St. Augustine” as a “Communist and radical technique.” He also led a march of three hundred youth to the thoroughfare in St. Augustine where slaves had once been auctioned during the antebellum era. To ensure a nonviolent protest, Williams remembered that they confiscated all “their knives, and anything else that may cause trouble, even the youth’s pencils.” Half of the marchers separated to protest the discriminatory practices at the Ponce de Leon Hotel. The police, carrying cattle prods and accompanied by five German Shepherds, quickly entered the premises and arrested each demonstrator for trespassing and violating the "unwanted guest" statute that was passed to discourage protests against segregation. Later that night, with Hayling and Williams in jail, the St. Augustine chapter of the SCLC held a mass meeting and agreed on a set of demands, including the integration of all public facilities and accommodations, the establishment of an interracial committee to negotiate a compromise, and the release of all protesters immediately.[20]

Williams's arrest did little to deter him from initiating another protest five days later. The flamboyant rabble-rouser knew that national attention on the movement in St. Augustine had ebbed once the northern college students and the most prominent duo of the New England delegation, Peabody and Campbell, had left to resume their privileged lives in the Northeast. On April 5, 1964, Williams planned a mass meeting at First Baptist Church. Two hundred people gathered for a briefing on the next steps, but only twenty agreed to volunteer for a sit-in and invariably face arrest. It was clear to Williams that the fear of physical danger and economic reprisal were crippling the black community's response. Williams told the crowd that "If segregation barriers remain up in St. Augustine, it will be because Negroes here did not support the movement." He soon turned to the battle-tested strategy that had galvanized his constituency in Savannah the previous summer—the night march.[21]

Williams's decision to incorporate the dreaded night march into the St. Augustine movement had a twofold purpose: to place the city authorities into an uncomfortable position and to pressure Andrew Young, executive director of the SCLC, to impress upon Martin Luther King Jr. that the organization needed to lay siege to the city with a sweeping nonviolent direct-action campaign. Rev. C. T. Vivian, the SCLC's director of affiliates and Williams's colleague in St. Augustine, concluded that "the night marches which were inspired and led by Hosea rocked the city and increased the participation of the youth." According to Rev. Fred Shuttlesworth, leader of the Birmingham movement a year earlier and a member of the SCLC's Executive Board who took direction from Williams in planning protests in St. Augustine, "the daytime marches had special value, but to do it at night would create more attention." The night marches, the fearless Shuttlesworth maintained, would keep the community "in a state of unrest," especially the "police even though they had guns and dogs" for protection. King had arrived in St. Augustine on May 18 to personally observe the ongoing racial crisis but was convinced by Andrew Young not to participate

Hosea Williams seated behind Martin Luther King Jr. as King speaks at the Tabernacle Baptist Church in Selma, Alabama. February 1968. Alabama Department of Archives and History. Photo by Jim Peppler, *Southern Courier.*

in the night marches, because his presence posed a safety concern for everyone involved. "I was determined to keep Martin from demonstrating at night," said Young. admonishing King by suggesting, "If you're out there and they're shooting at you, they're liable to miss you and hit some of us." King heeded his confidant's advice and refrained from protesting at night. Although there for only one day, King believed that the city was a "small Birmingham," because of the hatred its city fathers harbored for Blacks seeking to be treated as first-class citizens. King returned on May 26 and proclaimed that a "long, hot summer" would grip the city if substantive steps to completely desegregate St. Augustine were not made immediately. Despite the extent of his sway in the SCLC, King still made decisions by committee before committing the organization's might and resources to a respective city. In that process of deliberation, he relied heavily on the counsel of Andrew Young, the conciliating moderate who was later appointed by President Jimmy Carter as ambassador to the United Nations.[22]

Young, Williams's supervisor, had made several visits to the city with without King and was determined to withdraw all national SCLC staff members from St. Augustine. According to Williams, "Andy came down there to kill the movement" because he feared that violence would ensue and ultimately threaten the passage of the civil rights legislation in Congress that was still stalled by a bloc of southern senators. Williams knew that Young, King's voice of reason and moderation, could persuade King to double down or pull the plug on a major SCLC campaign. Believing in the critical importance of an SCLC-led assault on segregation in St. Augustine, Williams thus took draconian measures to sway Young to his side. On June 9, Young arrived in St. Augustine and attended a mass meeting at the Shiloh Baptist Church, which was located in the heart of the city. After seeing his boss in the church, Williams announced the presence of Young to the audience and spoke directly to the women. "Now, I want one of you beautiful young ladies to lead the march tonight, walking beside the Rev. Andrew Young, our executive director, who has just arrived from Atlanta." "There was no way I could back out of leading [the march after] Hosea had set me up so beautifully," Young later admitted in his memoirs. In spite of having using his trademark chicanery to achieve his desired ends, Williams realized that Young would be exposed to imminent danger: "I knew the Klansmen [particularly Holstead "Hoss" Manucy and his "Ancient City Gun Club," which comprised members of the local KKK] was going to whoop us." Young, who admitted that he had not yet been assaulted in any civil rights march, would be compelled to advocate for the SCLC to mount a major civil rights initiative in the city. Williams, Young, and C. T. Vivian began marching, and as Williams correctly predicted, the protesters were met and seriously beaten by Manucy and his henchmen near the old slave market. Williams's calculations had yielded the answer he sought from Young. "After I had been beaten," Young recalled "I went behind the church and cried. . . . After that night I became Hosea's strongest advocate for a major campaign in St. Augustine." "It also dawned on me," said Young, "as it had on Hosea, that the country should be reminded why we needed the rapid passage of the civil rights bill. Birmingham was a year in the past and Americans have short memories."[23]

Williams had won his battle to persuade the SCLC's executive leadership to launch a large-scale offensive against segregation in St. Augustine. Less than one week after whites beat three members of the SCLC's Board of Directors during a night march, the organization shifted its staff and resources to the city. On June 11, 1964—on the first anniversary of George

Wallace's Stand in the Schoolhouse Door, Kennedy's nationally televised address to the nation on civil rights, and Medgar Evers's assassination in Jackson, Mississippi—Williams was arrested along with Martin Luther King Jr., SCLC Treasurer Ralph Abernathy, and Bernard Lee, an aide to King, after they attempted to eat in the segregated Monson Motor Lodge. The four had been released by the morning of June 15 in time to attend a mass meeting at the St. Paul AME Church, at which Jackie Robinson addressed a crowd of four hundred.

Robinson, who had integrated Major League Baseball in 1947, admonished the crowd that "now is the time for action." The former second baseman for the Brooklyn Dodgers also encouraged attendees to register to vote. "I ask you to register so we can vote Democratic . . . because if the Republicans nominate Barry Goldwater, they will say to the Negroes: 'we don't want your vote.'" Robinson, a former supporter of Vice President Richard M. Nixon during the 1960 presidential election and traditionally a supporter of the Republican Party, was convinced that a Goldwater presidency would be a major setback to the civil rights crusade; the Arizona senator had cast his lot with southern Democrats in opposing the Civil Rights Act. Robinson continued candidly: "I don't believe that we ought to allow Democrats or Republicans to take us for granted. We should keep them guessing." Robinson's words resonated with the Black audience, but they were not the only ones listening to the Hall of Famer who had courageously crossed baseball's color line. An internal memo to J. Edgar Hoover, director of the Federal Bureau of Investigation, reported that "enthusiasm was high" in St. Augustine. Although the Black community's commitment to the movement in the city had intensified, Williams did not relent in his efforts to make the campaign in St. Augustine a total war on discrimination.[24]

On June 18, only forty-eight hours after Jackie Robinson addressed civil rights supporters, Williams initiated what the *New York Times* identified as a "swimming pool dive-in" around noon at the Monson Motor Lodge. Police arrested forty-one demonstrators, including sixteen rabbis, for trespassing after five Blacks and two whites who were registered guests at the motel dove into the pool. One of the patrons, after being told to leave, informed members of management that "these [Blacks] are our guests. We are registered guests, and we want them to swim with us." According to the *Times*, Williams's strategic planning had yielded a "ruse that caught authorities and the enraged motel owner by surprise." The protest was led by Martin Luther King Jr., Williams, Fred Shuttlesworth, and C. T. Vivian. King, who watched the melee from across the street, spoke of how the demonstration had provoked "raw police brutality. . . . Cattle prods were used on our demonstrators and people were actually beaten" by law enforcement officers. However, it was the action of James Brock, the manager of the motel, that has gone down in history. Furious about the protest at his establishment, he poured two containers of muriatic acid, a chemical cleaning agent, into the pool in attempt to force the protesting swimmers out of the water. Brock, according to an FBI memorandum, allegedly yelled out that he was "cleaning the pool right now." The highly publicized incident compelled a grand jury, after hearing testimony from King and approximately twenty-five additional witnesses, to beseech King to make a good-faith effort to halt all demonstrations, including "wade-ins, "pray-ins," and night marches in the city for thirty days and for the SCLC president to leave St. Augustine during this cooling-off period. After the thirty-day period, the grand jury, composed of two Blacks, would reassemble and convene a ten-member biracial group to address some of the racially charged issues that had fueled the protests. King promptly rejected the proposal, announcing that demonstrations would continue indefinitely. Why should Black protesters concede their right to peaceably assemble, he reasoned, while members of the KKK were not asked to make any concessions?[25]

Although Williams orchestrated and led the protest march that led to the dive-in, he did not dive into the pool for two reasons: He did not know how to swim, and he could not afford to be arrested because he was scheduled to lead another protest that same night. Around 9:10 PM, Williams and approximately one hundred sixty-eight demonstrators, including six whites, marched in orderly fashion through an all-white community. When Williams called the marchers to a halt, white law officers insisted that the marchers proceed. "You came out here to march, so march," growled Sheriff L. O. Davis. Williams, for whom rebellion was second nature, ignored the sheriff's orders and was arrested for disobeying an officer. Although their leader was carried away from the scene, the protesters continued their predetermined march route toward the old slave market in downtown St. Augustine. The next day, Florida Governor C. Farris Bryant issued an executive order prohibiting any night marches between 8:30 PM and daybreak.[26]

With night marches off the table, Williams and the SCLC delegation continued to devise innovative methods of protest, as previous demonstrations had proved that defying statewide directives ran the risk of alienating the sympathy and goodwill of moderate whites. On the afternoon of

June 21, Williams, C. T. Vivian, and Birmingham campaign veteran and civil rights firebrand Rev. Fred Shuttlesworth led a series of "wade-ins" at St. Augustine's all-white beaches. Evidence suggests that Williams was behind this latest tactic; he had conducted "wade-ins" during the Savannah movement in 1963. His colleagues, Vivian and Shuttlesworth, had not taken part in similar protests as activists in Alabama and Tennessee, nor as staff members with the SCLC, as this was the organization's first major campaign in a city with beaches and a coastline. The wade-ins, which occurred several miles east of St. Augustine proper, lasted through June 29. They were peaceful at times, but on other occasions, they provoked violence orchestrated by the KKK and its leader, Hoss Manucy. During one wade-in Shuttlesworth, who could not swim, recalls how one Klansman who was already in the water told the demonstrators, "Come on in, niggers. . . . You all got the right to swim, so dammit, come in." Shuttlesworth turned to Vivian and Williams and said, "We must go into the water, but not as far as they are, because I can't swim and I am sure not going to take responsibility for drowning these kids." It is clear from Shuttlesworth's account that the Klansmen were attempting to lure the marchers deeper into the water to injure or possibly submerge them under the waves until they drowned. When demonstrators waded into the ocean to a point where the water reached their ankles, St. Augustine police, seeking to avoid what was already a public relations nightmare becoming an even greater black eye for the city's white power structure, intervened and dispersed the protest after several of the angry whites assaulted the protesters.[27]

The protests in St. Augustine caused significant damage to the city's principal revenue-generating industry: tourism. Before the demonstrations, nearly two million visitors vacationed yearly, providing eighty-five percent of St. Augustine's income, according to one estimate. By the last week of June, commerce was down as much as fifty percent for some businesses. For example, the *Victory II*, a popular sightseeing vessel, reported a fifty percent decrease in revenue from the previous year. The Patisserie Parisienne, a pastry shop popular with visitors, also suffered a fifty percent loss in business after it was forced to close each evening at 6:00 PM instead of 8:00 PM. Two other tourist attractions, the City Museum and Spanish Fort Castillo de San Marcos, saw thirty percent decreases in sales. Hotels and motels were not immune to the effects of the frequent demonstrations. One proprietor was quoted as saying that he had as "many cancellations as reservations" during one particular week. Another hotel manager declared that if "Martin Luther King does not stay away, the whole summer will be lost." By the end of 1964, a study commissioned by the State of Florida estimated that St. Augustine lost nearly five million dollars in revenue.[28]

By Tuesday, June 29, the unrelenting efforts of Williams and the SCLC to end segregation in St. Augustine had worn down lawmakers' preference for maintaining the status quo. Governor Bryant announced the formation of an anonymous biracial committee of four individuals to negotiate an acceptable compromise between the city fathers and representatives of the SCLC. King announced a fifteen-day moratorium on all demonstrations in the city with the expectation that an agreement would be reached within a relatively short period of time. The SCLC was acting in good faith, but Bryant admitted to St. Augustine's mayor, Dr. Joseph Shelley, that he had not yet appointed the committee that was promised in exchange for a cooling-off period by civil rights activists. On July 1, King told a reporter from the Associated Press that "The purpose of our direct action was to create a crisis" to apply pressure on the US Congress to pass the civil rights legislation. Lawmakers in Washington had finally broken the southern filibuster. King left that night for Washington DC, to attend President Johnson's ceremonial signing of the Civil Rights Act the next day at the White House.[29]

With the passage of the landmark Civil Rights Act of 1964, Blacks were finally able to begin enjoying the rights promised them by the Constitution's Fourteenth Amendment. Historian Alan Matusow, a strong critic of the Kennedy and Johnson Administrations, called the signing of the act "the greatest liberal achievement of the decade . . . because it accomplished legal equality in a region where it did not exist." Another historian, Steven F. Lawson, called the act "the most far-reaching civil rights statute since Reconstruction." The Civil Rights Act was crucial to southern equality because its statutory reach not only ended legal segregation in public accommodations but the legislation, in the words of economic historian Gavin Wright, also made "genuine progress in employment and school desegregation." Blacks could be treated, at least before the courts, as American citizens with the same rights as whites in the public sphere. The federal government's role in passing and implementing these changes was, according to Lawson, "indispensable." Although the role of the judicial and executive branches in bringing about sweeping social reform had expanded dramatically in the decade from 1954 to 1964, federal activism from above almost always came in direct response to constant grassroots pressure from below by civil rights organizations.[30]

No single individual or organization was responsible for this landmark legislation. Gavin Wright was correct when he argued that the act was not just the result of "pure historical accidents." It can be argued, however, that Hosea Williams was among the principal protagonists in the last act of a drama that aired in the national and international media and displayed the gross injustices encountered by Blacks in America's oldest city during the debate, filibuster, and passage of the Civil Rights Act of 1964. The bill had been introduced by President Kennedy before his assassination, but it took President Johnson, a former Senate majority leader and skillful parliamentarian, to woo Republicans such as Illinois Senator Everett Dirksen and break the back of southern opposition that had stalled the passage of the Civil Rights Act. Biographer Robert Caro anointed Johnson as the "greatest champion that the liberal senators . . . and millions of black Americans" had working on their behalf in the federal government since Abraham Lincoln. However, the federal government did not operate in a vacuum. It had to be pressured by civil rights groups to guarantee the rights that were already promised in the amended Constitution. Williams, with his brashness and cold calculations, helped to bring the movement in St. Augustine to a boil at just the right time to show the world during the height of the Cold War that his country's self-professed image as a "beacon of democracy" was a veneer concealing the ugly rot of racism beneath. Presidents Kennedy and Johnson, Martin Luther King Jr., Senator Everett Dirksen, and other individuals have routinely drawn praise for their roles in winning passage of the Civil Rights Act, and historians have often drawn a straight line of causality between SCLC-led protests in Birmingham in 1963 and legislative victory. In Andrew Young's estimation, however, it was several months of continuous marching and demonstrations in St. Augustine that played a critical role in raising the national awareness for the need for a sweeping civil rights act.[31]

On August 9, 1964, Williams was arrested back in Savannah on a contempt of court charge for failing to appear in court to answer for a speeding citation. Grady Braddock, Savannah's chief of police, arrived at Williams's home on Gilbert Street and arrested him at around 11:15 AM, while he was sitting in his car scribbling ideas on a piece of paper for the SCLC convention that was going to be held in Savannah the following month. Williams was a national celebrity by now. He was recognized throughout the United States as Martin Luther King Jr.'s rabble-rousing lieutenant who had just turned St. Augustine upside down in the same manner as he had in Savannah the previous summer. He had officially become one of the most recognizable faces of the Black freedom struggle of the 1960s, but that notoriety made him an easy target for law enforcement. Throughout his activist trajectory he would face arrests, often on trumped-up charges. By September 1964, Martin Luther King Jr. and the SCLC were convinced that Williams's organizational and motivational skills, honed in some of the most brutal environments in the South, were worthy of recognition and promotion.[32]

Martin Luther King Jr. and the SCLC arrived in Savannah on September 29, 1964, to hold the organization's eighth annual convention. The landscape of America's civil rights struggle had shifted profoundly since the Montgomery bus boycott that had given birth to the SCLC. Williams and the Southeastern Georgia Crusade for Voters were designated as hosts. C. T. Vivian, who had forged a bond with Williams during the St. Augustine movement, served as the convention coordinator. The Tennessee native announced that five hundred delegates were scheduled to attend, as well as an additional one thousand representatives from the organization's two hundred seventeen affiliates from twenty-five states and Washington, DC. The SCLC honored Williams as the organization's "Man of the Year" and recognized the Crusade for Voters as "Affiliate of the Year." Williams and the Crusade, according to King in his annual report, had registered eight thousand voters during the previous fiscal year. King also hinted to attendees who filled to capacity the Butler Presbyterian Church that the SCLC would devote more direct-action techniques to securing the right to vote in the year ahead. King noted the recent departure of Wyatt Tee Walker, his former executive assistant who had served in the position since 1960. Walker's leadership style led historian Adam Fairclough to identify the executive as an "intolerant martinet." SCLC lieutenants and staff members, many of them ego-driven themselves, harbored a deep dislike for Walker because of his seeming inability to work peacefully with those directly under his supervision.[33]

Walker's resignation precipitated an organizational shake-up of the SCLC executive staff that ultimately created space for Williams within King's intimate inner circle. King promoted Andrew Young and Hosea Williams. Young, a shrewd and affable diplomat, assumed the position vacated by Walker. On December 18, Williams was elevated to Young's former position as SCLC's chief political organizer with the title of director of political education and voter registration. Williams knew that his promotion held special significance and potential. What he identified as the SCLC "Executive Planning Committee" had convened a few weeks earlier and had decided that the next major SCLC-led campaign would focus on the right to vote. Before the end of the year, Williams had left his wife and four children in Savannah for Atlanta. Whites in Chatham County likely breathed a collective sigh of relief that the boisterous and arrogant agitator was now Atlanta's headache.[34]

After passage of the Civil Rights Act, the fight to secure Blacks' unrestricted access to the ballot became the SCLC's driving force. On November 10, King and the SCLC staff gathered for a retreat at Birmingham's Gaston Motel to develop the organization's programing initiatives through the middle of 1965. Williams, as SCLC's director of voter registration and political education, was asked to submit to the executive staff a proposed departmental budget and program on November 30, covering the period from January 1 to June 30, 1965. Any subsequent campaigns relative to voting rights would fall under his direction. Although SCLC's president professed his burning commitment to "instill the philosophy of nonviolence in the North," King conceded that voting rights and Black political empowerment would be the focus of the organization's agenda in 1965. As the group met in Room 13 on the second floor in what, as Williams suggested, King referred to as the "upper room," the SCLC's executive leadership mulled over the choice of cities in which to stage the next major protest. Hard-won lessons from Albany, Georgia, Birmingham, and St. Augustine had impressed upon King and his lieutenants the importance of selecting municipal targets with care. "Selma was not at the top of the list at that time," recalled Williams. As the foremost experienced organizer in the area of voting rights based on his campaign in Savannah, he believed that the SCLC should channel its resources to larger cities, where whites were unlikely to mount staunch opposition to the registration of Black voters.[35]

The next day, Mrs. Amelia Boynton, a civil rights activist in Selma whom Andrew Young described as a "steel magnolia," spoke to those gathered in Birmingham and shared her impression that SNCC, reeling from the defeat of the Mississippi Freedom Democratic Party at the hands of President Johnson at the Democratic National Convention in 1964 in Atlantic City, was experiencing heightened internal dissension. SNCC, she asserted, had practically ceased to operate in Selma. Because of an organizational void in a city that had all of the necessary elements in place for a sustained and successful protest, Boynton highlighted the need for SCLC to tackle the issue of voting rights in Selma, as Jim Clark had, in Williams's words, "beat SNCC out of Selma." With these conclusions, Hosea Williams and the SCLC were heading into Selma, and, as a result, into history.[36]

FIVE
Selma and the Voting Rights Act, 1965

Selma, the seat of Dallas County, is located along Highway 80, west of Montgomery, Alabama. SNCC had held a presence in the city since the fall of 1963 after being invited by the Dallas County Voters League (DCVL). After a series of protests to desegregate movie theaters that failed to comply with the 1964 Civil Rights Act, James Hare, a local circuit court judge, issued an injunction barring more than three people from assembling in the city. According to then-SNCC Chairman John Lewis, Hare's ruling, coupled with the organization's commitment in Mississippi, led virtually all protest activity to reach a "standstill." Hosea Williams, in his candid and biting description of SNCC's diminishing presence in its own territory, put it more bluntly: "Jim Clark had beat SNCC and run them out of Selma. SNCC did not even have an office in Selma." Clark, the rabidly segregationist sheriff, "would let the deputies go in churches and spy to see whether they was talking about going to Heaven or civil rights," recalled Williams. Because SNCC had been "whipped" in Selma, Ralph Abernathy and the remainder of the committee agreed that this city would be the organization's rallying point to dismantle voting inequality in the South.[1]

Selma, Alabama, was an ideal city to launch a movement to secure access to the ballot. The city had all the key elements for what Adam Fairclough described as a "sociodrama" and could therefore draw a large press presence. The leading actor was Sheriff Jim Clark. Hosea Williams described Clark as a "role model racist" who was physically a "big, muscular, and handsome" man. Williams suggests that Clark carried an aura of distinction that epitomized a heroic, respectable government official. "Whether he had on a suit and tie or whether he had on his uniform, he looked like a general out of Washington," Williams said, but Sheriff Clark had serious psychological shortcomings. "His mind would snap. He could be talking with you and just all at once he would go berserk. He would lose control. He tried to play sane because the press was out there," but he was ultimately unable to control his fury and hatred for Blacks, said Williams. Selma whites embraced Clark as their defender, a sheriff who would protect them from what they saw as the threat posed by outsiders and impressionable local Blacks. For Williams and SCLC, however, the city was chosen as an ideal protest site because of its ruthless suppression of the democratic rights of its Black citizens.[2]

On November 30, 1964, while the SCLC was still drafting its tactical approach to dismantling the barriers to vote in Selma, Williams submitted his budget and programming outline to the executive staff. The position paper would provide the SCLC's roadmap for its voting rights initiatives and the template for the Summer Community Organization and Political Education (SCOPE) program. The report covered the operational cost of a sustained voter registration program and political education program in sixty southern counties that had a Black population of at least fifty percent. The report also identified six southern counties with large cities where there was potential for a doubling of the Black vote. Williams's analysis of the discriminatory voting conditions was informed by a comprehensive statistical survey of nine hundred ten counties within ten southern states: Alabama, Arkansas, Florida, Georgia, Louisiana, Mississippi, North Carolina, South Carolina, Tennessee, and Virginia. He and his staff used twenty-four criteria when selecting the "Project Counties" that were ripe for purposeful protests. Williams identified the most significant criteria as: "Percent of Negroes Registered, "Negro Percentage of Voting Population," "Facility of Registration," "Size and Geographical Location of County," and "Degree of Cooperation of Local Negroes and Existence of Active (SCLC) Affiliates." Williams emphasized to the executive staff that "all of the counties selected lie in the Black Belt of the South" because these areas were most vulnerable to "illiteracy, poverty and disease." In addition, the Blacks in the Black Belt southern counties had to contend with "frequent police brutality . . . trickery, dishonesty and open intimidation from registrars." If the SCLC desired to be successful in their ambitious effort to alter the political landscape, Williams argued, the organization must give him the flexibility to incorporate his program, which entailed a "vigorous registration campaign which will be carried out simultaneously with political education."[3]

The SCLC needed to remedy the lack of political education in the Black Belt counties. "Numerous counties across the South do not have an acute

Hosea Williams addressing a crowd in Eutaw, Alabama. November 10, 1965. Alabama Department of Archives and History. Photo by Jim Peppler, *Southern Courier.*

registration problem but desperately need political education," he wrote." Blacks needed to understand the necessity of their participation in the political process because, without it, any subsequent victories at the ballot box would prove hollow. He cited the Black community's tendency to elect "Negro 'Uncle Toms'" instead of electing "many qualified candidates" to further their interests, including "white liberals." It was vital to educate the "uninformed electorate," even in those areas where white hostility to Black voting was not as intense as in counties in Alabama and Mississippi. Williams also blamed the lack of political education for "many qualified Negro candidates" and "right-thinking white candidates" opting not to seek public office. The ultimate result of an "uninformed electorate" was "Negroes not receiving their fair, just, and equal share of education, jobs, decent salaries and justice in the courts," Williams wrote. Selma, Alabama, needed a strong direct-action and political education and voter registration program, he concluded.[4]

The City of Selma, along with the rest of Alabama and the Deep South, fit what the esteemed political scientist, V. O. Key, described in his seminal study, *Southern Politics in State and Nation.* Key posited that "the coin of southern politics has two sides: on one is seen the relations of the South as a whole with the rest of the nation; on the other, the political battle within each state. And the two aspects are, like the faces of a coin, closely connected." In a similar vein, the historian Numan V. Bartley has written that "the region has its own traditions, its own myths and symbols, its own images vis-a-vis the rest of the nation." Key and Bartley both described a region dominated by whites and firmly committed to perpetuating its relegation of all people of African ancestry to the lower rungs of society. The South, and certainly the State of Alabama, had perfected, by 1965, a system that kept Blacks from asserting their rights as citizens through rigid and brutal repression.[5]

Race and its interconnectedness to politics in Alabama since the end of Reconstruction provide a framework for understanding the challenges that Williams and the SCLC faced when focusing on Selma and the State of Alabama in 1965. The voices and presence of Blacks in the political process in Alabama had long been muted by the cries of white supremacy as well as crafty techniques used to exclude them from voting and from seeking and holding elected office. Beyond threats and physical intimidation, the "Big Mules" and planters in the state used various mechanisms to subordinate Blacks and render them voiceless and powerless in the governance of municipal and statewide policies. The Big Mules promoted the interests of the state's banking institutions, railroads, and large-scale industry from their positions of unchecked power from Birmingham, the state's commercial epicenter. Together with white planters, they controlled the politics of Alabama.

Of all the nefarious schemes adopted by Alabama's ruling elite, none were as effective as the 1901 Constitution, a document that has yet to be revised to reflect the modernizing trends embraced by most other states in the former Confederacy. According to John B. Knox, a lawyer from Anniston, Alabama, and president of the convention that drafted the state's governing charter, the primary aim of the conference was to codify white supremacy and remove the socially undesirable and intellectually inferior Negro from any participatory role in state politics through disfranchisement. The convention president's words merit quotation at length:

> The Negro is not discriminated against on account of his race, but on the account of his intelligence and his moral condition. There is a difference between the uneducated white man and the ignorant Negro. There is in the white man an inherited capacity for government, which is wholly wanting in the Negro. Before the art of reading and writing

> was known, the Anglo-Saxon had established an orderly system of government. The Negro on the other hand is descended from a race lowest in intelligence and moral perceptions of all races of man.[6]

John Knox's prose captures the tone, tenor, and spirit of the pervading attitude toward Negroes among the white citizenry in Alabama, especially the one hundred fifty-five delegates who had gathered to etch into the Constitution the most ingenious and insidious suffrage limitations in any modern democratic society. The cumulative poll tax, literacy test, residency requirements, and the white primary—the latter being more pernicious to Black voters until it was struck down by the US Supreme Court in its landmark decision in *Smith v. Allwright* on April 3, 1944—were the collective handiwork of the ninety-six lawyers, two former governors, and two former state attorneys general who crafted the restrictions within the state's governing charter. Together, these provisions removed Blacks from the body politic in Alabama for the next sixty-plus years. The voting restrictions imposed on Blacks by the 1901 Constitution nullified the first Reconstruction Act of 1867, which had granted 104,517 Alabama Blacks the right to vote. By 1903, only two thousand nine hundred eighty Blacks had access to the ballot in the entire state. By the middle of the 1960s, the statistics of Black voter registration had barely improved, even where Blacks made up the bulk of the population.[7]

Alabama's seventeen-county Black Belt, which comprised seventy percent of the state's Black population, was particularly affected by the state's constitutional restrictions. As the movement kicked off in Selma, no Blacks were registered to vote in Wilcox County. Hale County had registered less than four percent of the Black voting-age population on its rolls. Both Perry and Choctaw Counties could claim no more than seven percent of its Black residents as registered. By December 1964, fewer than three hundred fifty Blacks were registered in Dallas County. Although Blacks made up half of Selma's twenty-eight thousand residents, only one hundred fifty-six Blacks were registered to vote. Statistics from Dallas's neighboring county, Lowndes, were even worse. In the county known as "Bloody Lowndes" because of whites' unpunished and unabated violence toward Blacks since the end of Reconstruction, none of the county's five-thousand Blacks of voting age were registered to exercise the suffrage. Any suggestion that poor whites in these counties were apathetic insofar as voting was concerned loses credibility when considering that each of these counties, with the exception of Dallas, had a white registration of at least ninety percent. Andrew Young suggests that the number of registered white voters in Wilcox County surpassed that in other counties in the Black Belt, because their registration of its white citizens surpassed one hundred percent, as it registered voters who were no longer alive.[8]

The SCLC entered Selma in 1964 with two goals: heightening the awareness of the voting inequities that existed in the city and ultimately expanding voting rights to all Blacks within Dallas County and beyond. SCLC's Director of Affiliates C. T. Vivian said that "We wanted to raise the issue of voting to the point where we could take it outside the Black Belt. . . . We were using Selma as a way to shake Alabama . . . so that it would be no longer a Selma issue or even an Alabama issue but a national issue." Before the year concluded, King had tapped James Bevel, a former member of SNCC and an advocate of a statewide campaign in Alabama, to develop a plan of direct action to implement throughout the state. Bevel, described by the historian Adam Fairclough as "Arrogant, argumentative, and insubordinate," was the highest ranking SCLC staff member in Alabama. He supervised the field staff, including Williams, for the campaign. Bevel's initial job was, according to Williams, to "meet with the black preachers and other religious folk" to rally support for the campaign scheduled to begin on January 2, 1965.[9]

Martin Luther King Jr. and members of the SCLC's executive committee officially launched the Selma campaign on January 2, 1965, at Brown Chapel AME Church. Under the leadership of its pastor, P. H. Lewis, Brown Chapel would house many mass meetings over the next few months. The kickoff meeting, unlawful under Judge Hare's order, attracted an overflow audience. "You couldn't get near the church, you couldn't get in and out of the church," said Williams about the first meeting. King took pains to remind the congregation that only three hundred Blacks were registered to vote throughout the county. The recent Nobel laureate argued that the tactics used to disfranchise Blacks were nothing less than "deliberate attempts to freeze voter registration at their present undemocratic levels." This initial meeting, King continued, was the commencement of a "determined, organized, mobilized campaign to get the right to vote everywhere in Alabama." He hinted to the seven hundred people in attendance that imminent appeals to Governor George C. Wallace would likely fail to yield any substantive results. Even if Wallace failed to remedy the injustices, however, "we will appeal to the legislature. If the legislature does not listen we will seek to arouse the federal government by marching by the thousands to the places of registration," shouted King from the pulpit that cold night.[10]

Hosea Williams, James Bevel, and Andrew Young were King's top lieutenants who had a sustained presence in Selma from the beginning of the Selma campaign. "The SCLC people—Hosea, Bevel, and Young—mainly were essentially calling the shots," wrote John Lewis. By 1965, the three were all battle-tested activists who had faced death while agitating for Black equality. Williams, who turned thirty-nine three days after King's kickoff speech, was the oldest and most experienced civil rights activist of the three men. He was the only one of the three men to have led a major civil rights campaign before arriving in Selma. Young, six years younger than Williams and four years older than Bevel, did not begin participating in organized civil rights protests until joining SNCC in 1960. The twenty-eight-year-old Bevel had played a crucial role in the Birmingham campaign in 1963. The three had also attended college before 1965. All three were college graduates with four academic degrees between them. Williams had earned a bachelor's degree in chemistry from Morris Brown College in 1951. Young had earned a bachelor's degree in biology from Howard University the same year and a bachelor of divinity degree from Hartford Theological Seminary in 1955. Bevel received his bachelor's degree from American Baptist Theological Seminary in 1961. Bevel and Young were also ministers, ordained in 1955 and 1959, respectively. That Williams was King's only lieutenant who was not a minister likely triggered some underlying tension with Bevel, but it was not the source of the group's primary differences. Class and education may have trumped ministerial status. The lieutenants knew that Williams was a successful chemist in a space that was exclusive to whites in the South. On the other hand, all possessed towering egos, which resulted in constant discord and ideological differences. "You have to have ego to stay in the movement," Williams observed, "Ain't no money out there, ain't no nothing—you've got to have an ego to stay in the movement."[11]

The most contentious relationship existed between Williams and Bevel. According to Andrew Young, "each felt that the other was a menace to the movement, each was prone to let his own personal competition and his own 'movement image' interfere" with the ultimate goals of the civil rights struggle. Their relationship got off to a bad start in 1964, Williams later recalled. "Bevel tried to kill the movement in Savannah . . . that's when we really hit heads." Bevel felt that "I was too militant" and that "I was careless with the lives of people," said Williams. The disdain was certainly mutual: Bevel constantly spoke of Williams in a derisive and condescending manner. "Bevel thought of Williams only as a pesticide chemist who had no real understanding of nonviolence other than 'putting niggers in jail to get on television,'" wrote Taylor Branch. Conversely, Williams viewed Bevel as a conning trickster who, at vital moments during the movement, lacked courage. He said, "Bevel didn't really believe in exposing himself to danger. Bevel didn't go to jail but one time and he got tricked that time . . . Bevel liked to get up at the mass rallies and was great at it . . . He'd preach like hell and get the people inspired, but when we had to face Jim Clark and hit them streets, Bevel wasn't there."[12]

The director of voter registration and political education also viewed Andrew Young, the SCLC's executive director, with a similar disdain that led to numerous disagreements. Williams and Young had worked together in both the Savannah and St. Augustine movements. By Young's own admission, "I was always looking for the easiest way to freedom." Williams reached the conclusion that Young was a soft "Uncle Tom" because of his designated role as King's chief compromiser and diplomat, which often required him to take a moderate approach when dealing with the white power structure in cities where the SCLC demonstrated. "I depend on you to bring a certain kind of common sense to staff meetings, and you know it," King told Young in one meeting. King continued: "I need you to take as conservative a position as possible, then I can have plenty of room to come down in the middle." Tom Houck, a white northerner and personal driver to King, recalled that "Hosea was always on one side, Andy was on the other. And they would cuss each other out." Houck agreed with Williams. "In SCLC, you had two major factions—the Hosea Williams faction, which is the real militant faction, and the Andy Young faction, which is real conservative and only wants to pray and do nothing," Williams said in describing the tense personal dynamics in the civil rights organization. Young, reflecting on his and Williams's conflicted relationship remembered that "Hosea and I used to always clash. We were the opposites in SCLC. Hosea was always confrontational" with colleagues and just about anyone else who did not share his opinion. Dorothy Cotton, the only woman on SCLC's executive staff, later echoed Young's sentiments. She recalled a meeting when she was sitting next to King. "Williams walked into the executive staff meeting late. And Dr. King hunched me and said 'watch this meeting turn into a fight now that Hosea's here. . . . Hosea would bring a special kind of fighting energy to the table," she said. "Even though I might have wanted to put him in the trunk and sit on it sometime, but I also loved Hosea in a special kind of way like your naughty or rambunctious brother," Cotton continued. Although Williams and Young were diametrically opposed in their approaches to alleviating all of the vestiges of slavery and segregation, King skillfully harnessed their respective talents by utilizing patience and attentiveness. Dorothy Cotton touted King's ability to listen to all competing factions within his team of "wild horses" and make decisions with scholarly objectivity. King also knew how to leverage his "wild horses" to seek a desired outcome with recalcitrant segregationists. White city leaders' willingness to negotiate with Young and to make concessions did not come about because they had a change of heart and embraced Black equality. They were often more intent on ridding their cities of Williams's unrelenting protests and dreaded night marches.[13]

King appointed Williams, Young, and Bevel to lead the protests in effort in Selma in early 1965, but the evidence suggests that Williams—in theory, a subordinate to Young and an organizational equal with Bevel—became the de facto man in charge. As John Lewis observed, Williams became the "ringmaster" of the voting rights campaign. Taking a shot at Bevel and Young, Williams maintained that "People ain't dumb. They want a leader that's going to lead, going to get out front." He continued, "They don't want you to stand in that church and preach to them and tell them how to march downtown and face Jim Clark. They want you to get up there and say, 'You come on, we'll show you how to face Jim Clark.'" Because the Black citizens in Selma had witnessed Williams's willingness to stand with them in battle, he had, in his words, "unspokenly became the leader of the Selma movement."[14]

Although the SCLC has received a lot of the credit relative to the Selma movement, it is worth noting SNCC's place in the city before March 1965. SNCC had worked to register Blacks in the city who, by 1962, constituted less than 3% of registered voters. SNCC staged "Freedom Day" on October 18, 1963, where, according to some estimates, nearly eight hundred Blacks showed up at the Dallas County Courthouse and stood in line all day to register to vote. Only five Blacks had been allowed to proceed through the line by the time the courthouse closed. This disheartening statistic further dramatized the need for a concerted campaign in the city. Amelia Boynton and the Rev. Frederick Reese wanted to invite King and SCLC to Selma. Although some SNCC staffers agreed with Reese and Boynton, another faction within the organization did not want King in the city while they were trying to "reclaim their territory" after reestablishing a presence in Selma. As Williams recalled, "It was a duel between SNCC and SCLC" from that point. Some SNCC staffers had a deep disregard for the SCLC leader. For some members in SNCC, their "number one goal in their life was to embarrass Martin Luther King Jr," said Williams in 1991. Lewis, in the minority, believed that Dr. King should be invited to Selma. His stance was another factor that led to the friction between him and other SNCC members.[15]

On Monday, January 18, Williams registered at Selma's historic Albert Hotel, only recently desegregated under the 1964 Civil Rights Act. Within 24 hours, he had been arrested after leading a voter registration drive march on the Dallas County Courthouse. Selma police detained Williams and seventy fellow protesters, after they refused to move from in front of the courthouse and into a nearby alley, until they were allowed to attempt to take the unpassable literacy test—a requirement for Black applicants. Along with Williams and Boynton, John Lewis was also carried away to the county jail for protesting to register to vote. During this particular protest, Dr. King, who was across the street from the courthouse, watched Sherriff Jim Clark roughly handle Amelia Boynton, the activist who had persuaded SCLC to campaign in Selma the previous November. Clark roughly grabbed her by the collar of her fur coat and pushed her toward one of his deputies before shoving her into a waiting police vehicle. The treatment of Boynton led King to tell reporters that her arrest was "one of the most inhumane things I have ever seen." Although Clark was known for mistreating Black men and women in public, Williams insisted that he was far more brutal toward Black prisoners while inside the jail. He recalled, "They used to arrest us. . . . The jail was on the third or fourth floor, and they would stop the elevator between floors and actually stuck cattle prods in the women's vaginas and cattle prods in our rectums, while constantly beating us between floors."[16]

After the mass arrest on January 19, a period of relative quiet existed in Selma until February 1. The next three weeks were not as tranquil. Authorities arrested King and his most trusted confidant, Ralph Abernathy, on the first day of February after they led two hundred sixty-three other protesters in refusing to adhere to the parade ordinance that had been issued by Judge Hare in 1964 in his attempt to rid Selma of SNCC. Later that evening, Sheriff Clark arrested an additional seven hundred demonstrators as they sought to register at the Dallas County Courthouse. Williams was not among the demonstrators arrested; he was still actively involved in protests to secure the right to vote. He was leading nearly six hundred marchers in adjacent Perry County, where less than eight percent of its Black residents were registered.

Two days later, Malcolm X, a former firebrand within the militant Nation of Islam arrived in Selma to observe the conditions of Blacks in Selma. It is inaccurate to assume that Malcolm X did not respect King and his nonviolent philosophy. "Malcolm liked King, and King liked Malcolm, but there was no association," Williams said. After the conversation, Williams said that it was evident that the former disciple of Elijah Muhammad had "made a tremendous impact on King." Speaking of his own respect for perhaps the only figure who was more revered than him in certain Black communities for his militancy before 1966, Williams stated that "I was quite a Malcolm X fan and to classify me as nonviolent was sort of overbearing because I was bent the other way." Malcolm X had evidently impressed more than Williams and King. After the meeting, the staff persuaded Malcolm X to address a crowd at Brown Chapel. He told Williams and other staffers that, after his message, "You should usher me to the car and let me leave because if one of those crackers hit me, I'm going to try to kill him." This was Williams's first and last time to meet the Muslim minister. Williams asserts that Malcolm X and King met again on Auburn Avenue in Atlanta several weeks later, shortly before Black Muslims assassinated the thirty-nine-year-old Malcolm on February 22, in Harlem's Audubon Ballroom.[17]

Williams's participation in events in Dallas County and surrounding areas throughout the rest of February further exposed him to the further violence that would climax on March 7. "We began demonstrating in six or seven surrounding counties" to confuse law enforcement, he said. On February 17, he was standing behind his colleague, C. T. Vivian, when Vivian angrily hurled comparisons to Adolf Hitler at Sheriff Clark. "Before I knew it, Clark hauls off and hits C. T. in the mouth," Williams recalled. Vivian had studied Clark and knew that he could bait the demented lawman to assault him with the television cameras rolling. Later that evening, news stations showed the footage across the nation, and the newspaper headlines read "Taunted Sheriff Hits Rights Aide." Once again, a brutal Alabama lawman attracted national attention to the plight of Black Americans in the state.

Violence escalated two days later when Williams, Vivian, and James Orange led a nighttime march of four hundred protesters in Marion, Alabama. After lawmen and local vigilantes attacked the marchers, Jimmie Lee Jackson, a twenty-six-year-old Black man, and his mother fled into a local café. When state police charged into Mac's Café and began shoving Jackson's mother. Hosea recalled Jackson telling the officers, "that if you got to beat somebody, beat me. Please don't beat my mother." Highway patrolman James Bonard Fowler pulled out his pistol and shot Jackson in the stomach. The young man was not "known as a civil rights leader or a person who outright opposed the power structure. He wasn't known as a bad guy, a thug, or a criminal," Williams recalled. Along with Jackson, city police and a mob of club-swinging hastily deputized whites injured more than a dozen of the marchers, including Richard Valeriani, an NBC correspondent covering the demonstration. The white cameraman was struck in the head with an ax handle. The network aired footage of him recuperating in the hospital the next day. Jackson suffered the most serious injury, however. After Jackson was wounded, he was taken to a nearby white hospital in Marion but denied medical assistance because he was Black. "We brought him back to the hospital in Selma," remembered Williams. At Good Samaritan Hospital, Dr. William Dinkins, a Black physician, performed an exploratory laparotomy, a procedure that required a large incision to gain access into the abdominal cavity. Dr. Dinkins traced the bullet's path down the intestinal tract, sewing up any wounds and removing bullet fragments in the process. The operation was "successful," Dinkins recalled. Over the next few days, Jackson seemed to be recovering and, according to a hospital spokesman, "making encouraging" progress. A week after the shooting, however, he suddenly developed a high fever, and Dr. Dinkins detected a severe infection in his abdomen. Doctors began performing surgery to remove the infection around 2:30 AM on February 26. Jackson was pronounced dead seven hours later. Jackson's death outraged Blacks, including local activist, Mrs. Lucy Foster, who discussed marching to Montgomery with Jackson's lifeless body and delivering the remains to George Wallace at the Governor's Mansion. Bevel, who was recovering from pneumonia at the time of the shooting, also recommended marching to the state's capital city. "I," said Bevel, "recommended that people walk from Marion to Montgomery, which would give them time to work out in terms of what energy and thinking through their hostility and resentments, and get back focus on the issue."[18]

A series of legal exchanges between the SCLC and Alabama's Governor Wallace followed the February 18 police assault on marchers in Marion. Wallace, who had angrily denounced the Marion protestors and defended local authorities, was adamant in public statements and in conversation with his advisers that the civil rights organization would not be allowed to make the eighty-mile march from the city where Jackson was shot to Montgomery, Alabama. Shortly after Jackson's shooting, King hurriedly sent a telegram to Nicholas Katzenbach, the US Attorney General. The SCLC president wrote that Black demonstrators were "literally under house arrest in Zion Methodist Church" under "the threat death of further brutality." King implored the country's chief judicial officer to provide federal protection as the marchers sought the basic right to vote. The attorney general issued a brief reply to King later that afternoon. "Department attorneys," Katzenbach said, "and agents of the FBI have been on the scene in both Selma and Marion" investigating the incidents that he mentioned. George Wallace, on the other hand, continued to refer to the marchers as "professional agitators" and subsequently banned all nighttime marchers—the very demonstrations that Williams had devised and utilized as leverage to force the cities of Savannah and St. Augustine into making political concessions. At Jackson's memorial service on March 3, Bevel, with King's acquiescence, announced to the mourners that a march had been scheduled for Sunday, March 7, to protest not only the murder of Jackson but also for the right to vote. The night before the march to Montgomery was to take place, Governor Wallace banned the trek to Montgomery. Wallace's political instincts to keep the marchers in Selma undergirded his logic for an eleventh-hour decree. "His best bet," said Ralph Abernathy, "would be to use his power as governor" to ensure that the protesters would never reach the capital city. "That way, any violence would be attributed to Sheriff Clark and his hometown boys rather than to Wallace's Montgomery-based state troopers."[19]

Wallace, far from a political novice, was torn by conflicting emotions. He knew intuitively that if the marchers were stopped for any reason, especially by violence, that he and his state would be the subjects of national abhorrence for obstructing Blacks from practicing both their First Amendment and Fifteenth Amendment rights. However, he was also intent on avoiding the appearance that he had capitulated to the demands of King and his followers. The death of Jimmie Lee Jackson, along with the SCLC's overriding goal to bring national attention to Selma and Alabama's denial of Blacks' right to vote, would ultimately set the stage for what would become Williams's defining hour as a civil rights activist.[20]

On Saturday March 6, while Governor Wallace was meeting with his advisers and with state law enforcement officials in an attempt to halt the march on Montgomery, the defiant Hosea Williams used the organizational skills he had honed in earlier protest marches to ensure that his nonviolent troops had enough supplies on their civil rights excursion to the Cradle of the Confederacy. "I got in my car that Saturday and drove to Montgomery measuring miles," recalled Williams. Determining the mileage was only one component of the preparation for the march. Williams also had to make a decision as to "where we can stop and have lunch, where we could stop for breaks, and where we could spend the night. . . . I also had to figure out what bushes would make a good bathroom area." After carefully examining the route from Selma, Williams arrived at the MIA office on Dorsey Street on the west side of Montgomery, a space that had been secured by E. D. Nixon ten years earlier during the bus boycott. There, Williams was informed that Dr. King had been trying to contact him. Once Williams spoke with the SCLC's president that evening, he was informed that "Daddy King," Martin Luther King Jr.'s father and co-pastor at Ebenezer Baptist Church in Atlanta, was ill and unable to preach the next day, making it impossible for the younger King to lead the march as previously planned.

"Call the march off today, Hosea," King said while on a conference call with Bayard Rustin, C. T. Vivian, Ralph Abernathy, Andy Young, Dorothy Cotton, and Pastor P. H. Lewis of Brown Chapel. King, a leader who made decisions based on consensus, toward the end of the conversation said, "I won't" stay in Atlanta and preach "if you all said I shouldn't." King then called for a vote. Each caller, with the exception of Williams, supported King's initial decision not to proceed with the march. "No, Doc, I can't support you. . . . You don't know how well organized we are," Williams told the SCLC president. Disturbed by his subordinate's persistence to proceed without him, King, very sternly, told Williams: "You're not with me, son. Hosea, you need to pray. You need to get with me." Still trying to persuade King to allow the march, Williams said, "I'm telling you now. We'd better lead that march or they're going without us." King finally ended the debate. "No," he told Williams. "Go down there and tell them that the march is off. Ordered!" By 9:00 PM, the principals had agreed not to march—or so most participants thought. An angry Williams "drove back to Selma [from Montgomery] in twenty minutes . . . thinking how I can outsmart them, how I can trick them to do what I want."[21]

After arriving in Selma around 9:30 PM on March 6, Williams realized that his best and only chance to sway King was to rely on his colleague, co-organizer and archenemy, James Bevel. Williams believed that he had an unlikely ally in Bevel because the march on Montgomery was the latter's brainchild. Williams's reliance on Bevel was out of desperation. "Lord, how can I get out of this since I promised to get the people back to work on Monday?" Williams thought to himself. Another factor that gave rise to his increasing anxiety was the level of participation. "We see the people coming in from the counties . . . and we ain't got nowhere to put them, nowhere," he recalled. If the march was postponed until Monday, he reasoned, he and the SCLC would lose vital support and momentum. Aware of the stakes, Bevel, Williams's unlikely ally, decided to call King, hoping to change the latter's perspective on the import of marching the next day. Standing outside of the closed office door, Williams recalled, "I could hear Bevel and King arguing. Bevel got loud with King. Then he quiets down." Bevel walked out of the office and said to Williams, "Okay, you got it. Go ahead and march." Jubilant, "I kissed Bevel on the cheek," said Williams. He used the rest of the night to gather those who were willing to march the next day. While Williams was finalizing logistics, Bevel, as both men had agreed after the call with King, was designated to inform Pastor Harris about King's change of heart. Bevel neglected to follow up with Harris. Williams's nemesis knew that King had not consented to the march, and he did not want to be held responsible for disobeying King—ultimately leaving Williams to carry the blame and plausibly face termination as a consequence for insubordination.[22]

Early Sunday morning, March 7, after working on march logistics through the night, Williams, defying King, proceeded to prepare his followers for the fifty-four-mile journey to Montgomery. Pastor Harris allowed Williams to address a crowd of nearly five hundred people during Brown Chapel's Sunday morning worship service. "I had people jumping all over the benches that morning," Williams told one interviewer. In another recollection, Williams remembered that "I just really went wild in that pulpit . . . people were jumping all upside the wall." After firing up the crowd with a song and a brief but passionate charge, Williams told his audience that the march would commence at 3:00 PM. Harris, shocked by Williams's announcement (and still under the impression that there would be no march), questioned the anxious activist about his plans to lead the march. After Williams assured the pastor that King had given his permission, the preacher responded by saying, "You crazy. You crazy. You know King done called that march off." After calling Williams a "liar," Harris quickly called King in Atlanta to seek confirmation regarding his claims. King hung up with Harris and then called Ralph Abernathy; both were shocked that Williams had seemingly disobeyed a top-down directive.[23]

King and Abernathy contacted Andy Young, the executive director, to intervene in a futile attempt to halt the march. "I received a call from Martin instructing me to rush over to Selma and postpone the march until

Monday," said Young. Young left Atlanta on an 8:00 AM chartered plane to Montgomery. Williams met an angry and frustrated Young at the airport in Selma. "We are going to deal with you, Hosea. This is one time you have overstepped your boundaries," said Young. Williams was befuddled by the accusation. He told Young that Bevel had assured him that King had authorized the march. Williams and Young confronted Bevel to see who was at fault. "Shit," Bevel said, "I ain't told Hosea nothing like that." Young then called King and briefed him on the state of affairs: "We can't stop it," Young said to King, "He got them too fired up. They will go without us." Young also warned his boss that a press corps had assembled around Brown Chapel. Reneging on leading the march would damage crucial relationships with the media on whom they relied to disseminate news of barbaric injustices to the rest of the nation. After hearing the details from Young, whom King trusted to give wise and prudent counsel, the latter "reluctantly gave his assent," recalled Young.[24]

King's acquiescence to allow what had evolved into an inevitable march led to an extraordinary train of events that altered the history of the United States relative to Black Americans' rights to vote. John Lewis, the chairman of SNCC, who had not had a major role in planning this particular march, agreed to lead the protest alongside a representative from the SCLC. Williams, Bevel, and Young were told by King to choose from among themselves who would represent the organization as the other two needed to be able to lead any crisis management initiative that may arise as a result. The trio conducted a coin flip, with heads determining who would replace King at the front of the line. "I knew that I had won. They knew I knew," said Williams after the second coin flip. Although Bevel and Young knew that Williams wanted the limelight, especially since the media had gathered in Selma, Williams felt that neither wanted to lead the march in the first place. "Andy knew damn well he wasn't going to lead that march," said Williams. "Bevel certainly was not going to lead it either." The date of the march had approached so quickly since the idea was conceived only a few days earlier. "The march came up on us so fast. I had two trucks, about ten to fifteen sleeping bags . . . and only four cases of boiled eggs" for over four hundred people, remembered Williams. None of the prepared items would be utilized.[25]

Shortly before 4:00 PM, Hosea Williams, John Lewis, and James Bevel assembled nearly five hundred twenty-five marchers at Brown Chapel. Lewis read a statement to the press expressing why the marchers were protesting the injustices that dominated the lives of Blacks in Alabama.

Hosea Williams and John Lewis leading marchers across the Edmund Pettus Bridge on March 7, 1965. Alabama Department of Archives and History. Donated by Alabama Media Group. Photo by Tom Lankford, *Birmingham News*.

Everyone in the delegation bent their knees while Young prayed for God's mercies. Williams and Lewis, both dressed in dark slacks, neckties, and black dress shoes and wearing full-length raincoats to protect themselves from the cold wind that swept in from the Alabama River, led a double column followed by Amelia Boynton, Albert Turner, Bob Mants, Marie Foster, and hundreds of teenagers, teachers, and other professionals. After a nearly silent walk six blocks over to Selma's Broad Street, the marchers turned south toward the Selma bridge spanning the Alabama River. There, they encountered fifty Alabama State Troopers, dressed in glistening blue uniforms, who were stationed at the end of the Edmund Pettus Bridge and armed with handguns, billy clubs, and cattle prods. Approximately thirty-six volunteer "posse men," fifteen of whom were mounted on horseback, flanked the troopers from the side and the back. The troopers put on their gas masks. Williams and Lewis, still at the front of the line, stopped within fifty feet of the officers. "John, they are going to gas us," said Williams to his co-leader. With a kind of gallows humor, he glanced at the Alabama River flowing under the bridge and softly added, "John, can you swim?"[26]

As they halted, Major John Cloud lifted his megaphone. "Your march," said Cloud, "is not conducive to the public safety. You are ordered to disperse and go back to your church or to your homes." Williams was the only marcher who spoke and directed comments to Cloud. "May we have a word with the Major?" asked Hosea. Cloud responded, "There is no word to be had." Williams and Major Cloud repeated the lines two more times. "You have two minutes to turn around and go back to your church," concluded Cloud, but in less than one minute, the major shouted, "Troopers advance." Williams, then clinched his nostrils with his right thumb and index finger as the troopers dashed forward and plowed through the first ten rows of marchers. "Some of the troopers had even tried to push people off the bridge and into the ravine and water," he recalled. Shortly after the shoving began, the troopers released their first round of tear gas, composed of the explosive substance C-4, an agent effective in causing nausea. "It was so thick you absolutely couldn't see anything," Williams said.

Marchers began coughing and screaming. Women and kids were weeping uncontrollably. A second gas attack followed almost immediately after the first round. Ben Clark, Williams's lieutenant from Savannah, was carrying a little girl named Sheyann Webb (later Webb-Christburg) who was barely nine years old. Clark, only five feet, three inches tall and weighing one-hundred thirty-five pounds, could not move fast enough with the child. Williams grabbed the girl as he heard the horses' hooves pounding on the pavement. Sheyann yelled to the veteran SCLC activist, "Put me down!" As she later remembered ruefully, "He wasn't running fast enough." She ran all the way to the relative safety of her home in the George Washington Carver housing project. A woman rushed toward Williams and threw a blanket so that he could cover his head. "Hosea," she screamed, "they're going to kill you—you're the one they want." He fled into the nearby home of a Black family where he hid for almost an hour. By the time the eleven-minute attack had ended, some of the marchers had scattered throughout the nearby Carver project homes, while others sought refuge at Brown Chapel and neighboring First Baptist Church. The latter's parsonage resembled a "MASH unit," recalled Lewis who suffered from a fractured skull, as did Amelia Boynton. (Both temporarily lost consciousness.) Other demonstrators with fractured legs, arms, and ribs and with bloodied heads were carried to the Good Samaritan Hospital, the largest Black medical facility in Selma, and to Burwell Infirmary, a smaller Black health care facility.[27]

As injuries were being documented to ensure that there were no fatalities, Williams, Bevel, and Young telephoned King, who was still at Ebenezer Baptist Church where he had preached that morning. King was "horrified" at what he heard, Young recalled. Williams, King, Young, and Bevel decided that they should seek federal protection and immediately begin planning for the march from Selma to Montgomery. Later that evening, Williams spoke at a mass meeting that he, Lewis, and others convened at Brown Chapel. Williams, according to the *New York Times*, yelled from the same pulpit where he had announced the march that morning: "I want to tell you that the Germans never were inhuman as the state troopers of Alabama." While participants milled around the church, ABC aired fifteen minutes of footage showing beatings from the march during its showing of *Judgment at Nuremberg*, a documentary highlighting the atrocities sanctioned by Nazi Germany during World War II. Some viewers undoubtedly saw parallels between the events in Selma and those of Adolf Hitler's Third Reich. Once again, the SCLC succeeded in dramatizing the conditions in Alabama to the nation, launching a wave of sympathy and support throughout the United States. The country, including members of Congress, were horrified at what had flashed across their television screens that Sunday night. "I think their attitude was, 'Oh, my God, we've just got to, got to get on top of this problem, we can't continue to . . . be distracted by race . . . we've got to solve the problem," Attorney General Katzenbach recalled.[28]

Williams described the next two weeks as "crisis-packed." "We immediately set to work preparing for a second Selma-to-Montgomery march. . . ." Williams, said Young, "assumed responsibility for logistics." According to John Lewis, "Hosea never stopped. Apparently, he started planning for the continuation of the march" as soon as the chaos ended on Sunday. "He," Lewis continued, "became the leader and ringmaster more than anyone else." Early on the morning of March 8, Williams, as the lead plaintiff, filed suit in the US District Court Middle District of Alabama against Governor George Wallace; Al Lingo, the Director of the Alabama Public Safety Department; and Sheriff Jim Clark. Seasoned civil rights attorneys Fred D. Gray, Solomon Seay, James Nabrit III, and Jack Greenberg served as counsel. In *Williams v. Wallace*, the plaintiffs filed motions for a temporary restraining order and a preliminary injunction to nullify Governor Wallace's March 6 proclamation banning any marches in Selma—an act that Judge Johnson would later declare crossed the "constitutional boundary line." Initially, however, Judge Johnson told the plaintiffs that he would not immediately enjoin the defendants from blocking any subsequent marches until he held hearings later that week. Pointedly, Johnson strongly recommended that the SCLC postpone the march scheduled for Tuesday. After filing the motion at the federal courthouse in Montgomery, Williams traveled a few miles to the MIA's headquarters on Dorsey Street to plan strategy for new demonstrations to demand the right to vote and a redress of grievances.[29]

On Monday evening, after spending Sunday night sleeping on the kitchen floor in the Brown Chapel parsonage, Williams met with King, Young, Bevel, and SNCC members Lewis, Willie Ricks, and Fay Bellamy to discuss how to channel the momentum that had reached a crescendo only twenty-four hours earlier. Engaged in the teleconference meeting from Washington, DC, was US Attorney General Nicholas Katzenbach. With Katzenbach dissenting, the meeting participants initially decided to march to Montgomery the following day until they realized the logistical nightmares that would follow a hastily planned fifty-four-mile march that could easily span four or five days. Planning was complicated by the fact that over four hundred priests, ministers, and rabbis had already arrived from throughout the country in Selma in response to King's plea to support the demonstration. For example, Williams said, "We had to find places for them, and figure out how to feed them." Moreover, Judge Johnson, whom the SCLC needed as an impartial ally, had cautioned them against marching until he could hear testimony later in the week and, as Katzenbach made clear, the Johnson Administration vehemently opposed a march the next day. As a compromise with the White House and the Justice Department, King, with the counsel of his senior leadership, including Williams, agreed to lead a symbolic march close to Haistens Mattress and Awning Company on Tuesday. Haistens was located just before the Edmund Pettus Bridge. Once the fifteen hundred marchers, one third of whom were clergymen, reached the bridge, they knelt in prayer and marched back to Brown Chapel. With the exception of King and the leadership team, marchers believed that the march would proceed to Montgomery. Many, according to Williams, "felt betrayed." Others, including SNCC's Jim Forman, were "livid," according to Lewis. Although the demonstrators were visibly frustrated with King and the SCLC, some officials with the Justice Department claimed that King's actions were unpredictable. "We really didn't know whether Dr. King would turn around and go back or whether there would be another outbreak of violence," Nicholas Katzenbach later recalled.[30]

Although the march on Tuesday, March 9, was a brief and peaceful exercise of the protesters, constitutional right to assemble, violence befell an unexpected victim in Rev. James Reeb, a thirty-eight-year-old white Unitarian minister from Boston, Massachusetts. After the march, Reeb had dinner around 7:00 PM with Williams and other SCLC staff members at

Hosea Williams addressing a crowd in front of Brown Chapel in Selma, Alabama, on "Turnaround Tuesday." March 9, 1965. Alabama Department of Archives and History. Donated by Alabama Media Group. Photo by Spider Martin, *Birmingham News*.

Walker's Café, a Black-owned restaurant specializing in soul food on Selma's Washington Street. "The place was jammed," Williams remembered. After eating, Reeb and two additional Unitarian ministers left and walked toward the Silver Moon Café—a place Williams identified as a "real redneck" establishment. Four white men approached the holy trio as they walked down Washington Street. One of the white toughs hit Reeb in the head with what Williams described as a "huge wrench." (The two ministers accompanying Reeb later said it was a three-foot-long pipe, or perhaps a wooden club.) The men also attacked Reeb's friends. "One lost his glasses and couldn't see a damn thing," remembered Williams. The culprits quickly ran away after the attack; shortly afterward, Reeb slipped into a coma. Dr. William Dinkins, the same Black physician who treated Jimmie Lee Jackson on February 18, ordered Reeb transported to the University Medical Center in Birmingham, but transportation problems, including mechanical failure with one ambulance, prevented Reeb from promptly receiving the medical care for his severe injury, and the ambulance did not arrive until 11:00 PM. In Birmingham, Reeb underwent emergency surgery to treat several skull fractures that precipitated a blood clot on the left side of his brain. He died two days later, at 7:55 PM. Reeb's death further galvanized support for the conditions in Selma. "The national outcry was incredible. . . . There was a lot more fuss over Rev. Reeb's death than over the death of Jimmie Lee Jackson," Williams acidly noted. The White House did not officially acknowledge Jackson's death. President Johnson authorized a military aircraft to transport Rev. Reeb's wife to Birmingham, said Williams, while "Jimmie Lee's mama and his granddaddy were back on their 'little nothing' farm," already practically forgotten.[31]

The next week was arguably one of the most hectic and demanding seven days of Williams's tenure in SCLC. King instructed him to formulate a logistical plan to be submitted to Judge Frank Johnson for the latter's consideration when deciding to permit the march to Montgomery. "What a job," he told King. However, his military training from his days with a quartermaster truck company during the Allied Occupation of Europe and his experiences in leading highly publicized civil rights demonstrations during the previous three years in Savannah and St. Augustine gave him the background needed to create a logistical plan that could pass judiciary muster. That plan was also important in shaping Lyndon Johnson's deliberations, because Alabama officials had insisted in hearings on March 16 and 17 that a march from Selma to Montgomery was not conducive to the safety of the public. Thousands of marchers presented one problem; protecting, feeding and providing toilet facilities presented other obstacles. Moreover, not only did Williams have to construct a plan that conformed to state and county parade procedures, but he also had to anticipate and preempt Wallace's and Lingo's arguments while devising a proposal within a very short window of time. Williams solicited the assistance of Attorneys Greenberg and Nabrit to ensure that his proposal, which was submitted to Judge Johnson on March 17, did not break any laws, a misstep that would have been used by the defendants to halt any plans for the march and thereby bring the movement's momentum to a halt.[32]

Over the next few days, Williams devised a detailed logistical plan that included the dates, times, routes, and the mileage that would be covered each day of the march. He also laid out the support services that would be available to the marchers: food, truckborne washing and toilet facilities, litter and garbage pickup by truck along the route, ambulance and first-aid service, and communication services by "walkie-talkie." Finally, Williams spelled out what would happen once the marchers reached the state capitol in Montgomery.

His logistical plan, as outlined below, is worth quoting at length:

- The march will commence on Friday, March 19, 1965 at 10:30 AM or any day thereafter provided that plaintiffs will provide at least 48 hours advance notice of the march to Defendants, the United States, and the Court.

- The number of persons marching will be as follows:
  - There will be no limitation on the number of marchers within the Cities of Selma and Montgomery and along the 4-lane portions of Route 80-East between Selma and Montgomery.
  - The number of marchers will not exceed 300 persons on the 2-lane portion of Route 80.

- Approximate distances covered each day:
  - First day-march approximately 11 miles stopping at a designated private field with permission of owner which has already been granted;
  - Second day-march approximately 11 miles stopping at a designated field with permission of the owner which already has been granted;
  - Third day-march approximately 17 miles stopping at a designated building and adjoining field with permission of owners which has already been granted;
  - Fourth day-march 8 miles to the western part of Montgomery stopping at an area tentatively selected and to be designated;
  - Fifth day-march from western part of Montgomery to the Capitol;
  - Large tents will be erected at the campsites by professionals. Meetings and song festivals may be held at campsites.

- March routes:
  - Route of march in the City of Selma: Starting at Brown's Chapel AME Church on Sylvan Street proceeding South on Sylvan to Alabama, then West on Alabama to
  - Broad (Highway 80-East), then South on Broad Street across Edmund Pettus Bridge along Highway 80-East to Montgomery. The march in the City will be conducted in the streets.
  - Route in the City of Montgomery: Marchers will enter the City following Route 80 until it becomes Fairview Avenue and continue on Fairview to Oak Street turning North on Oak Street to Jeff Davis Avenue; then East on Jeff Davis to Holt Street; then North on Holt to Mobile Street; then on Mobile to Montgomery; then Northeast

on Montgomery to Court Square then up Dexter Avenue to Capitol. The March in the City will be in the streets.

- On the highway, the marchers will proceed on shoulders of the road walking on the left side facing automobile traffic. They will march along road shoulders two abreast and employ single files at places where the shoulder is narrow and on bridges without sidewalks. The marchers will be organized in separate groups of approximately 50 persons (or less) and each group will be under the supervision of a designated group leader.

- Upon reaching Montgomery: A mass meeting will be held in front of the Alabama State Capitol on the day the marchers enter Montgomery. There will be a speakers' stand with loud speakers in the street in front of the Capitol. The audience will be on the sidewalks and in the street in front of the Capitol as well as on the Capitol steps. The audience will be directed not to walk on the grass around the Capitol unless the state permits this. The formal program will be conducted between approximately . . . noon and 3:00 PM.

- Following the completion of the outdoor program:
  - Not more than 20 persons will enter the Capitol Building, proceed to the Governor's office, seek an audience with the Governor and present a petition.
  - Transportation away from the Capitol grounds will be provided by leaders of the march to various destinations including transportation terminals.[33]

Williams's detailed plan won the approval of Judge Johnson. On March 18, 1965, at approximately 4:42 PM, Judge Johnson signed the order declaring that the march could proceed. Williams's plan called for the march to commence Sunday, March 21. Late Friday night, Governor Wallace, who had exhausted his appeals to enjoin the march, wired President Johnson at his ranch in Johnson City, Texas, informing him that the State of Alabama could not afford to pay the costs associated with providing six thousand one hundred seventy-one men, four hundred eighty vehicles, and eighteen buses to provide "maximum security" for the five-day march. "This was just what Johnson was waiting for," said Williams. Judge Johnson responded that Wallace was shirking his "solemn responsibility" to protect the marchers, and President Johnson, immediately federalized nineteen hundred Alabama National Guardsmen. The president also directed one thousand full-time US Army personnel to be distributed along the fifty-four-mile route from Selma to Montgomery. To ensure that trained investigators were present, Johnson also dispatched one hundred Federal Bureau of Investigation agents and one hundred US Marshals to be on duty throughout the duration of the protest.[34]

On the morning of Sunday, March 21, exactly two weeks to the minute since Williams had delivered his impassioned speech to congregants at Brown Chapel AME, he and a diverse group of approximately four thousand demonstrators prepared to leave for the first leg of the four-day march. "When it finally got started, it was pretty tame. I was so busy, I probably missed a lot," Williams said. The huge number of out-of-town participants strained even the best laid plans. Alexander Aldrich, chairman of the Special Cabinet Committee on Civil Rights in the administration of New York Governor Nelson Rockefeller, described the events at Brown Chapel as "chaotic." "Nobody seemed to know what was happening," said Aldrich. "A group of Rabbis were sitting in folding undertaker's chairs beside the pulpit." Sitting next to the clergymen was prominent NAACP attorney Constance Baker Motley, while movement supporter and renowned entertainer Harry Belafonte gave an interview to reporters a few steps away from Motley. "Lots and Lots," Aldrich said, "of other brass, and hundreds of kids, plain folks, white and Negro," came to support the epic protest.[35]

Three hours behind schedule, Williams and the estimated four thousand marchers left the steps of Brown Chapel. "It was a perfect day to walk: cool and sunny, without a single bug, and just enough breeze," said one observer. Williams had little opportunity to enjoy the beautiful weather. Although he realized that "excitement was in the air," his job was to ensure that the march proceeded smoothly. Despite the delayed start, the *New York Times* called Williams's logistical arrangements "elaborate." What was elaborate also proved to be expensive. As Williams told a reporter, the four-day march would cost the SCLC at least thirty thousand dollars. These funds would ensure that marchers were afforded suitable accommodations. Food was one of the largest expenditures. For thousands of people, lunch consisted of peanut butter and jelly sandwiches, oranges, and protein-filled energy bars. "It really was like a military operation," the march director proudly recalled. Marchers eligible for support had SCLC-issued credentials. "The badge of honor was a red arm-band. This signified that you had been selected to march the whole way and it entitled you to supper and bedding," said Aldrich. White ministers from across the country were pressed into service as mess sergeants, wearing name tags that read "Fishes and Loaves." To accommodate the large crowd, Williams had arranged for meals such as spaghetti and meatballs, applesauce, green beans, and coffee to be cooked and prepared in Selma and brought out "hot" to the marchers on yellow Hertz trucks. "The lines moves surprisingly fast," said Williams. More important, one observer commented, "They never ran out of food, and it was always on time." Williams did not discriminate in assigning jobs in any area where there was a need. "I had a bunch of upper-class white folks and some priests and nuns that I gave the shittiest jobs to—the worse jobs of the march, taking care of the sanitary facilities and emptying slop buckets and garbage cans," he said.[36]

The first day ended at 6:00 PM after the "mile-long line" of demonstrators had marched eight miles under the protection of what reporters called "carbine-carrying" soldiers. Judge Johnson had decreed that no more than three hundred individuals could march on the two-lane highway. During this section of the march, the three hundred of the four thousand marchers slept in four eight-foot-long tents on a cow pasture owned by Black farmer David Hall. The forty to fifty volunteers from San Francisco Theological Seminary, had, in Williams's words, "the most strenuous job of all," moving and erecting the tents each day. In the near-freezing temperature, trucks shuttled the remainder of the marchers back to Selma while the group that Williams called the "special 300" retired to sleep on air mattresses and Sears and Roebuck sleeping bags in tents illuminated by one bulb and heated by two kerosene heaters. Most marchers felt confident, knowing that they were protected by troops and federal agents, but Governor Wallace had warned that he would do nothing to protect the "outside agitators," and there were disturbing instances along the route the first day. Some whites drove by with signs saying "Too bad, Reeb," a reference to the white Unitarian minister who died on March 11. Another group of angry whites shouted out to a group of nuns, "Go back where you came from. You are going to burn in hell with the rest of them goddamn niggers."[37]

The next three days presented challenges that tested the marchers' commitment and resolve to finish the march. The marchers had walked fourteen miles on the second day compared with eight miles on the first leg. The dinner of chili beans and sauce, saltines, fruit, and bread arrived "rather cold," said Alexander Aldrich, as they camped out much farther than the kitchen in Selma. If the food was not as tasty, one marcher maintained that "everything was beautifully organized." The third day, Tuesday, March 23, a pouring rain made the march and sleeping uncomfortable for the three hundred marchers. Resting in Lowndesboro, Alabama, after walking eleven miles, the "soggy but spirited" demonstrators, as one commentator described them, pressed on and camped within twenty miles of their final destination. Harris Wofford, a former aide to President John F. Kennedy and then assistant to President Johnson, was present and helped Selma activist Marie Foster carry her bags throughout the rainy day. The rain had transformed the dirt into mud six inches deep. Before sleeping under two tents, the marchers ate pork and beans and spiced tea. Although King and Abernathy had left to raise money for the campaign, Williams displayed his ability to lead independently. He kept the march moving smoothly, in spite of the weather. March 24 was "very hot," compelling marchers to begin each day by coating their faces with zinc oxide, a sun-blocking agent. For breakfast, marchers consumed cereal and coffee. On the fourth day, the three hundred marchers reached the four-lane highway where, under Judge Johnson's decree, additional marchers could peacefully participate.[38]

Marchers who had participated in the march since the delegation left Brown Chapel on Sunday morning sometimes met additional marchers with scorn. Once the original marchers got on the four-lane road, they were joined by protesters who were viewed as "comfort-loving dilettantes who were attempting to use the march to for their own show-business reasons," one marcher recalled. "It took a real effort of will to remember that we ourselves must look the same way to the Montgomery 'Bloody Sunday' veterans and all of the SCLC regulars," Aldrich said. Approximately fifteen thousand marchers reached the last campsite at the City of St. Jude, a Catholic school and hospital in Montgomery that Williams described as "forbidding looking." They enjoyed a variety show sponsored by Harry Belafonte, gospel music legend Mahalia Jackson, actor Nipsey Russell, and singing trio Peter, Paul and Mary—providing an experience that Williams compared to the entertainment that military soldiers received abroad—using coffins as a stage. "With all the newcomers," Williams said, "this night was the first time we were really swamped . . . the crunch of all these new people was too much to handle."[39]

The fifty-four-mile protest reached its climax after more than thirty thousand marchers, including two Nobel Peace Prize winners, several US congressmen and entertainers, made the three-and-one-half-mile walk from St. Jude to the Alabama State Capitol on Dexter Avenue, less than one hundred yards from Dexter Avenue Baptist Church—the only church that King pastored a decade earlier. Marchers started out that morning eight abreast, fighting to keep the lines organized until they made it to the Capitol. Williams, Martin Luther King Jr. and his wife, Coretta, took the lead with Ralph and Juanita Abernathy. Marchers knew that they were witnessing a historic moment in the history of the United States, as they saw the stars and bars of the Confederate flag atop the dome of the Capitol building—with a spot on its portico identifying where Jefferson Davis had taken his oath as the president of the Confederacy in 1861. As the huge procession reached the capitol, Williams had little time to reflect on his achievement; he was still busy ensuring that the march remained orderly when the demonstrators reached the Capitol around 2:00 PM.

King spoke from a podium that had been erected on a flatbed truck, because state officials had denied him permission to address the crowd from the steps of the Capitol. As King had done so many times before, he used the gift of oratory that had produced his "I Have a Dream" speech two years earlier to prophesize to Blacks that "no lie can live forever" and that "the arc of the moral universe is long but it bends toward justice." "How long," King asked his listeners, would it be before they received a redress of their grievances. "How long? Not long," he promised the marchers in a call and response that rang out over the vast crowd.

With this speech, King ended what Andrew Young called the "strongest single dramatization of the need for new legislation protecting the right to the ballot for all citizens." Young neglected to mention that the march was also the most expensive demonstration relative to the expenses incurred by the SCLC and the federal government. Once the costs had been itemized, the SCLC had accumulated a bill of fifty thousand dollars. The organization's financial obligation was miniscule compared with the cost incurred by the Department of Defense. Two months after the march ended, sources from the Pentagon reported that the Department of Defense had paid five hundred ten thousand dollars to protect the marchers. The bulk of the bill covered the pay and allowances of the Alabama National Guardsmen and US Army soldiers.[40]

John Lewis was right when he said that it was Williams, more than anyone else, who made the march a success. Although other SCLC and SNCC staff had a hand in the Selma campaign, Williams had been a constant presence in Selma since he entered the city as King's advance man in January 1965, at a time when SNCC had virtually no operations in the city. He had been the moving force in orchestrating every major episode of the 1965 campaign, particularly Bloody Sunday and the actual march from Selma. He could justly claim that not only had he been beaten on the Edmund Pettus Bridge, but he had also rallied to prepare the proposal that gave Judge Frank Johnson the confidence to permit the march to go forward. It was Bloody Sunday and the Selma-to-Montgomery march that galvanized support in the judiciary, legislative, and executive branches of the federal government for a voting rights bill—landmark legislation that was signed by President Johnson on August 6, 1965. The Voting Rights Act made literacy tests illegal as a perquisite to vote, and it also authorized the US Attorney General to block state and local authorities from using the poll tax, the white voucher system and other subjective measures that were arbitrarily applied to aspiring Black voters. In spite of the promises of fair voting practices that had been codified by the new legislation, Hosea Williams and the SCLC did not rest on their laurels.[41]

The march from Selma to Montgomery was relatively free of any serious incidents of violence until Viola Liuzzo was murdered around 8:30 PM on March 25 while driving her Oldsmobile along Highway 80 in rural Lowndes County, approximately 26 miles east of Selma—coincidentally along the same route that marchers walked in an earlier trek of the journey to Montgomery. Liuzzo, a thirty-nine-year-old mother of five children, and student at Wayne State University, had driven south from Detroit, Michigan, to participate in the march for voting rights after Bloody Sunday in response to King's nationwide call when she suffered from bullet wounds to the temple and neck. Liuzzo had been accompanied by nineteen-year-old Leroy Moton, a Black barber, who was in the car when the two were returning to Montgomery after shuttling protesters in Selma. In less than seventeen hours, four Klansmen—Collie Leroy Wilkins Jr., Gary Thomas Rowe, William Orville Eaton, and Eugene Thomas—were arrested for the senseless murder. Rowe was an FBI informant who later testified that Wilkins was the shooter. Wilkins, Eaton, and Thomas were later found guilty by an all-white jury in Alabama and sentenced to ten years in prison for depriving Liuzzo of her civil rights. This murder was a tragic ending to the march from Selma to Montgomery.[42]

SIX

SCOPE, SNCC, and Black Power, 1965–1966

The success of the march from Selma to Montgomery had given Hosea Williams justly deserved cachet and credibility. As the SCLC's director of voter education and political education, he was determined to use his prominence to lead an ambitious effort to increase Black political participation. Although many of the barriers to the ballot would be eliminated by the passage of the Voting Rights Act, many Blacks, observed Andrew Young, "had gotten used to not having a vote and often could not believe that their vote would mean anything." On March 31, six days after the march from Selma to Montgomery concluded, Williams pitched the idea of the SCOPE initiative at an SCLC meeting at Maryland's Lord Baltimore Hotel. Operation SCOPE, said Willliams, would be a regionwide push to register Black voters in one hundred twenty rural southern counties and ten southeastern cities with the help of five hundred northern college students screened by their own colleges and universities. SCOPE, Williams remarked, had three goals: mass voter registration; community organization; and political education, which, Williams said, "is my pet project and first love . . . if we could get people educated politically [we would not have to devote so many resources to voter registration campaigns because] an educated electorate would respond to issues" without having to be instructed to do so. "Organizing our people" for political purposes is important, Williams said, "but to eradicate evil and accomplish the good that come from our communities" is the key goal with the community organization phase of SCOPE.[1]

Operation SCOPE, a bold and ambitious endeavor, gave Williams operational latitude and a very large budget, much to the chagrin of other executive staff members and program directors. Although King was a vocal supporter of the project, some members of the SCLC's executive staff shuddered at the possibility of Williams becoming too powerful. The Deep

South personnel would be transferred from the supervision of "the mercurial Bevel to the explosive Williams," wrote David Garrow. Bevel felt that King's endorsement of SCOPE might prove detrimental not just to the SCLC but also to southern Blacks as well. Bevel called SCOPE a "scheme" that caused a naive Dr. King to divert over five hundred thousand to a project that "threw the movement off because," he believed, SCLC "should have pursued the educating of people so that they could functionally carry out good government from the precinct, through the beats on up to the legislative districts, to the counties." Williams maintained that jealousy on behalf of his colleagues was the true source of the tension among SCLC staff members, especially Bevel. "King gave me the leeway, and that's when the executive staff basically turned out against me. They accused King of giving me much more than my rightful share of the income of the organization," said Williams. SCLC Program Director Randolph Blackwell and Stanley Levinson, a white northern businessman and trusted advisor to King, warned in May 1965, that SCOPE's budget of one hundred thousand dollars per month budget was exorbitant. King may have been pressured to defend Williams's programs because he believed that increasing the Black electorate would invariably lead to an increase in the election of moderate representation on the local, state, and federal levels. King was also well aware that SCLC's fortuitous financial circumstances were, in large measure, due to the Selma campaign that Williams had organized. SCLC had generated more than $1.5 million in contributions during the previous ten months, with the bulk of the donations coming in response to the campaign in Dallas County.[2]

Operation SCOPE got off to a fast start in Chicago in April 1965. Williams landed at O'Hare International Airport at noon on Saturday, April 17, to fulfill a twofold mission: to register some of the five hundred students chosen to participate in the ten-week SCOPE initiative that was scheduled to begin the next month and to highlight the correlation between southern and northern race-based discrimination at the Good Friday–Passover "Witness against Willis" rally. The demonstration targeted Superintendent of Chicago Schools Dr. Benjamin Coppage Willis. Willis was accused of perpetuating segregation in the city's public schools eleven years after the *Brown v. Board of Education* decision by keeping Black schools in Chicago's inner city overcrowded while holding white schools well below capacity levels. Adamant about keeping the races separated, Willis reduced the overcrowding of inner-city schools by using six hundred twenty-five mobile classrooms, known as "Willis Wagons," instead of busing Black students to white neighborhoods. At the march, Williams told a large crowd: "Ben Willis is as big a racist as Governor George C. Wallace, he is just more sophisticated." Williams used his oratory to recruit students and to publicize his ambition to add one million Blacks to the voter rolls in South Carolina, Alabama, Georgia, Florida, and Virginia. By the next month, Williams had recruited the desired number of volunteers to kick off the inaugural SCOPE.[3]

On Tuesday, June 14, nearly five hundred students from approximately sixty colleges and universities throughout the United States arrived in the downtown district of Atlanta, Georgia, to attend orientation. The students, mostly white, began a six-day seminar in the Atlanta University Center, a consortium of historically Black colleges and universities, including Spelman College, Morehouse College, Morris Brown College, Clark College, and Atlanta University. Nuns and college professors from the University of Chicago were also present, including Dr. John Hope Franklin. Franklin, the noted Black historian who, by 1965, had authored *The Militant South: 1800–1861* and within two years would publish his seminal work, *From Slavery to Freedom: A History of African Americans*, was the keynote speaker. Franklin spoke about his graduate-level seminars emphasizing the mythical horrors of Reconstruction and the perpetuation of the planter oligarchy. The narrative that projected the South as battered and unable to perpetuate their dominance in the region was false. The notion that the "South was under the foot of a foreign power" was untenable, Franklin told the five hundred collegians.[4]

Dr. King addressed the SCOPE workers two days later in the gymnasium of Morris Brown College, Williams's undergraduate alma mater. King's speech, which was the highlight of the orientation, addressed a variety of issues during the question-and-answer period. King spoke about the importance of the labor movement, specifically the need for the minimum wage to be raised to at least two dollars an hour. "Labor and the civil rights movement go hand in hand," said the SCLC president. King also encouraged the students not to be discouraged by the "outside" status that they would encounter while working in the rural southern communities. "Don't pay any attention to this outsider business. Anyone who lives in the United States cannot be considered an outsider in any section of the United States," claimed King, who spoke of the significance of SCOPE and the students' role in making history. SCOPE, he maintained, was "one of the most significant developments in our struggle" for equality. He told the students, "You are here because history is being made and this generation of students" is poised to lead the civil rights revolution. Williams concluded the program by reminding the students of the special currency of voter registration and political education.[5]

Williams officially announced tentative assignments to thirty-seven southern counties for twenty-eight SCOPE college chapters at the David T. Howard High School in Atlanta. Although forty-two colleges were represented, only twenty-eight actually had established chapters on campus. Some of the colleges and universities represented included the University of Missouri; the University of California, Los Angeles (UCLA); Cornell University; Indiana University; University of California, Berkeley; and Marquette University. Johnson C. Smith University was the only participating Black institution. Law enforcement officers in Virginia, North Carolina, South Carolina, Georgia, Alabama, and Florida would be more tolerant of northern white students canvassing their cities to register voters than of Black students. Black students were more likely to be harmed than white pupils. The pupils got a chance to see Williams's "explosive" side when Stoney Cooks, one of the key staff members who had recruited many of the students for the project, attempted to assign the students to their respective counties. Most of them had made arrangements to work in areas where they had friends or family connections. Williams, likely affronted by Cooks's zeal, told the young staffer, "Little nigger, who put you in charge? You just got here. . . . You don't know any more than these other kids." Nevertheless, Cooks stayed on board with Operation SCOPE and made a meaningful impact once he was transferred to Alabama.[6]

The first two months of the SCOPE project saw beatings and instances of intimidation in Alabama, Georgia, and Virginia. Three SCOPE workers were seriously injured before the end of June, including Jimmie Lee Jones, who sustained permanent damage to his eyes after he was assaulted in Liberty County, Georgia. On June 28, white SCOPE worker Mike Farley was beaten in jail after a correctional officer bribed a white inmate. In Alabama's Wilcox County, the mayor threatened to arrest any SCOPE workers who were seen at the Antioch Baptist Church after dark and to charge them with being a public nuisance. Sheriff Jenkins threatened to permanently shut down the church if the pastor continued to allow civil rights meetings. Tactics aimed to intimidate SCOPE workers intensified during the following month. On July 6, a SCOPE worker was choked by a deputy in Marengo County, Alabama, for taking pictures. Two days later in Wilcox County, Alabama, whites shot at three SCOPE workers who escaped unwounded. Hatred for SCOPE workers reached the Chesapeake.

On July 21, one restaurant in Sussex County, Virginia, placed a sign on its door with the words "Closed on Account of Niggers." Local officials deplored the presence of SCOPE workers. In Marengo County, Alabama, local officials filed an injunction preventing assembly at the Morning Star Baptist Church on any day except Sunday. Even on Sunday, the church was required to submit a list of the names, addresses, and the amount of money each person contributed to the collection. The county endorsed an ordinance barring people from clapping their hands or singing in streets to discourage protest marches. Patrons or protesters, officials decreed, would be arrested in the downtown shopping district if they carried less than three dollars in their pockets.[7]

Operation SCOPE continued to suffer setbacks in August, with its workers encountering threats and beatings. Before the month concluded, SCOPE's internal files recorded over twenty incidents of brutality and intimidation. On August 2, 1965, four days before President Johnson signed the Voting Rights Act and five days before riots erupted in Los Angeles, four SCOPE workers were beaten in Luverne, Alabama. A gang of white toughs attacked Blacks Bruce Hartford, SCOPE director for Crenshaw, Alabama; and Dunbar Reed, when Hartford attempted to obtain information on his colleague at the sheriff's office after the latter had been arrested and transported to the city jail for protesting at a restaurant. Reed was testing the restaurant's compliance with the Civil Rights Act, which had been passed the previous year. He was subsequently released. Although the two Black men were arrested, the whites who initiated the assault were not detained. Later that same day in Athens, Georgia, Chris Clark, the director of SCOPE in Clarke County, reported to local authorities that Howard Sims, a North Georgian Klansmen who had previously been indicted for the murder of an educator from Washington, DC, had followed and threatened to kill him for shuttling Blacks to the county courthouse to register. Seven SCOPE workers and two hundred local Blacks were arrested after they attempted to register in Allendale, South Carolina, on August 2. The protesters arrived at the courthouse at 9:00 AM, but by the end of the day, only fifty-five applications had been processed. The registrar's office was only open once every thirty calendar days. In Georgia, two SCOPE workers were also hospitalized after being beaten by state troopers. Two days later on August 4, SCOPE workers William Rau and Darb Wiggins were beaten by J. W. Sewell, a representative in the Georgia General Assembly and Dr. Don Holloway, a physician who resided in Plains, Georgia.[8]

By the end of August, SCOPE's visibility in its targeted locales was undeniable. Helped by five secretaries, he was managing one hundred eighty staff members and had seventy-six projects going on simultaneously. Williams had failed to meet the benchmarks he outlined to the board when he formally proposed the program at the Lord Baltimore Hotel on March 31. He maintained that six hundred fifty students participated during the inaugural summer, yet evidence suggests that approximately three hundred students actually committed to the effort. Williams also fell shy of his goal of registering voters. SCOPE and SCLC suggested that close to twenty-six thousand voters were added throughout Georgia, Alabama, Virginia, South Carolina, and North Carolina. These numbers must be seen in perspective with the delayed passage of the Voting Rights Act, which, according to Williams's prelaunch projection, would have been critical to the success of the program. Without the legislation, many prospective Black voters were still barred from voting because federal examiners had yet to be disbursed to the southern counties falling under the jurisdiction of the Voting Rights Act. The late passage of the landmark legislation caused another problem for Williams—the volunteers did not have much they could do. "So I had all these kids going South . . . demonstrating around other things, which I had to do to keep them busy," Williams said.[9]

By the autumn of 1965, Williams and the SCOPE program faced serious criticism. Several members of SCLC's executive staff questioned the results of the program. Mismanagement only fueled James Bevel's and other staff members' perceptions that the project was a "scheme." Accusations that the initiative was a failure are difficult to prove, even fifty years later. Demonstrating that SCOPE needed more oversight is not as challenging to authenticate. From June through August, five SCOPE workers were arrested on charges ranging from reckless driving, driving without a license, and writing bad checks. Although the number of arrests were miniscule in relation to the number of volunteers, opponents used these statistics as ammunition to kill the program. These misdemeanors were trumped in late August, when Leon Hall and Richard Smith were arrested and accused of stealing a two-foot by four-foot safe containing $202,545 in checks. Hall and Smith resided in the SCOPE branch office at 563 Johnson Avenue in Atlanta (coincidentally a home that was previously rented by Martin Luther King Jr.). Their arrest confirmed to some critics that Williams, as director of the project, had not used effective screening methods when recruiting SCOPE workers.[10]

Hosea Williams speaking to an audience at the Maggie Street Baptist Church in Montgomery, Alabama. February 1968. Alabama Department of Archives and History. Photo by Jim Peppler, *Southern Courier.*

Once the first summer of Operation SCOPE concluded in September 1965, the SCLC convened for a two-day executive staff meeting at the Atlanta Airport Hilton Inn to discuss the advantages and disadvantages of attempting to the launch civil rights protests in the North. Dr. King had strongly considered taking the movement to Chicago. Andrew Young argued that no one involved in the discussion could "claim purity of motive." He suggested that Williams initially favored a move to Chicago to remove Bevel, his chief rival, from the South. Given the competition between the two lieutenants, it is plausible that Young correctly remembered the deliberations. However, even he and Bayard Rustin believed that a move to Chicago would be disastrous and echoed the sentiments later voiced by Williams, who believed that the SCLC was making a tactical error in relocating civil rights demonstrations to a northern geography. "I remember when King decided to go to Chicago. He was pressured by Jim Bevel and Jesse Jackson," said Williams. Bevel and Jackson, he thought, were anxious to break away from SCLC and begin their own national movement. Both men "just about forced King into Chicago to protect his flanks or SCLC's flanks," he recalled. Williams, though intimately involved with the conversations regarding a northern campaign, may have oversimplified the complexities and the factors undergirding a sustained commitment in the Windy City.[11]

The riots in Watts, California, in August 1965, five days after President Johnson signed the Voting Rights Act, sped up and guided SCLC's decision to mount a campaign in Chicago. King, Young, and other staffers visited with the Black leadership in Watts after the SCLC leader had returned from a vacation in Puerto Rico. What he saw in the aftermath of the violence was troubling. King saw the violent protests as a direct threat to the philosophy and methods of nonviolence. Although the SCLC believed that the tactical application of nonviolence could be applied throughout the nation, King, Young, and other staffers also knew that tackling poverty and economic marginalization of the urban North was essential. SCLC, Young recalled in 1980, had "analyzed the problem in the North as one of relative lack of progress . . . the problems in the North were economic and the relative lack of change produced a kind of restlessness . . . We knew that we would eventually have to get into the economic problems. . . because the War on Poverty had not produced any results for the man on the streets in the North." SCLC, in Young's thinking, had long believed that economic reform was impossible to accomplish before voting reform because the racist southern senators had a paralyzing grip on the US Senate's committee structure. Moreover, King understood that the SCLC would be derelict in their moral duty if they did not forge ahead with a campaign in the North. New York, Philadelphia, and Cleveland were untenable. That Bevel and Jackson may have had internal motives for King beginning a campaign in Chicago only strengthened King's resolve in light of his own philosophical convictions and willingness to preserve SCLC's reputation as the moral arbiter of the movement.[12] The director of voter education and political education, Williams, also grumbled that a sustained northern movement might compromise future contributions. "Much of the money we received to carry on the civil rights movement was from the North. Just about eighty-five to ninety percent of our white volunteers came from the North." He made a grim prediction: "Now when you take the struggle to their back door," he told King at an SCLC strategy meeting, "they are going to desert you." Williams was also against taking the movement to Chicago prematurely because of fears for the communities SCLC was leaving behind. He knew firsthand the negative views that whites in southern towns harbored against King and his followers. "Most of those towns we went into,"—most recently, Selma—"the blacks really stood up with us. . . . The whites would wait until we leave town" and then exact physical brutality and economic reprisals against local Blacks, Williams said. He urged the SCLC executive committee to have the organization maintain a presence in the towns where they led campaigns, arguing that it was morally incumbent upon them to remain "until things sizzled down." Only then, he maintained, would the organization "reach a level of respectability in the community." The SCLC officially kicked off its Chicago campaign on January 6, 1966—one day after Williams's fortieth birthday. True to his convictions, he initially remained in Alabama.[13]

Williams's commitment to realizing Black political equality through the expansion of an intelligent Black electorate ensured that he would continue to administer the organization's voter registration and political education projects in Alabama's Black Belt in 1966. He kicked off the year in Jefferson County, Alabama, as a continuation of SCLC's "Christmas Project," which had been initiated on December 20, 1965. No federal registrars had been sent to the county surrounding Birmingham in accord with provisions of the Voting Rights Act. Because there was no federal oversight, Hosea contended that local officials continued to erect barriers to keep Blacks from exercising the franchise during the recently renewed voting rights drive in Bessemer, a city eighteen miles southwest of Birmingham. "Bessemer officials," Williams claimed, "are purposely sabotaging our drive. When you make someone wait in line for five hours, they may not want to come back and vote again." During the first week of January, Williams estimated that the voter registration drive had encouraged four thousand prospective voters to attempt to register in Bessemer, but only two thousand four hundred twenty-five had been successfully added to the voter rolls because of the Board of Registrar's "delaying tactics and inadequate facilities." Although more than two thousand Black voters had been registered to vote because of the efforts of Williams's Department of Voter Registration and Education, Jefferson County still had almost ninety thousand unregistered Blacks. This large number of potential Black voters, Williams asserted, "could be a deciding factor in whether Alabama will have a fruitful or detrimental future."[14]

Williams and the SCLC responded to the city's stalling tactics by leading a series of demonstrations in Birmingham. Known pejoratively as "Bombingham" because of local Klansmen's efforts to bomb the homes of protesting Blacks, the city had long had an active population of Blacks who had opposed the discriminatory devices used by its city fathers long before Williams and the SCLC became involved in the city's fight for civil and voting rights. The historian and Alabama native Glenn T. Eskew argues in *But for Birmingham: The Local and National Movements in the Civil Rights Struggle* that an assertive group of Black attorneys and civil

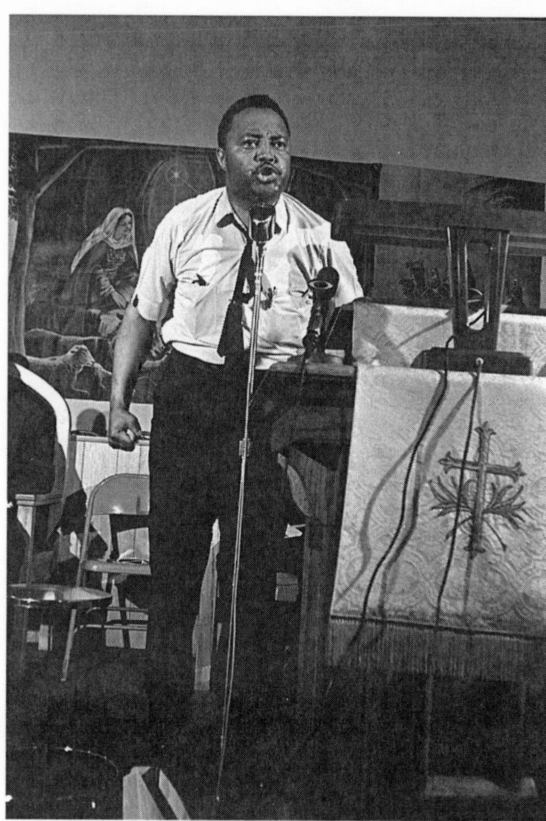

Hosea Williams speaking to an audience at St. Paul AME Church in Birmingham, Alabama. ca. 1965. Alabama Department of Archives and History. Photo by Jim Peppler, *Southern Courier*

rights activists, including lawyer and friend of NAACP General Counsel Arthur D. Shores and civil rights warrior Fred Shuttlesworth, were among those who "organized new indigenous protest groups in the 1950s and 1960s that demanded equal and immediate access to the system." Rev. Shuttlesworth, who had aligned himself with the SCLC in 1963 and worked with Williams in 1964 during the St. Augustine movement, was now continuing to work with him to implement fair voting practices in the city.[15]

Williams and Shuttlesworth opted to use the former's preferred tactic on January 4, 1966, staging a night march. More than one hundred "handclapping, hymn-singing Negroes," according to *The New York Times*, marched in "chilling" rain and temperatures to protest Birmingham's continued defiance of the Voting Rights Act. This demonstration, the first nighttime mass protest in Birmingham since the "powerful days" of the spring 1963 demonstrations, began at the St. Paul AME Church and followed on the heels of a demonstration earlier in the day. Williams urged

Rev. Fred Shuttlesworth, Bernard Lee, Martin Luther King Jr., and Hosea Williams at voter education rally. Kelly Ingram Park (former site of fire hose and police dog attacks), Birmingham, Alabama. 1966. Stanford University Libraries, Department of Special Collections and University Archives. Photo by Bob Fitch.

those in attendance at the mass meeting to stand up against the city until they had been granted full access to the ballot. The demonstrators left the church and marched to the Jefferson County Courthouse, where Williams led them in songs and a prayer. "We want six-day registration sessions and nighttime neighborhood registration," Shuttlesworth yelled to the one hundred twenty Blacks who had gathered at the courthouse. "If we don't get it, we may have all night vigils at the courthouse and might pull children out of school to help us demonstrate." The latter option, resurrecting the specter of the "Children's Crusade" from 1963, would soon stir controversy between Williams and the wealthiest Black in the city, businessman A. G. Gaston.[16]

Because the city fathers refused to grant the demands voiced by Shuttlesworth at the January 4 demonstration, Williams led a demonstration one week later involving several hundred Black students. Police became involved after they claimed Black students from Birmingham's Parker High School destroyed a chain link fence around the school's perimeter so that they could join an ongoing demonstration for voter rights. According to the school's principal, Robert C. Johnson, five civil rights workers entered the school building and began opening the doors to the classrooms and urging students to leave the premises to protest. Police fired shots in the air, citing as the pretext for their escalation claims that Blacks were throwing rocks and pieces of iron. Williams demurred, saying that "The students did not throw rocks at the police. . . . The students began running because the police came out their cars waving billy clubs." He led two more separate protests later that afternoon, which saw seven hundred demonstrators marching to the Birmingham City Hall in the afternoon and to the Jefferson County Courthouse that same night. During the night demonstration, he encouraged the students to refrain from going to school the following day. "Don't go in the schools. Turn the schools inside out from the outside—make tomorrow a school holiday," Williams told the pupils. His unabashed militancy in using children to demonstrate against local authorities had the same effect as it had during the Savannah movement in 1963 and in Birmingham in April and May of that same year: Some members of the Black elite condemned the tactics.[17]

Hosea Williams, Fred Shuttlesworth, and other demonstrators marching to the Jefferson County courthouse in Birmingham, Alabama, to protest the incarceration of Martin Luther King Jr. and several other civil rights leaders. October 30, 1967. Alabama Department of Archives and History. Photo by Jim Peppler, *Southern Courier*.

Williams, as the SCLC's director of voter registration and political education, was fighting battles on multiple fronts in Alabama's Black Belt with other civil rights organizations, particularly SNCC. SNCC's presence had grown stronger after the march from Selma to Montgomery one year earlier. SCLC, composed primarily of middle-class preachers and other professionals, stood philosophically to the right of SNCC. Most SNCC activists had yet to turn thirty, and as their adviser, Ella Baker opposed traditional leadership hierarchies. SNCC's Alabama operation, particularly in the Black Belt, cannot be discussed separately from Stokely Carmichael. Historian Peniel Joseph referred to Carmichael as the "hipster hero" whose telegenic smile and charisma enabled him to hypnotize the high and the humble. Another historian, Hassan Kwame Jeffries, wrote that Carmichael "was as comfortable breaking bread with black sharecroppers as he was with the white elite." By early 1966, the twenty-four-year-old native Trinidadian and Howard University graduate had become a civil rights veteran after serving in Mississippi as one of SNCC's field secretaries in 1962 and 1963 and as SNCC's project director in the Mississippi Delta in 1964. Carmichael shared the philosophy of many of the SNCC cohort. Meaningful and sustainable progress for Blacks could only be a reality if Blacks secured political power outside of the Democratic Party—which he asserted was "the most treacherous enemy of the Negro people." Blacks had run a hard campaign in Lowndes County to get Blacks elected to the Agricultural Stabilization and Conservation Service Committee. Black farmers appeared to be in the majority, yet they were unable to elect their candidates to four of the five committee seats. "We don't know, but we feel sure that we were cheated at the ballot box," said local activist John Hulett. "We did it fair and square. We believed in them [White Democrats in Lowndes County] and they cheated us." The leader continued: "They step on us, they take us for granted and we're completely irrelevant." Carmichael's appraisal of the political milieu in Alabama was clear: "There's no room for Negroes in the same party as Wallace."[18]

Williams and the SCLC were diametrically opposed to the idea of a third party in Alabama. He wanted to work from within the Democratic and Republican parties to secure gains for Blacks by electing white moderates. On January 15, 1966, forty-eight hours after the protests at Jefferson County's Parker High School, Williams made the one-hundred-eighty-mile journey from Birmingham to attend a meeting at the St. Paul Christian Methodist Episcopal Church that had been hastily called by the SCLC affiliate in Lowndes County after hearing about SNCC's role in organizing the recently established Lowndes County Freedom Organization (LCFO). LCFO, a third political party, had organized locals in Lowndes County. They chose as its ballot symbol a grimacing black panther, obviously influenced by the mascot of Clark College, the sister school of Williams's alma mater in the Atlanta University Center.[19]

Williams confronted Carmichael as the latter encouraged those in attendance to launch similar independent parties similar to the LCFO. At the meeting, Williams called Carmichael's idea a "bed for the black nationalist or the Black Muslim" that would force even moderate whites to align with the extreme right wing of any party that opposed Black advancement. Carmichael responded that the Democratic Party is "not a black man's party, but white people aren't going to come over before they think they can get something out of it." He displayed the Alabama Democratic Party's logo—a crowing rooster with the slogan "White Supremacy for the Right." "If you're registered in the Democratic Party," said Carmichael, "you back this!" As Carmichael passed out LCFO literature with a grin on his face, he held up the black panther emblem and unapologetically told those in attendance that the panther "can't be tamed. Once he gets going, ain't nothing going to stop him. He's one MEAN cat!" SNCC and the LCFO reasoned that the logo was appropriate because the black panther only defends itself when its life its endangered by hostile forces. Once threatened, it uses all of its strength to fight for its survival.[20]

Williams and the SCLC believed that the LCFO was jeopardizing the gains of the Voting Rights Act and Blacks' chances of electing moderate whites. A non-white government dredged up fears created during Reconstruction when the threat of "Negro domination" terrified white southerners. Williams wondered what might happen if Carmichael and SNCC saw their vision of localized Black political dominance realized: "Will they treat white folks like the white folks treated them? Will they hate the white folks the way white folks hated them?" Williams attacked SNCC's mathematics. "We are only thirty-five percent of the people in Alabama, and ten percent in the nation," he said. "We can't go pitting race against race." In an uncharacteristic manner, Williams willingly revealed his concern: "There ain't no Negro in Alabama, including ourselves that knows one iota about politics. Politics is a science" that whites invented and Blacks had not had sufficient time to truly understand. Williams believed that Carmichael and SNCC were unknowingly "[creating] a monster in Alabama . . . that will be detrimental to generations of Negroes unborn."[21]

Each approach had merit. Historian Susan Youngblood Ashmore argued that although SNCC's approach could yield positive results in the Alabama Black Belt counties because of the high Black population, SCLC's strategy was more appealing on the state and national levels because it called for more inclusion. "We must let the Negro vote hang there like a ripe fruit, and whoever is willing to give the Negro the most freedom can pick it," Williams said. "We may not be able to elect a black man, but God knows we can say what white man," he continued. Unwilling to lose the gains as a result of the Voting Rights Act, historian Hassan Jeffries suggested that Williams and the SCLC deplored the third-party initiative because they themselves wanted to chart the course of the Black electorate in the wake of the Voting Rights Act. The organization moved quickly to checkmate more militant and estranged idealists. Williams and the SCLC aligned themselves with the conservative Alabama Democratic Conference (ADC). The ADC, the state's first Black political caucus, had been founded in 1960 to ensure that John F. Kennedy received Alabama's Black vote for the presidency. According to Joe Reed, a protégé of Rufus Lewis, chairman of the organization in 1966, the "ADC may have been partisan as hell but we knew that whites still had the numerical majority in the state and it was practical to align with whites on the moderate end of the Democratic Party spectrum."[22]

Williams was well aware of the potential in organizing a Black voting bloc appealing to Blacks who were uncomfortable in embracing the militant LCFO. On March 5, 1966, Williams left his work in Birmingham, leading what Dr. King called the "most significant voting drive in the South," to preside over a major political organizing meeting at the St. Paul CME Church in Selma. Over one hundred fifty leaders from nineteen counties (including fifteen from the Black Belt) and several large cites assembled for over four hours to discuss the most efficient method to unify the Black vote in Alabama. Representatives claimed that their fiefdoms could deliver between one hundred twenty thousand and one hundred thirty thousand Black votes in the upcoming May 3 primary. However, representatives from Mobile and Montgomery, the second and third largest cities in terms of Black voting strength after Birmingham, did not attend. The state's three largest cities, bases for Isom Clemon, Rufus Lewis, and Orzell Billingsley, founders and officers of the ADC, did not show up for the meeting. The ADC was not the only organization that opted not to participate. "I talked to John Patton, head of NAACP voter registration in Alabama," said Williams. "Patton's response was, 'We've already got a statewide organization.'" Although Williams organized what would become known as the

Martin Luther King III (second from left), Martin Luther King Jr., Yolanda King, and Hosea Williams. Gadsden, Alabama. 1966. Stanford University Libraries, Department of Special Collections and University Archives. Photo by Bob Fitch.

Confederation of Alabama Political Organizations (COAPO), he insisted that the COAPO would be a statewide effort administered by Blacks in Alabama. "This is not an SCLC organization," Williams declared; "We invited every organization in the state that we knew about." He believed that all of the disparate groups held potential for considerable sway in their respective counties. "We must bring them all together," he said. Williams intended using COAPO to strike bargains with moderate white democrats in exchange for support from the Black voting bloc. Once the candidate was elected, he or she would express the proper gratitude by distributing jobs and political favors to loyal Black groups. "We've got to say, 'White Folks, what you going to give us?' We've been selling our votes all along," said Williams. "Now we've got to sell it for freedom."[23]

COAPO worked to realize three goals. First, as Williams said, the organization sought "to rid Alabama's body politic of racism, whereby an electorate could vote for a candidate on the basis of how he deals with issues involving human dignity rather than emotions." To counter the rhetoric of SNCC and the LCFO and simultaneously appease moderate whites, Williams promised that the organization did not intend to "take the government away from the white folks, but we do intend to prove to them that black folks can't mess it up any more than they already have." Second, COAPO wanted to use the strength of its bloc vote to elect Attorney General Richmond Flowers to succeed George Wallace as governor of Alabama, as the incumbent was constitutionally barred from running in three successive elections. Flowers, a white moderate by standards of the times, had vocally supported the removal of the "White Supremacy for the Right" slogan from the Alabama Democratic Party's logo. Blacks had to vote together to oust Wallace, Dr. King said. "For all these years whites have bloc-voted to keep us down. Now we got to bloc vote to get ourselves out of this dilemma." Finally, the organization committed to support Black candidates in Black Belt counties where the numerical majority favored Blacks and where the SCLC had strong organizational roots.[24]

Although Williams protested that COAPO was not an SCLC effort, the former bore a striking organizational resemblance to the CCCV that he had begun in Savannah. COAPO was structured on five levels: county, state representative, US Senate and Congressional districts, and other statewide elective offices. Each county unit had three divisions—an interview committee, a political guidance committee, and a patronage committee—composed of Black business professionals, organized labor, the religious sector, political and civic forces, and youth. The interview committee was responsible for gauging the political thinking of the constituents in the county and then interviewing the office seekers to determine whether the candidate would represent voters' interests. The political guidance committee, after consulting with the interview committee, was responsible for making an official recommendation to the patronage committee based on the candidate's ability to win and honor his campaign promises. The patronage committee's task was to inform the candidate of the organization's willingness not only to provide an official endorsement but also to ensure that the politician remained true to the pledges made on the campaign stump. The ADC was "partisan as hell," Williams said, but COAPO was nonpartisan, which, he hoped, would "prevent the greatest mistake Negro politicians made . . . when they were duped into the party of Abraham Lincoln, thereby allowing all whites to rush into the Democratic Party." Williams's fear of Blacks "being duped" affected how he viewed successful Black businessman who opposed the methods that he believed were necessary to achieve full freedom.[25]

The months before the May 3 primary were hectic for Williams as he traveled continuously from Lowndes and Dallas Counties to Birmingham to lead voter registration drives. Accompanying demonstrations often demanded the use of high school students in Jefferson County. Williams and Black Birmingham millionaire businessman A. G. Gaston were opposed to each other's methods of pursuing full equality for Blacks in Birmingham. Gaston had been born in a log cabin in 1892 in Demopolis, Alabama. He moved to Birmingham and began working at US Steel for $3.10 a day. He later built his wealth by starting burial societies for Birmingham Blacks. By the 1960s, Gaston owned thirteen funeral homes and a string of motels. The entrepreneur was conservative politically but strategically used his wealth to quell racial discord in Birmingham. He had bailed King and SCLC staff members out of jail in 1966 and allowed them to lodge for free in his hotel while they conducted civil rights demonstrations in Birmingham. Gaston, a powerful figure who had a relationship with city officials because of his wealth, was adamantly opposed to using children in demonstrations. Williams was taking the kids out of school, "you know, marching," said Gaston. "I thought that was unnecessary. In fact, my idea was the kids, many of them, didn't know what it was all about to start with," Gaston remembered. Williams viewed Gaston as a typical "head house nigger" afraid of losing his prestige and community standing with the white power structure. Williams, Gaston said, called him a "Super Uncle Tom" for opposing the student demonstrations. Gaston, recalled Williams, "is running off at his mouth too much." Williams placed the Black millionaire in the same category as whites who delayed the progress of Black equality. "If we have to work on brother Gaston, I'm going to work on him just like I work on the fat cat white man downtown," Williams grumbled. Gaston believed that Williams was ungrateful for his generosity. "The guys couldn't eat, they had no place to stay and eat, other than [me], they couldn't do nothing but get up, 'cause I was feeding them and putting them up down there," Gaston said in 1985.[26]

In spite of the tension between Williams and Gaston, the voter registration drives in Birmingham yielded promising results. Although Gaston disagreed with the tactics used by Williams, he admitted that the SCLC's director of voter registration and political education used the students "very effectively." Dr. King maintained that "The voter registration drive was the most significant ever to take place in the South." The drive's success was the result of two factors: Williams's no-holds-barred approach and the assistance of the federal government. Federal registrars finally arrived in Jefferson County on January 24. By February 8, fifteen thousand additional voters had added their names to the voter rolls in the county—eight thousand more voters than the seven thousand three hundred twelve voters who had been added during the four months from August to November 1965. By the time Williams and the SCLC left Jefferson County in the middle of March, the SCLC claimed to have registered thirty-nine thousand forty Blacks. In total, fifty-nine thousand Blacks were now registered to cast their ballots in Jefferson County before the March 15 deadline for the May 3 primary. In spite of the surge in registered Black voters since the SCLC began the "Christmas Project" on December 22, 1965, Williams coveted not just the tail of the proverbial pig but the whole hog. He was displeased with the fact that thousands of Blacks were still not registered. "Most unregistered negroes cannot afford to leave their jobs in order to register during normal working hours," Williams said, "and those who can, could not afford to pay for transportation to distant registration places." The drive was far from a failure, however. Success had come at a price that was not as steep as anticipated. There were only nineteen arrests and twenty injuries associated with this particular voter registration drive. Williams was hoping that his laborious canvassing and leading voter registration drives before the May 3 primary would yield substantive political gains.[27]

Alabama Blacks were dealt a devastating blow when the votes were tallied after the primary. Pundits had suggested that Blacks could be victorious in almost twenty-five contests in the Black Belt because of the record number of registered Black voters. Despite the addition of one hundred twenty-two thousand Blacks to the voter rolls, which now totaled two hundred thirty-five thousand, no Black candidate was elected to office. Moderate candidates for statewide office were defeated by large margins, and white voters who might not ordinarily have voted rallied around the segregationist cause. Lurleen Wallace, the wife of the incumbent governor, stood in as gubernatorial candidate for her husband and won a landslide victory over her opponents, US Representative James D. Martin and Alabama Attorney General Richmond M. Flowers. A tally of three thousand three hundred seventy-one of the state's three thousand six hundred fifty-four voting precincts revealed that Wallace received three hundred ninety-nine thousand twenty-four votes, whereas her opponents collectively received three hundred sixty-four thousand one hundred seventy-six votes. She would not even have to face a runoff election. The shellacking was attributed to two factors: voter suppression tactics, including the disqualification of eligible Black voters, and permitting whites who were not authorized to vote to cast ballots. Polling places were also switched without adequate notification to Black voters. Also, White backlash and fear of a Black voting bloc in the wake of the Voting Rights Act had caused one hundred ten thousand new white voters to register during the previous year. The implications from the race were clear: Blacks' hope of an alliance with moderate white candidates in exchange for votes and political patronage were trumped, because moderate candidates believed that a close link with the Black cause would result in political suicide. Commenting on the election, Dr. King said, "It seems obvious that white Alabamians are desperately grasping for a way to return to the old days of white supremacy." Williams was quoted in the *New York Times*, saying that Blacks "probably would go fishing" at election time in November if white candidates chose not to make concessions to receive the Black votes.[28]

On June 6, 1966, news that James Meredith had been shot in Mississippi during what he identified as his "March Against Fear" interrupted an SCLC staff meeting at the organization's headquarters on Auburn Avenue in Atlanta. Meredith, described as a "loner" by historian John Dittmer, was the first Black person to enroll at the University of Mississippi almost four years earlier. Three days after attending the White House Conference on Civil Rights, he embarked on a one-man march "to challenge the overriding fear" and to encourage Black Mississippians to remove the psychological fetters that straitjacketed them while fighting against the state's discriminatory tactics. SCLC staffers first assumed that Meredith had been fatally wounded on the second of his planned sixteen-day, 220-mile pilgrimage from Memphis to Jackson, Mississippi. "If they killed James Meredith, we gotta do something," Williams said to Dr. King and Andrew Young. Young, whom King always relied on to take the conservative route, wanted to ponder the best course of action, as he believed that initiating another campaign while still involved in the fight against poverty in Chicago would be too demanding. Williams was vehemently opposed to waiting on anything. The SCLC should board a plane immediately and "decide what to do on the way to Memphis," he said to Young. Williams, King, Bernard Lee, and Ralph Abernathy left Atlanta the next morning on a rocky flight for Memphis. The pilot cautioned that the flight would be turbulent. Williams remarked, "it'll be a lot more turbulent on the ground once we arrive in the Magnolia State."[29]

Williams hoped to play the same pivotal role in the Meredith March as he had while organizing the trek from Selma to Montgomery in 1965. Andrew Young suggests that Williams was eager to take a leading role in Mississippi to eclipse Bevel, who was handling the SCLC campaign in Chicago. "I felt Hosea saw the Meredith March as a perfect opportunity to get something dramatic going in the South accompanied by an army of reporters," said Young. "Hosea would have much of the limelight to himself." Williams readily admitted that he thrived on the attention afforded to him: "I did find a lot of satisfaction . . . I liked the limelight. It was appealing to me. I found out that civil rights leaders were about as attractive to women as playboys were." Egotistical motives aside, he began working on the logistics of the march on June 7 after King received permission from Meredith to continue his trek after visiting with him in his room at William F. Bowld Hospital in Memphis, Tennessee. The SCLC delegation, along with SNCC and CORE, agreed to resume Meredith's march at the point where he had been gunned down by buckshot. Williams rented a car, and just as he did in Selma in preparation for the march to Montgomery, drove along US Route 51 to Jackson, appraising the possible locations for camping grounds. King, who was staying at the Black-owned Lorraine Motel in Memphis reached out to contacts from around the country and asked SCLC loyalists to descend upon Mississippi.[30]

Williams, King, and other staff members did not waste any time. Joining SCLC were the recently elected chairman of SNCC, Stokely Carmichael, and Floyd McKissick of CORE. They began the march near the Tennessee state line in sweltering subtropical heat on Highway 51, the road Meredith identified as "the classic route of the Mississippi Negro, a concrete river heading away from home" when Blacks were scrambling to head North and leave Mississippi. As Williams, King, Lawson, Abernathy, and sixteen others marched through DeSoto County, they stopped for lunch at the Black-owned "Hole-In-The Ground" restaurant, recalled Leroy Johnson, a high school junior in 1966. The marchers, numbering about twenty on the first day, covered approximately six miles before stopping near Coldwater, Mississippi. Williams, with his deep baritone voice, led the marchers in the movement anthem, "We Shall Overcome," and Lawson gave the benediction before the leaders reassembled later for a mass meeting at Centenary Methodist Church back in Memphis. "Pray that our feet may never turn back. We will see a thousand, yea ten thousand of feet, marching toward Jackson, Mississippi," Lawson prayed.[31]

The leaders of the five major civil rights organizations gathered in King's room at the Lorraine Motel to discuss strategy and possible objectives for the march. King, Roy Wilkins of the NAACP, Whitney Young of the National Urban League, Carmichael, and McKissick grouped themselves around the table. Carmichael was also accompanied by Cleveland Sellers and Stanley Wise. According to at least one account, Wilkins and

Hosea Williams, Bernard Lee, Martin Luther King Jr., and Stokely Carmichael enjoy a moment of levity during the Meredith March. June 1966. Stanford University Libraries, Department of Special Collections and University Archives. Photo by Bob Fitch.

Whitney Young took umbrage at Sellers's and Wise's attendance at the meeting. "Martin, you know we talk with generals," said Young, Wilkins quipped, "not with rank and file." Sellers and Wise attending this meeting with Carmichael and the other heads of the major civil rights groups was another reminder of SNCC's philosophy of inclusion regarding its Black members' participation in the organization's decision-making process. Although Williams was only a lieutenant to King, he, too, was invited in the meeting to discuss tactics. "I was always suspicious of what was going to happen, so I watched them," said Williams. He still resented Wilkins for the latter's role in keeping him off the NAACP National Board of Directors in 1963 for his allegiance to King and the SCLC. Wilkins suggested that each organization should have one vote on major issues and argued that the march should be squarely focused on passage of the pending civil rights legislation. Whitney Young agreed and requested that voter registration campaign or direct-action techniques be mandated during the march. When Carmichael drafted a manifesto portraying President Johnson as an opponent of the civil rights movement, Wilkins and Young refused to sign the document. Carmichael intended to upset the movement's elder statesmen so they would refuse to participate. Carmichael outlined his strategy:

> SNCC and CORE goes to the left. NAACP and Urban League goes to the right. And then King is allowed to walk down the middle. So we recognized from the beginning if we eliminate from this march, NAACP and Urban League and if you have SNCC and CORE and King, if SNCC and CORE is on the left, King cannot stay on the right. He will be forced to move closer to SNCC and CORE.[32]

Carmichael insulted Wilkins and Young and even hurled curse words at the venerable leaders. Both packed up their briefcases and left for New York, vowing not to work with Carmichael and SNCC again. King, according to Carmichael, did little to halt their departure. Carmichael asserted that King was happy because "he would in fact have the limelight over myself and McKissick.[33]

The SCLC, particularly Andrew Young and Hosea Williams, distrusted Carmichael and felt that he would attempt to undermine King and his leadership. Before the Meredith March, Carmichael was largely unknown to the national media, since the recently ousted John Lewis had been the chairman of SNCC. "He went right to work attempting to establish a more militant image for himself and SNCC," said Andrew Young of the upstart. "We felt a lot of the focus on his distinct image had to do with his resentment of Martin's preeminence and of the overwhelming media focus on Martin." Williams confirmed Young's thoughts shortly after the initial meeting concluded with Wilkins and Whitney Young. He stumbled upon a closed-door conversation between Carmichael and McKissick, and he heard the former say, "We got him. . . . Now, let me tell you. We've got to keep King. If we lose King, we lose the press." Carmichael, according to Williams, then referred to King as a "son of a bitch" whom he would "make look like the greatest Uncle Tom in the world and make him denounce nonviolence" when the delegation arrived at the conclusion of the march in Jackson. "I knew what we had on our hands, so I went to work," said Williams.[34]

As march coordinator, Williams managed the campaign headquarters at Centenary Methodist Church in Memphis, where Lawson served as pastor. Almost immediately, the sponsors found themselves forty-seven hundred dollars in the red. Large tents and portable toilets represented the largest expenditures at six hundred dollars per day. Another major expense of two thousand dollars was the installation and usage of unlimited AT&T long-distance service. Williams was relentless at soliciting donations and financial advances. Costs escalated because of rights activity. Williams had to "bully, beg and persuade" the right donors, according to one observer.[35]

The second week of the march would radically alter the course of the Black freedom struggle. Hosea Williams was at the center of the planning and implementation. By June 14, Flag Day, the marchers had arrived in Grenada, Mississippi. The night before, "I found about a thousand American flags," Williams recalled. Mississippian James Eastland, the staunch segregationist and powerful US Senator and chairman of the Senate's Judiciary Committee, called the march a "circus." Although the marchers did camp under circus tents, the march had very serious civil rights goals. Voters registered in numbers unheard of the state. Over seven hundred new Black voters were added to the voting rolls during the delegation's trek through Grenada alone. Williams was at the forefront of the protests. He led three hundred demonstrators during one of his infamous night marches to the Grenada County Courthouse. One reporter observed that Williams's "voice could be heard for blocks" before the group's arrival at the courthouse just after 9:00 PM. Robert Green of SCLC joined a crowd of demonstrators who had surrounded a memorial to Confederate President Jefferson Davis and yelled, "We're tired of seeing the rebel flags. Give me the flag of the United States, the flag of freedom." Although historian Peniel Joseph suggests that Grenada was a "feel good story" of the Meredith March, any good feelings that existed between Williams and the rival organizations were slowly eroding. Williams asserted that SCLC and SNCC openly quarreled during the demonstration. "Grenada's where it really broke, that's where we really clashed . . . SNCC tried to take over the courthouse there." Willie Ricks, SNCC's advance man, had confiscated some of the flags that Williams had given to the marchers in celebration of Flag Day. "They went over there and built a fire and burned the flags. And they looked around, every damn person still had a flag," Williams recalled, "Goddamn, you got me," Ricks told Williams. It was evident that the rift was widening.[36]

On Thursday, June 16, the tenth day of the Meredith March, Carmichael had been arrested for trespassing at the Stone Street Negro Elementary School. The school had been declared ineligible as a campsite for the marchers. Willie Ricks, whom Williams claimed was "to Stokely what I was to King," assumed leadership of SNCC staffers as Greenwood police detained his leader. Ricks's role was to manage from twenty to forty people and to travel to plantations to speak to sharecroppers "and to throw out Black Power and to give little Black Power speeches to get the reaction," Carmichael recalled. Ricks had determined that the time was ripe to

Eva Grace Lemon (7 years old), Martin Luther King Jr., Aretha Willis (7 years old); background: Andy Young, Hosea Williams, march to integrate schools, Grenada, MS. 1966. Stanford University Libraries, Department of Special Collections and University Archives. Photo by Bob Fitch.

"drop it [Black Power] now," Carmichael remembered. It is worth noting that Carmichael had already had a connection with the residents of Greenwood before his introduction of the phrase "Black Power." Carmichael's commitment throughout the Delta, the epicenter of SNCC's organizing in Mississippi, was deep and undeterred. Protesters at Broad Street Park knew that he had been arrested in earlier civil rights campaigns, most notably during 1964, when he was SNCC's project director in the Delta. He was immensely popular with those whom he met during his frequent stints in the local jails and in other public spaces. Greenwood residents were drawn to him because they believed that this charismatic leader spoke a language of liberation that they understood and found relatable. Carmichael had been arrested in 1964 during Freedom Summer and had also served as director of one of SNCC's projects.[37]

After Carmichael was released from jail, he made his way to Broad Street Park, and in the words of his biographer, "into history." Ricks had already primed the crowd. Carmichael stepped before those who had gathered and reminded them of his dedication to the city of Greenwood and the state's Second Congressional District. He told them that he had been arrested multiple times and would not be incarcerated again. "The only way we gonna stop them white men from whuppin' us is to take over. What we gonna start saying now is Black Power!" Reminiscent of the Black church's call-and-response dialogue between minister and congregants, Carmichael called whites in Mississippi unrepentant racists who refused to treat Blacks as citizens. When he asked "What do we want?" the Blacks fervently responded, "Black Power!" Although Carmichael did not invent the phrase or do Ricks's laborious leg work of introducing the slogan to Black Mississippians, he became an instant media sensation with the national news media. "Black Power," Carmichael declared, meant "Negroes taking over the governments in the counties where Negroes have a majority." Ricks argued that the phrase was "a more specific way of saying what we mean. When we say we want freedom, we mean we want black power." Williams concluded: "I don't think you'd ever heard talk of Stokely Carmichael if it hadn't been for Willie Ricks."[38]

After walking twelve miles, Hosea and the SCLC held a joint rally with SNCC the following day at the Leflore County Courthouse in Greenwood, Mississippi. With more than eight hundred marchers in attendance, Williams became increasingly vocal about Black Power without directly using the phrase. "We want what God wants everyone to have. The movement is

Erecting tent shelter: Stokely Carmichael, Floyd McKissick (with cigarette), Martin Luther King Jr., Hosea Williams, and others. Stanford University Libraries, Department of Special Collections and University Archives. Photo by Bob Fitch.

Willie Ricks, Bernard Lee, Martin Luther King Jr., Stokely Carmichael, Andrew Young, and Hosea Williams lead march through small Mississippi town. June 1966. Stanford University Libraries, Department of Special Collections and University Archives. Photo by Bob Fitch.

not taking the sword from one man's hand and putting it in his own hand," Williams told a *Southern Courier* reporter before the rally. The demonstration almost reached a violent climax after a white service station attendant turned a high-pressure water hose on unsuspecting marchers. A white ally of the march wrested the hose away and drenched the attendant. Angered, he ran and returned with a pistol and billy club. Andrew Young quickly intervened and restored order. The presence of Medgar Evers's accused assassin, Byron De La Beckwith, also heightened tension at the rally. De La Beckwith wandered around the courthouse grounds inquiring about the presence of the slain activist's brother, Charles Evers. Carmichael, unfazed by the white supremacist, continued to build on the momentum from the preceding night. "The only way we can change things is with the ballot. That's Black Power," he said. Ricks and Williams continued to yell competing chants "Black Power" and "Freedom Now" to the hundreds who had gathered at the park. Williams, a fierce advocate for Blacks' unrestricted access to the ballot promised "Once we get that vote and put black faces in those uniforms . . . we will whip those policemen across the head with it." His motivational pitch to the audience should not be interpreted to reflect a nonexistent proclivity for violence. Williams was simply expressing that Blacks with a ballot in their hands would have a considerable degree of power and influence in their communities over who policed their neighborhoods by voting in elected officials who represented their interests. SCLC and SNCC leaders attempted to downplay the longstanding discord between the two organizations.[39]

Williams did not refute the idea of "Black Power." Quite the contrary. In an oral history years later after the Meredith March, he clearly expressed his feelings about Black Power. His quote merits quotation at length:

> I think Black Power is probably one of the greatest instruments of Black survival. I think the failure of Black Power has been due to the interpretation of the white power structure that Black Power is violence. That Black Power is hating white people. To me, Black Power is synonymous with Black survival. And Black Power does not mean hating white folks. Black Power is not anti-white, but it is pro-Black. Black Power is not the enslavement of white people, but Black Power is controlling the destinies of Black people. I think the main failure as far as the Black community is the true absence of Black Power.[40]

To Williams, Black Power was not a rallying cry for vengeance through violence. He disagreed with Carmichael's and Ricks's application in reality because he embraced nonviolence as a way of life. Moreover, mass violence could not yield the desired outcomes because it was untenable. He maintained that SNCC, and, by extension, Carmichael and Ricks, ultimately failed because they lacked patience, specifically when it came to practicing nonviolence. Williams said that the "youngsters in SNCC could not relate [to] the progress of Blacks and could see it in no way commensurate with the suffering." In other words, the prolonged sufferings did not match the perceived gains that had been made by 1966. SNCC, Williams claimed, believed that "there must be another way and they resorted to violence, therefore bringing about the black militant movement and the Black Panthers." Derisively, Williams believed that SNCC had been "duped" by taking violence to the streets as a method to address their frustration with the systemic inequalities wrought by racism in America. As a result, members of the Black Panthers were "cold blooded murdered like flies with public opinion on the side of the power structure."[41]

The marchers, estimated by journalists of the *Southern Courier* to be between fifteen thousand and twenty thousand, finally entered Jackson, Mississippi, on June 26 for a rally at the Mississippi State Capitol Building.

Leading the eight-mile processional from Tougaloo College were Hosea Williams, Dr. King, James Meredith, Floyd McKissick, and other civil rights activists, each donning hats and short-sleeved white shirts in a futile attempt to moderate the hot and hazy Mississippi climate. Factionalism continued to determine the role of each organization at the Mississippi State Capitol. Charles Evers, the state's NAACP field secretary and brother of slain civil rights worker Medgar Evers, was barred from speaking at the final rally because the NAACP refused to sign the "march manifesto" that had been authored by Carmichael a few weeks earlier. Meredith did not minimize the contentious relationship when he addressed the crowd. "From what you've seen on television and what you have read in the newspaper, you might assume that I had been shot by a Negro," said Meredith. Williams did not address the crowd, but King spoke with a profound sense of pessimism. The "dream" of which he spoke in Washington, DC, three years earlier "had become a nightmare." Although Blacks were still poor and treated as second-class citizens, King said, he still believed that "even here in Mississippi, justice will come to all of God's children." Carmichael also spoke. Although he did not use the term "Black Power," he forcefully reasserted that "blacks must build a power base in this country so strong that we will bring them [Whites] to their knees every time they mess with us." Although the intrusion of Black Power and discord between the organizations led the media and hostile politicians to paint the two-week-long protest as a failure, twenty-eight hundred seventy-seven Blacks were registered by county registrars, and federal examining officers registered an additional twelve hundred Black voters. In total, the march led to the registration of four thousand seventy-seven new Black voters—the highest two-week total in twentieth-century Mississippi.[42]

Confusion and a lack of solidarity plagued the major civil rights organizations after the march climaxed at the Mississippi State Capitol. Later that evening at a meeting at Pratt Memorial Methodist Church, Bob Smith, a SNCC staffer, hit Williams, and four of his colleagues continued the assault. The disagreement apparently began after contributions totaling more than eight hundred dollars were stolen from a collection at the church, which Williams vehemently denied was the work of angry SCLC staffers. Within two days, Dr. King announced the SCLC would "go it alone" during the duration of the summer-long campaign in Mississippi that had initially been a joint effort between SCLC, SNCC, and CORE. The ideological disagreements over "Black Power" represented only one component of the dissension. The SCLC, SNCC, and CORE (the NAACP and the National

Urban League did not play a significant role in the march after the meeting at the Lorraine Motel) could not agree on which organization would assume certain expenses that accompanied the march. Andrew Young maintained that SCLC had agreed to handle the bulk of the expenses but "ended up having to pay practically all of them." SNCC and CORE, vying for the attention that ultimately overshadowed SCLC's presence on the march after the Black Power speech, were unable to "pay a share" of the expenses "because of a shortage of funds," said Young. The fourteen hundred dollars collected in oversized liquor boxes was only a fraction of expenses estimated to be near twenty-five thousand dollars. Williams said that he was "burned up" over the many disagreements during the march and vowed never to work with SNCC and CORE again.[43]

The historian Aram Goudsouzian summed up the fivefold effect of the march: "In popular memory the Meredith march won resonance for the rise of Stokely Carmichael, the evolution of Martin Luther King, the bizarre crusade of James Meredith, the alienation of Lyndon Johnson and the rage of black militants." Although Carmichael had paid his dues by working tirelessly in Mississippi and Alabama, his rise in the public conscience had at least two results. Known to some SNCC staffers as Stokely "Starmichael," his celebrity generated desperately needed funds for the organization while causing internal discord because of his short temperament and unilateral decision making on organizational policy. Although the media offered varying interpretations of Black Power, Richard Bone of the *Times* suggested that the phrase had "Nothing to do with black supremacy, but much to do with manhood and self-reliance." Other media outlets were not as accepting.[44]

Williams was tapped by Dr. King to remain in Grenada, Mississippi, throughout the summer to direct the Mississippi Summer Project, a program of direct action aimed at ensuring that the state enforced the Civil and Voting Rights Acts. Grenada had a population of eight thousand, forty-eight percent of which were Black. Williams argued that, "Grenada could easily become the nation's number one civil rights problem." However, he and the ten SCLC staffers and four volunteers realized that organization and political mobilization would pose significant challenges. Local authorities were firmly committed to prohibiting Blacks from exercising basic rights guaranteed by the US Constitution and the new legislation. After the Meredith March, officials in Grenada had promised march leaders that demonstrators would be allowed to assemble peaceably as long as no one ran afoul of the laws. However, sixty-six people were arrested within the first seven days of the campaign. King accused the city fathers of reneging on their pledges to lengthen voter registration hours, desegregate facilities in the courthouse, and extend police protection to Blacks seeking to vote and demonstrate. They have "gone back on every promise," King said. He threatened to return to Grenada after Williams and one hundred other demonstrators were beaten and jailed for marching to the county courthouse on July 7, less than two weeks after the Meredith March concluded on June 26.[45]

The city of Grenada had made a three hundred sixty-degree turn. City fathers flatly refused to compromise with Williams. "There will be no concessions of any type or degree made to anyone anywhere," said Sheriff Suggs Ingram. He was particularly hostile to Williams and his staff because Ingram felt that "they had it easy" during the two-week Meredith March. Williams, as King's "kamikaze," was willing to engage in dangerous direct-action tactics, including the night march. However, the promise of the publicity that had followed previous demonstrations was not enough to convince his ten staff workers to subject themselves to the inevitable brutality that would follow. Williams accordingly altered his strategy and incorporated tactics that were not as dangerous as after-dark demonstrations.[46]

On July 13, Williams orchestrated a "swim-in" at Grenada Lake. He decided to transform a street march into a splash party because the temperatures in the Mississippi heat reached one hundred one degrees. Approximately fifty Blacks swam in a lake that was being managed by the US Corps of Army Engineers. The lake was technically open to both Blacks and whites; however, intimidation from local whites had ensured that Blacks stayed away from the technically integrated body of water. Although no violence occurred, twenty whites appeared willing to stand at the side of the lake in the blazing Mississippi heat rather than swim. At the conclusion of the hour-long protest, Williams next proposed a boycott of all white stores in Grenada. He told approximately 130 Blacks at the Bell Flower Baptist Church that "Clothes don't make the man." He challenged all Blacks to cancel their credit accounts with all white stores until Grenada became an "open city." Unlike SNCC, SCLC welcomed participation from liberal whites. Before the conclusion of the mass meeting, Williams publicly acknowledged the presence of Ron Gordon, a white eighteen-year-old freshman at the University of California. In an apparent rebuff to SNCC, which had all but expelled many of its white volunteers, Williams said, "I am glad to see these young white civil rights workers down here."[47]

Carmichael and the rest of SNCC's delegation were also in Grenada but were not invited to attend the rally at Bell Flower Baptist Church. Observers speculated that the radical adherents of Black Power were barred from SCLC events because both organizations were still vying for control of the freedom campaign in Grenada. Williams and Carmichael had spoken before the rally, but Stokely was told that he would not be permitted to speak because he planned to encourage Blacks in attendance not to march. "I've had it all with the marching just to get your head beat in," Carmichael told reporters as he stood outside of the church. Williams articulated a very different philosophy from the pulpit: "As long as there's man, there's going to be a need to dramatize the injustices." He promised the crowd, which had grown to approximately three hundred, "We're going to turn Grenada upside down and then set it right-side up."[48]

On August 8, Hosea Williams and an estimated three hundred fifty demonstrators were violently attacked by a gang of young white toughs after beginning their march from the Chat and Chew Café on Union Street. The mob of whites, either sanctioned or tolerated by Grenada's city fathers, hurled bricks, bottles, and pipes at the defenseless marchers as they gathered at the courthouse square. Williams was injured after he was struck on the knee with a canister of tear gas. Sheriff Ingram was under a court injunction to provide reasonable protection at the demonstration. He opted to disregard the order. In a statement to the press, Dr. King condemned Governor Paul Johnson and Senator James Eastland for permitting the police to sit idly by while protesters were assaulted. "If such an atrocity had been committed against white persons," King said from the SCLC's convention in Jackson, Mississippi, "the state authorities would have crushed the oppressors with National Guardsmen." Williams, though badly injured, cautioned protesters leaning toward Carmichael's more militant crusade. "The only chance whites got is for Negroes to turn violent," he said. "The minute the police start throwing tear gas on us and the Negroes start throwing bottles, rocks and bricks, you gonna end up in slavery for a century." Williams's warning exhibited by the same common sense he had shown to civil rights activists in Lowndes County in January after the LCFO chose the snarling black panther as its symbol. Black demonstrators in the northern Mississippi town continued their advocacy of nonviolence, and the Grenada police still refused to protect them or their children.[49]

By 1966, twelve years after *Brown v. Board of Education*, Black and white schools in Mississippi and most of the South remained segregated. However, in the summer of 1966, US District Judge Claude Clayton, authorized a "freedom of choice" proposal designed to allow Black students in Grenada to attend John Rundle High School and Lizzie Horn Elementary School. The number of students expected to exercise the option to attend the two schools exceeded the total that school and county officials had expected. When the school year officially began on September 12, ten days after the schools had been scheduled to open, approximately one hundred fifty Black students entered the schools without incident. However, another fifty students were not permitted to attend classes. Anticipating trouble, school officials authorized both schools to close at noon. Approximately sixty Black pupils under the age of eighteen were brutally beaten by a white mob as they attempted to leave the campuses. Thirty-three children suffered serious injuries. United Press International (UPI) reporter Robert Gordon later testified in Clayton's court, that "white men were beating people with ax handles, chains, and whatever" until police intervened and said, "okay boys . . . they've had enough." A doctor testified that one student had a skull fracture. Even the conservative Judge Clayton was disheartened by the attacks on the children. He referred to the event as "senseless" and savage." "I am astonished that such violence could have happened once," said Clayton. "I am absolutely amazed that it could have happened as many times as it did with no greater reaction [from law enforcement] than was shown by the record." Police Chief Pat Ray testified that he was in his cruiser without a radio for almost two hours and was unaware of the attack. He proposed that the Mississippi Highway Patrol should assume responsibility for the protection of the students until the tension subsided. Evidently, the threat of the Mississippi Highway Patrol was effective, as one man shouted at a city council meeting, "You get the highway patrol out of here and in twenty-four hours there won't be a nigger left."[50]

On September 20, one week after the students were beaten, Williams led a delegation of approximately one hundred sixty-two students to the Rundle High School and Lizzie Horn Elementary School under the guard of FBI agents and the Mississippi Highway Patrol. The number of students enrolled represented approximately ten percent of the student population at both schools. Once the students arrived, they were shocked to discover that they were assigned to classes based on gender, but the integration of both schools was seen as a momentary victory for Williams and the SCLC. During the next two years, historian John Dittmer suggests that fewer than eight thousand pupils were enrolled in Mississippi schools previously reserved for white students—less than four percent of the Black students between the ages of six and eighteen in the Magnolia State.[51]

Williams seldom used one method of direct action when leading major civil rights campaigns in southern cities. Although protest marches were crucial, he also masterminded a series of successful boycotts to cripple the white establishment. Grenada, Mississippi, was no different. The *Southern Courier* called the boycott "very effective." Many Black patrons refused to shop in stores that did not have the "Grenada County Freedom Movement Approves" sign in its window. During the two-month boycott of some white and Black establishments, at least three stores were forced to close down. One storeowner lamented that, before the boycott, his establishment brought in close to one thousand five hundred dollars per week. By the end of September, his weekly sales barely reached five hundred dollars. However, the success of the boycott could not be sustained because SCLC staff was unable to remain in the northern Mississippi town beyond October—a concern that SNCC had expressed since the beginning of SCLC's entry into the Delta—foreshadowing the premature exit from Chicago in the future [52]

SNCC's commitment and success with Delta residents can, in some respects, be attributed to its bottom-up approach to leadership that was indistinguishable from Ella Baker's philosophy. She opposed traditional leadership hierarchies. According to native Mississippian and SNCC Field Secretary Charles McLaurin, Baker frequently drilled into the youth that "Strong people do not need strong leaders. Local people need to be involved in the decision making." Moreover, Baker had networks with the YMCA and other community organizations that she used to construct informal networks to facilitate outreach and engagement strategies. McLaurin suggested that this framework allowed SNCC to host voter registration efforts that yielded an estimated ten thousand people.[53]

As Williams and his staff left Mississippi, they could claim a few victories. During one of the last mass meetings, one staffer maintained that "We've gotten hundreds of people registered in [Grenada], we've done integrated every school in the county, and the boycott has almost broken whitey down." However, local activists were not prepared to assume the responsibility of the campaign without Williams and the support of the SCLC. Williams and the SCLC had not built a framework that would enable their projects to endure in the absence of the organization's leadership because of its top-down leadership philosophy. Williams was not necessarily an adherent to Baker's "Strong people do not need strong leaders" mantra. Williams had always wanted full control of every project and was unwilling to cede any measure of power in the projects which he was involved. Failing to empower the locals halted the type of progress that any community could make after the bright lights and news coverage that followed King, Williams, and other SCLC staffers and directors had exited. To echo the point, one Grenada attorney suggested that the SCLC did not permit local Blacks to have a voice when critical decisions were made about the objectives of the campaign. Dittmer suggests that Mississippi did not differ that much after the Meredith March. Segregation, oppression, and depression still characterized every aspect of Black life. Once again, the SCLC appeared to have excited a community that longed for social change only to be reminded of the bleak prospects for meaningful change.[54]

Williams was tired and desperately wanted to spend time with his wife and four children. Barbara, his eldest daughter was eighteen and preparing to go off to college by the end of the year. Elizabeth, his second eldest child, was now fourteen years old and eager to make plans for her fifteenth birthday party in the following February. Hosea Jr. and Andre, born in 1955 and 1956, respectively, were now eleven and ten years old. Williams's youngest daughter, Yolanda, was only six and in her first quarter as a first grader. Williams realized that his children were growing up without him as he spent more time on the road than at home. However, when King decided to appoint Williams to lead a major voting rights drive in very hostile territory, he accepted his first long-term northern assignment.[55]

SEVEN

Chicago, the Kentucky Derby, and the Poor People's Campaign

Martin Luther King Jr. unleashed Hosea Williams, his "bull in a china shop," into Chicago and Louisville, Kentucky, to create maximum havoc around the open housing. The "bull" saw the muleta of structural racism intertwined with housing segregation. The Williams-led protests were most effective in Louisville and most destructive to the "downtown power structure." He orchestrated protests around the "No Housing, No Derby" rallying cry during "Derby Week." He and his staffers developed "trial runs" during some of the lesser races during "Derby Week," where some of his lieutenants ran across the race tracks near the galloping thoroughbreds to raise awareness of the housing issue.

Andrew Young announced to the media on September 1, 1965, that the SCLC decided to initiate its first northern campaign in Chicago. King's deliberate decision to use the nonviolent direct-action strategy to eliminate slums in the Windy City as part of the "Chicago Plan" was not difficult for him to make, despite internal opposition within the SCLC. SCLC staff and outside advisors, including Bayard Rustin, argued that the organization's efforts would not resonate in northern cities. Moreover, staff, including Williams, believed that King and the SCLC would be subjected to donor backlash, because a large segment of the organization's northern benefactors were reflexively resistant to protests on their home turf. King was not swayed. That James Bevel, SCLC's mercurial director of direct action, had moved to Chicago in 1965 likely strengthened King's resolve to extend SCLC's footprint to this city, which had a complex history of protests for racial equality.[1]

When King arrived in Chicago at the invitation of Albert Raby of the Coordinating Council of Community Organizations (CCCO), he and the SCLC were not working on unplowed ground. Raby, in the words of the historian James Ralph, believed that the movement in Chicago "was not ablaze, but burning out," evidence supporting the argument that activists grappled with a confluence of factors over an extended time that may have doused the fire fueling the civil rights protests without eliminating the heat supply. Black Chicagoans were not subjected to the exact indignities endured by their co-sufferers in the South. De jure segregation did not exist in the city as in Montgomery, St. Augustine, or Birmingham. Financially, the median income for Black families was nearly five thousand dollars, a figure higher than that for Black households in the South. However, public school policy that caused massive and exclusive overcrowding in Black schools was the source of Blacks' unrelenting consternation and cause for protests by the early 1960s. Middle- and working-class Blacks led boycotts of the schools and organized to remove public officials from elected office. However, by the time King arrived in 1966, local Black activists were gridlocked.[2]

On December 2, 1966, Dr. King announced that the Chicago freedom movement was mobilizing to launch an "intensive" voter registration and voter motivation campaign as part of an overall strategy to address the poverty and inadequate housing on Chicago's predominately Black South Side. King emphasized that registration and education of voters were the hallmarks of an informed electorate. King asserted that, although the freedom movement was "staunchly-nonpartisan," it "never claimed to be nonpolitical." The SCLC president tapped Hosea Williams to lead the effort. "Mr. Williams . . . has been responsible for registering hundreds of thousands of Negroes throughout the South," said King. "We are grateful that he has consented to leading our voter drive here." Williams had previously expressed his disagreement to King and other SCLC executives about a campaign in Chicago, because such an effort would lead to the erosion of northern support. "King came and pleaded with me," remembered Williams. "I had not been in Chicago. I'd go there for a march, speech, but I had not been considered part of the Chicago movement." SCLC had not been successful in Chicago before Williams's arrival in late 1966 because the whole situation was a "tightrope," recalled Andrew Young.[3]

Soon-to-be four-term Mayor Richard Daley presented the most formidable obstacle to reform in Chicago. "Daley resented King" and the SCLC coming to town, said longtime Chicago activist John McDermott. "He was angry at the notion that Chicago was just like Mobile or Montgomery or Birmingham. He saw this as a progressive northern city that had progressive policies. He [Daley] thought of himself as a northern Democrat." He even persuaded certain vendors to defray costs for SCLC events. However, the CCCO, a coalition of nearly seventy-five civil rights organizations, believed that substantive change in Chicago could not be achieved unless Daley was defeated. "SCLC could not take on the responsibility of running Daley out of Chicago," protested Young. SCLC was unable to untie the proverbial Gordian knot. "I was to go up there and really bail them out" because "SCLC was leaving Chicago in really sad shape," said Williams. In spite of Williams's successful record of creating meaningful change in hostile cities, he could not have realized that his initiative to educate and empower Chicago's Black electorate would be stillborn.[4]

Williams's mission in the Chicago freedom movement was to focus on key elections of aldermen scheduled to be held in February. He needed to rely on his quick wit and understanding of the criminal element to maneuver around the underbelly of Chicago's more confrontational splinter groups. He would need to contend with a militant Black Muslim faction in the city that was determined to rid Chicago of King and his nonviolent philosophy. He also had to work around the second tier of semiorganized crime syndicates. "Only a fool would take the gangs on in Chicago—which I did," said Williams. "I had an army with me. A very, could-be violent army," he remembered. Although he believed in nonviolence, "I had gangsters by my side" in Chicago, he said. His chief enforcer was Lester "Big Lester" Hankerson, who had worked to keep hustlers in check in seaports along near Savannah, Georgia. "Big Lester," said Williams, "was known for grabbing you by the head and kicking all your teeth out with his knee." Williams's inner circle also included Willie Bolden, another one of his captains from the campaign in Savannah. Although Williams did worry that the radical Black elements could jeopardize his safety, he still prepared to grapple with unforeseen obstacles.[5]

Williams and twelve SCLC staff members kicked off the citywide voter registration drive at a mass meeting on December 20 at Bethel Baptist Church. He started off at a significant disadvantage because SCLC and CCCO had been unable to produce the forty-five-thousand-dollar budget needed to finance Williams's strategy of creating a vibrant presence in eighteen of the city's fifty wards, devoting significant energy and resources to two-thirds of these wards, and finally whittling down the number to five or six that evidenced the most promise. Williams advised attendees at a

Song leaders Lester Hankerson, J. T. Johnson, and Hosea Williams. Birmingham, Alabama. 1965. Stanford University. Libraries. Department of Special Collections and University Archives. Photo by Bob Fitch.

steering committee meeting that the approach they had formulated to organize potential voters around certain issues should be revised. Williams's experiences in Savannah, St. Augustine, Selma, Birmingham, and Grenada suggested that "people vote against before they vote for—urban renewal, welfare, education and economic exploitation." The issue most likely to rally Black voters and get them to the polls was the prospect of electing aldermen more sympathetic to their interests in the administration of the city.[6]

On December 20, Williams's skills were tested just before the beginning of the first major rally at Bethel Baptist Church. An unnamed leader of the local Black Nationalist faction interrupted him at the church and told him that they would not be allowed to hold the meeting. "You've got to be kidding me," Williams said to the young radical. "'No, Hosea,'" he said. "'I'm not kidding. No bullshit at all. We're going to tear this meeting up.'" Immediately, Williams recalled, about twenty-five or thirty allies of the Black Nationalist movement stood up. "There's going to be blood. Every one of them got loaded guns," said the young thug. "Every goddamn one of them is ready to die." Williams held both hands up to quell the discord. After a prolonged discussion between Williams and the young Black Nationalist in the church's basement, both sides resolved their issues for the time, and Congressman John Conyers, the young Black representative from Detroit, Michigan, addressed the crowd about the importance of voting.[7]

Shortly after the mass meeting concluded, Williams flew to Atlanta to spend time with his family and celebrate his forty-first birthday. Upon his return to Chicago, he teamed with Albert Raby of the CCCO and worked out of that organization's headquarters at 366 E. 47th Street on Chicago's South Side. The initiative homed in on young people from ages twelve to twenty to motivate older members of the community to vote in the upcoming elections. Williams created the themes for the campaign: "Register and Vote . . . For me!" and "I'm too Young to go and Vote. . . . What's Your Excuse?" The first voting registration drive, dubbed the "Vote-A-Baloo," took place at Orchestra Hall on January 13. The "Vote-A-Baloo" was actually a rally to encourage approximately two thousand youth to "pledge themselves to carry the voter registration campaign to adults in their various communities, "said Williams. Popular singers entertained; most notably, Jean Pace of the Staple Singers. Williams acknowledged that Black Chicagoans carried significant untapped electoral power, but he was concerned about their willingness to actively participate in the political process. "The Negroes' desire for better political representation must be reckoned with," said Williams. "But this will not happen until the Negro voters become aware" of the collective control they possess in local affairs. Approximately one million of the city's one and a half million residents were Black. A National Urban League study revealed that, four years earlier, only six hundred thirty thousand eligible Blacks to vote were registered. Only forty-seven percent, or two hundred ninety-six thousand one hundred, had actually voted, compared with seventy-eight percent of whites who cast ballots. His guarded optimism turned into vocal pessimism after disappointing results from the "Vote-A-Baloo."[8]

Williams's displeasure with Chicago's Black electorate and the overall conditions of the "Windy City" made him lambast local Blacks in the media. "It's cold here," he said. He expressed a deep dissatisfaction for Black apathy and the lack of efficient organization. "I don't like Chicago, he said. "We're [SCLC] used to working with people who want to be freed. The Chicago Negro," Williams lamented, "isn't concerned about what the power structure is doing to him." Williams was not the only SCLC staff member to experience mounting frustration at the unwillingness to cooperate.

Hosea Williams planning Chicago civil rights campaign in 1966. He is holding a map of the city in his hand. Stanford University Libraries, Department of Special Collections and University Archives. Photo by Bob Fitch.

Leon Hall, a staffer from Montgomery, Alabama, reported that a Black woman attacked him with an icepick as he canvassed for voters in one of the South Side's dilapidated tenements. Williams's chief enforcer, "Big Lester" Hankersen, maintained that Black "people won't even talk to us." Although Hankersen had been assaulted in Grenada and in Alabama while working with Williams, he suggested that he would "rather be working there" because "people in Chicago are not interested in first-class citizenship." After observing Daley's operation and the apathy of Blacks, Williams concluded that "There is no difference between the Daley Machine in Chicago and the Wallace machine in Alabama." Blacks in Alabama expressed a greater desire to be free of restrictions than Chicagoans who appeared beaten down and unwilling to fight. Williams asserted that he had "never seen such hopelessness. The Negroes of Chicago have a greater feeling of powerlessness than any I ever saw," he said. "They don't participate in the governmental process because they are beaten down psychologically."[9]

Rev. Delton W. Franz, the thirty-five-year-old white pastor of the Woodlawn Mennonite Church on Chicago's South Side, argued that the perceived apathy among Blacks reliant on some form of governmental assistance resulted from fear. "Every welfare recipient is afraid to oppose the wishes of the precinct captain," said Rev. Franz. Blacks who received housing assistance also chose to remain apolitical. "Everyone living in public housing is afraid," Rev. Franz recalled. "They have been told that the machine alderman is the one who insures them living quarters."

Williams's remarks drew the ire of the SCLC's executive leadership and movement supporters. Andrew Young and Stanley Levinson, one of King's closest northern candidates, called King while he was vacationing in the Caribbean to consider the best way to repair the breach caused by Williams's candor. Levinson suggested that Williams be terminated. King, although furious with his wayward lieutenant, balked at taking such a draconian measure. In a meeting in Chicago, "they [Young and Levinson] demanded that King fire me, and I got so angry. I wanted to fight so bad . . . I'm up here giving my life, putting my life on the line, and I was not appreciated for willing to make the ultimate sacrifice," Williams recalled. Although he had a tough exterior, he could still be hurt. Talk of his being fired reminded him of Roy Wilkins's refusing to seat him on the NAACP's National Board of Directors. "I got so crazy. I ran out . . . ran down the street crying," said Williams. Abernathy ran after him and told him, "King will stick with you." In a futile attempt to register as many Blacks as possible before the January 30 deadline, Williams, Abernathy, and Young lobbied Daley and the Cook County Registrar for off-site voter registration with the assistance of deputy registrars, recalled Young.[10]

The last-minute efforts to expand Chicago's Black electorate were derailed by the Chicago blizzard of 1967. The snow affected northeast Illinois and the northwest section of Indiana. SCLC had set a goal of raising thirty thousand dollars to finance the Chicago Freedom Movement. On January 26, the day of the fundraiser, Williams recalled that city was blanketed with snow by 3:00 PM. "I ain't never seen so much snow . . . with the exception of what I had seen in Germany," Williams said. "We nearly froze to death." Daley ordered city workers to work around the clock to clear the streets. By the end of January, the two-month voter registration drive had succeeded in registering only several hundred new voters.[11]

The election took place on February 28, 1967. Williams, in one last effort to encourage local Blacks to elect new aldermen, encouraged Black voters to shun the Chicago's Democratic Party and vote for independent candidates. "I urge every Negro with a view toward the future to vote for the full slate of independent candidates," said Williams. The *Chicago Defender* quoted his characterization of the city government as a "dictatorship" reinforced by Black aldermen whose allegiance to the political machine prevented them from ably and honestly representing the interests of constituents. Williams maintained that voters had elected an "undue" number of white councilmen, as Blacks represented thirty-two percent of the city's population but were only represented by twelve percent of the city councilmen. Young disagreed with Williams's directive that Blacks abandon the Democratic Party. "It would have been far better for Chicago if blacks had been encouraged to register in large numbers and vote Democratic," said Young, many years later. On the whole, the Chicago freedom movement campaign met with little success by the time SCLC left the city. The aldermen elected were part of Mayor Daley's political machine.[12]

The SCLC-led campaign did not accomplish its stated goals to "end slums" or to make Chicago an "open city." From the onset of the campaign, the scope was too broad, and the objective was too lofty and unrealistic. Moreover, SCLC may not have clearly seen the long tentacles of the structural racism that touched every nook and cranny of Chicago society. Racism was the fulcrum upon which every government institution in the city turned. Second, SCLC was a victim of its successes in Birmingham, St. Augustine, and Selma. King's and SCLC's presence immediately heightened expectations beyond what was possible without, at minimum, a three-year commitment with hundreds of staff members and several million dollars at their disposal. It is worth noting that SCLC devoted twenty months to the campaign in Chicago—more than any previous campaign before or since the initiative in the Windy City. Third, and perhaps most important, SCLC's top-down approach prevented the organization from developing local leaders who could continue the initiative without King and other staffers—a pattern that reflects in some ways the outcome in the Mississippi Delta. Nevertheless, James Ralph notes that SCLC received several substantial grants in 1966 and 1967, respectively: a four-million-dollar grant from the Department of Housing and Urban Development to developing housing initiatives, as well as a grant of one hundred thousand dollars from the US Office of Education to raise the educational functioning levels and measurable skills through an adult education program. Ralph ably sums up the complexities in Chicago: "SCLC is more properly regarded as the resuscitator of a dying movement in 1965 rather than as the hidden assassin by 1967."[13]

The SCLC had already shifted its focus to fair housing by 1967. The separate housing markets for Blacks and whites was essential to the creation and maintenance of slums in the Windy City. Chicago Blacks were disproportionately harmed by having to pay the "color tax" because of limited housing options and lower wages compared with their white counterparts in and around the city. The campaign around fair housing was consequential. King believed that the debate around open housing would supply much-needed enthusiasm to the movement while also influencing President Johnson and lawmakers to move decisively in favor of national legislation that specifically targeted equal housing opportunities for Blacks. SCLC had already held large rallies in Chicago, including an event at Soldier Field that was attended by an estimated thirty thousand Black and white Chicagoans. That Williams and his staff pivoted to a fair housing platform in early 1967 was part of a much larger national conversation that would have lasting implications.[14]

Shortly after the disappointing elections, Williams and his staff left Chicago and made the five-hour drive to Louisville, Kentucky, at the request of Rev. A. D. King, Dr. Martin Luther King Jr.'s younger brother. They were charged with assisting the SCLC's Kentucky affiliate in its protest of the city council's reluctance to eliminate discriminatory tactics in housing. The open housing movement in Louisville had its origins in 1963, when the West End Community Council (WECC), a local mix of Black and white residents, formed a coalition to stop the pernicious practices of "blockbusting" and "white flight." Both phenomena adversely affected property values and the overall community climate. In 1964 the white population in Louisville was 310,717. The city's Black population numbered seventy-eight thousand three hundred twenty-seven, a mere eighteen percent of the city's residents. A. D. King, who was simultaneously serving as pastor of Zion Baptist Church and chair of the Kentucky Christian Leadership Conference (KCLC), requested the SCLC's assistance in early 1967. Tensions had heightened between the Black leadership and the city leadership over a bill presented to the board of aldermen in September 1966. The legislation called for fines and jail sentences for any individual or entity discriminating "because of race, color, creed, or national origin in the sale, rental, or financing of housing by salesmen, lenders, or mortgage bankers." The Louisville Real Estate Board and the county's board of aldermen led the opposition to the penalty mandating jail sentences.[15]

Back-and-forth proposals between the Black leadership and the city fathers finally precipitated the demonstrations that Mayor Kenneth Schmied, the county board of aldermen, and business owners dreaded. On March 7, exactly one year after Bloody Sunday in Selma, Williams led the first march of the Louisville fair housing campaign to Mayor Schmied's furniture store, the American Home Supply Company. At the conclusion of the demonstration, Williams left Kentucky and drove to Atlanta for an SCLC staff meeting to address lingering personnel issues. In his absence, the local Black leadership, including Rev. Fred Sampson, Rev. Leo Lessor, and Rev. A. D. King, picked up where Hosea left off by leading marches to the homes of Schmied and the board of aldermen. The protests showed that Blacks in Louisville were committed to pressuring the city fathers through nonviolent direct action.[16]

Williams and other members of the executive staff were summoned by King to a meeting to discuss the discord among the leadership and the rank and file. Williams outlined the problems he saw with the organization in a memo to King, dated March 8, 1967. The SCLC's "volunteers and followers" were dwindling primarily because of the organization's blemished reputation in southern Black communities. After they organized, staff mobilized and motivated Blacks "to forthrightly confront their oppressors and then run and leave the same negroes at the mercy of their oppressors," wrote Williams. "People" feel as if they are "secondary to our primary objectives—building images, getting publicity and raising funds." The SCLC "failed to bring about meaningful change," continued Williams, because the leadership in the previous "battle fronts and campaign grounds . . . seriously question whether or not their communities were better or worsened by our presence." Williams respectfully suggested that King was out of touch with what was happening. Leaders hesitated to voice their true feelings about SCLC in large measure because of the "fascination" of King's "mere presence."[17]

In the same memo, Williams addressed the issues relative to staff problems, which he described as "unbelievable." The organization was wasting approximately twenty-three thousand dollars in "salaries and subsistence" on people who had not been involved with SCLC's functions in almost three months. He also enumerated what he thought to be the most pressing personnel issues that hindered the SCLC's operational efficiency and effectiveness in the North and South:

> One of the first problems we must eliminate, is the feeling of the "Northern" (Bevel) and "Southern" (Hosea) staff. Our entire staff must unquestionably understand that all of us are a part of SCLC's staff, period. You must make it crystal clear that every SCLC staff member must respect responsibilities assigned. Some say that I have gone too far in this area, but I still can demand a fair amount of respect from the Southern Field Staff. At least, I have not lost them completely.

> There is proof that other executives have gone much too far in the opposite direction. An example is Rev. Bevel and how he relates to the staff working with him in Chicago. Bevel allowed this question of staff independence and staff choice to get out of hand. He got himself in a position of not being able to require anything from the vast majority of the staff assigned to him. Another example is Rev. Young who has allowed the staff to question his authority and his position on staff independence to the point that he is unable to require many staff members to function to the degree which is necessary if SCLC is going to bring about meaningful change. Remember, one of our greatest problems in the Chicago Voter registration drive was the fact that regular Chicago staff (definitely including Debbie) had been taught indirectly to disrespect my position and authority just as the staff working in the South had been unintentionally taught indirectly to disrespect the position and authority of certain other executive members.[18]

As a possible remedy, Williams asked whether someone could devise an "efficient means of apprising [King] of the total scope of operations." King agreed that Williams had made several valid points. He also informed SCLC executives during the two-day meeting on March 9–10 that a series of candidates should be considered to serve as executive director. Williams warned King that the "field staff is retired" and that a sixty-day "rest and study" break would go a long way in rejuvenating the staff's depleted energy. King did not embrace this last suggestion, because he and other members of the executive staff, after due consideration, had decided to initiate a major SCLC campaign in Louisville, Kentucky, as the date loomed for the annual Kentucky Derby.[19]

As King's "kamikaze," Hosea Williams was eager to force the city of Louisville into a compromise on the housing issue by using the threat of demonstrations at the nation's most celebrated horse race at Churchill Downs. As part of a series of nonviolent direct-action demonstrations, Williams; Rev. A. D. King; and other SCLC staffers, including J. T. Johnson, Henry Brownlee, Phil Goober, Mike Whitman, Mike Bibler, and Winters Knott led a sit-in at the City Council's meeting room on March 14. The demonstrators were dragged away, and some were beaten. After the protest at City Hall, Williams thoroughly reexamined the housing situation in Louisville and developed a plan to force the city to adopt a strong housing legislative agenda.[20]

Williams's five-point plan, modeled on the civil and voting rights protest campaigns he had organized since the 1950s, outlined the most specific details of the Louisville strategy. Tactics demanded an organized field office and a strong staff. Williams obviously stressed the need for office supplies: a mimeograph machine, paper cutter, and two telephone lines with one phone per line. He also called for one thousand index cards, poster boards, mimeograph ink, and buttons with the words "Get Rid of Slums." Williams appointed J. T. Johnson, an SCLC staffer who had worked in St. Augustine and other project areas, as second in command. Henry Brownlee, another veteran staffer, would head the production department. Williams assigned Bibler, Whitman, and Robert Sims to rally high school and college students. Knott and "Big Lester" Hankerson were assigned to work the street corners and manage the block workers.

Under the "Ideas" section of his proposal, Williams planned to have night marches throughout the city, followed by mass meetings that would be publicized two days in advance. To encourage the youth to participate, Williams suggested hosting "block dances" and "street rallies." He recognized that many of Louisville's Black residents might not be fully informed on the housing issue, so he planned to prepare a "master leaflet" to outline the most important points. A leaflet would be effective, but radio would be even more efficient. Williams stressed the importance of securing four radio spots that would not only highlight "yesterday's and last night's activities" but would also inform the listeners of "today's and tonight's activities." He had to grapple with the same problems that reduced the efficiency of the national SCLC. Under the "Problems" heading of his plan, he wrote, "Staff does not feel free to go out and do what is necessary to get the job done." Williams also recognized that many of the men were not firmly focused because they were constantly "chasing young girls." He also cited transportation and the inability to raise funds for the campaign as impediments to success in Louisville.[21]

Williams was firmly committed to assisting the local Black leadership in passing a suitable fair housing ordinance. "Derby or no derby," Hosea said, "there's going to be some hell in Louisville until a housing bill is passed." The specific tactics he recommended reflected experience gained from the campaigns he had led in other southern cities hostile to fair and equitable treatment of Black citizens. He proposed "drive-ins" around Churchill Downs. Cooperating drivers would drive their cars as slowly as the law allowed to prevent horse owners from arriving at their stables before the race began. As a secondary and, perhaps more dangerous, method of protest against the city's failure to enact fair housing legislation, Hosea suggested that protesters actually launch themselves onto the racetrack and "sit in" on the final stretch of the contest, halting the race altogether.[22]

Although Williams and his staff were limited by a lack of resources, they were still able to galvanize enough support within Louisville to stage successive protests for the next month. The city fathers unintentionally united liberal and conservative forces within the Black community after three tactical missteps. First, on April 11, the board of aldermen defeated another open ordinance proposal submitted by Mayor Schmied that shielded buildings where owners lived. The mayor's amended version also exempted all apartment complexes for the first year after they were constructed. Second, several violent attacks against peaceful Black demonstrators rallied the professional, or "responsible," elements of the Black community to embrace a more direct form of protest. Finally, Jefferson County's Circuit Judge Marvin J. Sternberg, issued an injunction barring Williams's night marches outright and limiting the size of daytime demonstrations to one hundred fifty persons.[23]

By April 29, nearly five hundred protesters had been arrested on a wide variety of charges. The most serious, "banding together to commit a felony," a violation that carried a maximum penalty of one year in jail, was levied against forty-two demonstrators. One week before the ninety-third running of the Kentucky Derby, Louisville and the city's Black leadership were still stuck at an impasse because both sides were unable to reach a compromise on the open housing ordinance. Williams informed several hundred advocates of fair housing legislation that Stokely Carmichael of SNCC and CORE National Director Floyd McKissick, would be in Louisville the following week to assist with demonstrations during "Derby Week." Williams and A. D. King, with the assistance of Carmichael and McKissick, planned to protest along the Pegasus Parade route on Thursday, May 4—an effective threat, as close to two hundred thousand spectators annually attended the race.

Referred to as demonstration "technicians" by Ben A. Franklin of the *New York Times*, the four activists, in a manner reminiscent of Williams's strategy in St. Augustine to embarrass that city as it was celebrating its Quadricentennial in 1964, planned to use the Kentucky Derby and the city's fear of losing tourism-generated revenue to force the mayor and board of aldermen to enact a fair housing measure. Anxiety concerning the ability of the police to control both large crowds and demonstrators drove the lawmakers and Derby organizers' decision to limit the week's activities. Local lawmakers reasoned that the threat of protests during the weeklong activities outweighed the economic advantages promised by the parade and, therefore, decided to cancel it. Other "Derby Week" activities continued as planned. Williams decided to conduct "trial runs." During one of the lesser races held on May 1, six of Williams's staff members, led by Robert Sims, jumped on the racetrack and bolted across the path of racing thoroughbreds. The young demonstrators were immediately arrested, but the protest heightened tension among law enforcement officers and Louisville's leadership community as May 6 approached.[24]

Williams and his staffers in Louisville were firmly committed to creating a major nonviolent disturbance during the Kentucky Derby. Advocates of the radical approach had adopted as their policy, "No housing, no derby." To their dismay, however, Dr. King and local moderate Black leaders in Louisville decided on the night of May 5 to cancel any demonstrations during the nation's most celebrated horse race the following day. "We were going to break up that damn Kentucky Derby" until King intervened, Williams said later. King's opposition was rooted in the fear that riots and severe injury would be the inevitable result of the protest. Although Williams did not break ranks with King this time, his staffers were not as willing to genuflect to the SCLC president's will. They had long anticipated disturbing the Derby. They decided to refrain from engaging in any additional demonstrations in the hopes that city officials would relent and authorize a fair housing measure that both parties could accept.[25]

The fervor for direct action waned. Local advocates for fair housing decided to turn to the ballot as a remedy for the city's reluctance to advance a satisfactory fair housing ordinance. One historian maintained that the number of nighttime demonstrators dwindled from a few hundred to between fifty and seventy-five after King decided not to protest at the Kentucky Derby. Demonstrations were soon limited to one per week while the main focus of local organizations, such as the Committee on Open Housing (COH), shifted to conducting voter registration drives to oust the current aldermen in the upcoming municipal elections and elect candidates who would push an acceptable ordinance to passage. Georgia Davis, chairman of the All Citizens Voter Registration Crusade, announced that, as of July 15, 1967, more than twenty-six thousand eligible Blacks were not registered to vote in Jefferson County. She pledged in a letter to Vernon Jordan, the president of the Southern Regional Council, that she and other volunteers would commit to register no less than twenty thousand Blacks by September 9, the last day to register voters in time for the November 7 statewide and countywide elections. The registration efforts netted a gain of one thousand one hundred fifteen voters in Louisville's West End district alone.[26]

The Black community used the ballot to its advantage during the November 7 election to the county board of aldermen. After the votes were tallied, Democrats occupied eleven of the twelve seats on the county board of aldermen. Louise Reynolds, a Black woman and six-term incumbent, had been the only alderman to advocate for fair housing legislation the previous spring; she became the only candidate to retain her seat. On December 13, 1967, the board finally passed an open housing ordinance by a nine-to-three margin, which declared that racial discrimination in selling, purchasing, exchanging, renting, or leasing and withholding housing accommodations from any perspective buyer or renter on the basis of race was illegal and punishable by five hundred dollars per offense. With the law's passage, Louisville, Kentucky, became one of only a few southern cities to pass a fair housing ordinance before President Johnson signed the Civil Rights Act of 1968 into law the next year. Dr. King called the new open housing law another example of how racial progress can be achieved through aggressive, nonviolent action."[27]

Although Williams played an integral role in the planning and demonstrations in Louisville and should have enjoyed the triumph that resulted from a very demanding campaign, his pent-up frustration with the SCLC executive leadership compelled him to submit his resignation to Dr. King on the same day the ordinance passed in Kentucky. As he recalled, "I called Ralph [Abernathy] that night and I said 'Ralph, I want you to take my resignation to Martin. I've decided that I'm going back to private life.'" Williams cited the "mental and physical requirements of his position" as the reason for his desire to leave. He emphasized his dedication to King and the causes they both held dear. "I have acted somewhat in a sacrificial manner," he wrote, "and the assistance I have given SCLC has aided in bringing about meaningful social change in the South and throughout the world." Evidence suggests that Williams felt as if he had been snubbed by Dr. King after the SCLC president made several personnel changes, particularly the hiring of William Rutherford."[28]

King appointed William Rutherford, a PhD, as executive director of the SCLC during the organization's four-day staff retreat in late November in Frogmore, South Carolina, two and a half weeks before Williams submitted his resignation. Rutherford was brought in to "serve as a manager in mounting, developing, and installing certain management systems that hadn't existed before," said King. Williams believed that Rutherford's hiring had an unspoken purpose relative to his position in King's inner circle. "I always will believe [that] one of Bill's jobs was to get rid of me at the organization," said Williams. After the changes were made, King polled the other staffers to gauge their support. Williams informed King of his displeasure. "You mean to tell me that you would bring a man in as executive director over me?" Williams asked. "He ain't never had one day's experience in civil rights." At the time of the Frogmore retreat, Williams was the director of seventy-six projects and had a combined staff of one hundred eighty people scattered throughout the South. Williams's offices were managed by five secretaries. After the retreat, his staff was reduced to eight. Adding additional insult, his chief secretary, Terrie Randolph, had been moved to Rutherford's office. Williams had not been "micromanaged" since he arrived in SCLC and felt that Rutherford was "juvenile" in the execution of his duties as executive director. "I was going crazy. I tried everything I could do. . . . He stayed on my ass all the time," said Williams.[29]

On December 14, one day after Williams submitted his resignation, he had lunch with Abernathy and King at the Regency Hotel in downtown Atlanta. King realized that the launching of the Poor People's Campaign had not taken off as expected. The SCLC executive had announced the initiative in Atlanta on December 4. The Poor People's Campaign, he had planned, would be geared to "secure at least jobs or income for all," King said. "They ain't got the damn thing off the ground," Williams thought to himself. King likely realized that Williams's absence would create a major void in the areas of planning and mobilizing thousands of participants in ten major cities and five rural communities. King, according to Williams, practically begged to keep him on the staff. "I was wrong about you," King told him. "I'm asking you not to leave me. If you leave me, I don't know what I'm going to do. I need you. This program will never work without you." King wanted to solve two significant problems at the same time: Make Williams happy and move the Poor People's Campaign forward. King decided to incorporate several phases into the campaign. He placed Williams as head of mobilization, which, in theory, placed many of the former staff members back under his supervision. "That was just to get me back in power," said Williams. "They knew if they got me back in power nobody else was going to take it away from me."[30]

Hosea Williams entered 1968 with a renewed purpose as the SCLC's director of mobilization for what would be Dr. King's last campaign. On January 4, one day before Williams's forty-second birthday, Rutherford and Bernard LaFayette jointly penned a memorandum to "All SCLC Staff Members," informing them that their presence was mandatory at the organization's staff retreat, January 14–16, at Ebenezer Baptist Church, where Dr. King served as co-pastor alongside his father, Martin Luther King Sr. The retreat, according to Rutherford and LaFayette was a "must if the Washington Poor People's Campaign [was] to be a success." Excuses other than "grave sickness" or death would not be an acceptable reason to be absent. On January 10, Williams followed up with a more specific memorandum to fifty staff members throughout eighteen cities. He informed everyone that they would receive their specific Poor People's Campaign staff assignments on Sunday, January 14. To avoid hotel expenses, Williams planned to lodge visiting staff members in private homes. Three meals would be provided on January 15 and January 16. Williams capped each break at thirty minutes during the three-day mandatory staff meeting.[31]

Scheduled to begin in April, the campaign as King envisioned it would be geared to securing "jobs or income." Williams, along with Bevel and Jesse Jackson, complained throughout the retreat that King's objective was both too ambitious and ambiguous. Bevel and Jackson were the most hostile opponents of King's strategy for two reasons: They wanted to remain in Chicago to manage "Operation Breadbasket," and they also desired to be autonomous from King and the SCLC. According to Williams, "Jesse was using Bevel. I don't think they were going in nothing else where King was going to be the leader. I think they had come to the time of challenging King's leadership." He maintained, "Bevel was experienced. Jesse was not considered back then." He suggested that both men were using possible flaws in the Poor People's Campaign to expose deficiencies in King's leadership. Williams believed that their disdain for King and the campaign had more to do with their desire to lead than their contempt for King's strategy. Bevel felt that the SCLC should harness all of its energies and resources to resist the Vietnam War, which King had publicly opposed for the first time in 1967. "The War was a substitute," said Williams. "If he [Bevel] hadn't chosen the war, he was going to choose something else. Hadn't been for Chicago [it] would have been another city. . . . Like Stokely, they didn't believe that King deserved to be at the pinnacle." King believed that Bevel and Jackson's opposition was influenced more by their disloyalty than their analysis of the scope of the Poor People's Campaign. In spite of the internal discord, King held fast to his strategy.[32]

Bevel and Jackson wanted the SCLC to create a lengthy list of demands on paper to present to the federal government. King demurred. The SCLC president confided to them and to other staff members who had not been involved in the campaigns in Montgomery and Birmingham that specificity could be a hindrance when attempting to arouse the conscience of the nation insofar as poverty was concerned. "The people we are going to be mobilizing," King said, "are not going to be fired up on the basis of a long list of demands." "Denial and deprivation" meant that the disinherited could not be motivated by lengthy proclamations. "If you go there with a demand for negative income tax, they don't know the meaning of negative, they don't know the meaning of income, they don't know the meaning of tax," King said. "But they do know that something is wrong with their lives and in their situations." King was adamant that emphasizing "jobs" and "income" gave SCLC a strategic advantage not only with the impoverished but also with the other hostile forces within the civil rights movement and the federal government. He truly believed that jobs and increased income were "so possible, so achievable, so pure, so simple, that even the backlash can't do much to deny it." Jobs and income were so "non-token and so basic to life that even the black nationalists can't disagree with it that much."[33]

Williams sprang into action to galvanize support for the Poor People's Campaign, but he saw several impediments that might slow his mobilization of staff and volunteers. Most of the issues were internal. In a four-page memorandum placed on LaFayette's desk around 5:00 AM on February 11, Williams wrote that he was "very disturbed" about the progress of the Campaign. He told LaFayette, the program administrator for the Poor People's Campaign, that he was "hamstrung" and could not properly oversee the initiative because the staff had not yet been notified that he had been tapped to direct the mobilization phase. "None of the staff [are] keeping me informed of their activities, and many of them are not even in touch with me," Williams wrote. He complained that staff members at the executive level, including LaFayette, Rutherford, and Young, were receiving and analyzing reports of mobilization activities as well as "approving budgets and leave of absences," and he "didn't know anything about it." Williams suggested eight recommendations to LaFayette with the hope that the program administrator would quickly move to remedy the lack of communication throughout SCLC and the overall lack of progress of the campaign. First, Williams asked that Rutherford and Young write a letter to all field staff informing them of his appointment as chief of field staff supervision.

Young sent out a memo the following day that addressed Williams's request. He wrote to all staff members that "Mr. Hosea Williams will serve as Field Director and be in charge of the mobilization aspects." Young had underlined the sentence in the memorandum that indicated that Williams would be "Over all Supervisory of Field Staff and Recruiting of Personnel for Washington."[34]

Williams's seven remaining recommendations to LaFayette were focused on strengthening his own control of the project. The second recommendation called for LaFayette to approve a "minimal budget" to mobilize and recruit volunteers in eight cities where funds were scarce and local enthusiasm was low. Recommendations three and four called for a "systematic reporting system" to ensure that staff members were not exaggerating statistics from their work and the hiring of two additional secretaries to the Department of Voter Registration and Political Education to assist Williams in evaluating the field staff. Another recommendation called for the recruitment of "better staff and personnel in Baltimore, Maryland, and other areas surrounding Washington, DC." Williams believed that this action might influence "certain black militants" who were determined to destroy the Poor People's Campaign. The sixth recommendation called for the SCLC's office in Washington, DC, to be staffed with a "full-time administrative secretary, typist and a clerk" within the next three days. Recommendation seven called for all executive staff members to submit their itineraries to Williams's office three weeks in advance so that their schedules "would not conflict with nonviolent workshops, orientation of local leaders and mass meeting speaking engagements." Williams's last recommendation to LaFayette suggested that all funds be made payable to the SCLC's national office. "I feel it would be much easier for staff to raise funds to finance their projects if this is done," he wrote. He believed that contributors would be more likely to contribute "respectable" amounts if they felt that the monies were written in the "care of the President, Dr. King."[35]

The Action Committee of the Poor People's Campaign met at Pascal's Motor Hotel in Atlanta, on February 11. Eighteen people attended, including Hosea Williams, Dr. King, Jesse Jackson, James Bevel, Bernard Lee, Dorothy Cotton, William Rutherford, Andrew Young, and Rev. Joseph Lowery. "We are not doing our homework," King said. He was "disturbed" by the fact that the groups of people important to the campaign had not been satisfactorily recruited. "We have not recruited twenty people who will go and stay with us," King said.

Bernard Lee, a graduate of Alabama State College and confidant to King, suggested that the campaign be called off. Rutherford agreed and said that it "should be called off or call off everything else." King said that some staff members seemed not to know where to go, whereas others were just not being supervised and asked Williams to address this problem. According to Williams, recruitment of the poor was limited by "inadequate numbers and quality of staff in Washington" as well as "coordination." Williams also complained that the memo notifying the staff of his authority over the campaign had not been sent out. After discussing the issues surrounding recruiting poor people, the debate about budget appropriations for the campaign intensified between Dr. King, Williams, and Rutherford. "Bill [Rutherford]" said King, "will have the final okay to approve requisitions." Williams told King that he was "making a mistake . . . requisitions should come to my office and I in turn will submit them to Bill." King relented. Williams kept pushing. "Could you give a certain time limit on approval?" he asked King, "We cannot wait to get these projects on the move." King assured Williams that his budget would be reviewed tomorrow. "I cannot agree to this arrangement," Rutherford said to King and Williams. King asked why. "I cannot work things out with Hosea," Rutherford said. "I can just see now hours and hours arguing over every penny. I would go out and raise $10,000 than disburse it." King suggested that the budget be "tentatively approved" and then discussed at the next meeting.[36]

Five days after penning the lengthy missive to LaFayette, Williams traveled with Dr. King on an SCLC tour throughout Alabama and Mississippi to galvanize support for the Poor People's Campaign. On one stop of the tour in Montgomery, Williams flanked King as the SCLC president addressed a crowd of about seventy attendees at the Maggie Street Baptist Church. America as a country "has lost its sense of direction," as evidenced by its willingness to "spend one-half million dollars to kill every Viet Cong, and fifty-three dollars to help poor people," said King. Williams also traveled with King to Selma, where the latter spoke at Tabernacle Baptist Church. King recalled the struggles and triumphs in Selma and asked the congregants if they would be willing to follow him into Washington for the Poor People's Campaign. The crowd, which included Amelia Boynton and SCLC State Field Director Albert Turner, expressed their support for the organization's attack on poverty. After touring with King, Williams returned to Atlanta to stay on top of the campaign.[37]

Williams had also spent time in Savannah recruiting volunteers for the Poor People's Campaign. Because of FBI Director J. Edgar Hoover, the notorious racist and unrelenting enemy of King and the SCLC, Williams's recruitment efforts on his former turf met little success. The Bureau used its COINTELPRO methods to deter potential recruits from joining the protest in the Nation's Capital. The FBI utilized local media outlets that were friendly to their smear campaign to portray Williams as a naïve idealist whose inabilities as an organizer would cause them to be stranded and alone in a big city without the proper support. These strategically planted stories dissuaded Black Savannahians from signing up to join the campaign.[38]

On March 5, Williams penned a memorandum to "All Project Leaders and Field Staff Involved in the Mobilization of Field Troops for the Washington Poor People's Campaign." He informed all recipients of the correspondence that they should tell donors to make checks payable to the SCLC's national office and address them to William Rutherford. He reminded staff members of their responsibility to organize their "ministers and churches support committee" to ensure that a "certain amount of money can be raised" and donated to SCLC. Although Williams emphasized that churches should play an active role in organizing the poor in their areas, they should also be donors. It is clear from this correspondence that Williams was firmly focused on increasing the number of contributors to enable him to effectively mobilize the initiative. "Get your business and professional people organized," he wrote. "Most of them will not march, go to jail, or to Washington, but they must furnish their money." Staff members should not just lobby professional individuals, they must approach businesses. "Every business should make a large pledge," he wrote. Although Williams's approach to fundraising may appear to be excessively coercive, he should be viewed as a skilled and experienced civil rights activist who had the ability to see around the proverbial corners. He knew that once a movement was launched, white merchants routinely escalated prices on items necessary to support the mobilization of thousands of individuals.[39]

Three days later, on March 8, Williams outlined the specific staff requirements that would make Dr. King's next venture a success. The "People to People" tour, an initiative of the Poor People's Campaign, connected King with impoverished inner-city residents in hopes that his presence could not only dramatize the plight of the poor for the media but also encourage those most vulnerable to travel to Washington. Williams wrote to the staff that the tour must be "informative and educational for the haves, but much more so for the have nots." His memorandum emphasized that the agenda in big cities had to focus on ministers, businesses and professionals, youth and young adult Black militants, poor people, and mass meetings. He reminded the staff that Dr. King's role was not to organize their respective communities. King's role, Williams said, was simply to "stimulate . . . stimulate that what you have already organized and mobilized." Although he had previously articulated that the participation of ministers, churches, and the business communities was vital, he re-emphasized the dire need for financial support. "Cash and checks are better," Williams wrote, "but reputable pledges are acceptable." As a shrewd publicity technique, he indicated in the memo that once King arrived in a town, he would meet with business owners. During the meeting, a business should hang a sign on the establishment saying, "Closed, meeting with King, and the Washington Poor People's Campaign." Williams also understood the effectiveness of involving the youth and young adults. He instructed staff members to organize an outdoor mass meeting that would attract other local high school and college students. He suggested that staff members should also orchestrate a "sympathy march," which would garner much-needed publicity after King spoke in their respective city. Williams took great pains in this memo to inform the staff of the importance of the grassroots leaders.[40]

Williams stood firm in his conviction that the "grassroots leaders and the poor were the most important" elements for the staff to engage. "This is where you must personally give your time," he wrote. He encouraged the staff to gather a very large crowd of the poor who could present their "demands" to Dr. King so that he could carry them with him to Washington. This particular meeting, Williams suggested, would be the "longest and most important" assembly during the tour. He wrote that, after the meeting, King would need to have lunch in a "real poor" neighborhood that would require him to walk on the streets and visit several houses. "See if you can find a home," he wrote, "where a simple soul food dinner can be prepared for six to eight persons." For practical purposes, those residing in the chosen home would be the only residents notified of King's visit. Williams pointed out that the element of surprise was very important. "Do not let the other people know that Dr. King will be visiting their home," he wrote. "They will try to clean up and dress up. He would like to catch them in their natural habitat." Whether he intended to be ironic or chose his words unwittingly, his language for an internal memorandum was troubling, given the embedded zoological semantic connotations.[41]

Hosea Williams understood that the mass meeting had been a staple of the civil rights movement. It enabled leaders to communicate their objectives to the attendees and also to serve as a tool to revitalize the participation in the face of intimidation. He wrote that the mass meeting must "be representative and huge. . . . Your largest church should be overcrowded." He ordered that sections in the churches should be organized according to socioeconomic standing. Professionals, welfare mothers, and ministers should sit in their own sections. "Congregations should stand when ministers present [their offerings]," wrote Williams. This was an obviously an attempt to encourage the minister and congregation to give a substantial amount if they wanted to avoid being perceived as lazy or unwilling to give. He emphasized that the mass meeting should be "simple and short" and should consist of three parts: the collection, Dr. King's speech, and a mock trial. Dr. King would not only address the congregants, but he would also serve as a judge. The objective would be to put "America on trial for robbery and exploitation of the poor," Williams wrote. Specifically, he wrote in the advisory memorandum to staff members, "America will be tried for violating the Declaration of Independence . . . and be tried for stealing 4 million mules and eighty million acres of land" after the Civil War.[42]

Williams was obviously working under very time-specific deadlines while heading up the mobilization department for a massive campaign. Circumstances often mandated that he be in several places simultaneously. The demands on his time in Atlanta led to citations—and occasionally even arrests—for reckless driving. Unlike King, Williams did not have a personal driver to ensure that he was safely and quickly transported to meetings and other obligations. On March 14, Williams was cited and arrested for driving eighty-five miles per hour in a forty-five mile per hour zone between Glenwood Avenue and Second Avenue, less than five miles from his home at 8 East Lake Avenue. Officers C. T. Bruce and C. E. Lovell also charged Williams with making an improper lane change and passing over the yellow line. After being detained for several hours, he was released from the DeKalb County Jail on a three-hundred-dollar bond. He later resolved the citation by paying a fine.[43]

The campaign shifted to Memphis, Tennessee, after Rev. James Lawson, pastor of Centenary Methodist Church in that city, appealed to King to support thirteen hundred striking sanitation workers. The exploited workers had been in a dispute with city fathers opposed to their desire to have better pay, safer working conditions, and a recognized union to allow collective bargaining power after two Black sanitation workers in their thirties, Echol Cole and Robert Walker, were crushed to death in their garbage compactor as a result of malfunctioning equipment. Their deaths might have been prevented if the city had replaced defective equipment in the fleet's garbage trucks after two men were killed in 1964. That Cole and Walker were so underpaid that they could not afford the city's life insurance policy, nor were they entitled to workmen's compensation as hourly employees, was demonstration of the department's devaluation of Black labor. At the time of the strike, Black men constituted ninety percent of Memphis's sanitation workers. Memphis Mayor Henry Loeb, a World War II veteran, whom Andy Young referred to as "obstinate and inflexible," agreed to offer the sanitation workers a twenty-cent-per-hour raise in pay, from $1.60 to $1.80. However, he refused to formally recognize the union or to allow for union dues to be withheld from workers' paychecks. The Black community, led by Lawson, initiated a boycott of the downtown stores and two of the city's largest newspapers in an attempt to force the city into recognition of the union.[44]

The campaign in Memphis to assist the sanitation workers clearly demonstrated the interconnectedness of race and class and the explicit message to Black employees that their arguments for redress were not worthy of serious consideration. Four years earlier, the largest public-sector union in the United States, the American Federation of State, County and Municipal Employees (AFSCME), started a local union, Local 1733, in the city. The charter did not compel city officials to enter into binding agreements. Not only did Mayor Loeb resist signing any contracts with Local 1733, but he also reinforced the economic exploitation of Black sanitation workers through intentional municipal labor policies that primarily affected the Black working class. By the time King and the SCLC arrived, Blacks constituted 40 percent of the city's population. Nearly 60 percent of the Black community lived in abject poverty. One scholar compared the exploitation of the Black workers to "plantation-like conditions."[45]

The unskilled Black laborers in the Memphis Department of Public Works were dehumanized and delegitimized each day they reported to work. The department on the whole and the white supervisors did not realize the dignity in Black labor. Sanitation workers were not issued city uniforms or gloves. Black men were routinely sent home without pay if they were late by a minute or two. The workers had to carry trash in a tub on their head. Their faces were blanketed with flies and maggots. Black workers were not afforded basic amenities such as having a bathroom where they could wash up. There was not a reserved location for Black workers to consume their lunch during the allotted fifteen minutes. Workers, on occasion, were forced to eat their lunch in the garbage compactors. Workers were not paid overtime, despite working for more than twelve hours.

Black workers were sent home with two hours' pay when it rained, whereas White supervisors were paid their regular wages regardless of the weather conditions. Worse, Black sanitation workers did not have job security and served simply at the pleasure of their arbitrary white supervisors, who had the latitude to fire them for the slightest perceived transgression.[46]

King arrived in Memphis on March 18 with the conviction that the Johnson Administration's War on Poverty was withering as a result of the nation's commitment in Vietnam. King spoke before a crowd of almost ten thousand people at the Mason Temple. The event was a success, and the SCLC leader returned to Tennessee's largest city to lead a demonstration on Thursday, March 28, after a previously scheduled visit on March 22 had been derailed because of an unexpected snowstorm. The march was a disaster. Violence erupted as King led an estimated six thousand marchers from the Clayborne AME Church to City Hall in support of sanitation workers. Policemen used mace and tear gas to disperse the crowd after a small number of teenagers, who not been instructed in what to expect in the demonstrations and had little civil rights march experience, defied King's and Lawson's insistence on nonviolent discipline and started breaking windows. A policeman gunned down Larry Payne with a shotgun. Police claimed that the sixteen-year-old Black teenager had brandished a knife after being confronted while looting, but at least one eyewitness claimed that Payne's hands were in the air when the officer fatally shot him in the stomach. As many as fifty others were injured in the melee. Although SCLC had not organized the march and might have attempted to disassociate the organization from the riotlike atmosphere, King vowed to return to Memphis the following week. He insisted that nonviolence was the only viable strategy for confronting Memphis's white power structure.[47]

Williams initially resisted King's request that all SCLC high-ranking staff members leave their individual projects and return with him to assist the protesting sanitation workers. Young later suggested that Williams had succumbed to his own "egomania" and was adamant about not returning to Memphis. In Andrew Young's recollection, "Hosea wanted to focus on voter registration and running Black candidates for state offices." Williams remembered events differently; looking back on the decision nearly a quarter century later, he insinuated that the SCLC president was having his own ego battle. "King wanted to go back to Memphis to save that King name. . . . That was the only march he ever led that was not organized by his staff," Williams recalled. However, he swallowed his opposition to the march and left for Memphis to join King, Young, and Abernathy on April 3.

They checked into the Black-owned, two-story Lorraine Motel located on Mulberry Street—a familiar place for King as he had stayed there as early as the 1950s when lodging overnight in Memphis. That night, King reluctantly agreed to speak at the Mason Temple before a crowd of approximately three thousand people. The SCLC leader, looking haggard, delivered a poignant but very gloomy speech on that cold, rainy night. He spoke of the many threats against his life and sounded fatalistic, themes that he had often discussed privately over the years, seeming to suggest that his days were numbered. In his rich, baritone voice with the speaking cadence that he had perfected over years as a southern Baptist minister and seasoned civil rights orator, he entered his peroration. The Bible's Old Testament Exodus narrative of a chosen people freed from captivity had always struck a chord with adherents of Afro-Christianity from slavery through the grim years of the nadir and Jim Crow. King inserted himself squarely into that liberation narrative, evoking Moses's mountaintop experience, as enthusiastic members of the audience shouted out during pauses in his phrasing:

> I just want to do God's will. And He's allowed me to go up to the mountain. And I've looked over. And I've seen the Promised Land. I may not get there with you. But I want you to know tonight, that we, as a people, will get to the Promised Land.

In words that eerily foreshadowed his death and have resonated with prophetic force in the decades since, he claimed he was "not worried about anything. I'm not fearing any man. '*Mine eyes have seen the glory of the coming of the Lord.*'" As his words echoed around the cavernous rafters of Mason Temple, the crowd erupted in deafening cheers in response to the same words from "The Battle Hymn of the Republic" that had shaped the stirring conclusion of King's antiphonal "How long? Not long!/Our God Is Marching On" speech at the conclusion of the march from Selma to Montgomery at the Alabama Statehouse three years earlier. King collapsed into his chair assisted by Jesse Jackson and Ralph Abernathy. He was visibly exhausted. It was the last public address he would deliver.[48]

After the speech, King, Young, Williams, and Abernathy went to the home of Benjamin Hooks, a prominent Memphis minister and lawyer, to discuss the sanitation strike well into the morning.[49] Williams began the following day, Thursday, April 4, with a 10:30 AM meeting in the Lorraine Motel's room 315, with SCLC staffers Bevel and James Orange and a group of black militants, including Charles and Richard Cabbage, John Burl Smith, and Milton Mack. King wanted the four militants to serve as marshals for the march that had been scheduled for Monday, April 8. Charles Cabbage, a graduate of Morehouse College, King's alma mater, attempted to leverage his reputation with the youth in Memphis to remain nonviolent in exchange for a large donation from King and the SCLC to the "Invaders," a militant organization. Cabbage insisted that if law enforcement or white toughs attempted to endanger the marchers, he could not rule out the use of "tactical violence," his definition of self-defense. When Dr. King entered the meeting after being briefed by his staffers, he told Cabbage and the Invaders that SCLC could not work with the group if they refused to abide by nonviolent discipline on the march. King was torn, for he believed that Invaders' presence would be effective in quelling possible disruptions among the youth who had not been exposed to SCLC's nonviolent workshops. The group disbanded without reaching an acceptable resolution.

Later that afternoon, Williams proposed that Cabbage and Smith be placed on the SCLC's payroll. According to one historian, Williams believed that "exposure to Dr. King and the staff would give them the idea of being nonviolent." Ralph Abernathy recalled that King became "grim and businesslike" after being notified of Williams's idea to hire the young militants as march marshals. King remonstrated, "Hosea, no one should be on our payroll that accepts violence as a means of social change. The only way to have a world at peace is through nonviolence." Sensing that he could not persuade King to accept the hire, Williams abandoned his advocacy for the young militants.[50]

Hosea Williams's life and the course of the modern civil rights movement were irrevocably altered around 6:00 PM on April 4, 1968, when an assassin shot and killed King as he stood on the balcony outside room 306 of the Lorraine Motel. The high-velocity bullet, purportedly fired by James Earl Ray, struck the Nobel laureate on the right side of his face near his chin, dropping King immediately. He was likely immediately paralyzed, as the bullet traveled from his jaw and severed his spinal cord before the projectile lodged in his back. Williams was putting the key into the door of his assigned motel room, 210, when he looked up and saw his leader's feet hanging over the edge of the concrete balcony above. Quickly realizing what had happened, he rushed, along with other SCLC staffers, to King's side. "All of his side of his face was shot off," Williams told an unnamed interviewer that evening.

Someone called emergency medical personnel at 6:03 PM. An ambulance arrived on the scene almost simultaneously with the first call; a police officer had already alerted the local dispatcher. The paramedics hurriedly placed King on a stretcher and loaded him into their vehicle. Abernathy, King's closest confidant, and SCLC staffer Bernard Lee rode in the back of the ambulance with King to nearby St. Joseph's Hospital. Williams remained at the hotel with A. D. King, the SCLC leader's younger brother, with whom he had recently worked in the open housing campaign in Kentucky the previous year. The two were together when they heard that the Rev. Dr. Martin Luther King Jr. was pronounced dead at 7:05 PM. The universally recognized leader of the modern Black freedom struggle and arguably the most eloquent orator of the twentieth century had been silenced.[51]

Riots and civil unrest plagued the city of Memphis and numerous other cities after King's assassination had been confirmed, including major disturbances in Chicago and Louisville, whose racism-blighted urban geography was very familiar to Williams because of his involvement with SCLC's recent campaigns in those cities. As one of King's top aides, Williams played a critical role over the following days, working to ensure a continuity of leadership within the SCLC and assisting with plans for his fallen leader's funeral.

Around 1:00 AM on April 5, Williams and other top SCLC lieutenants met with R. C. Lewis, owner of the Memphis funeral home that had routinely provided King with a limousine and driver while they were in the city. They chose a suitable coffin to transport King back to Atlanta. After this morbid yet necessary procedure, King's top aides, including Williams, met in a room at the Lorraine Motel into the early hours of the following day. In a scene that might have evoked a mafia succession had it not been for the SCLC's ethos of nonviolence, they each pledged their fealty to Abernathy as King's appointed successor as the organization's president.

As the meeting continued, they also briefly discussed possible funeral arrangements for what would inevitably be a massive logistical operation for the City of Atlanta, the King family, and the SCLC. Staffers, according to Andrew Young, wanted to recommend to King's wife, Coretta, that two services be planned: one for family and SCLC insiders and a second ceremony for the public, including heads of state and other persons of means and influence. King had died in Memphis advocating for the economic uplift of the sanitation workers—a testament to his commitment to fight for the downtrodden—and the larger Poor People's Campaign was still a work in progress. However, in an initial discussion of funeral arrangements,

Williams quickly came to feel that this constituency of "have nots" and the nameless poor was largely being ignored by some SCLC staffers and the King family.[52]

King's death while fighting for the poor had a profound impact on Williams, which drove him from that moment on to be the one of the most fervent supporters of the poor as a civil rights activist and humanitarian. He maintained that April 4 "was the most unforgettable day in [his] life" and that his commitment to improve the lot of poor Americans had begun with his unyielding support for the nation's underclass to have the same access to King's service as the powerful and affluent members of society. On April 6, Williams rode with A. D. King to the latter's parents' home in Atlanta, where arrangements were being made for the funeral. Dr. King's parents; Coretta Scott King and her sister, Edythe Scott Bagley; and King's spiritual and intellectual mentor and former Morehouse College president, Dr. Benjamin E. Mays, were all present.

"I sat there and they could only see this man Martin Luther King Jr. as an intellectual being in his middle class setting," Williams recalled. The group planning the funeral were wedded to the idea of dividing the church into three sections: Ebenezer Baptist Church's membership, King family members, and "VIP's." "Where would the poor people be?" asked Hosea. "Who?" asked some of the people in attendance. Williams responded: "THE POOR PEOPLE! I WANT TO KNOW WHERE THEY WILL BE?" According to Williams, an unnamed attendee at the planning session said, "We don't quite understand." Williams clarified his advocacy for the poor: "THE PEOPLE THAT MARTIN DIED FOR. THE PEOPLE THAT HE REALLY LOVED. THE PEOPLE THAT HE DWELT AMONG. THE PEOPLE THAT HE WORKED FOR. WHERE WILL THEY BE?" The sentiment among the King family and Mays was that "the church is too small and we don't have any space for them." Williams's passionate plea fell on deaf ears. The beneficiaries of King's last crusade would not be permitted to attend the service at Ebenezer.[53]

Williams, then, took a different approach. "I proposed that when the funeral in the church was over that we'll take the symbol of the poor in this nation—the mule and wagon—and take his body back to Morehouse." Williams awaited a response from the small group that had assembled in "Daddy" King's living room, those he now saw as elitists. "You can't put Martin Luther King's body on no mule and wagon," someone responded. "I finally acted like Hosea Williams," said the fiery rabble-rouser. "Okay, YA'LL HAVE THE FUNERAL. WHEN THAT BODY COME OUT OF THE CHURCH, IT WILL BELONG TO US. WE'LL TAKE OVER," Williams remembered roaring.[54]

Two services were held for Dr. King in Atlanta on Tuesday, April 9. An estimated fifty thousand mourners, including Vice President of the United States Hubert Humphrey; Senator Robert Kennedy; and Jacqueline Kennedy, the widow of the slain thirty-fifth president of the United States. Two days earlier, President Lyndon Johnson had declared a national day of mourning. Eastern Airlines reported that approximately thirty-three chartered planes had made arrangements to land in the city so that their passengers could attend the services. The first service, which had been planned to not exceed half an hour, took place at 10:30 AM in the thirteen-hundred-seat Ebenezer Baptist Church. Stretching three times as long as it was intended, the observance inside the church featured a eulogy from Ralph Abernathy in which he referred to the assassination of King and its aftermath as "one of the darkest hours of mankind."

The voice of the SCLC's slain leader then echoed from beyond the grave, as in a recording of one of his last sermons—"The Drum Major Instinct," delivered at Ebenezer Baptist just two months before—King again touched on themes of mortality and asked that, at his funeral, there should be no discussion of his awards and honors. "And if you get somebody to deliver the eulogy, tell them not to talk too long."

> I'd like somebody to mention that day that Martin Luther King Jr. tried to give his life serving others. I'd like for somebody to say that day that [I] tried to love somebody. I want you to say that day that I tried to be right on the [Vietnam] war question. I want you to be able to say that day that I did try to feed the hungry. . . . I want you to say that I tried to love and serve humanity. Yes, if you want to say that I was a drum major, say that I was a drum major for justice. Say that I was a drum major for peace. I was a drum major for righteousness. And all of the other shallow things will not matter. . . . I just want to leave a committed life behind. . . .
>
> Yes, Jesus, I want to be on your right or your left side, not for any selfish reason. . . . not in terms of some political kingdom or ambition. . . . I just want to be there in love and in justice and in truth and in commitment to others, so that we can make of this old world a new world.

When the service was over, Williams, wearing blue dungarees and a white shirt, directed pallbearers to place the slain leader's body on the wagon drawn by two Georgia mules that he had procured from a Black farmer and friend to Dr. King, Dan Young. His symbolic evocation of the "Poor People's Campaign" took place against the wishes of Coretta Scott

Pallbearers, including Hosea Williams, T. Y. Rogers, and James Orange around Martin Luther King Jr.'s casket at Southview Cemetery in Atlanta, Georgia. April 9, 1968. Alabama Department of Archives and History. Photo by Jim Peppler, *Southern Courier*.

King. The elites had had their funeral, and now the poor people would have theirs. The processional, led by Rev. Abernathy and members of the King family, left Ebenezer approximately at noon, when the temperature was around eighty degrees. Williams guided the wagon bearing the African mahogany coffin slowly along the three-and-a-half-mile route from Auburn Avenue through Courtland and Hunter Streets and finally to the

Jesse Jackson, Ralph Abernathy, Andrew Young, and Hosea Williams at the committal service for Martin Luther King Jr's remains at Southview Cemetery. April 9, 1968. Stanford University Libraries, Department of Special Collections and University Archives. Photo by Bob Fitch.

Morehouse Chapel, arriving nearly three hours later. Seven hundred forty city policemen, one hundred firemen, and several thousand soldiers from the Georgia National Guard lined the streets to ensure the protection of the mourners and the funeral cortege; more than one hundred thousand people lined the procession's route. Dr. Benjamin E. Mays, standing on the same platform as he did when King attended Tuesday morning chapel services in Sale Hall as an undergraduate, told the crowd: "I make bold to assert that it took more courage for King to practice nonviolence than it took for the assassin to fire the fatal shot. The assassin is a coward: he committed his foul act and fled. . . . When Martin disobeyed an unjust law he accepted the consequence. He never ran away."

After the service, King's body was transported by a black hearse to Southview cemetery on Atlanta's West Side for a private interment ceremony. Rev. Abernathy solemnly pronounced the final benediction for his best friend: "The cemetery is too small for his spirit, but we submit his body to the ground. . . . No coffin, no crypt. No stone can hold his greatness." King's body was lowered into the Georgia soil. The crowd of family, SCLC staffers, and a few friends dispersed.[55]

Hosea Williams and the thirty-four members of the SCLC Board of Directors had to put their grief and disbelief aside less than two hours after the burial of their fallen leader as they assembled for the first time since February 6. Joseph Lowery, chairman of the board, called the meeting to order at 7:00 PM at the Mount Moriah Baptist Church in Atlanta, Georgia. Rev. Benjamin Hooks of Memphis, Tennessee, moved to officially confirm Ralph Abernathy as president. The motion was seconded and carried unanimously. The Board then elected Cirilo McSween to the position of treasurer, which had been occupied by Abernathy since the SCLC's founding in 1957. The Board also decided to adopt three recommendations advanced by Abernathy: The SCLC should pay all expenses associated with the burial of Martin Luther King Jr.; the SCLC should pay a salary of twelve thousand dollars for one year to Coretta Scott King; and, likely in a strategic move to increase fundraising, the organization should suspend the rules and bylaws and elect King's widow and Harry Belafonte to the Board. Perhaps the most important suggestion for consideration was made by Board member Charles Morgan, who requested that the Board not back away from the Poor People's Campaign because a decision to do so might give the perception that the SCLC's agenda can be thwarted by "shooting the leader." The meeting adjourned at 11:30 PM.[56]

After nearly three years of debate, procedural obfuscation, and delay, members of Congress, in what some historians have seen as a paroxysm of guilt, reconciled minor differences and passed the Civil Rights Bill of 1968 against the national backdrop of the King funeral. Often referred to as the Fair Housing Act, the legislation was signed into law by President Johnson on April 11. Although it was rightfully perceived to be weak by Williams and many other activists, the bill was, in some respects, a "symbolic victory" for movement leaders who had fought in Louisville, Chicago, and countless other communities to end discrimination in the renting and selling of homes based on race, sex, religion, color, or national origin. In the history of the long civil rights movement, however, the fruits of such symbolic victories typically offered a meager harvest at the grassroots. Many activists could not fully appreciate the bill because the federal government's powers of enforcement left many opportunities for the exploitation of the very people the bill was intended to protect. The bill's passage came at a time when the flames of racial unrest were still literally smoldering in the aftermath of King's assassination. Washington, DC, had seen violence and destruction on a mammoth scale.

The Fair Housing Act certainly was not seen as substantive enough to result in calling off the Poor People's Campaign. Williams knew that this effort would require their uninterrupted attention if it was to be a success, especially since the federal government had to be pushed to compromise if any meaningful measures would be enacted to help the poor.[57]

Williams and the organization's board had a renewed vigor to finish King's final campaign. All signs pointed to a successful protest in Washington that could poignantly dramatize the plight of the poor. SCLC's coffers were overflowing, a direct mail campaign for contributions had yielded nearly five hundred thousand dollars per month. Three thousand poor volunteers were now easily recruited to make the trek and peaceably assemble in the nation's capital. However, the internal strife surrounding the practicality of nonviolence as a philosophy and method to achieve social harmony was now tearing the very fabric of the SCLC. The leaders, including Williams, were publicly denying that any rift existed. "There is absolutely no truth" to the rumors, said Williams. He told a reporter from the *Chicago Defender*, less than three weeks after King was gunned down, "SCLC is more united now than it has ever been in its history due to the absence and the love of Dr. King who made us what we are today." However, his words to the reporter were ominous: "There is no question in our mind that the least bit of disunity could very well destroy us." Evidence indicates that Williams was one of the lieutenants voicing acceptance of violence as a means to awaken America. Reporters Drew Pearson and Jack Anderson suggested to the *Chicago Defender* that Williams cited the riots in the aftermath of King's death as proof that violent eruptions in urban areas were the most successful strategies to gain attention for the nation's poor citizens. Williams maintained that Pearson's and Anderson's accusation was "the biggest lie that he had ever been told." Although Williams was adamant that he had not embraced violence, other distractions were taking a toll on the SCLC as they strategized around how to effectively manage the Poor People's Campaign.[58]

The Poor People's Campaign was never quite able to capture the effectiveness of previous demonstrations, in spite of Williams's undaunted optimism and his willingness to assume several demanding roles. "Elements that were dead set against us are now prone to be more cooperative," he said.

"We find ourselves in a new position, and we hope we can make the best of it." Williams, whom one reporter identified as "bombastic" and as "not only inviting trouble, but giving it a bear hug," was the director of mobilization. On May 31, while leading a mule train to Washington, he was notified that he would replace Jesse Jackson as the director of Resurrection City, a makeshift town erected on the Mall at the Lincoln Memorial to house the three thousand poor demonstrators who had assembled to redress their grievances with the federal government. Jackson, who had replaced Bevel, was demoted by Abernathy because of the young Chicagoan's inability to subordinate his own desire for publicity. Announcing the personnel shift, Young called the move a "shifting of gears" instead of demotion, in his attempt to quell any rumors that the SCLC was imploding. The move did not have an impact on the type of protests that would accompany the mass demonstration. Less than one hour after the personnel shift had been announced, Williams led a two-hour demonstration in the auditorium of a building occupied by the Department of Health, Education and Welfare, after he and approximately five hundred demonstrators were not allowed to meet with Department Secretary William Cohen. Secretary Cohen was in the building but declined to meet with Williams and his delegation of poor protesters. Williams told officials that "we [will] stay here until he comes to see us." The crowd enthusiastically endorsed their leader's persistence after he told representatives that "We're ready to bleed if necessary, we're ready to go to jail if necessary and we're even ready to die if necessary." Around 6:00 PM, Secretary Cohen finally addressed the demonstrators and told them that he would support a welfare system that would evenly assist the nation's poor, regardless of race.[59]

Williams was not pleased with the federal government's reluctance to make meaningful changes to improve the lot of the poor. On June 2, he declared that protests would take a more militant approach. "The picnic is over," Williams yelled to several hundred demonstrators outside the grounds of Resurrection City. Williams was not afraid of being beaten by police or going to jail. "The police want to use those billies," he said. "We'll give them a chance." He emphasized that the number of demonstrators could range from ten to five hundred, and the demonstrations would have a twofold purpose. "Sometimes we'll be going to make a point," said Williams, "and sometimes we'll be going to jail." After rallying the three hundred protesters outside of the campsite, Williams led a march to the Department of Agriculture to demand that officials answer questions regarding the "dumping of tons of food in the ocean while black people starve in Mississippi and Alabama." Williams also wanted answers as to why James Eastland, the powerful US senator and rabid segregationist from Mississippi, was reportedly paid to support policies that benefited big business instead of the poor citizens who were suffering in his state from poverty and malnutrition. It was clear that Williams was firmly committed to seeing the Poor People's Campaign to the end.[60]

The rest of the month was dominated by a national tragedy that would drastically affect the SCLC's fight to achieve full equality for Blacks, as well as for poor whites. On June 5, Senator Bobby Kennedy, a perceived ally of the poor, was assassinated in Los Angeles, California, in the kitchen of the Ambassador Hotel after giving a victory speech after he had been declared the winner of the California Democratic Party presidential primary. Democrats could not hope to nominate another presidential candidate strong enough to defeat Richard Nixon in November's general election. Nixon's election to the White House in November would usher in the beginning of a neoconservative movement that owed much of its strategy to George C. Wallace. Dan T. Carter suggested in *The Politics of Rage: George Wallace, the Origins of the New Conservatism and the Transformation of American Politics*, that the former governor of Alabama was the "most influential loser in American politics." Wallace brilliantly combined racism with a rancid form of populism that articulated the fears of blue-collar Democrats: a refashioned fear of Negro domination. Nixon, far more polished than the segregationist governor, cloaked Wallace's racist rhetoric in terms such as busing, quotas, and affirmative action. Nixon's promise to "bring us together" by modifying Johnson's Great Society reforms laid the groundwork for the political realignment in 1972. With the help of former Johnson aide Daniel Patrick Moynihan, Nixon brought loyal Democrats into the Republican Party by placing a renewed emphasis on controlling crime and drugs, code words that stimulated the nostalgic yearnings of southern blue-collar whites willing to sacrifice their own economic interests on the altar of white supremacy.[61]

The Poor People's Campaign continued on a downward spiral because of internal squabbles resulting from power struggles, with Williams often contributing to the disunion. On June 7, Bayard Rustin, the mastermind of the 1963 March on Washington, threatened to resign as campaign coordinator after Abernathy and Williams made statements to a newspaper reporter stating that Rustin did not have full authority to mobilize the protest. Rustin warned that he would abandon his efforts if the SCLC did not give him "complete authority" over the protest within twenty-four hours, as the campaign's climax on June 19 was speedily approaching. Rustin was an invaluable asset; he had worked tirelessly to bring order to the chaos surrounding the campaign. On June 2, Rustin issued a report titled "A Call to Americans of Goodwill." The manifesto, which had so far only been approved by Andrew Young, clearly outlined a set of demands that the poor should take to Congress. The economic bill of rights called for Congress to recommit the government to the Full Employment Act of 1946 and to repeal the restrictions that limited the number of families that could receive welfare assistance. Rustin also called for President Johnson to grant several demands, including the incorporation of food distribution programs in severely affected areas; expansion of the food stamp program; assistance for poor farmers in establishing cooperatives; incorporation of programs to assist poor mothers and children in rural areas, and a halt of the US Department of Agriculture's discriminatory practices, which prevented Blacks from receiving just benefits.

Williams, according to newspaper columnist Ethel Payne, "had publicly denounced Rustin and claimed that he was the real boss of the show." Co-workers were unsure who had the report and were happy that he had neglected to address the issues surrounding Vietnam and had not clearly identified the demands of other minorities. Rustin also failed to mention some of the proposals recommended by the Kerner Commission that had been released in February 1968, just weeks before King's death in Memphis. Williams referred to Rustin's demands as "a bunch of jazz and nonsense." Rustin resigned after Abernathy failed to give him an unqualified endorsement and latitude to direct the campaign. Abernathy appointed Sterling Tucker, executive director of the Washington Urban League, to replace Rustin and assume the directorship of the June 19 mass protest.[62]

The Poor People's Campaign of 1968 came to a pitiful end on June 24. The local Washington police cleared the Mall by the Lincoln Memorial and seized the mule train that Williams had secured. The National Parks Service asked for payment of a bill totaling seventy-one thousand dollars to cover the costs associated with managing the grounds for the previous four weeks. Andrew Young appeared to rejoice that the whole ordeal was over. He said, "Whoever cleared us out may have done us a favor." In the end, the Poor People's Campaign was a failure. The absence of King's steady hand at the helm was compounded by Abernathy's utter inability to lead effectively and to manage the "team of rivals"—SCLC's lieutenants—as his predecessor had before him. Williams, Bevel, and Jackson were, unable at best or unwilling at worst to be controlled by anyone but Dr. King. Egos, personal agendas, and the awesome burden of trying to lead in King's place took a heavy toll. SCLC was unable to force the federal government into making any meaningful compromises that would significantly address the plight of the poor. The executive and legislative branches virtually ignored demands. King had been silenced, and his lieutenants would be unable to mobilize the masses as in previous campaigns.[63]

Williams was a loyal lieutenant to Martin Luther King Jr. and was willing to lead dangerous demonstrations without regard to his own personal safety. He proudly wore the badge of King's "Kamikaze." The most dangerous and effective protests from 1964 through 1968 had been organized and led by Hosea Williams. His leadership in St. Augustine, Selma, and Mississippi was a testament to his willingness to die for the cause, to a degree surpassed only by Martin Luther King Jr. These experiences would guide Williams for the rest of his life as he entered the world of local and state politics. Most important, although Williams had, at times, grappled with poverty and dislocation, King's assassination in Memphis was the transformative episode that had the most impact in thrusting him into a leadership position, which he often occupied alone, in a full-frontal assault on poverty in America.

EIGHT

The Movement Continues, 1968–1974

1968 was a year of revolution that was characterized by rebellion against the policies, politics, and people that had hitherto guided America since the end of World War II. Mark Kurlansky, in *1968: The Year That Rocked the World*, suggested that 1968 represented "a spontaneous combustion of rebellious spirits." William Chafe, in *The Unfinished Journey: America Since World War II*, put it succinctly: "1968 witnessed a cresting of forces committed to social change that had been building since the 1950s." These forces to which Chafe referred were the ideals espoused by the liberal consensus. The core maxims of the liberal consensus are summed up squarely by Godfrey Hodgson in his analysis of twentieth-century liberalism in *America in Our Time: From World War II to Nixon—What Happened and Why*. He posited that the bedrock of the foundation of the consensus consisted of the following fundamental ideas: Unlike communism, American capitalism is democratic, and it improves the economic conditions in society, which consequently advances social causes; all interests are synchronized and inseparably linked together. There is no longer a clear demarcation in society, because the working class benefits from the system of free enterprise; the biggest potential threat to this social utopia is the spread of communism; and the United States is the true harbinger of democracy and must ensure that the rest of the world is made safe for the cultivation of republicanism. By 1968, the widespread agreement with this liberal ideology among northern liberals, the universities, organized labor, the churches and synagogues, the federal bureaucracy, and the business sector had finally fragmented and crumbled under the unbearable weight of poverty, racism, and the Vietnam War. This troubling trifecta, amplified and made available to the world via mass media, forced liberals to accept the fact that their sanguinity insofar as their recommendations for eradicating social problems through capitalism and democracy had been found wanting. In a sense, America was forced to look at herself in the mirror and accept the grim picture that her experiment in liberalism had failed. Failures also give rise to readjustment, and Hosea Williams and the SCLC continued to figure out what appeared to be the insoluble paradox of poverty and racism in the United States.[1]

Williams and the SCLC were obviously forced to readjust after the assassination of their unquestioned leader, Martin Luther King Jr. Abernathy, King's closest ally in the modern Black freedom struggle, had been elected president to succeed the fallen leader. Abernathy was no Martin Luther King, however. The former appeared to lack the latter's charisma, eloquence, and ability to, in the words of Williams's oldest daughter, Barbara Williams Emerson, "tame the wild horses." The "wild horses," including Hosea Williams, Andrew Young, Jesse Jackson, and James Bevel, felt that no one had earned the right to lead them as had King. The impact of the egos and eccentricity relative to Abernathy's ability to lead cannot be understated. Williams maintained that each of the top lieutenants could have been worthy successors to King with the right support staff. "If the rest of them would support that person," Williams said, "just like all of us had supported King, Abernathy would have ended up just as great a leader as Martin." Because Abernathy was forced to lead without the executive staff's vitally important support, the new president's tenure was virtually stillborn. "I think Abernathy was a great leader, but I still think the executive staff deserted him soon after King was buried . . . he was the captain of a ship without the crew," said Williams—who, on the contrary, worked well and very closely with Abernathy.[2]

The working and personal relationships of Williams and Abernathy were strengthened by their similar backgrounds before aligning with Martin Luther King and the SCLC. "I was always closer to Ralph than I was to King. I believe Ralph had a more genuine appreciation for me than King," said Williams. His mutual affinity with Abernathy was likely the result of their shared experiences. Both men, born in 1926, were reared in rural southern towns but lived in relative comfort. Williams, the older by only two months, came of age in Attapulgus, Georgia, two hundred forty miles northwest of Abernathy's hometown in Linden, Alabama. Next to the geographical similarities, Willliams and Abernathy were influenced primarily by strong, entrepreneurial male figures who were widely respected in their communities. Hosea Williams's grandfather, Turner Williams, owned a barbershop and a café and was the Bainbridge bootlegger. Turner Williams's financial independence allowed him to own nearly two hundred acres of land in South Georgia. Abernathy's father, Willie L. Abernathy, was also self-sufficient. He was a farmer who had worked hard enough to have the deed to five hundred acres of land. Abernathy described his father as being "stern," honest, and "the most dominant figure" in his life.[3]

Williams and Abernathy also shared in common their service in World War II and their postwar academic experiences. Both men began their enlistment with physicals at Fort Benning just outside Columbus, Georgia. Abernathy joined in 1944, shortly after his eighteenth birthday. Williams also enlisted in 1944, a few months after he turned eighteen. Both men spent time in Germany near the end of the war. Williams, a private in the 41st Infantry, was almost killed on February 5, 1945, when he and twelve other Black soldiers attempted to rescue British service members in Einbeck, Germany. All of Williams's fellow platoon members were killed. Abernathy, however, never had to engage in lethal or physical combat with the Axis powers. Both men also dealt with a near-fatal bout of rheumatic fever during their enlistment. Williams's illness hospitalized him for nearly four months in 1944, and Abernathy's earned him an honorable discharge in 1945. Williams and Abernathy shared yet another experience in common: education. Both men earned undergraduate and graduate degrees at historically Black colleges and universities (HBCUs) after returning home from war-torn Europe. Williams earned a bachelor of science degree and a master of science degree in chemistry from Morris Brown College and Atlanta University in 1951 and 1952, respectively. Abernathy, on the other hand, was awarded a bachelor of science degree in mathematics in 1950 from Alabama State College in Montgomery, Alabama, and a master of science degree from Atlanta University in 1951. With these similarities in background, it is little wonder why Williams and Abernathy could relate to each other as co-laborers in the fight to secure equitable treatment for Blacks.[4]

Williams and Abernathy worked together in the SCLC's first major campaign of 1969, which targeted wage inequality and the demand for union recognition in Charleston, South Carolina. Labor historians Leon Fink and Brian Greenberg argued that the Charleston movement was "one of the South's most disruptive and bitter labor confrontations since the 1930s." Charleston was reminiscent of Savannah, Georgia, and St. Augustine, Florida: cities where Williams lead major civil rights crusades in the early and middle 1960s. Charleston was steeped in history that dated back to the colonial area. Founded in 1670, the city was preparing to celebrate its tricentennial when Dave Livingston, a white progressive, sought SCLC's assistance in March after twelve South Carolina Medical College Hospital workers were fired for attempting to organize a labor union. South Carolina was a staunch anti-union state, and because state law prohibited an agent of the state or a municipal government from negotiating with a union—in this case, Local 1199B—blue-collar hospital workers basically had no leverage in negotiating their wage of $1.30 per hour. Nearly four hundred workers began striking on March 20, 1969, in protest to have their union recognized by the city and state governments.[5]

Williams was not an architect of the campaign in Charleston, as his energy was being expended in preparing for the second phase of the Poor People's Campaign in Alabama and Mississippi, which had been launched on the first anniversary of King's assassination. "I was not for coming to Charleston," said Williams. "It was dealing with too small of an item—the integration of hospitals. It was co-opted by the unions and the unions were no longer our friends." However, Abernathy sought his assistance in addressing a mass rally at the Memorial Baptist Church, because the movement for union recognition had not reached the desired results. "Hosea had come to Charleston because he had heard I was in trouble. Loyal as always, he wanted to share in the danger," Abernathy recalled. Williams was never asked to have a major role in the city's labor strike, which consisted mostly of Black women. "I was only supposed to come up there and make a speech and depart," said Williams. Evidently, his reputation as the bombastic "bull in a china closet" had preceded him. He said of his arrival, "I got off the plane and I saw all the state troopers and the militiamen. . . . They had scared the people to death about me." Williams met with Abernathy before the mass meeting and convinced his colleague that the demonstrations should continue at night, although Robert McNair, the governor of South Carolina, had imposed a curfew that banned demonstrations from 9:00 PM to 5:00 AM. Williams eventually addressed the crowd at Memorial Baptist Church before the march and had "set the folks on fire" in the process. Abernathy, who had previously chosen not to march that night, changed his mind and marched with Williams into the streets of Charleston. Both men, along with fifty-eight demonstrators, had been beaten, but the two SCLC activists were the only ones placed in the city jail and charged with a felony for inciting a riot.[6]

Williams and Abernathy were committed to fasting together while they were locked up for nearly three weeks. Both men had their resolve and commitment to the striking workers tested after only a few days in the local jail on a felonious charge. Bail was set for the two at fifty thousand dollars each. "We could no more get one hundred thousand than we could get one million dollars," Abernathy grimly said. Their lawyers approached the quagmire as if the charges were without foundation. The attorney first conferred with Williams, who was occupying a cell next to his old friend, and informed the old warhorse that the ranking legal officer in the Ninth Judicial Circuit had reduced the bail by forty-five thousand dollars—making the task of bailing him out of jail significantly easier. Williams initially accepted the offer until Abernathy impressed upon him and the lawyers that they should not pay a fine, because no crime had been committed. "I think we should stick to our guns," said Abernathy. Williams, forever loyal to his leader and the causes for which he valued, confirmed his willingness to stay in jail after Abernathy convinced him of the righteousness of the campaign. "Mr. President," said Williams from the adjacent cell, "are you going to stay in?" Abernathy's response was certain: Yes! "We said we were going to fast and die until that strike ended," recalled Williams. The strike finally ended on June 24, after the American Federation of Labor and Congress of Industrial Organizations (AFL-CIO) lent their influential support to the striking workers by threatening to shut down Charleston's harbors. The city considered this threat to be credible, and, if carried out, it could prove disastrous in light of the fact that the city's port had generated close to five hundred million dollars through a combination of import and export shipping the following year. On June 24, 1969, Director of Personnel Charles Fennessey issued a statement declaring that the South Carolina General Assembly had passed a blanketed minimum wage general appropriations bill that made it unlawful to pay any state employee less than $1.60 per hour. The state couched the legislation in a pay raise that affected all state employees, so that it could not be seen as bowing to the workers' demands. As part of the compromise, the state also agreed to create a systematic grievance procedure to address future concerns relative to pay equity. Williams and Abernathy were bailed out shortly after the settlement was announced. The campaign, according to Williams, could only be viewed as a minimal success, because its impact was only local—unlike the movements in Birmingham, St. Augustine, and Selma.[7]

Williams's unyielding assault against poverty and economic inequality, which he believed was the direct result of the federal government's alienation of the impoverished, continued in the next month as the National Aeronautical Space Association (NASA) was preparing to launch a manned spacecraft to the moon. President John F. Kennedy formally announced his vision for the United States to place a man on the moon on May 25, 1961, beginning what historian Ralph Martin identified as the "real birth" of the country's unsleeping devotion to conquer space. NASA's budget the next year was a whopping $1.7 billion dollars, with more than one-third of the funds being devoted to manned space programs. The following year, the space program's budget was increased to $3.7 billion dollars. By the time astronauts Neil Armstrong and Edwin "Buzz" Aldrin prepared for their epic lunar launch on July 15, 1969, the federal government had spent an estimated twenty-four billion dollars on the space program—an absurdity to Hosea Williams, who was playing a crucial role in the second edition of the Poor People's Campaign. In protest, Williams secured a train of mules from Georgia—the forlorn symbol of the poor—and rallied twenty-five families from twenty-five US Congressional districts to participate in "Moon Hunger" demonstrations at Cape Kennedy during the firing of Apollo 11. Lilly Belle Holt and her nine children were one such family for whom Williams spoke. "This woman," he said, "gets $82 a month and lives in a one-room shack" in Social Circle, Georgia. "This demonstration," he continued, "was not in protest of America's ability to explore outer space, but was to dramatize our government's ability to choose priorities." Williams believed that the United States's willingness to perpetuate war abroad and poverty at home was, in large measure, the fault of the legislative branch. The demonstrations at Cape Kennedy "dramatized the inequity in Congress' appropriation to put a man on the moon in comparison to keeping him alive or allowing him to survive on earth," Williams said. Although Williams and the twenty-five impoverished families were disruptive and kept attention on the poor during one of the man's greatest feats, no one was arrested or beaten. Abernathy and the SCLC made the lunar launch and the protests against the fiscal appropriations for the project a crucial component of the organization's convention the following month in Charleston, South Carolina.[8]

Williams was still serving two critical functions within the SCLC during the summer of 1969. He was spearheading the second Poor People's Campaign and leading the organization's Department of Voter Registration and Political Education. He outlined the previous year's accomplishments and his vision to improve the plight of the poor through effective political participation in his annual report to the Board of Directors at the SCLC's Twelfth Annual Convention in Charleston, South Carolina. Beginning almost one month after the protest at Cape Kennedy, the convention's theme was "Billions for the Moon and Pennies for the Poor." Since the last convention, Williams had dramatized the plight of the poor at the Democratic National Convention in Chicago (with a mule train). He had devoted his department's time and resources to assisting the Small Business Administration's National Black Advisory Council to create "Project Own" a government program that increased federally guaranteed loans to poor Blacks from twelve hundred to ten thousand loans in less than one year. He led a "Poor People's Land Grab Plant In" in Mississippi, a demonstration that entailed hundreds of poor people marching across the state and into Sunflower County to the farm of rabid racist US Senator James Eastland in an attempt to impress upon him that the impoverished should be given fertile land to farm, especially the families on his planation who were receiving welfare checks of less than sixty dollars per month. Last, Williams and the Department of Voter Registration and Political Education organized statewide marches in Georgia and delivered a "Poor People's Manifesto" to segregationist Governor Lester Maddox, demanding an end to "poverty, illiteracy and disease." Williams did not spare the "Wild Man from Sugar Creek": He also marched on the home of the powerful U S Senator Richard B. Russell, whom he described as the "supporter of all anti-movement forces" and the ultimate symbol of corruption in politics because he endorsed billions of dollars to what Williams called the "fabulously rich" in the form of federal subsidies. In spite of what he believed to be government corruption, Williams still believed that power in politics would solve the problems of the poor.[9]

Williams wrote in his report to the board at the twelfth convention that "The real issue of the poor [was] one of REPRESENTATIVE GOVERNMENT." He maintained that the civil rights and voting bills were landmark legislative enactments, but the conditions of the poor had "hardly changed." Although Blacks could now eat at lunch counters and attend integrated schools on a token basis, the withholding patronage campaigns and voter registration drives throughout the country were failing to meet the overall objective of improving the lots of society's most vulnerable: poor Blacks. "The poor," Williams posited, "are still left out of the mainstream of decision making in almost every walk of life." He pointed out that there were a little more than seventy southern counties in the South where Blacks made up at least fifty percent of the population. Williams calculated that at least one thousand six hundred ninety-five progressive Black officials within the seventy-county sample had to be elected to make a meaningful difference in the southern political sphere. However, there were only three hundred sixty Black elected officials throughout the South, with many of the officeholders coming from urban metropolises: for example, Atlanta, Augusta, and Savannah, Georgia, and Charleston, South Carolina. Although voter registration drives during the previous seven years had been "good," Williams wrote, he and the SCLC had missed the mark because they failed to realize that "To register a potential voter without politically educating him meant that we should have spent as much work and money getting him to vote as we did in motivating him to register." He continued, "a politically educated potential voter will not only get himself registered, but he will vote." More pointedly and important in galvanizing strength and support to eradicate poverty, the politically educated voter will vote, Williams believed, "according to issues rather than emotions." Williams believed that he had found the answer in the formula that he had used in Greene County, Alabama.[10]

Williams believed that Greene County, Alabama, could serve as a template for Blacks to follow if they wished to gain electoral power. Before 1965, fewer than fifty Blacks were registered. By 1966, a strong voter registration campaign had increased the Black voter rolls to three thousand eight hundred seventy-five. In that year, eight Blacks ran for elective office, but only one Black candidate, the Rev. Peter Kirskey, was successful in his bid for a seat on the Greene County Board of Education. The Black candidates had lost because of political chicanery. "On election day in 1966, a lot of plantation owners," Williams recalled, "loaded up their farm hands and took them to another county to work for friends so they could not vote." Two years later, seven Black candidates ran for office but were unlawfully left of the ballots for the school board and county commission by Probate Judge J. Dennis Herndon because they were candidates from the National Democratic Party of Alabama (NDPA)—a party that staunchly opposed segregation and the governorship of George C. Wallace. The candidates filed suit, and the US Supreme Court ordered a special election for July 29, 1969. At the time of the special election, Blacks in the county had outnumbered whites ten thousand to three thousand but were, according to Williams, "totally controlled by the white masters." Local Blacks called Williams and sixteen of his disciples into the county ten days before the election to register and educate the potential Black voters. During a conversation with Martin Waldron of the *New York Times,* while dressed in a checkered jumpsuit and donning an afro and full beard shortly before the election, he told the reporter that "We have to win this election, for it will decide the fate of Black people's ability to participate in politics." Williams's method of political education in Greene County for this election revolved around one issue: jobs. Blacks wanted to work but feared economic reprisals from whites. Williams kept telling local Blacks that "If we get the county commission, there will be jobs for everybody. . . . There will be a flow of federal funds and industry into this county."[11]

On July 30, the persistent voting registration drives and political education paid off. Two Black candidates, Robert Hines and J. A. Posey, joined Reverend Kirksey on the Greene County School Board. Harry Means, Frenchie Burton, and Vassie Knotts won election to the Greene County Board of Commissioners. This election marked the first time in the county's one-hundred-fifty-three-year history, which predated the era of Reconstruction, that Blacks were in control of county politics. The election was historic, transcending the bounds of Alabama. Greene County was the only county in the South that was controlled by Blacks. After the election results had been certified by county election officials under the watchful eyes of Department of Justice staff members, Williams gave the crowd a "soul power salute"—a clinched fist in the air with his arm at a slight bend. He had earned the right to gloat, especially since local journalists and candidates credited him and the SCLC for educating and motivating the Black masses in the county to register and vote, notwithstanding physical intimidation and the threat of economic reprisals. Obviously, this success in Alabama would influence his strategy to empower Blacks politically in the future.[12]

Since 1964, Hosea Williams had not only been a part of but also spearheaded some of the SCLC's greatest triumphs as the organization fought to secure civil and political rights for Blacks. However, like some of his colleagues, the battles had taken their tolls on him mentally and physically. By January 1970, Williams was forty-six years old and a seventeen-year veteran of the civil rights struggle. Andrew Young succinctly summed up the condition of SCLC and its workers in a January interview: "We're not healthy . . . we're an exhausted organization right now . . . the toll of a decade or more for some of us in the movement is beginning to tell on all of us in terms of physical health." Williams was no exception. Full bearded and weighing nearly two hundred forty pounds, he had been battling bronchial pneumonia since November 1969. Young suggested that the organization would refrain from launching any major campaigns on the scale of Birmingham or Selma until 1971 and squarely focus in the interim on voter registration and political education. This strategy would not lighten Williams's load, because he still directed the department that oversaw a portion of the organization's programmatic thrust.[13]

Williams's commitment to the poor and disinherited remained relentless in spite of the heavy demands on his schedule as an activist, father, and husband. In spite of the rhetoric, he never publicly embraced the notion that Blacks should be allowed special entitlements. He plainly made his point when he served as the keynote speaker at the beginning of the National Association for Community Development (NACD) on April 24, 1970, in Memphis, Tennessee. The NACD, founded in 1965, provided educational services as well as information and technical assistance for the nation's community developers. Williams told approximately five hundred people from across the country that the most effective way to eradicate poverty among Blacks was to stop expecting help from the federal government. "If you really do something," he told the audience, "you're going to get tired." The federal programs, in his opinion, did not lead to any meaningful changes for the poor, because that was not the intent. "The problem with all federal programs is that they were never designed to help poor people," said Williams. The speech in Memphis was important, because this was the first time he publicly embraced the words "Black Power." He maintained that "what we're really talking about in organizing is power, Black Power." To steer clear of accusations that he was wedded to the former Carmichael faction of SNCC, Williams followed up his statement with saying that "If the poor whites ever get their heads together, they'll be talking poor white power." Forever wedded to the belief that power is the byproduct of politically educating the people on society's lower economic rungs, he encouraged people to start organizing at the bottom, as those on the top would be forced to recognize the united voice of the masses. Williams hoped to motivate the attendees to organize locally by presenting them with a grim reality: "The United States may be a rich man's heaven, but it is certainly a poor man's hell."[14]

Williams was not averse to using his fiery preaching and gift for applying calculated disruptive tactics as tools to dramatize the plight of the poor in some of America's cities that were known as symbols of the country's wealth. On January 23, 1971, he led a delegation of SCLC staffers into Daytona Beach, Florida. Williams was summoned to what one editor described as a "racially divided seaside resort town" to organize laborers who were earning as little as thirty dollars per week. Local Black leaders had been requesting for Williams and the SCLC to come to the city for at least two years before January 1971. The city fathers had been unwilling to address the wage issue because they had not been effectively pressured. "We have been waiting for the local power structure to move in that direction, but the situation is getting worse," Williams told a reporter. Although Williams was part of the advance team that was assigned to raise awareness in the city before Abernathy and other staffers from the negotiation team, he vowed to "stay a week, a month, a year, whatever it takes." The city and state officials raised the wage by fifteen percent as a result of the SCLC's efforts. After the Daytona protest, Williams left the Sunshine State and began preparing for demonstrations in New York around the time of the third anniversary of Dr. King's assassination.[15]

Williams did not hesitate to cite hypocrisy within the religious establishment insofar as its treatment of the poor was concerned. As part of SCLC's first major campaign since 1968, Williams, wearing African beads around his neck while dressed in blue jeans and a vest, was arrested on April 4, 1971, after he charged into the St. Patrick's Cathedral in New York City during the 10:00 AM Palm Sunday service as part of the SCLC's "March Against Repression," which would be a weeklong demonstration against wealth and big business. As Bishop Joseph Flannelly led a procession of junior clerics to bless a stack of palms, Williams, alone, while twelve of his disciples stood outside, stopped the flow of the service when he told the bishop that he was "coming to him as Christ came on Palm Sunday." The congregation, visibly disturbed by Williams's intrusion into their exclusive Fifth Avenue establishment, was aghast. Unmoved, Williams continued his ecclesiastical indictment: "How could the church continue to preach the Gospel of Jesus and continue to have holdings in big companies that oppress people in South Africa?" he growled. He was bailed out after spending a few hours in jail, allowing him to lead a mule-train march on Wall Street—the financial capital of the world.[16]

Williams's native Georgia was not spared when he entered Columbus, Georgia, on June 19 while on leave from his paid position as the SCLC's national program director. He led approximately five hundred residents of the city in a fifteen-block march from the Black YMCA and ended at a mass rally at the Muscogee County Courthouse in protest of the firing of thirteen Black policemen, who were terminated for picketing police headquarters in uniform in May for equal treatment relative to pay and promotion using the same criteria as for white officers. City officials claimed that policy prohibited officers from picketing any establishment while in uniform after the mass firing. Although thirty-eight Black policemen remained on the force, none had ascended to the ranks of captain or lieutenant, and only one Black policeman reached the rank of sergeant. After speaking for more than an hour in the hot Columbus sun, Williams made five demands to the local leaders on the threat of a boycott of the city: reinstatement of all officers; the promotion of all thirty Black policemen who remained on the force; the appointment of a biracial "citizen's police review board"; the desegregation of all jail facilities; and an increase in the representation of Black officers by thirty-five percent. Protesters set at least nineteen fires the next day, Sunday, June 20. An abandoned warehouse, a liquor store, and a grocery store were severely damaged. Major J. R. Allen blamed Williams: "The leader of this band of invaders sowed seeds of hate, collected his contributions and left town." Major Allen was not the only government official to castigate the hellraising Williams.[17]

Governor Jimmy Carter condemned Williams and attempted to brand him as the responsible party for the unrest. Carter's seething frustration with Williams was a carryover from Williams calling him a "racist" from the steps of the State Capitol on June 5, warning that if Carter did not recalibrate his strategic priorities for Black Georgians by "mending his racist ways in about two weeks," he would lead a mass protest in Atlanta. Williams and members of the Black Leadership Coalition met almost two weeks later in the governor's office, after a Black male inmate was found hanging in his cell in Macon County. Williams demanded that Carter suspend the sheriff, but Carter was not empowered to do by statute. Carter rebuffed. Williams insisted during the thirty-minute meeting that Blacks enjoyed better conditions in the state during rabid segregationist Lester Maddox's tenure as governor. He also accused Carter of failing to address the needs of Black citizens because of his laser focus on his goal of rapid mass transit in Atlanta. By the time of the Columbus incident, Carter had already formed an impression of the headstrong Williams. Sitting behind his desk and a handcrafted Georgia state flag with the Confederate battle emblem, Gov. Carter stated, "I personally do not think that Hosea Williams is seeking a solution. He's not trying to establish communications between the blacks and the whites. I think he is trying to get publicity for himself and to create dissension." A local unnamed white minister summed it up this way: "I don't know if it is intentional or not, but that man Williams carries the germs of violence and disorder with him."[18]

There is little doubt that Williams sought publicity to dramatize the plight for Blacks in Columbus, Georgia. As he had shown many times before 1971, white segregationists in power did not automatically cede to the demands of Blacks, who, in their perception, did not deserve equal protection and opportunity. Asserting that Williams was spreading hate and purposely retarding progress with race relations is not accurate. He did not encourage arsonous activity or violence in any form. He continued to espouse the nonviolent teachings of Martin Luther King and believed that this technique would move the community closer to the goal of equality. "There is one way you can lose this," Williams advised a group that was picketing downtown, "and that is get violent. That's just what they want." Although the economic boycott of white businesses was met with moderate success because of minimal participation, Blacks in Columbus were no longer willing to use a different method to address their grievances. An older Black woman said, "I'm glad to see blacks get some spunk in them around here."[19]

Williams's public references to heaven and hell as reward and punishment during his speech in New York in April may have had to do with his mounting desire to be formally recognized as a minister. He had long been referred to as "Reverend" while working with the clergy-dominated SCLC. Each of King's closest lieutenants, Abernathy, Young, Jackson, and Bevel, had all been ordained. Evidence suggests that Williams was not entering the Christian ministry for self-promotion. He apparently heard the "call" from God to preach the Word. Although Williams had defected to the Presbyterian denomination in the early 1960s, he returned to the Baptist church, the denomination of his childhood, after he returned in 1970 from the SCLC-sponsored Goodwill Brotherhood Tour, during which he visited Africa, South Vietnam, India, Japan, and the People's Republic of China. On the morning of December 12, 1971, Williams preached his trial sermon at the 10:45 AM service at West Hunter Street Baptist Church, the house of worship that had been pastored by his friend and SCLC colleague, Ralph Abernathy, since 1961. The scriptural basis for his message, "Is Christianity too Important to be Left in the Hands of Today's Christians?" came from the Old Testament book of Genesis, twenty-first chapter, eighteenth verse: "Arise, lift up the lad and hold him fast with your hand; and I will make him a great nation." Williams's sermon was heavily influenced by his trip to communist China. "I went to China as a Christian," said Williams to the congregation, "and I have returned a better Christian. Recognizing the religious hypocrisy of America, it makes me wonder whether or not God has decided to entrust the regeneration of man into the hands of nonbelievers." Williams also incorporated his compassion for, and the church's distancing of, the poor. He chided the religious establishments for turning their backs on the poor—the very people among whom Jesus dwelled.[20]

Invitations for the forty-six-year-old Hosea Williams to speak as minister and SCLC's national program director increased in 1972. Most of the invitations he received were for him to speak in churches and universities in the North and Midwest. Williams, accompanied by his wife, Juanita, attended the Ecumenical Conference in Kansas City, Missouri, from January 12 to January 16. On January 30, he was in Louisville, Kentucky, to speak at the Community Methodist Church. The week of February 7 to February 10 was busy, as his schedule required him to speak at four universities. Williams spoke about his world trip at the University of Minnesota on the February 7th. On the following day, he was in Columbia, South Carolina, speaking on the four-year anniversary of the Orangeburg, South Carolina, massacre. He caught a late flight and arrived in Thibodeaux, Louisiana, to lecture about his world travels at Nicholas State University. He finished the week in Clarksville, Tennessee, at Austin Peay College with a lecture titled "Problems of Black People in Our Society." One week later, Williams spoke at the University of Evansville in Evansville, Indiana. On February 18, Williams spoke at Washington, DC's Catholic University at the request of Robert Perry.[21]

By the middle of 1972, Williams was widely perceived to be the chief avenger of the poor. His visibility as a civil rights activist and former lieutenant to the late Martin Luther King Jr. gave Williams a certain degree of respectability with the Black working class. Besides his name and face recognition, he had mastered the ability to communicate at a level at which society's most oppressed could easily relate, regardless of exposure and education. These factors were evidence to him that he should run for public office. Williams decided to run for one of Georgia's seats in the US Senate after the death of longtime senator and powerful chairman of that body's Armed Services Committee, Richard B. Russell. Two years before Williams decided to make his bid for the seat in early 1972, approximately 3.3 million out of almost 5 million voting-age Blacks were registered to vote. Because of the increase in registered Black voters as a result of the Voting Rights Act of 1965, 1,200 Blacks were serving as elected officials throughout the United States. Of this number, 528 Blacks had been elected to public office in eleven southern states. Nineteen Black officials were serving as mayors, and thirty-one Blacks were holding seats in state legislatures. Williams was facing a formidable foe in the senate race's perceived frontrunner, Georgia State Representative Sam Nunn.[22]

Williams knew from the beginning of the Senate campaign that the prospects of defeating Nunn and other white candidates were not very good. However, he confidently argued that he "never ran in an election for an office to win that [he] did not win." Williams maintained that he ran in this campaign because apathy and fright still kept Blacks in Georgia from being actively involved in the political process. He said, "I ran as a means of education because in a lot of Georgia's cities and counties, even though federal legislation existed, blacks were afraid although the laws made it easier for them to participate." He campaigned in the cities as well as through Georgia's Black Belt—the (fifteen-county) rural region throughout the state that contained sixty-six percent of the Black population. He believed that it was essential for Black residents in this part of the state to take an active role in electoral politics because they could be a decisive factor in statewide elections, as all of the Black Belt counties contained a population where eligible Black voters approached fifty percent. He sensed that Blacks throughout Georgia had better jobs than in previous decades but were not making the best of the opportunities that he and his co-laborers in the modern Black freedom struggle had fought to secure. "I wanted to prove to them that the opportunity was there and that they needed to seize the chance. . . . And that was one of the reasons why I ran," said Williams. He also believed that his reputation as a fiery agitator and feared civil rights activist would force other candidates to, at the very least, "discuss issues relevant to Black people," conversations that they would otherwise have ignored.[23]

Hosea had his hand on the pulse of the southern electorate and knew from his experiences in organizing throughout the Deep South that the Black vote, particularly in Georgia, represented untapped electoral power. By February 1972, Georgia was leading the eleven-state southern bloc at the state level, with two senators and thirteen representatives. According to the Voter Education Project (VEP), eight hundred seventy-three Blacks were serving terms as elected public officials—an addition of three hundred forty-five since 1970. "The continued upswing in the total number of Blacks in public office over the past six years is an indication that blacks are beginning to acquire the kind of political sophistication which will enable them to begin to control their own destinies," said former SNCC Chairman and Director of the VEP John Lewis. However, Lewis shared Williams's sentiments relative to the number of Blacks who were steering clear of politics. "We must be aware, said Lewis, "that the number of blacks in office constitutes only a fraction of elected positions in the South." However, Williams was cautiously optimistic about Blacks making a meaningful difference in electoral politics in light of the fact that fifteen Black legislators, six county officers, thirty-one elected city officials, one judge, and ten school board members were serving the state in an elected capacity.[24]

Williams's balancing of his duties with the local SCLC while campaigning for the US Senate came at a time when the organization was grappling with the loss of two critical and recognized executive staffers. By July, Williams and Abernathy were King's only remaining lieutenants from the classical phase of the modern civil rights movement. Jesse Jackson, widely believed to be the most charismatic and dynamic aide to King, quit after a forced leave of absence in the midst of the board's inquiry into his unauthorized establishment of corporations under the SCLC. Referring to Jackson, Williams posited that he was impatient and had no respect for movement elders. "He destroyed himself because he lacked patience and had no respect for Ralph—for age . . . he refused to wait in the so-called line of opportunity," Williams said. Jackson, according to Williams, lost his chance to lead SCLC because "he destroyed himself by trying to crush those who had come before him." Joseph Lowery, chairman of the board and SCLC co-founder, suggested that Jackson's "personal ambition" kept him from following "organizational policy." Andrew Young was another SCLC defector. By spring of 1972, he was devoting most of his energies to what would ultimately become a successful bid for the US Congressional seat from Georgia's Fifth District. The departures of Jackson and Young appeared to give Williams unchallenged primacy within the organization, as his tenure at SCLC's epicenter was now second to Abernathy. However, he had to deal with Joseph Lowery, —the dictatorial chairman of the board whom Williams believed lacked the requisite battlefield experience to lead.[25]

Williams was determined to continue in his role as being a voice for the voiceless while campaigning for the US Senate in spite of being criticized by SCLC board members and other middle-class Blacks. In April, three months before the election primary, Williams led a series of demonstrations at southwest Atlanta's Holy Family Hospital to protest the facility's treatment of its employees in spite of the fact that affluent Blacks were employed by and benefited from its operations. The hospital had been established as an integrated facility in 1964 and was one of the first hospitals in the Deep South to allow Black and white physicians to labor for the infirmed as equals. Blacks constituted ninety percent of the staff, but the hospital administration was still white. Williams had originally decided to stay away from the labor dispute until his wife, Juanita, was injured in a car wreck and needed medical assistance. "I went over there to see my wife at that hospital, and those women came in and asked me to assist them because the white administration was treating them unfairly," he recalled. "I told them I could not be bothered. . . . And they started crying in that room and I gave in." On April 25, Williams; Rev. Joseph Boone, director of the Metro Summit Leadership Congress; Al McClure, director of the Atlanta NAACP; and Rev. Arthur Langford, assistant pastor of the Free for All Baptist Church, pitched a rented tent on the grounds of the Catholic-owned hospital. The four pledged to hold prayer vigils and live only on salt water until the hospital incorporated fair wages for its employees and rehired staffers who were wrongly terminated for attempting to form a union the previous month. Williams told a reporter for *The Atlanta Voice* that the vigil's purpose was to "cast the devil out of the devilish hospital administrators"; namely, the board of trustees and Lee Nichols, the facility's highest ranking officer. Williams stayed on the hospital grounds for seventeen days "without eating a mouthful," he claimed later. Andy Young, who was an influential voice on the Atlanta Community Commission and also campaigning for the Georgia's Fifth Congressional seat at the time, was brought in to broker a compromise between the two sides. On April 27, Lee Nichols fired shots into the tent, striking Langford and former SNCC staffer, Willie Ricks. Both men survived. Nichols was subsequently arrested. Within two months, the hospital granted all of the striking workers' demands: the reinstatement of the twelve registered and practical nurses with retroactive pay and fringe benefits; also, the hospital workers were allowed to form a recognized union. Williams's leadership in this strike did not sit well with the Black power structure in the city.[26]

Williams's work as chief avenger of the poor in Atlanta was frowned upon by national SCLC Board Chairman Joseph Lowery and other Black community leaders who believed that direct-action techniques, especially against companies with support from Atlanta's conservative Black leadership, were not only archaic but unnecessary. As a result of the discord between Williams and Lowery, by June 1972, Williams was in the middle of a board-imposed, nine-month leave of absence from his duties as SCLC's national program director and was unsure whether he would be permanently relieved of his duties. At the time, he was also founding president of the SCLC's affiliate in DeKalb County, Georgia, a perceived threat to the national organizational base. The burly and combative warhorse continued to fight on behalf of Black workers in spite of Lowery. Williams assumed the leadership in protesting against Citizen's Trust Bank, the largest Black-operated financial institution in Atlanta, after the bank fired five Black women for conducting a "sick-out." The women initiated the protest after their requests for raises were denied without cause. Williams spearheaded a series of pickets at the bank in downtown Atlanta after Lowery forbade SCLC from becoming involved in the demonstration. Lowery then moved to begin an Atlanta chapter of the organization to usurp Williams's chapter. The national board chairman had also directed an employee to empty Williams's office and transfer his assistant, Terrie Randolph, to another department within SCLC. When asked about the changes, Williams stated, "They moved my things out of my office because they said they needed space, but I know that's not true. . . . If there's anything brewing now it's nothing but petty jealousy."[27]

Williams, while in the midst of serious internal contention at SCLC, was also still campaigning in advance of the August 8 Democratic primary for Georgia's US Senate seat and received a favorable endorsement from Maynard Jackson, Atlanta's first Black Vice Mayor. Jackson, who would become the first Black mayor of a major Deep South city the following year, wrote Williams a very complimentary letter that was published in *The Atlanta Voice*:

> It gives me a great deal of pleasure to endorse your candidacy because your candidacy represents a clear alternative to the Wallacism that is sweeping our home state. Your candidacy represents a chance for change. Hundreds of thousands of Georgians can now share the hope of being represented by someone who will fight for the human rights of the little man, the forgotten man.

In spite of this gracious endorsement, Williams came in fourth place in the Democratic primary. Although Williams lost his bid for the US Senate, it was clear that his work in pushing voter registration and political education campaigns throughout the South led to changes in Georgia. Andrew Young, his former SCLC colleague, defeated a white alderman, Wyche Fowler, in the former's second bid for the seat. Young captured 60.3 percent of the thirty-five thousand nine hundred twenty-six votes that were cast. Three months later, Young defeated Republican challenger Rodney Cook in the general election, becoming Georgia's first Black US Representative since Jefferson Franklin Long's election.[28]

Williams continued to work on behalf of Atlanta's underclass after he was defeated in his quest to be Georgia's first Black senator. On August 18, Williams organized and encouraged approximately eight hundred workers, many of whom were Black, to initiate a work stoppage at the Mead Packaging Company, an affiliate of the Mead Corporation, to force the organization to grant the demonstrators three specific demands: the right to approve all new company rules; a safety committee chosen by the workers who would have the authority to shut down worksites that pose a safety threat; and an agreement from the Mead Corporation to give a considerable amount of its minor construction jobs to Blacks and an immediate pay raise of fifty cents per hour. At the time of the strike, the average hourly pay rate was $3.60. The lowest hourly pay rate was $2.85, and the highest was $4.30. The strike appeared to be breaking the company's will to resist the demands. Officials at Mead maintained that the strike was "substantially [affecting] operations." Hence, company lawyers filed suit in the Fulton County court to lessen the impact of the protest, especially as some demonstrators issued threats and took pictures of the license plates of workers who desired to work under the current conditions. Judge Claude Shaw issued an injunction that only permitted two persons to picket outside the company's entrance on Marietta Street. Responding to the order, Williams loudly proclaimed, "I feel that the orders violate my constitutional rights and if necessary, I will go to jail. We will continue to picket." Leo Banatar, vice president and general manager of the plant in Atlanta, was adamant that the company refused to negotiate with Williams because the old warhorse was not a part of a recognized union.[29]

Williams's modus operandi mandated that he disobey Judge Shaw's ruling. He was arrested on Friday, September 15, on charges for inciting a riot, simple assault, and simple battery on an officer, R. T. Bradfield. He bonded out on September 18 and was wearing a sign that read "Metro-Dekalb SCLC Fights Back." Williams maintained that the charges were "trumped up." He told newsmen on the Fulton County jail steps that "I was illegally jailed and illegally held because I had committed no crime and will pay no fine. If justly convicted, I am prepared to spend every day in prison." Williams suspected that members of Atlanta's power structure, including the Executive Committee of the Chamber of Commerce and *The Atlanta Constitution*, were responsible for encouraging his arrest. He said that he signed his bond only after one of his top aides, Tyrone Brooks, admitted that the job of organizing the workers would not be possible if Williams was in jail. "It was the first time I've ever demanded anything of him, but we need him to help mobilize the people, said Brooks."[30]

Williams continued to organize and motivate the striking workers in the midst of negotiations. By September 30, both sides were moving closer to an amicable compromise. At a meeting on the night of September 26, the workers turned down a company offer to hire approximately one hundred workers who had been suspended or terminated as a result of their participation in demonstrations against the organization. The company also rejected the employees' demands relative to a better pension plan and for sick leave, a better insurance plan, and retroactive pay for all workers who played a role in the protests. Mead and the employees debated over the points of contention for the next two weeks. On October 17, Williams held a press conference at the Wheat Street Baptist Church Education Building, announcing the signing of a covenant with the Caucus of Rank and File Workers of the Mead Corporation. "We did not gain everything sought, but we gained a whole lot more than we had when we began," said Williams. He gave Mead six months to address and implement the forty-two demands presented to them by the Mead Caucus of Rank and File Workers. If the demands had not been satisfactorily addressed within six months, the workers vowed to initiate a nationwide strike and, with Williams's assistance, organize a boycott of all Mead products. The immediate concessions, however, included a pay raise of fifty cents per hour and the right to address safety concerns at dangerous worksites. After the truce was made public, Williams asserted that he was ready to spearhead a boycott during the Christmas season that "would dry up downtown like a prune." When asked why he risked his freedom for the striking company workers, Williams replied that "The rich live well but the poor live in hell."[31]

In 1972, Williams had been instrumental in successfully forcing concessions from Holy Family Hospital and Mead—the latter, a Fortune 500 Company. However, his most notable fight that year on behalf of the "forgotten man" was against the largest retailer in the United States: Sears, Roebuck, and Company. Williams had organized the employee walkout at the Sears retail location in Atlanta while he was simultaneously managing the work stoppage with Mead. Black employees had long complained of racial discrimination in the areas of promotion and general workplace maltreatment. After several weeks of unyielding demonstrations, the retail giant agreed to grant thirty-three demands to the striking workers to avoid further public relations problems. One of the granted demands was the recognition of Dr. King's birthday as a legal holiday (fourteen years before Reagan made King's birthday a national holiday). Perhaps Sears's most important concession dealt with the placement of Blacks in vacant positions as they became available until Blacks were equally represented in the Atlanta store relative to their population in the city. If Blacks constituted sixty percent of the Atlanta citizenry, they would have sixty percent of the available jobs. One local newspaper maintained that the "Settlement of this racial labor dispute is the greatest victory for black people in Atlanta" since the passage of the Voting Rights Act of 1965. Williams called the signed covenant between Sears, SCLC, and the workers "the most revolutionary document signed by Blacks and the corporate structure in the history of this nation . . . because it forces Sears to redistribute some of the profit it takes back into the ghetto in an effort to rebuild an economic base controlled by blacks." Although the settlement looked good on paper, Blacks were still victims of subtle discriminatory tactics used by the company. Louella Fluker, one of the three Blacks hired to work at Sears in the West End Mall, argued that whites would void a selling transaction initiated by Blacks and credit the sale to white employees. To keep white managers honest, Fluker recalled, "I would say I was Hosea's niece to get more respect." This is just one example of how Atlanta retailers, large and small, feared the repercussions of having to deal with the bombastic Hosea Williams.[32]

By November 1972, Williams had proven to be a committed crusader for whom Maynard Jackson referred to as the "forgotten man." His legendary triumphs against major corporations were testaments to his willingness to fight on behalf Atlanta's disinherited. Not only did the burly warhorse wage what seemed to be unwinnable wars with Fortune 500 firms, but Williams also directly attacked hunger, a more complex quandary. He was originally driven to initiate a program to feed Atlanta's hungry in 1971 but lacked a suitable venue. By 1972, he had built a strong relationship with Rev. Williams Holmes Borders, the longtime pastor of Atlanta's Wheat Street Baptist Church. On Friday, November 17, Williams and his SCLC chapter held a ribbon-cutting ceremony in celebration of the grand opening of the Poor People's Chow House in the Wheat Street Baptist Church's Education Building, a free food program for the city's hungry adults and children. He maintained that thousands of children were unnecessarily starving in the most prosperous country in the world. He argued that poverty had no respect for color. "We found out there are many whites, as well as blacks, who live off what they can steal. Many women have to sell their bodies to get enough to feed their children," said Williams. God, he believed, was unhappy about the country's mistreatment of the poor. Williams's commitment and sensitivity to aiding the impoverished was heightened in 1968 with the initiation of the SCLC's Poor People's Campaign and King's assassination in Memphis while fighting for a living wage for garbage workers. However, he spoke of one particular incident that renewed his vigor to live up to his Christian obligation to feed those who had nothing to eat.

> I came up on this idea one day when I was working in Vine City and came across two dirty, raggedy, unshaved, black drunkard looking men who asked me for a quarter. I looked down at them and asked what did they want for a quarter? They replied, "We want some chow, man." I told them they just wanted a quarter just to buy some more wine. That stuff was killing them, therefore, I was not going to give them anything. One of the men staggered up and said, "Man, damn, a drink? My belly hurts. I want something to eat." Then I noticed just a step away was a ghetto grocery store. I turned, walked in and ordered one loaf of bread and a pound of bologna. I returned to the men and said, okay, you all are so hungry, now eat. They snatched the bread out of the sack. Before I could unwrap the bologna, those men had begun devouring the dry bread. I stood watching them cram wads of bread down their throats. Finally, it dawned on me—these men were not hungry, they were starving.[33]

The end of 1972 was a busy time for Williams. On November 28, only eleven days after the ribbon-cutting ceremony for the Poor People's Chow House, he announced the formation of the Poor People's Union. Williams suggested that the Union, a leadership responsibility that he shared with National SCLC President Ralph Abernathy and the Distributive Workers of America (DWA), had one encompassing objective: Eliminate what he believed to be America's number one problem—poverty—by giving the working poor the latitude and leverage to influence decisions relative to their employment. "The idea of the Poor People's Union," said Williams, "grew out of the fact that, generally speaking, there is no viable, nationally organized labor movement for the poor today." He maintained that leaders of labor had formed an "unholy alliance" with conservative corporate chieftains, often at the expense of the interests of those whom the unions pledged to protect. Williams envisioned the Poor People's Union as playing a crucial role in improving the quality of life for individual families and in the communities where they lived. The Union provided medical and dental insurance, a savings and loan program designed to teach the working poor about making sound fiduciary investments, and political action programs designed to make the working poor informed members of a growing Black electorate. Although Williams worked unrelentingly on behalf of working poor adults in Atlanta, the burly and bombastic activist had a tender spot in his heart for children—especially during the holiday season.[34]

Williams and the Metro Atlanta-DeKalb SCLC hosted a three-day Christmas party for the underprivileged children and their parents from December 22 to December 25. Williams lobbied businesses and individuals for enough money and in-kind contributions to feed Christmas dinner to four hundred eighty-two families. He even convinced eighteen individual families to open up their homes to feed the less fortunate. Catering especially to the children, Williams dressed up as a Black Santa Claus and gave away seven hundred wrapped presents to kids who would not have otherwise received a present. He said, "The true meaning of Christmas was exemplified by those who gave so that our Christmas program could be a success." He ended the year on a high note: His initiative to fight on behalf of the forgotten man by feeding the hungry and to fight on behalf of employees who were being discriminated against in the workplace was fulfilling his inner mission to be a voice for the voiceless. His vision of continuing Dr. King's attack on poverty, racism, and economic inequality differed from that of Coretta Scott King, the former SCLC's president's widow and legal executor of the estate of Williams's former boss.[35]

Williams's opposition to, and irritation with, Coretta Scott King, the grand matron of the movement, was primarily rooted in her handling of monetary contributions that, he believed, belonged to the national SCLC. When King was alive, Williams maintained, "twenty percent of the checks that came into SCLC were addressed to Martin Luther King Jr." Shortly after Dr. King's death in 1968, hundreds of thousands of dollars were donated to SCLC in the name of Martin Luther King Jr. as a way to continue the fallen leader's work. Because the checks and money orders were written to "Martin Luther King," the SCLC did not have the legal latitude to deposit the checks into SCLC accounts. Therefore, lawyers advised SCLC officials to establish the Martin Luther King Jr. Foundation to legally accept the sizable donations pouring in during the aftermath of the assassination. Problems immediately surfaced because Dr. King died intestate. Therefore, his estate was put in the trust of the courts. Coretta Scott King probated the estate, and, as his widow, she was awarded the legal rights to his name, likeness, and sole ownership of the Martin Luther King Jr. Foundation, which, by 1969, had approximately seven hundred thousand dollars. King's widow, then, proceeded to fundraise throughout the nation and the world in the name of her husband to build the Martin Luther King Jr. Memorial Center in Atlanta, a living memorial to the former SCLC president and clearinghouse for his papers and artifacts. According to Williams, "Coretta raised the money without letting the public know that the money was only going to the Center and not being used at all by the Southern Christian Leadership Conference to keep the action side of his programs going." Because Coretta Scott King had the name and the monetary contributions, some of SCLC's prominent board members defected to work with her, which effectively weakened the economic base of the organization that her husband co-founded in 1957. "The best thing I can relate it to," Williams said, "was those who gambled over the garments of Christ."[36]

Hosea Williams aired his disdain for Mrs. King publicly in January 1973 during a press conference he called after she hosted a large benefit concert on January 15 at Atlanta's Omni Coliseum in honor of what would have been Dr. King's forty-fourth birthday. Williams was upset that none of the funds, including an unexpected $1.7 million dollar contribution from the Department of Housing and Urban Development (HUD) and the seventy-five-thousand-dollar gross from the concert, had been earmarked for the SCLC. Mrs. King's self-serving interests, Williams said, "forces us in the SCLC Atlanta Chapter to break our silence on what is truly happening to the works of Dr. King." King's widow rebutted, saying that Williams's statements were "filled with misconceptions." Mrs. King argued that she had raised millions of dollars "exclusively for the SCLC during and after [her] husband's lifetime." She cited numerous fundraising initiatives, including "freedom concerts, fundraising dinners and Madison Square Garden Memorial Meetings" as evidence of her previous commitments to share resources with the SCLC. By February 1973, Mrs. King had secured nearly three million dollars for the construction project. On the other hand, the SCLC was suffering financially and hardly able to mount any substantive campaigns on the national level. Although Williams believed that Mrs. King could have made more meaningful contributions to the SCLC, he said in 1991 that he did not "hate Coretta. I grossly disagree with her prostituting Dr. King's legacy and claiming to be [its] custodian."[37]

Williams did not allow his frustration with Mrs. King to thwart his attempts to improve the quality of life for Atlanta Blacks who were languishing in the workplace while their white counterparts were steadily climbing the ladder of upward mobility. Shortly before the fifth anniversary of Dr. King's assassination in 1973, Black employers from Rich's department store in Atlanta approached Williams about leading a strike and boycott of the exclusive retail store in advance of the Easter holiday. The workers complained about poor general working conditions and what one unidentified employee termed "starvation" wages. The Black workers also complained about the lack of promotional opportunities for employees of color. In

1973, Rich's only employed three Black executives out of three hundred. Before he agreed to spearhead what was destined to be a prolonged protest requiring jail and bail, he told the willing protesters to do two things: Register a formal set of complaints, and then bring him a list of demands. The demands, he told them, "must be strong enough to cure all of your ills." Once the strikers came back to him a few days later with concise and relevant demands, he sprang into action. "I developed a leaflet from the demands and spread them amongst the employers," Williams recalled. Most of the Black employers were made aware of the pending demonstration and proceeded to use various methods of creative tension.[38]

Williams spearheaded the withholding patronage campaign in the same way as he did in Savannah and St. Augustine during the early sixties. He chose to begin the strike right before the Easter holiday in an attempt to devastate Rich's bottom line during one of its busiest shopping seasons. One woman picketing the store expressed her angst about missing out on the thirty-percent discount but was firmly committed to refraining from shopping in the store until both sides reached an amicable compromise. Others shared her sentiment. Marchers, led by Williams, held a series of demonstrations, including a candlelight march from Wheat Street Baptist Church down Auburn Avenue to Rich's. Approximately two hundred "singing and chanting" demonstrators, wrote Bill Cutler of *The Atlanta Voice*, "marched around and around the store." One demonstrator loudly proclaimed that, "We're on the case twenty-four hours. We don't shut down because the store shuts down." On April 11, 1973, Williams issued a list of thirty-seven demands to Rich's. On the following day, Rich's Chairman of the Board Harold Brockey claimed in a response that "many of the issues raised are totally unrelated to Rich's employees." For example, one demand that Williams listed was for the store to deposit a minimum of one million dollars into Black banks. Although some compared this particular demand to extortion, Williams, on the contrary suggested that "Black banks need to survive and a large company like Rich's, which makes a large profit from the black community, has a responsibility to the black community." This particular demand may not have been directly related specifically to the store's employees. However, the twenty-second demand, which stated "That all associate and supervisory level vacancies be posted in a conspicuous location prior to being filled for at least one week" was not being embraced at a time when ninety-nine percent of the Black workers were at the associate level, the lowest position within the institutional hierarchy. Williams and the demonstrators, displeased with the pace of negotiations, moved forward with a more direct approach to dramatize the plight of the Black workers.[39]

Williams proposed a more drastic measure to get the attention of the department store's executives and the Atlanta community. He asked the president of the store, Richard Rich, for a meeting to discuss the demands and ways to end the labor dispute. Rich declined. He and other executives attempted to spin the narrative of the strike by suggesting that "the strike was a Hosea Williams confrontation with Rich's and not a Rich's employee confrontation with management," according to Earnie Brown, a spokesman for the demonstration. Determined to keep the store on the defensive, Williams led an in-store protest on April 18th. He fondly recalled, "I went up about three or four flights of stairs and about eight of us went up there to the conference room and conducted a "lay-in." We just spread out in the middle of the floor." Glenda Elaine Brown, a Rich's employee, and "lay-in" participant, stated that "We completely took over the business office and we just fell out in the floor." Brown, a longtime associate of Williams, maintained that she immediately recognized his "boldness" and "genuine love for people." Ms. Brown was not the only Rich's striker who was captivated enough by Williams to risk their jobs and freedom. Approximately sixty of the one hundred two demonstrators and sympathizers who participated in phases of the protest that morning were arrested on two charges: criminal trespassing and inciting turmoil. A few days later, Charles Allen Lingo, a white SCLC field worker, secured their releases. Although the picketing continued, Rich's had been successful in securing an injunction barring more than three demonstrators from protesting near any store entrance, because the protesters were alleged to have coerced and threatened other employers and customers with physical violence for patronizing or cooperating with Rich's.[40]

The "lay-in" only added to Rich's mounting frustration with its employees and with Williams. At an April 19 meeting at Emory University, Richard Rich, chairman of the executive committee of Rich's department stores, called Williams an "extortionist," "drunkard," and a "charlatan." Williams is reported to have said that "I may take a drink every now and then, but not enough to be called a drunkard. I might pass the collection plate every now and then. But I ain't never been to Charlotte." The following day, Williams announced that he intended to file a six-million-dollar lawsuit against Rich if he failed to issue a public apology, as the remarks, Williams maintained, caused emotional distress to him and his family. Rich refused. Williams's attorneys, Joe Wyatt and Al Horn, filed a suit in the Fulton

County Superior Court against Rich for defamation of character, slander, and making false statements against the old warhorse. Williams did not believe that the suit would be successful. However, his strategy was focused on keeping the striking workers' demand for fair and equitable treatment in public discourse. The suit lingered and was ultimately dismissed in 1976 after Rich passed away.[41]

Williams's strategy to keep the pressure on Rich's by using strategies to ensure that the media continued to follow the protest began to yield positive results. On Tuesday, May 22, seven weeks into the strike, he announced that store employees had agreed to meet at the Wheat Street Baptist Church's Educational Building with representatives of Rich's board to evaluate several proposals from the company. As a matter of good faith, Williams issued a twenty-four-hour moratorium on picketing the stores. He was adamant that the protest was still in effect and would not be permanently called off until a satisfactory compromise was reached. However, he reasoned that that the temporary suspension of strike activities would give the workers "a chance to evaluate, accept, or reject management's answers to our demands." Within two days, the strike had officially ended after Rich's agreed to address most of the employee's demands. The most important demands—the promotion of Blacks into supervisory roles and a seventy-cent wage increase across the board—was implemented within sixty days. Although Rich's did not respond favorably to every demand, Williams still considered the two-month-long demonstration a "major victory" for Blacks in Atlanta and for labor.[42]

After his success in securing meaningful concessions from Mead, Holy Family Hospital, and Rich's, Hosea Williams once again considered running for elective office. In 1973, less than twelve hours before the qualifying deadline, he entered the race to become the first president of the Atlanta City Council—a recent position created by the city charter. Williams maintained that he sought the post after the continuous prodding of friends and associates and their commitment to raise the funds necessary to run his campaign. He declined to publicly mention the people who persuaded him to run. However, he emphasized in an interview with the *Atlanta Voice* that he "could never be a conventional politician, nor could [he] run a conventional campaign." The reporter, aware of Williams's combative nature and unwillingness to compromise, told the aspiring politician that voters are looking for the city council president to possess skill at "mediation" and "reconciliation." Williams posited that he was a "misunderstood" man and cited his success at leading negotiations with upper management at Mead,

Rich's, and Sears and Roebuck. He also emphasized the need for local control down to the ward level of city affairs. "I am a states' righter at heart . . . I'm only against states' rights when people in power use that power of the states to infringe upon one's rights because of his race, creed or color."[43]

Race played a critical role in the city primaries on October 2, 1973. At the time of the election, 206,267 Atlanta citizens were eligible to vote. Of this total, 100,496 (approximately 48.7 percent) were Black, and the remaining 105,770 (51.3 percent) were white. However, only 108,622 ballots were cast during the election. Of the forty-one precincts sampled, Williams secured 45%–69% of the Black vote in majority Black precincts. Whereas his primary competitors, Wyche Fowler and Wade Mitchell—both white liberals—increased their vote total by winning 6%–25% and 13%–29%, respectively, of the Black vote, Williams did not win more than 10% of the white vote. Another high-profile Black candidate for office, Maynard Jackson, received a large share of the Black vote in almost all of the Black precincts in his quest to become the city's first Black mayor and only Black to preside over a state capital city anywhere in the country. For example, in the Harrel Road precinct, 9C, Jackson secured 94.5% of the Black vote, whereas Williams collected only 56%. In another precinct, 10F, near Frederick Douglass High School, Jackson secured 92.6% and Williams collected only 55.3% of the Black vote. At precinct 10L, near the West Manor vicinity, Jackson captured 93.3% and Williams collected only 52% of the Black vote.[44]

Williams's reputation as a vocal opponent of the status quo and crusading image for the forgotten men, particularly Black men, was responsible for his loss in his second bid for elective office. It was painfully clear to him and his supporters that voters did not heed his appeal for them to consider his record instead of his rhetoric and continued protests of businesses, including Black-owned enterprises. During the runoff election on October 16, Williams received only 65.9% of the Black votes, whereas the winning candidate, Wyche Fowler, received approximately 85% of the white vote and 34.1% of the Black vote; this made it virtually impossible for Williams to be victorious, as he lacked appeal with conservative Black voters and virtually all of the white voters. For example, Jesse Hill, the prominent Black president of the Atlanta Life Insurance Company who had recently been appointed to Rich's Board of Directors, opposed Williams's candidacy in the aftermath of the seven-week-long demonstrations that he spearheaded at the store. Hill's blessing and support was critical for any aspiring Black person seeking political office in the cultural and commercial capital. Sam

Massell, Atlanta's first Jewish mayor and loser to Maynard Jackson in his bid to seek reelection, helped to further alienate the white community from Williams in hopes of persuading Black and white citizens to vote for both a white mayor and a white president of the Atlanta City Council by using race-baiting tactics to subtly warn Atlanta residents to avoid Black bloc voting. Massell stoked fears of a large Black voting bloc to white Atlantans. The defeated mayor referred to Williams as a "racist, a radical and an obstructionist without any capability to be president of the City Council."[45]

The *Atlanta Constitution* argued that Hosea Williams had been perceived as an "extortionist," "charlatan," "car thief," "drunkard," "liar," "professional noisemaker," and "middle-aged delinquent." By December 1973, Williams had reached the conclusion that he had to modify his image from a rabble-rousing, bombastic civil rights activist from the 1960s to a conciliator and mediator if he wanted to appeal to the sectors of the Atlanta electorate that chose to vote against him for the presidency of the Atlanta City Council. On December 1, eighteen years to the day that Rosa Parks was arrested for refusing to surrender her seat on a Montgomery bus, Williams announced that he and the Metro-Atlanta SCLC were embracing an alternative to their radical approach of picketing and marching as a first response to issues arising from the grievances of Blacks with the city and employers. He said that a "negotiate first, picket second" model would now be used when addressing labor and employment concerns with industries in Atlanta. However, an activist in his heart and soul, he said, "If we can't come to an agreement, we will go back into the streets picketing, marching and demonstrating." He even attempted to persuade white businessmen that he performed a favor for them by spearheading protests against Rich's, Mead, and Sears. In a modulated tone, he told an interviewer that "if Hosea had not been available, a Black Panther would have." Furthermore, in an attempt to shed his image as a stubborn and dogmatic leader, he also announced that he would be advised by a "Think Tank" composed of individuals from the business and political spheres to ensure that his methods to help victims in their redress of grievances were not only effective but also less controversial.[46]

Williams was obviously making an attempt to defend his administrative credentials to political pundits and voters by January 1974. He was now forty-eight years old and a grandfather. His hair was now graying, and his limp from being injured in World War II and the countless beatings on the frontlines of civil rights movement campaigns throughout the United States was more discernable. Age brought about a level of maturity that seemed to inform and strengthen his political and administrative insight. However, his personal battles with drinking continued to harm the image he was trying to rebuild. On January 8, a patrolman for the Atlanta Police witnessed Williams driving erratically on Piedmont Avenue and subsequently cited him for driving under the influence of alcohol and driving in the wrong direction on a one-way street. Per policy with the Atlanta Police Department at that time, anyone suspected of drunk driving is routinely arrested and detained in the Fulton County Jail. However, Lieutenant G. J. Krecko, a superior to the arresting officer, voided the tickets and allowed Williams to drive home. During an investigation conducted by the Department's Internal Affairs Division, Krecko argued that the DUI was questionable and would have not withstood legal scrutiny if the case had been heard in court. Krecko was levied a five-day suspension the following week, after investigators concluded that there was enough probable cause to arrest Williams. Although his citation did not stand and he was never arrested, the incident made the newspapers at a crucial time when he was considering a run for the Georgia General Assembly.[47]

Williams's timing in modifying his image and approach to crusading for the poor came at a time when the US Department of Justice, working within the authority vested in it by Section Five of the Voting Rights Act of 1965, had ordered the Georgia General Assembly to redistrict several predominately urban areas where representatives were hitherto elected at-large. Under the previous system, a metropolitan area could be totally represented by white legislators because their home district was overwhelmingly white. The Justice Department maintained that this previous districting invariably discriminated against Georgia's Black citizens, preventing them from having equal representation in the statehouse. The reapportionment bill, which passed on February 11, 1974, and created seven new majority Black districts, was welcomed by the Black Caucus of the Georgia General Assembly, as the new legislation was expected to increase the number of Black elected representatives at the state level. Former SNCC communications director and then-State Representative Julian Bond posited that "the bill could mean as many as ten new majority black districts." There were thirteen districts in the state where Blacks made up at least forty percent of the population. There were twenty-five additional districts where the Black population hovered near thirty percent. Williams was in the process of performing an exploratory committee to examine his viability as a candidate from Georgia's Fifty-Fourth District when his positive momentum was once again halted after yet another incident with the police.[48]

Hosea Williams was arrested on March 9 at Hartsfield International Airport after attempting to board a plane to attend the statewide Ministerial Alliance meeting in Pittsburgh, Pennsylvania, with a handgun. To make the legal matters worse, the pistol, discovered in his briefcase, had been reported stolen. Williams maintained that the thirty-eight-caliber pistol was confiscated from a hungry drunkard who came to the SCLC Food House for a hot meal. Williams insisted that he had placed the gun in his briefcase and forgot that he was carrying the weapon when he freely handed the briefcase to airport security personnel. Having flown many times before, he knew the procedures in place to prevent any passenger from boarding a plane with a gun. On May 11, after considering the evidence and Williams's verbal testimony, Municipal Court Judge Arthur Kaplan dismissed the possession of stolen property charge but ruled that enough evidence existed for the defendant to be bound over to the state court for attempting to carry the gun on the airplane. He was subsequently released on a bond of one thousand dollars while he awaited the criminal trial scheduled shortly after the election for the Georgia General Assembly.[49]

That spring turned into Atlanta's own version of a long, hot summer of 1974 spurred by several murders that thrust the city into a fierce battle for its soul. Williams, who called for a "Crusade to Save Atlanta," was squarely in the middle of these charged events. He led nonviolent protests throughout downtown Atlanta in the aftermath of the June 22 shooting death of seventeen-year-old Bowen Homes resident Brandon Gibson by three white policemen. On June 30, he was subsequently jailed and held on an excessive bond of ten thousand dollars, along with his son Andre and Rev. W. J. Stafford, on charges for inciting to riot, parading without a permit, and violation of the safe streets and sidewalks ordinances, respectively, during a mock funeral procession for Gibson. Williams vowed to embark on a fast and pledged "not to eat anything or drink anything other than water." While incarcerated on these misdemeanor charges at the Atlanta City Jail, Marcus Wayne Chenault, who referred to himself as "Servant Jacob" who had been "God sent," fatally shot Martin Luther King Jr.'s mother, Alberta Williams King, as she played "The Lord's Prayer" during the 10:30 AM morning service at Ebenezer Baptist Church. Chenault was apprehended and treated for minor cuts at Grady Hospital before he was detained on the third floor of the Atlanta City Jail—several cells away from Williams. SCLC President Ralph Abernathy spoke with Chenault while on his way to speak with Williams. During that conversation, the accused murderer confessed that Abernathy, along with Hosea Williams and Jesse

Jackson, were also on the "list" to be killed because of their Christian faith.[50]

As president of the Atlanta chapter of the SCLC since 1972, Williams was charged with steering the organization in the right direction amid ongoing challenges associated with funding and unexpected criminal interference while also simultaneously campaigning for a seat in the Georgia General Assembly. Thieves burglarized the SCLC's headquarters at 775 Hunter Street. The unknown perpetrators stole an estimated ten thousand dollars' worth of photography and office equipment during the heist. Williams, an astute businessman, had previously attempted to insure the building and its contents. However, the insurance premiums were cost prohibitive, because the headquarters were located in a "high-crime area." "This loss has immobilized us," said Williams. He continued, "We have nothing to work with and will have to ask for donations from people who have excess equipment." The burglary was a major setback at an inopportune time for the local chapter. The Atlanta SCLC was forced to temporarily suspend its operations on October 14. The disruption affected the free soup line, the Poor People's Clothing Center, and the SCLC's free legal aid clinic. In a solicitation letter dated October 21, 1974, Williams explained to supporters that weekly income had dropped below two hundred dollars, preventing the local chapter from covering staff salaries. Moreover, the organization was indebted to the tune of twelve thousand eight hundred thirty-five dollars in rental obligations, bonding fees, utilities, and other expenses necessary to ensure the efficient operation of the chapter. Williams was never ashamed to solicit financial support. He called for a "Save SCLC" fundraiser for October 26 at the local Mosley Park. Williams and the organization met only modest success by raising only approximately one thousand one hundred dollars.[51]

By the end of October, Williams was in the midst of campaigning for the Fifty-Fourth District in an election that saw twenty-three Blacks seeking office, including the incumbent, Rep. James Dean and Roland Perrin. The predominately Black district in DeKalb County included the Edgewood, Kirkwood, and East Lake communities, respectively. Blacks were optimistic about the election's outcome, because there were approximately 397,570 eligible Black voters in the state who could make a meaningful impact in the elections if they decided to vote in a contest in which state and political pundits were only expecting a forty-percent turnout among both Black and white prospective ballot casters. Of the twenty-three Black prospective political office holders, at least twelve would be successful in their bids for office, because they were running in districts that had a majority Black population of at least fifty percent. However, Williams was not as fortunate as Horace Tate and Julian Bond, both Blacks who were seeking bids for the Georgia State Senate without opposition. He was running in a crowded field with contenders including Paul Jones, a write-in candidate; Mildred Glover, a Black professor at Atlanta University; and Wade Harris, a college professor at Williams's alma mater, Morris Brown College.[52]

The aspiring state representative understood that the key to electoral victory to the Georgia House of Representatives was voter registration and turnout. On August 23, he met with approximately thirty-five community leaders to express the importance of political organizing, specifically in the predominately Black Fifty-Fourth District, which included the Kirkwood, Edgewood, and East Lake communities, respectively. Williams felt that he had a personal responsibility to increase political participation in the process, particularly since Blacks constituted approximately fourteen percent of the county's population. The Fifty-Fourth District "is probably the least registered (to vote) of any district in the state." He continued, "I'm embarrassed that Hosea Williams, who's been all over the country working in voter registration drives, should be elected to represent the least-registered in the district." He spoke from many years of experience to those who had gathered for this informational session, emphasizing the need for "get out the vote" efforts ahead of the September 3 runoff. DeKalb County had been a Republican stronghold because of a robust party presence and grip on the county commission. Williams insisted, with prophetic accuracy, that a robust registration and education effort, "can put Dekalb in the Democratic column, and we can keep it there." Williams believed that his election to the seat would show a powerful Black voting bloc in the presence of a strong local white Republican-dominated county.[53]

Unlike the other candidates, Williams was preparing for two criminal trials and, if found guilty, could spend nearly five years in jail. His trial for two separate incidents, which happened nearly eighteen months apart, began on October 21, 1974. Instead of a twelve-person jury, the judge selected a five-panel jury composed of four women and one man. Williams was being tried on the charges of attempting to board a plane with a concealed weapon, as well as simple battery against a police officer—the latter stemming from September 1972. He believed that he was being charged and being tried for his unyielding fight on behalf of the forgotten man. "I think this is the first time they are really trying to send me to jail," he said after the first day of the legal proceedings. "It is clear cut political repression. . . .

They want to silence me to see to it that I don't win the seat for the legislature." The initial charges, including creating a turmoil and inciting a riot, stemmed from an incident during a demonstration at the Martin Luther King Jr. Nursing Center on September 15, 1972, where Williams was protesting the mistreatment of elderly Black patients and intolerable working conditions. Williams argued that he asked R. T. Bradfield, an Atlanta Police Department officer, if he wanted to make a financial contribution to help fund the protest. Bradfield attempted to arrest Williams after informing him that the demonstration he was leading was illegal. The officer claimed that Williams resisted arrest and grabbed him, subsequently leaving bruises on both of Bradfield's thighs. Williams countered and stated that the officer had kicked him while purposely handcuffing him tight enough to cause significant swelling in his wrists. Williams's attorney, a skilled litigator for the American Civil Liberties Union (ACLU), filed a motion to dismiss the simple battery charge because his client did not have the right to a speedy trial. More germane to Williams's defense, Al Horn argued that the officer lied in his arrest report for reasons none other than to silence the poor's most vocal crusader.[54]

Two weeks after the trial began, two predominately Black juries, composed of five members each, acquitted Hosea Williams on all charges. The jury first found him not guilty on the simple battery charge on Officer Bratfield regarding the incident that took place at the intersection of Auburn Avenue and Boulevard in the southeastern section of Atlanta. Bratfield's statements were found to be inconsistent and largely without merit. The officer stated in one account that he had warned Williams and other picketers that they were not allowed to impede the flow of moving traffic by asking for contributions. However, Bratfield admitted in court that he had not warned Williams before the confrontation. Bratfield's statements about the battery charge were also contradictory: He initially posited that Williams grabbed his arms, but in court, Officer Bratfield told jurors that the fiery activist grabbed him by the testicles. He was unable to produce pictures of the scratches of his arms but did provide pictures of a scratch on his testicle—a mark that could have derived from a source other than Williams. The second jury unanimously cleared Williams of the possession and concealing of a weapon charge, as the Georgia Code dictated that the prosecution must prove that the defendant "knowingly carried" the weapon into a prohibited space. The security guard responsible for confiscating the weapon testified under oath that, when he confronted Williams about the weapon, the latter's remarks were: "I didn't know I had it . . . I'll take care of it." Although he was acquitted, Williams told a local reporter that he "has been persecuted . . . misused and taken advantage of."[55]

Williams emerged victorious in his criminal trials as well as in his bid for the Fifty-Fourth District's seat in the Georgia General Assembly as a member of the Democratic Party representing DeKalb County. He soundly defeated Paul Jones, a write-in candidate who was endorsed by conservative Blacks and the white establishment. Williams was not the only newly elected Black state legislator. A total of ten new Black legislators represented a forty-five percent increase in the number of legislative seats held by Blacks. Williams, age forty-eight, was the oldest and most battle-tested official in the Black legislative delegation. With this electoral victory, Rep. Williams joined Congressman Andrew Young and US Congressional Delegate Walter Fauntroy as the only members of Martin Luther King Jr.'s former executive leadership team elected to public office.[56]

NINE

Politics, Prosecution, and Persecution, 1975–1984

Representative-elect Hosea Williams began January 13 exhausted from a speaking engagement commemorating the life of Martin Luther King Jr. the night before at the First Presbyterian Church in Red Bank, New Jersey. Around 11:00 AM, he and other freshman legislators were officially sworn in as members of the 133rd General Assembly by six Georgia Supreme Court associate justices. The next order of business was the election of the speaker of the House of Representatives for the ensuing two-year term. Thomas "Tom" Murphy, by a margin of one hundred seventy-eight to zero, was unanimously reelected to the position for a second time and held on to the speaker's gavel for consecutive terms until 2003. The "Yellow Dog Democrat's" forty-year tenure made him the longest serving House speaker of any state legislature in the history of the United States. His unprecedented and unsurpassed grip on political power was likely attributed to his ability to intimidate potential usurpers through obstruction. According to Jim Galloway, "At the height of his power, Murphy could kill legislation with a glance and resurrect it with a nod of his head." It is likely that Rep. Williams sensed that the notoriously autocratic Murphy was politically agile, and he wisely sought to align himself with the House speaker, as the latter had skillfully built strategic alliances between Blacks and rural whites.[1]

Rep. Williams experienced Speaker Murphy's preferred method of parliamentary maneuvering on his first day under the gold dome. The headline of an article in *The Atlanta Constitution*, "Verbal Storms Only Thunder as House Opens," aptly highlights the unusually mild weather for opening day of the legislative session while covering the spirited sparring between Speaker Murphy and Minority Leader Mike Egan of Atlanta. The Republican legislator wanted to grant open access to committee meetings—a position that Speaker Murphy vehemently opposed. Speaker Murphy did not allow Egan to speak without interrupting him several times from the Speaker's stand, erected high above the House floor. With noticeable frustration, Speaker Murphy raised his voice and asked, "For what purpose does the gentleman rise?" Murphy banged his gavel to silence Egan and told him that the matter he brought before the body was beyond debate because the chair was following the rules adopted during the previous legislative session. Speaker Murphy's anger was also directed toward other Republicans who supported Egan. The House voted 122–52 to keep the committee meetings closed. Williams likely voted in the affirmative as a matter of obligation to the Democratic caucus, and he sensed that this vote did not warrant a disagreement with the Speaker on his first day in the great chamber before receiving his first committee assignments—a significant prize and pathway of many legislators to gain greater visibility within their respective districts.[2]

Speaker Murphy doled out committee assignments on the first day of the legislative session. Of the twenty-seven committees, Rep. Williams served on the Industry, Insurance, and Special Judiciary Committees. He was also asked to serve on several subcommittees, including Tourist Relations, Insurance, Health, Life and Accident Insurance, and Inquiry and Investigation. Rep. Williams's background in civil and voting rights, as well his previous and future encounters with law enforcement, may have influenced his ambitions to serve on the Motor Vehicles, and Legislative and Congressional Reapportionment Committees, where he could have directly influenced legislation that he felt could address the systemic racism and inequality that perpetually marginalized Black citizens in Georgia.[3]

Rep. Williams made some pointed analyses after his first two weeks in the legislative chamber, calling his baptism by fire in the General Assembly "one of the most revealing spells" in his life. Rep. Williams was convinced that crucial decisions were not truly considered on the floor of the legislature but were already decided by a "well-organized clique" of wealthy and connected individuals long before the measures were formally introduced through the formal parliamentary procedures. His personal observations of the "highly paid lawyers" whose principal function was to steer legislation that benefitted the white "power structure" and to "prevent laws from passing that will truly help poor people" certainly strengthened his resolve to work for those who did not have a voice. He believed, in 1975, that the Georgia citizenry would be better served if the legislature convened once every five years, as that body was already bought by the "big rich companies and the super-rich whites." In essence, the legislature was replete with "sold-out" representatives who were not accountable to the people.

He would use the terms “sold out,” “highly paid,” and “power structure” in his frequent rails against Black and white politicians in his ensuing years as an elected official in metropolitan Atlanta. A deeper analysis of Williams’s thinking encourages comparison to future Republican President Donald Trump, who, as part of his 2016 campaign, promised to rid the nation of the exclusive and hidden government known as the “Deep State.” Williams believed that the only remedy to cure the legislature of this secret world was for Blacks and whites, regardless of class status, to unite together by not only attending legislative sessions but also forging a coalition to penetrate the clandestine society by running for office.[4]

Local Black elected officials, particularly Mayor Maynard Jackson, were often the subject of Rep. Williams’s attacks for their perceived failure to fight for the poor and disinherited. Jackson and Williams had a politically sensitive love-hate relationship that may have been subtly influenced by the mayor’s cosmopolitan, upper-middle-class rearing as part of Atlanta’s Black royalty. Speaking to the Atlanta Jaycees, Williams said that the mayor’s success and legacy would suffer if he failed to remove himself from the “intellectual rich clique.” Echoing a populist refrain, Williams added that “If Atlanta is to become the world’s next great city, the next mayor must come from the rank and file.” He disingenuously told members in the audience that he was not interested in becoming the mayor of Atlanta. Responding to an attendee’s question about a possible run for the mayor’s office during the next election, “I’m a much better kingmaker than I could ever be a king.” Citing his reasons for why he might not make a good mayor of a city with Atlanta’s profile, he followed with a more believable answer, “I talk too much.”[5]

Despite his strong feelings against the “local Deep State,” evidence suggests that Rep. Williams embraced his new role as a lawmaker with considerable verve and vigor, despite his unfamiliarity with the legislative machinations. “It’s confusing—all these buttons you have to push to vote and all the notebooks you have to keep track of. I didn’t know what the hell I was doing, voting on one amendment to an amendment of some resolution,” said Williams. Moreover, his freshman status and notoriety as a civil rights activist did not stymie him from building bipartisan support with white legislators during his first term. Probably undetected by some of Williams’s fellow legislators, fate and circumstance enabled him to usher his first bill to passage by a margin of 165–2 on March 7, 1975—ten years to the day of the march from Selma to Montgomery for the right to vote. The measure made it illegal for utility companies to suspend service if the customer was behind on their payments for an appliance bought from the company.[6]

The ten-year anniversary of the march from Selma to Montgomery must have drowned the civil and voting rights activist-legislator in a torrent of emotions, as he likely considered all that had transpired since he, John Lewis, and others were beaten on the Edmund Pettus Bridge. The assassination of his friend and leader, Martin Luther King Jr., Andrew Young's electoral victory to the US Congress representing Georgia's Fifth Congressional District, and his own election to the Georgia General Assembly likely reminded him of the significant gains that Blacks had made regarding access to the ballot since that fateful day in March 1965. Despite his singular successes, sacrifices, and contributions to the struggle for freedom, Rep. Williams felt not only unappreciated by those who benefited from his valor on the battlefields of freedom but also purposely targeted by local police and other law enforcement agencies, specifically, the Georgia Department of Public Safety.

Williams's well-publicized encounters with the Georgia Department of Public Safety during the 1970s did not necessarily begin in 1975. He had been arrested at least twenty times since 1965 because of multiple moving violations and hazardous driving patterns. His driver's license was suspended because he had accumulated twenty driving error points within a two-year period. Under state law, fifteen points was the maximum amount allowed before officials could legally issue a suspension order and require drivers to surrender their licenses. According to the Department of Public Safety Commissioner, Col. Herman Cofer, Williams received six points for a speeding arrest on January 6, 1973 in Alabama; two points for driving on the wrong side of the road in Atlanta three months later; three points on a charge of speeding in his own legislative district in DeKalb County on May 19; three points for running a traffic light in Atlanta on June 2, 1973; and six points for a speeding charge in Atlanta on October 30, 1974. These charges resulted in Williams being charged as a "habitual violator," a felony offense in the State of Georgia that would have required him to surrender his seat in the General Assembly.[7]

Rep. Williams's legal troubles related to his alleged erratic driving patterns continued on May 28, 1975, when he had to formally answer to the charges against him. The local prosecutor provided evidence that most of Williams's violations were speeding tickets and other moving violations. Williams was cited twice for driving at least thirty miles above the posted speed limit and cited an additional two times for driving twenty miles above the legal limit in Georgia and Alabama. After testimony, DeKalb County Superior Court Judge Clyde Henley permanently revoked the legislator's driver's license after he was found guilty as a "habitual violator" of the state's driving statues. According to Georgia law, he was eligible to apply to have his license reinstated in five years. According to Georgia law, Williams would be subjected to a felony charge if he was caught driving an automobile before May 28, 1980.[8]

Blacks in Georgia and throughout the South had long contended that they were subjected to overpolicing and blatant retaliatory tactics as part of the growing prison industrial complex as a way of keeping vocal and unruly Blacks in their "place." Rep. Williams maintained that the arrests and some of the subsequent charges were in retaliation for his unapologetic leadership in civil and voting rights campaigns. As five picketers protested in front of the county courthouse with signs in support of the beleaguered but unbowed activist, he addressed the matter directly to Judge Henley during the May 28 hearing. "I was the guy who always got the folks marching. I swear upon the Bible that most of them [arrests] were because of my civil rights activities." Williams contended that he was not always innocent of the charges against him. "In some of them I was definitely guilty," he confessed. "But this is an attempt to punish me, to harass me, and to get me in line politically." Williams's lawyer, Glenn Zell, argued that his client was subjected to double jeopardy because the defendant had his license suspended in 1966, and some of the same driving charges that he was convicted of nearly ten years earlier were being used against him during the current trial. Attorney Zell also questioned the constitutionality of Georgia's "habitual violator" statute. Judge Henley refused to rule on the legality of the legal decree. Zell proceeded to challenge the application of the law. Zell correctly, but unsuccessfully, argued that the law was applied to his client on "ex post facto" grounds, maintaining that the statute "invokes a penalty by adding violations that occur before the date of the law," which was passed in 1972.[9]

Williams was a savvy public relations mastermind, a skillset that he constantly refined during many campaigns and protests during the classical phase of the civil rights movement. During his most recent skirmish with law enforcement, he strategically cultivated an image depicting the massive machinery of state government using its might to mute the state's most vocal supporter of marginalized communities. On June 7, 1975, one week after his license revocation hearing, Rep. Williams issued, for "IMMEDIATE RELEASE," a press statement on official Georgia House of Representatives letterhead condemning Judge Henley's decision. Forever invoking the golden name of the martyred Martin Luther King Jr., the headline read "DR. KING'S AIDE STILL FIGHTING." The press release included a picture of the two hundred thirty–pound Williams with a large, neatly groomed afro and wearing a light-colored suit and dress shoes, riding a ten-speed bike. Williams had recently purchased the bike so he could travel within the city without a driver's license while simultaneously provoking more conversations from sympathizers to rally support for his cause. Emphasizing that he had compiled a history-breaking record of ninety-nine arrests since the early 1960s, the old and defiant warhorse wrote that "I will not be silenced if I have to ride a bike or even skate for the rights of Black and poor people." He finished the press release with a statement that merits quotation at length:

> I could have saved my license had I gone down "Uncle Tomming" to the Governor or the Chairman of the County Commission. They've tried every possible way in the world to control me, but if Dr. King could give his life, I can certainly give up a driver's license. I'll never turn back; I'll continue fighting for the rights of my people until we are free or until I'm dead. I MAY NOT HAVE A DRIVER'S LICENSE, BUT I HAVE MY DIGNITY AND MY SELF-RESPECT.[10]

Rep. Williams's unfinished legal woes during the summer of 1975 did not prevent him from balancing his roles as president of the Atlanta chapter of the SCLC and a new business opportunity that allowed him to utilize his entrepreneurial acumen and academic training as a research chemist. He purchased the Kingwell Chemical Corporation for twenty-five thousand dollars three months earlier and held a ceremonial ribbon cutting ceremony on August 6 at the company's only location on Browns Ferry Road, located on the southern edge of the City of Atlanta. Several people of note attended the event, including Mayor Maynard Jackson. Williams wore a navy blue suit with red stitching along the seams and a matching necktie to the event that officially launched him in his new positions to the public as owner and president. Although his wardrobe reflected the traditional conservative attire of the corporate elite, he insisted that he was still the same Hosea Williams. He noted that he would lead the company, which had thirty-two employees, without compensation. Perhaps jokingly and with a sense of half-hearted humility, he insisted that "I'm not in this business to get rich." However, what was beyond dispute was his commitment to Blacks' and whites' upward mobility. "I'm not leaving the movement," he said. "This is a new dimension of the movement." He continued,

"If economic liberation of the masses of blacks and poor whites is ever to be realized, we must create new and better jobs by entering the mainstream of American economic life." Conceivably, Williams, who was a deft pragmatist at his core, understood the benefit of appealing to customers of all shades. "We are not running a Black company. We are running an economic company," he stated. Although Williams's tenure as owner and president ended the following year, his attempt to plant his feet in the unfamiliar corporate world reaffirmed his twin messages that economic and political empowerment were inseparable.[11]

The last four months of 1975 included Williams's alleged participation in a police chase, which started a city saga that included multiple arrests, the impaneling of a grand jury, and a police officer being charged with neglect of duty. The peculiar train of events began two weeks after Williams's ceremonial ribbon cutting at Kingwell. On Sunday, August 31, Rep. Williams was accused of driving a rented Oldsmobile Cutlass that was allegedly involved in a police chase in Cabbagetown, a neighborhood slightly east of downtown Atlanta. Williams knew that this was a felonious offense that carried a mandatory jail sentence of one to five years, as well as the forfeiture of his seat in the Georgia House of Representatives, if convicted. On September 19, the grand jury formally indicted Williams on a charge of driving with a revoked license despite Williams's full-throated denial. Williams referred to the "red-neck racist" whites who testified against him as vigilantes in a "witch hunt." Patrolman C. R. Ables, the officer who pursued the speeding Cutlass, wrote a report indicating that he never witnessed the state legislator driving the vehicle, as he briefly lost sight of the automobile during the chase. As a result of the formal charge, Williams arranged to turn himself in at 11:00 AM on September 25 at West Hunter Street Baptist Church. The planned arrest was similar to previous detentions. "He's always one of the easiest arrests," said an unidentified deputy who had previously participated in Williams's "planned apprehensions." Rep. Williams was released on one thousand dollars bail shortly after being booked into the Fulton County Jail.[12]

Patrolman Ables's puzzling actions after the incident ignited a controversy that led to a reprimand by his superiors. He asserted that he never charged Williams, despite seeing the two-hundred-thirty-pound forty-nine-year-old jump a fence and run after Williams was spotted standing next to the Cutlass in a private driveway on Powell Street. The officer's initial report was strange, considering that Williams told him on the scene that "I'll get someone to come back and get the car." Fearful of a citizens' complaint, Patrolman Ables asserted that "I may have pursued it further if it were not Hosea." A three-member internal panel recommended to Commissioner Reginald Eaves that Ables be charged with neglect of duty and refusing to discuss the incident with superior officers. Assistant District Attorney William Weller concluded after a police investigation and review of an unnamed policeman's written report that Williams was indeed driving the vehicle.[13]

The claims of impartiality from Rep. Williams and his supporters had merit, but the circumstantial evidence in the case suggested that he was likely driving the car without a driver's license in spite of the officer's trepidation about charging the local legend with the felony. Police Captain Herman Griner, Ables's commanding officer, said, "We could not, through the officer and witnesses, place Williams behind the wheel of the car on a public street." The local solicitor argued to the police "that they did not have a case." Some of Williams's supporters, including his movement comrade and friend, Rev. Ralph D. Abernathy, believed, or at least publicly stated, that the indictment was the result of racial discrimination. Abernathy and others, including Black policemen, had witnessed for years what they perceived as systemic racism in the treatment of Blacks in the City of Atlanta and throughout the Deep South. In a prepared statement, Abernathy wrote, "If this case had involved anyone other than Hosea Williams that the Atlanta Police investigated and gave a clean bill of health to, it would have been the end of it." He continued, "We are not going to sit by and allow a good courageous American like Hosea Williams be crucified by racism." The Afro-American Patrolmen's League also threw their support behind Williams. The Black Atlanta policemen issued a statement saying, "We believe these charges are the result of deliberate political persecution . . . our discontent [is]with this case's lack of evidence and disregard for the officer's report that could not place Reverend Hosea Williams at the scene." Along with contributing to the "Hosea Williams Legal Defense Fund," the Black police officers also offered to transport Williams anywhere within the city limits during their off-duty hours. This support speaks to the affection that many Blacks had for the man whom they referred to simply as "Hosey." It is worth noting that, during the same period, Rep. Williams was the most vocal opponent of a city annexation plan that would have minimized the Black vote in Atlanta from sixty percent to thirty-eight percent. Expecting a protracted legal battle, the comedian and civil rights activist,

Dick Gregory, agreed to raise funds for Williams's legal defense fund to pay for the latter's representation by Atlanta City Councilman and future foe Marvin Arrington.[14]

Rep. Williams entered 1976 with a serious legal case looming over his head while grappling with personal and SCLC-related financial challenges. The Atlanta SCLC chapter, formed in 1972 and the only local branch that Ralph Abernathy granted a charter to operate in the country, was forced to cease business operations indefinitely one year after a disruption in services for similar reasons. Donations the previous year had allowed the organization to eliminate all but one thousand dollars of a debt of twelve thousand dollars. Williams blamed the financial woes on the community as well as on Coretta Scott King. "If all the people we helped with demonstrations gave us 50 cents a month," he maintained, "we'd be in good shape." He directed much of his criticism to Martin Luther King Jr.'s widow, believing that she used her late husband and the movement to promote her own agenda and not the movement that he championed. Usually unbothered by criticism, a close friend stated that, "Hosea really got to her." Williams's frustration with the lack of what he thought was sufficient support from Mrs. King was likely exacerbated by his own financial problems. He declared bankruptcy, informing the federal district court in Atlanta that he had a total debt of $190,547.31, with assets of only $55,284. He reported that he only earned seven thousand dollars annually as a state legislator and two thousand dollars in honoraria fees he received as a minister and activist.[15]

The old warhorse and protector of the "little man, the forgotten man," did not allow his own financial plight prevent him from leading protests in behalf of one hundred taxicab drivers in Atlanta. The drivers were upset after an encounter with Atlanta police at the Hartsfield Airport that led to the arrests of two taxicab drivers for allegedly illegally parking in an unauthorized space in close proximity to an area known as the "bullpen," the airport location where drivers picked up fares. This latest incident was another component of a strained relationship with the city administrators. The drivers constantly balked at a local ordinance that prevented anyone from acquiring a business license unless they owned at least fifty vehicles—an unlikely possibility for small operators. Sympathetic to their conditions, Williams met with the drivers at the Wheat Street Baptist Church and assisted in drawing up their demands. In response to the protest, Mayor Jackson's administration agreed to create a commission to review the drivers' grievances. Jackson promised to do "everything possible" to find an equitable resolution. The assurances did not resolve the drivers' or Williams' frustrations with an administration they perceived as hostile to the interests of the "working man." The disgruntled drivers planned to stage a "cruise-in" on one of the city's busiest thoroughfares, Peachtree Street. Williams said the protest "will show some nonviolent strength" that the drivers possessed as leveraging tools with the city.[16]

Williams kept a hectic, fast-paced schedule. The next day after the taxicab driver protestations, Williams was also asked to help Black contractors secure federal contracts to build the twenty-four-story Richard B. Russell Federal Building in downtown Atlanta. He and other activists demanded of the General Services Administration (GSA) that Black contractors be awarded at least twenty percent of the contracts. The GSA insisted that they would not make any decisions for at least twenty-four hours. In their efforts to preempt the agency from falling below the desired threshold of twenty percent of the contracts, Williams, representing the National SCLC, maintained that he and other activists were willing to address the matter in federal courts. He also promised to "have sit-ins, lie-ins, and sleep-ins," if necessary to ensure that Black contractors were treated fairly in the bidding process. Another leader, Rev. Ted Clark, insisted that, "Before a bulldozer moves one ounce of dirt, they'll have to move 10,000 blacks." Williams said during the meetings that, "Blacks have sixty-percent of the population in Atlanta, and it is only right to that we get a larger share of federal building projects." He was arrested two weeks later, on August 4, for protesting against the GSA because the federal department said that it could not guarantee a twenty percent share of the contract work. Hours after Williams was released, a contract worker for the department expressed some confidence that they will "reach or exceed" protesters' demands. Feeling victorious, Williams declared from the steps of the city hail in his boisterous voice, "The Richard Russell Building is just the beginning." He believed that the federal government had conspired to excluded Blacks, Native Americans, and Hispanics from contract work with the federal government and, likewise, vowed to mobilize these three groups across the country. Although Mayor Jackson and Congressman Andrew Young were critical in securing the project for the city, it is likely that the protesters' demands would not have been met without Rep. Williams leading the protests.[17]

The publicity that Williams generated in the summer and fall of 1976 probably helped him to secure another term in the General Assembly, as well as favorable consideration in his jury trial, which had been delayed since the previous year. He took seventy percent in his contest against his opponents in a lopsided three-way race for the opportunity to represent once again the Fifty-Fourth District. Rep. Williams was unable to bask in his electoral victory, as a guilty verdict in his felony trial on charges stemming from driving on a suspended license (after a DeKalb County superior judge declared him a habitual offender) would have prevented him from being seated in the legislature under Georgia law. He also faced up to five years in jail if found guilty on the felony charge. He took the witness stand in his own defense and attested that Horace Woodward, a deacon in his church, was driving the car on August 31, 1975. Two older women testified under oath that they witnessed Williams driving the car, despite the state representative's vehement denials to the contrary. Likely appealing to the ten women and two men in the jury (seven whites and five Blacks), he recited a refrain that would be the foundation of his defenses over the next twenty years: The trial is "not a prosecution, but a persecution." The defense attorneys made the same plea to the jury during closing arguments. The jurors deliberated for approximately nine hours before acquitting Williams on November 19, 1976. His attorneys, expecting a hung jury or a mistrial, were surprised by the verdict. So was Williams. He was speechless and purposely avoided the press after leaving the courthouse.[18]

Rep. Williams entered the beginning of a looming challenge with the Metropolitan Atlanta Rapid Transit Authority (MARTA) shortly after his trial, which continued into 1977, ultimately creating an impasse between him and SCLC Chairman Joseph Lowery, who was a member of the organization's board of directors. Martin Luther King Jr.'s defiant former lieutenant accused some MARTA contractors of hiring newly incorporated, in-name-only minority subcontractors as thinly veiled attempts to satisfy or circumvent the transit company's affirmative action stipulations. He had also accused MARTA executives for taking "kickbacks and payoffs" as part of a larger scheme with "pseudo joint ventures." He presented MARTA's general manager, Alan F. Kiepper, with a "declaration of grievances" after they had a testy exchange that included: the streamlining of procedures to prime contractors so minority contractors do not run short of operating funds; increased monitoring of the prime and subcontractors to ensure fair treatment; and ensuring that general contractors do not create in-name-only joint ventures to undermine the subcontractors. Rep. Williams and the Rev. Ted Clark asked for an "independent audit" of the amount of money MARTA paid to minority firms. Rev. Clark was certainly empowered by the number of Black elected officials. "We've got enough black folk to see things gets done," said Clark. He even threatened to "slap" a board member if they spoke down to him in a condescending fashion. Williams did not resort to using physical threats, but he did demand that MARTA hire a "neutral auditor" to review all financial contracts and transactions as he suspected the possible "fraudulent handling or misuse" of funds within MARTA's executive leadership. He was frustrated with MARTA's perceived indifference to his request on behalf of the Black citizens' group Joint Venture to Bring MARTA Into Compliance's request for a well-resourced independent auditor. On December 23, he told reporters that the group would plan a nonviolent direction campaign by marching on MARTA construction sites. "If you don't look around, I touch you on the shoulder. If you don't turn around, I pull you around. If you still don't come around, then I sock you," he said, while punching his right hand with his left fist. This was not a physical threat. Williams was likely referring to the potential of the Black citizens' group to lobby against MARTA receiving the one-percent sales tax during the General Assembly's next session.[19]

The threats led to a serious audit that was carried out by J. L. Tatum & Company, a Black certified public accounting firm. Williams and the Joint Venture to Bring MARTA into Compliance were right and wrong. The accounting firm discovered that, although the joint ventures were legitimate, "a wide variance in the amount of minority participation" was evident. Specifically, in one of the joint ventures between Gate City Electric Co. and E. C. Ernst, the smaller organization "appeared" to have "minimal" participation in the normal operations. In another joint venture between H&H Electrical and Maintenance Company and Henderson Electric Company, the minority business participated "in approximately 8 percent of the labor costs." A legislature held hearings in response to Rep. Williams's charges and the audit findings. Joseph Lowery, one of a few Black members on the MARTA board and chair of the committee that was responsible for minority programmatic initiatives, proposed guidelines to ensure the accuracy of the number of Black and white firms who bid on contract work with the transit giant. This was a consequential development. Rep. Williams waged a very public battle over Black participation with a powerful company that had ties to legislators and lobbyists. He forced MARTA to bend and adopt new guidelines that streamlined procedures and monitoring of joint ventures. Second, and most pertinent to the already strained relationship with Joseph Lowery, it put the latter in a precarious position as a paid MARTA board member who likely had to contend with competing forces within the company to "control" Williams to avoid negative publicity with patrons, legislators, and a growing faction of movement alumni who now embraced more sedate alternatives that appealed to middle-class Blacks instead of the picket-line method.[20]

The SCLC's twentieth annual convention in Atlanta in August 1977 revealed an ideological rift between Williams and Lowery that widened as the two vied for the organization's presidency, which had been vacated by Ralph Abernathy in February 1976 in his unsuccessful quest to represent Georgia's Fifth Congressional District. Lowery disingenuously maintained that he was not interested in the SCLC's top spot. Williams was not so quietly lobbying an arm of the SCLC who embraced his grassroots and flamboyant leadership. The "old guard," unquestionably led by Williams, believed that SCLC's relevancy would further diminish if they did not recalibrate the organization's strategic plan to include nonviolent, direct-action protests in the streets. Although Lowery, a co-founder of the SCLC, acting president, and chairman of the board, was theoretically a member of the "old guard," some in the organization believed that he was leading the charge to "intellectualize" the movement to satisfy the trio of Martin Luther King Sr., Coretta Scott King, and Andrew Young. One observer maintained that "They are trying to take SCLC out of the streets and put it into the black middle class." Tyrone Brooks, one of Williams's closest friends and associates since 1965, believed that the SCLC should not attempt to compete with the Urban League or the NAACP by appealing to middle-class sensibilities. "What we need is a person who is willing to face the power structure and fight for the little people," Brooks said before the beginning of the formal convention.[21]

One hundred delegates assembled at Ebenezer Baptist Church on August 18 to formally cast their vote for the next president of the SCLC. The nominating committee comprised four people who were named by the SCLC's Board of Directors and three who were appointed by Lowery. Before the formal voting began, Jesse Jackson, while glancing at Williams, admonished "self-appointed leaders who spend their time looking at themselves in the mirror." Abernathy then made a motion to vote to the slate of candidates in the form of a plea: "Let us 'disappoint the forces of evil, those who want to see us divided.'" The US Congressional delegate from DC, Walter Fauntroy, was named chairman of the board of directors. Abernathy was voted president emeritus for life. To quell dissension within the ranks the delegates selected Lowery as the President and chief spokesman of the organization. As a compromise, Williams, Lowery's chief rival, was voted to serve as executive director, a full-time role with a salary of twenty thousand dollars that required him to be responsible for the day-to-day operations of the organization. Williams had threatened to resign from SCLC if he were not given "chief administrative" responsibilities. After Abernathy's motion, Williams approached the platform and seconded the request to formalize the officers to assert himself as King's rightful heir: "In the name and unity as one of the true custodians of Martin Luther King, I'd like to second the motion." The convention attendees stood and celebrated as Lowery and Williams embraced each other in the pulpit that was once occupied by King. Williams later disclosed that the makeup of the committee stymied his chances of being elected president. "I didn't stand a ghost of a chance with that committee," Williams recalled after the convention. Despite the collective "kumbaya" moment, there were a lot of unanswered questions about the direction of the SCLC. Tyrone Brooks, emphasizing his desire to "stay on the streets" and "go to jail," posed a query that would later splinter the leadership: "Are we going to have a militant or a bourgeois, middle-class group?"[22]

Rep. Williams was forced to balance the mounting pressures of managing the day-to-day operations of the SCLC and assisting his wife, Juanita, in her run for the Atlanta City Council's Fifth District seat against incumbent Morris Finley. She understood that name recognition was the irreducible common denominator of many electoral victories. She agreed to have her name listed as "Mrs. Hosea Williams" on the ballot. Although Williams claimed that he was not actively involved in her campaign, Finley did not underestimate the state representative's savviness and unpredictability. "You never know what he's going to do. He's smart," said Finley. Williams wanted to build a political dynasty in metropolitan politics. He believed that they could address problems that long plagued the city and the Fifty-Fourth District. "With our political pull, we could stop all the shenanigans about who's responsible for what services in that area." Juanita maintained that she had "no" problems with Finley. She believed that she could be a more productive councilperson for the Fifth District. She thought that she was better qualified to bring the district's women into the calculus. Juanita was, in her words, "really trying to carry [her] campaign to women. I think women can get more done with problems that really affect the family than men [can]." 82.3% of the eight thousand six hundred seventy-two voters were Black. Nearly fifty-five percent were women. Finley had a formidable track record of success. The "Finley Ordinance" was a statute that both Williamses would have supported, because the law required all city contractors to spell out, in granular detail, their minority employment and affirmative action plans, respectively. Despite the

Williams's tag-team approach, Juanita lost the election on October 4 by a margin of one thousand five hundred fifty-three to nine hundred twelve votes, a difference of six hundred forty-one votes. Juanita was eventually elected to her husband's seat in the Georgia General Assembly, when he resigned the post and defeated Morris Finley for the Fifth District seat on the Atlanta City Council in 1985.[23]

Williams penned an editorial in the January 14, 1978, edition of *The Atlanta Journal* titled "King As Century's True Militant." This published missive was a literary shot across the bow to Lowery and the others who believed that the SCLC should embrace less radical forms of protests against injustice, especially in Atlanta, because of its carefully crafted image as a city "Too Busy to Hate." In the opening stanza, Williams asserted that King "was the truest militant I ever met." Malcolm X, he argued, spoke his powerful messages of Black empowerment from the comforting Harlem when King constantly "return[ed] to the battlefield to face the Pharaoh." Williams believed that King's courage was on best display during protest marches. He recalled a time in 1965 when he and King were scheduled to march from Brown Chapel to the courthouse to present a set of grievances to Sheriff Jim Clark. The goal was to provoke Clark to arrest King and Williams. By his own admission, Williams was scared to the point that he was "trembling." A "mob was spitting and cursing," but King "kept walking," despite the recent revelation that a white mob was awaiting the protesters inside the courthouse. Williams was unsuccessful in convincing King to leave the scene. King's response to his "wild man" was "No, I'm going to walk." Williams's message to Lowery and the board of directors was incandescently clear: Marching in the streets for justice was the method of his fallen friend and SCLC's founder. Moreover, Williams had already indicated his intentions as national director to carry King's mantle when he seconded the nomination motion at the convention in August, when he branded himself as one of King's "true custodians."[24]

Williams certainly wanted to revive the SCLC and restore the organization to its "golden era" by returning to the streets; however, he believed that Lowery and members of the board of directors were looking for a reason to discredit and terminate him from the position. The SCLC meeting minutes and correspondence with the staff of sixteen in 1978 project Williams as paranoid, constantly operating as if he knew that he did not have any job security. Staff were often caught in the middle of the cold war between Williams and Lowery. It is obvious from the minutes that Williams inherited an undisciplined staff. The full-time administrator, Claudette Matthews, captured the essence of the weekly staff meetings: "Rev. Williams [is] only happy with the performance of four people in office. He is not happy with [the rest] of staff"; "Rev. Williams has to get a hand on the organization because he has to make a report to the board in order that they may evaluate him"; "Rev. Williams stated that he is having serious problems with the president but is not giving up"; and "Rev. Williams stated he will ask the president to fill all positions or wipe them out because there are games being played on him." Perhaps what is most revealing about Williams's and Lowery's working relationship is best captured in the executive director's response to SCLC staffer Rev. Fred Taylor, who indicated his refusal to accept the position of associate director of chapters and affiliates because he did not like the director. According to Williams, Taylor said, "I didn't want to work for Joe and he didn't want me to work for him, but we are making it and he is the 'Boss.' I may not do everything he say, but be damn if I don't do most and I respect him as the boss."[25]

By 1978, Williams was an experienced leader who had supervised staff at some level for nearly fifteen years with the SCLC. He recruited some of the staff from Savannah with whom he was particularly close; specifically, Willie Bolden, Henry Brownlee, Ben Van Clark, Charles Clark, and Joseph "Big Lester" Hankerson. According to his trusted and loyal executive assistant, Terrie Randolph, he was "close to them and knew what they were capable of doing, but he treated all staff members the same." Although there was no such thing as "pay raises" and formal recognition, Williams was fiercely loyal to his sergeants. Bolden, nearly thirty-five years later, compared his then-boss to a military comrade whom he could trust his life to in a foxhole under heavy fire. "Everybody," said Bolden, "wants to have at least one friend like Hosea." He continued. "If I was in combat and they were bombing all around me, and Hosea Williams said 'Bolden take you a nap,' I would go to sleep. I knew when he said go to sleep that he had my back."[26]

The SCLC had well-documented financial challenges before and during Williams's executive directorship. The lack of adequate operating funds tends to compound tension in any organization, as well as reporting relationships. A correspondence trail between Williams and Mattie Brooks, the finance officer, highlights the confusion between the two foes. Williams notified Brooks that Lowery had authorized her to honor the executive director's signature by issuing checks "as long as the money [was] there," and he made the request through the SCLC's "official voucher procedure." In a response memo with the subject line: "Vouchers, Honoring Your Signature," Brooks informed Williams that she could not "comply with this request as I have been instructed by the President to do otherwise." She also indicated that she could only write "small checks" for him after additional discussion with Lowery. By using such vague and ambiguous language, Williams likely had to secure approval from Lowery for practically any amount at the president's discretion. Sensing a disconnect, Brooks requested a meeting with Williams and Lowery as soon as their schedules permitted. This exchange is evidence of mistrust between the two highest ranking members in the organization. Furthermore, claims of due back wages certainly did not ease the issues in the finance office, especially when the request was made by one of Williams's ardent loyalists. In a letter notarized by Williams's longtime and faithful assistant, Terrie Randolph, Tyrone Brooks claimed that he was owed $13,734.40 in four years of back wages. Once again, Mattie Brooks denied the request.[27]

Williams knew that the SCLC's national office was hemorrhaging financially and sought to combine his self-proclaimed "hustler" ingenuity with the laws passed by the General Assembly—specifically, the regulations regarding bingo—to ensure the organization's solvency. The incorporation of bingo was probably another source of contention between him and Lowery because of the latter's conservative views on gambling as a Methodist preacher who likely believed that this game was below his dignity and the dignity of the organization that he co-founded. However, he probably grudgingly respected Williams's unorthodox ability to leverage publicity and profit potential. On February 16, 1978, Rep. Williams voted on a bingo regulation bill in the Georgia House that passed 149–11. The principal authors maintained that the intent of the bill was to curtail "Mafia-type" influences with professional bingo operators by turning the operation into a free-standing, full-fledged gambling business. The measure would only permit nonprofit organizations and corporations tax exempted by the Internal Revenue Service and the Georgia Department of Revenue to secure a license to operate a game in the state. It is worth noting that, during debates, he said to his colleagues on the floor of the House: "I don't think we ought to get frantic and throw the baby out with the dish water." Within three months, he was actively discussing on record in staff meetings the possibility of bingo as an SCLC strategic priority as early as May 17. "Rev. Williams is trying to work on the chapter on Bingo. The new law," he continued, "wiped out all of the small organizations." It is worth mentioning that Williams's church, the Martin Luther King Jr. Poor People's Church of Love, grossed more than $4.2 million dollars between 1979 and 1991, making his business the largest private bingo operation in Georgia.[28]

Williams was invariably convinced that a successful bingo operation under the auspices of the SCLC would effectively remedy many of the organization's financial woes. Six months after he introduced the idea of bingo during an SCLC staff meeting, he announced that the SCLC was going to open an eighteen-thousand-square-foot bingo parlor at the Grant City Plaza on Candler Road in South DeKalb County. Officially named the Bingo Palace, Williams expected the operation to gross between "$7,000 and $8,000" per month. The Bingo Palace would only open twice each week for gaming. Lowery did not publicly endorse the endeavor, but he likely reluctantly authorized Williams to use approximately forty thousand dollars in SCLC funds to lease the large building and purchase the necessary machines. Lowery, a pragmatist, probably viewed the Bingo Palace as a way to generate a much-needed revenue stream to fund some of the organization's initiatives that generated positive publicity in Atlanta.[29]

There is no greater example of SCLC's need to develop creative revenue streams than Williams's perennial plea for donations each holiday season to support his Thanksgiving and Christmas projects to feed Atlanta's poor and provide toys to the city's needy children. 1978 marked the eighth year that Williams spearheaded what would become a touchstone in the city of Atlanta. Nearly three thousand children planned to attend a well-publicized party at Atlanta's Civic Center on Christmas Eve. However, Williams had only secured enough toys to give to five hundred children. Also, the SCLC had also planned to feed at least two thousand of Atlanta's poor in Wheat Street Baptist Church's education building, the site of many of Williams's holiday dinners for the city's less fortunate. With less than three days before Christmas, he had only collected enough food to feed approximately one hundred people. Discouraged, but not defeated, "We've just not been able to raise the necessary funds, toys or food to go through with this worthwhile project," Williams said. "Too many people depend on us too much for us to call these two events off."[30]

By the end of 1978, the SCLC was not the only civil rights organization grappling with significant financial hurdles: CORE and the NAACP were in similar or worse quandaries. CORE had not hosted a national convention in ten years, and the NAACP had incurred six hundred eighty-five thousand dollars in 1978 alone. Some organizational insiders believed that Blacks were no longer joining these organizations and making financial contributions in large measure because of the perception that the agencies were obsolete. Another reason, according to Paul Brock, a spokesman for the NAACP, was that Blacks no longer had a vested interest in the agencies and were passing the responsibility to others. "Someone else will give if I don't," Brock wrote. Leaders within these three organizations maintained that it was virtually impossible to locate one in ten people who previously supported SCLC, NAACP, and CORE during the classical phase of the civil rights movement to donate in 1978. Coupled with cash flow problems, SCLC and NAACP were grappling with ideological rifts from within. The NAACP forged an alliance with oil companies to counter President Carter's proposals to pressure large oil companies to shift to coal. The NAACP argued that this legislation would drive unemployment at a time when the organization was focusing on jobs. As within the SCLC, Williams was adamant that the twenty-one-year-old organization would experience a rebirth by forcing white power structures to end racially discriminatory practices through marching, picketing, and selective buying campaigns.[31]

The protesting techniques that Hosea Williams used to bend companies to the will of justice, as continued negative publicity related to his encounters with law enforcement, would be the unstated reasons that Lowery would use to dismiss the rebel from his executive directorship. Once involved, Williams entered into a public dispute about the treatment of a minority construction company, specifically, Southeast Grading Incorporated. Southeast was a subcontractor of the white-owned Mergentine/KVN Construction Company. Southeast claimed that Mergentine/KVN owed them approximately five hundred seventy-eight thousand dollars. MARTA was not directly responsible for the arrears but became involved because the contested dispute created public interest, gaslit by Williams. "MARTA is responsible for the death of more black contractors than we could probably organize in the next decade," Williams declared. Sticking to his proverbial guns and preferred method of nonviolent direct action, he promised to "lay in front of the bulldozer" and "march and picket" if MARTA did not intervene and apply significant pressure to ensure that Mergentine/KVN made Southeast Grading pay the amount that was owed. Lowery, a MARTA board member, was once again thrust in the middle of a Black-White debate by his firebrand and rebellious subordinate when he preferred a more subdued approach in the closed confines of the boardroom—one of the likely reasons why MARTA recruited the respected SCLC president—to preempt noisy protests from disgruntled, hellraising civil rights activists. Lowery responded to the protests with a calmer admonishment that was not directed at any party: "We have a moral responsibility not to let the big fish chew up and spit out the little fish."[32]

Rep. Williams was a vocal supporter for several bills because personal convictions during the One Hundred Thirty-Fourth General Assembly. He made an emotional plea to his colleagues in the legislature to make Martin Luther King Jr.'s birthday a state holiday at a time when thirteen other states were already celebrating the martyred leader's life and contributions with a statewide holiday observance. Bellowing through the great chamber, "It's more than Martin Luther King," he said, "I'm pleading you to deal with the dignity of a people." Despite his impassioned argument, the Georgia House defeated the proposal 94–52. The bill's critics used the same reasoning they used when the bill was presented to the floor in previous years: Passing the bill was too costly because of the amount of money the state had to pay employees for a day off from work. Rep. Williams was particularly interested in the passage of HB 1248, a bill that minimized the restrictions on reissuing driver's licenses to those who were declared to be habitual offenders. Before the law was passed, a habitual violator was required to wait for a period of five years before they were eligible to receive another license. The new bill only required habitual violators to wait for two years before they were eligible to apply for a new license. Additionally, the Department of Public Safety was authorized to issue a new "probationary" license to offenders to drive to and from work. Unfortunately, Rep. Williams became painfully and embarrassingly familiar with this statute throughout the remainder of his life; this often made him the source of contempt and derision.[33]

Rep. Williams's one hundred third arrest occurred four days before the bill's passage in the City of Atlanta, and three citations were issued: the felonious offense of driving with a suspended license as a "habitual offender"; making an improper lane change; and simple battery against Trooper T. L. Thornton, a Black officer, for an alleged altercation at the police station. Rep. Williams asserted that the four-year veteran of the force "beat him up." Once again Williams's ability to continue representing his constituents in the Georgia House of Representatives was at stake, as a felony conviction would translate to a minimum of one year and a maximum of five years in jail. Williams was formally indicted on the felony charge on May 1, 1979. He was set to stand trial for the second time in three years on the habitual violator charge. He eventually pleaded guilty and was ordered to pay a fine of one thousand dollars as part of a negotiated plea. He also received three years on probation. Most importantly, Fulton Superior Court Judge Osgood Williams gave him the heatshield of "first-offender" status, which protected him from being stripped of any of his civil rights. The unusually light sentence also carried a stipulation that Williams's probation can only be revoked if he was driving and not for being arrested for activities such as leading protests. This was one of the rare sentencings in which Williams did not accuse the judge of being partial and persecuting him for his storied civil rights activities. After the trial, he said that Judge Williams was "very fair in the sentencing." He invariably welcomed this favorable outcome during a very public termination as the SCLC's executive director.[34]

The board of directors, through Joseph Lowery, terminated Hosea Williams on March 27, 1979, for the stated reason of conflict of interests between his position as an elected state representative and his SCLC executive directorship. According to Lowery, Williams resisted two requests to resign from the legislature to give him more time to devote to SCLC's national efforts. The train of events after the official announcement was puzzling. Claud Young, chair of the SCLC's personnel committee, asserted that a termination letter was sent to Williams. Possibly in denial, Williams told a reporter that he had not received a letter and that any conclusions based on hearsay were unnecessarily presumptuous. "I'm sure I would have been consulted about it. Dr. Lowery would have called me in to talk about it," he said. There was not a conversation. Young insisted that Williams had agreed to relinquish his seat in the Georgia House of Representatives upon his election to the second highest ranking position in the national organization. Williams refuted that such an agreement existed, because it defied logic and political pragmatism. He felt that he was exempted from this stipulation, even if it was buried somewhere in the organization's governing bylaws. "Why would they not want me to serve in the legislature for those 40 days [that the General Assembly meets from January to March]?" He continued, with obvious entitlement: "I think it would add to the prestige and influence of the organization [for SCLC to have an officer in the legislature]. I was the one who marched and saw people get killed to get us here."[35]

Hosea Williams's nature was to defy authority. After all, this was one of the characteristics that buttressed his courage during the many civil rights movement campaigns of the 1950s and 1960s. Claud Young expressed that he did not believe that Williams could be subordinate to anyone, saying "He's on his own." Young's observations were telling. Perhaps what is most revealing is Young's belief, which was probably shared by others on the board of directors, that "When he gets ready to speak out on something, that's what he does . . . and that's not the way we operate." Young's statement indicates that, at the very least, Williams was terminated not simply for retaining his legislative position but also for his steadfast belief in picketing, marching, and protesting, despite the fact that these methods were no longer in vogue within the upper ranks of the organization. Williams probably believed that the blood that he spilled on battlefields in the South through his numerous acts of valor alongside Martin Luther King Jr., Ralph Abernathy, Andrew Young, C. T. Vivian (his chosen successor as executive director), and countless others purchased him enough political capital within the organization to guarantee him the appointment for as long as he desired. Williams was not vacating the role without a long and protracted struggle with Lowery and the board of directors. He promised to appeal his ouster at the SCLC's April 10 board meeting.[36]

The wounded warrior considered some draconian measures to counter what he perceived as a defeat. Williams vowed to "take his case to the people." He contemplated forming a new civil rights organization if his appeals were unsuccessful. He and his followers formed an ad hoc group, the National Committee to Save SCLC, to pressure the board of directors. Speaking as if the Committee had the upper hand and moral high ground, lead protagonist and faithful ally Tyrone Brooks said, "We want to give the other side an opportunity to repent. We want the other side to realize that we don't want this to become a Hosea issue. We don't want Hosea fired—but we don't want SCLC to die." Perhaps Brooks and other Williams supporters believed that the real reason for his firing was the result of an ideological schism. The bottom line of the friction was rooted in Williams's glory days and his street-fight approach to remedy current injustices vis-à-vis what Brooks referred to as the sellout, social club, similar to the "federal grant-getting" NAACP. During an interview at Paschal's restaurant in Atlanta, Williams contended that Lowery fired him to eliminate the vocal wing blocking him from rebranding the SCLC to resemble an organization that will be "accepted by an elitist crowd" that consists of Blacks and whites. Williams also suggested during this same interview that Lowery wanted to fill the SCLC with "well-educated intellectuals and theoreticians" while ridding the organization of the "crazies." It was the supposed "crazies," Williams believed, who were the "salt of the movement" who had guts—the foundation of any movement.[37]

The SCLC Board of Directors rejected Williams's appeal on April 10 at the organization's convention in Washington, DC. At least twenty of Williams's followers, led by Tyrone Brooks, protested the ruling. Shortly after Williams's hearing, the board unanimously voted to terminate Tyrone Brooks for "conduct unbecoming of a paid staff member." The thirteen-year veteran expected this outcome. "If Lowery does it to Hosea, he'll do it to me," Brooks said, before he was formally notified of his termination. Brooks would later join his friend and mentor in 1981 in the Georgia House of Representatives representing the Thirty-Fourth District. As for Williams, the nineteen-year veteran of the SCLC refused to vacate his office, claiming that his arrest record and tenure with the organization "give me the right to use this office." Lowery hired an armed security guard to patrol and remove him and his belongings from the SCLC's Auburn Avenue headquarters. Another Williams devotee, twenty-year veteran "Big" Lester Hankerson, punched a man in the face for barring him from the locked office. Williams had still refused to vacate the office nearly two months after his dismissal, prompting Lowery to file a court order to restrain Williams temporarily from going to the headquarters. His undignified departure brought to an end an era in the SCLC's history.[38]

An editorial in *The Atlanta Journal-Constitution* compared the beleaguered Hosea Williams to General George Patton: "Brilliant in war and clumsy and out of sorts during peace." The writer suggested that the movement had, indeed, moved from the streets to the courtroom. In many ways, Lowery and SCLC brass shared the sentiment of this unnamed writer of the piece that was published in the local paper one week after Williams was fired. Williams deserved to be fired, not because of the misconception that his tactics were antiquated but because he did breach an agreement to resign from the legislature based on SCLC's bylaws. Lowery's portfolio of civic and business activities sheds light on what may have been the root cause of the friction between him and his onetime subordinate. Lowery had ascended to the presidency of the SCLC while he was president of Enterprise Now, a federally funded initiative. He was also serving as the pastor of the conservative Central Methodist Church while also maintaining the position of partner in the Phoenix Parking Corporation. Phoenix was vying for a major contract with Hartsfield Airport during the same time he terminated Williams. However, Lowery's stated contention was that Williams did not devote enough time to SCLC's national operations. Lowery was more engaged in non-SCLC-related activities than Williams. At the very least, Williams used his position in the Georgia House of Representatives to do what Lowery and the board of directors believed was the best method of addressing the remaining vestiges of slavery and Jim Crow legislation. Williams was ahead of Lowery and some members of the SCLC Board of Directors. He understood that court action was often prompted by the pressure created by marching, picketing, and protesting. Perhaps Lowery, an astute pastor and seasoned activist who lacked the scars and limps of battle, believed that Williams's strategy was indeed effective. It simply jeopardized the material manifestations that accompanied the middle class and Atlanta's carefully tailored image as a progressive city devoid of the racism and bigotry that haunted Grenada, Albany, Birmingham, and other cities.[39]

Milovan Djilas wrote, in *Of Prisons and Ideas*, that "The way prisons are run and their inmates treated gives a faithful picture of a society, especially of the ideas and methods of whose who dominated that society." Williams had not read this book, but he certainly embraced Djilas's analysis of the prison industrial complex by the summer of 1979, when he and State Senator Julian Bond lead an eighty-mile, six-day march from Savannah to the Georgia State Prison at Reidsville nearly one year after an uprising in the maximum-security prison. The Coalition for a March on Reidsville, said Williams, had three goals: End the racist treatment of Black prisoners; free the six "Reidsville Brothers," the inmates charged with killing one white guard and two white inmates the previous summer; and permanently close the forty-one-year-old prison. Williams referred to the prison that once housed Martin Luther King Jr. in October 1960 for a misdemeanor as a "hell-hole and criminal producer. . . . It must be closed." The fact that officials had reduced the prison population and secured several million dollars to improve the facility did not deter Williams and his delegation.[40]

Williams and the remainder of the Coalition, including Ralph Abernathy, escorted by the Georgia State Patrol, began the six-day trek at the base of Tomochichi Rock in Savannah's Forsyth Park. Williams led many marches from the Rock during the 1960s when he was still employed as a chemist with the US Department of Agriculture's Bureau of Entomology and Plant Quarantine. Tragedy struck on the third day of the march, when nineteen-year-old Savannah native Arthur Ashley Norwood drowned in a river when he took a brief respite from the scorching sun. "It was over 100 degrees on the highway, with no trees," Williams said in a deeply somber tone. Speaking at a memorial service for Norwood on August 8, 1979, in the small city of Pembroke, Williams reflected on the value of Norwood's sacrifices: "We are not unmindful of what it means to give up a life." Although devastated, Williams used Norwood's life as a rallying cry to dramatize the plight of Reidsville prisoners and the overall treatment of prisoners throughout the nation as he and approximately forty-nine other marchers completed the trek to Reidsville on Friday, August 10. He and approximately sixty-five additional protesters, including Dick Gregory, were arrested the following day for failing to obey Superior Court Judge James

Finley's order prohibiting them from marching within one thousand yards of the prison when they proceeded to cross the Ohoopee River Bridge on State Highway 147. Gregory and Williams, as well as the state representative's two sons, Hosea II, known as "Junior," and Andre, remained in jail and vowed to continue on a hunger strike in protest of the imprisonment of the "Reidsville Brothers." Although the marchers did not encounter any violence, they did pass a burning cross and a few white antiprotesters waving Confederate flags.[41]

The Reidsville protest was largely considered a failure at the time because it did not lead to the release of the "Reidsville Brothers," nor did the prison close. The sentiment was not necessarily positive in Atlanta for those who followed the march in the press, despite the widespread sentiment that the prison should be closed or repurposed. The State of Georgia was in the middle of a multimillion-dollar remodeling campaign that was the direct result of the uprising that gained nationwide publicity that pressured the state, albeit through horrendous violence, to address the conditions that inmates complained about for decades. One observer in 1979 believed that Williams and his coalition were flowing some misguided priorities. The critic advised the protesters to "hold down the crime rate" so that Atlanta's youth will not end up in Reidsville or a similar facility. "Keeping folks from going to prison seems to make a lot more sense than protesting the existence of a prison," wrote an unnamed Atlanta resident shortly after the march began. There is some fact in this misleading point of advice as the observer tacitly acknowledges that everyone sentenced to prison was guilty. Williams and the coalition believed that despite an offender's guilt or innocence, they still deserved to be treated as human beings, regardless of the hue of their skin.[42]

Writing of Hosea Williams in 1974, SCLC staffer Rev. John Barber referred to the complex leader as a "man of many contradictions." More pointedly, Barber believed that Williams's consistent inconsistencies were the "secret of his survival." His eleven-day trip to Libya in September 1979 to meet with Col. Muammar Gaddafi and the Palestine Liberation Organization (PLO) in the aftermath of Andrew Young's forced resignation as United Nations Ambassador was a shock to some who knew and worked with Williams. The overseas trip was sponsored by the Libyan government, with some assistance from the Black Studies Department at the University of Washington. His "humanitarian" visit was focused on establishing an "Afro-American/Arab relationship" that could use Libyan wealth to "further the dream of the late Martin Luther King Jr.," he said, before departing a plane from New York with nineteen other black educators, businessmen, and politicians. He believed that a coalition would alter the lot of Blacks in the United States. Williams insisted, and took great pains to emphasize in all of his statements, that the collaboration was not "pro-Arab" or "anti-Jewish." He was keenly aware of the cultural sensitivities of the Jewish community but was not fearful of any potential backlash, particularly after he presented the anti-American leader of Libya, Col. Gaddafi, with a Martin Luther King Jr. peace medallion when the two met in Tripoli. Gaddafi was also a strong supporter of the PLO. "I'm not going to be intimidated by the Jews," he said. From Williams's perspective, the trip was also about proving that Blacks were politically nimble and intelligent enough and, likewise, had every responsibility to build strategic international partnerships that could improve their communities in a manner similar to the collaborations that Jews developed.[43]

Criticism of Williams's visit with the PLO was swift. However, he was not alone. Several movement alumni, including Jesse Jackson, Joseph Lowery, and Ralph Abernathy were accused in some quarters of taking the Middle East trip to further their own respective agendas, which invariably included soliciting money from the Libyan government. One critic even said that historians in 2020 may well view this trio of Black leaders as the "Neville Chamberlains of 1979" because of their supposed appeasement of PLO leaders. This was obviously a gross overstatement, because Jackson, Lowery, and Williams were not heads of state or even representatives of a sovereign government. The multivariate truth is that the trio was possibly aiding embattled movement alum Andrew Young in the aftermath of his resignation as Ambassador to the United Nations for having an unapproved, diplomatically sensitive meeting with the PLO and subsequently denying that the meeting occurred. Jackson was probably attempting to heighten his profile for a possible run for elective office in a statewide or national election, and Lowery and Williams were leveraging the publicity to show who was the better statesman and heir to the King legacy. There is also a possibility that Williams and Lowery were laying the foundation of a donor cultivation strategy that they hoped would yield a sizable donation for civil rights initiatives and a long-term relationship with another marginalized population.[44]

In 1980, Williams showed why he was the "man of many contradictions." He gave a full-throated endorsement of conservative Republican candidate for president, Ronald Reagan, over the Democratic incumbent, Jimmy Carter. Williams and Abernathy appeared at the "Victory 80" campaign rally in an affluent suburb of Detroit, Michigan, that included Reagan's running mate, George Bush; former President Gerald Ford, current Michigan Governor William G. Milliken, former Gov. George Romney, and former Senator Robert Griffin. When Reagan was asked about the endorsement after the rally, he said "I just didn't realize such a thing could happen. I was overwhelmed." The nominee was not the only one in shock. Coretta Scott King, after learning of the duo's endorsement, asserted that, if her husband were alive, "he would be out campaigning against Ronald Reagan." Mrs. King was a staunch supporter of Jimmy Carter, who had been friendly toward her while he was governor and president. The Martin Luther King Jr. Center for Nonviolent Social Change was being constructed at the time, with a substantial amount of federal funding. "If I was getting two or three million dollars a year for my project, I'd probably support Jimmy Carter too," Williams said.[45]

Whereas Williams believed in Reagan's phantom plan to help Black Americans, he had a deep-seated disdain for the incumbent that began during President Carter's tenure as governor of Georgia, after a supposed retraction of a campaign promise. "Jimmy sold me out," Williams said. Carter had allegedly pledged to appoint Blacks to selected positions in state government after the election and careful vetting of a list that Williams and the Georgia Voters League were to submit for consideration. At the time, there were very few Blacks, if any, serving on state boards and commissions. According to Rep. Williams, Carter had arranged to meet with him at noon the day after the election. Williams asserted that he arrived 30 minutes before the appointed time and witnessed Carter being chauffeured from the meeting location. Charlie Kirbo, a Carter aide with whom Williams was familiar because of their rearing in Bainbridge, Georgia, told Williams that he had "good news and bad news." Carter would not appoint a Black from his and the Georgia Voters League's list of potential appointees, but he would honor any financial commitments that were promised. Williams felt that he was duped because he campaigned for Carter around the state and lent his considerable degree of credibility with the "old guard" arm of the movement to convince skeptical Blacks of Carter's sincerity to support a Black agenda. By 1980, he was convinced that Carter was a "staunch conservative" who helped the rich get richer by "exploiting the poor." Carter had also failed to usher through the Georgia General Assembly or the US Congress a state or federal holiday observance in honor of Martin Luther King Jr. Rep. Williams also compared Carter's record as governor to that of axe-carrying Lester Maddox, saying that Carter did less for Blacks as governor "than the bigot racist Lester Maddox did when he was governor of Georgia." Worse, Williams claimed, Carter raised "black America's political hopes at an all-time high" but failed to honor any policy promises. Carter was not alone at fault. Williams thought that the national Democratic Party had long taken the Black vote for granted.[46]

Rep. Williams enjoyed White House access for a period of time, a visible perk that he did not have in the outgoing Carter Administration. The president-elect flew Williams and Abernathy to California, and the three met at Reagan's Los Angeles home on November 6. They did not discuss specifics, but the parties agreed to establish a national Black monitoring committee to periodically evaluate the progress of a pending policy agenda. Williams, Abernathy, and Charles Evers, the brother of slain NAACP Secretary Medgar Evers, met with Reagan on December 10, 1980, to discuss a Black agenda for consideration after he was sworn into office in January 1981. Rep. Williams poured cold water on any rumors that he would join the Reagan Administration in an official, paid capacity. "I don't want to be his Andrew Young," he said. Williams and the Black delegation did, however, present an economic development plan that could improve the Black private sector in business development—an agenda item that would directly benefit his growing business portfolio back home. He believed that the political gamble had paid off. "Suppose all of us had gone solidly and supported Jimmy Carter?" Williams asked. What a hell of a fix black people would be in, because none of us would have a line to the President." Despite his rebuke of Carter and Atlanta's Black establishment, including Andrew Young, Maynard Jackson, and Coretta Scott King, Rep. Williams remained a Democrat, despite his support of Reagan.[47]

Williams's endorsement of Reagan in 1980 is more complex than simply viewing Carter's records as governor and president of the United States. Carter had relationships with people whom he thought were more influential with middle-class and "respectable" Blacks; specifically, Andrew Young, Martin Luther King Sr., and Coretta Scott King. President Carter's appointment of Young as United Nations Ambassador and his support of Mrs. King's sprawling complex on Auburn Avenue to honor the life's work of her late husband created a politically sustainable relationship. Williams may have felt that the attention and courting received by King's family members and even Andrew Young were not necessarily justified. Williams's beatings and jailings throughout the Deep South, in his reasoning, were more instrumental in expanding the electorate to increase Carter's electoral chances for the governorship and the presidency than the movement-era contributions of Young and the Kings. Moreover, Williams, still a fiery-eyed agitator, was now an entrepreneur and employer who stood to benefit financially from Reagan's business-friendly policies. Although he was still deeply entrenched with the plight of the poor, he was also the president of a chemical company that supplied cleaning supplies to commercial and state agencies. What is more revealing is his growing admiration of the Coretta Scott King ally and successful president of Atlanta Life Insurance Company and the Atlanta Chamber of Commerce, Jesse Hill. "I think Jesse symbolizes what I'm trying to do with my own business. That is, with all the odds against you in this world, you can still make it if you have the tools and utilize them," Williams said. This was a modified and erroneous talking point of the Republican establishment. No one understood the contradictions better than the man who fed more poor people in Atlanta during the past ten years than any single person. Williams's unrelenting persistence over the remaining twenty years of his life for the causes to help the "little man" and racial justice—principles that Ronald Reagan and his administration did not embrace—leads any observer to believe that his support for the fortieth president was a politically advantageous ploy to raise his public profile while also addressing the legitimate grievance that he had with the national Democratic Party for ignoring its base of faithful Black voters.[48]

Rep. Williams's endorsement of Reagan during an election year did not cost him his seat in the Georgia House of Representatives with his predominately Black base of voters. He defeated James Finley in a tight race for the right to represent the heavily Democratic Fifty-Fourth District for a fourth and final term. Rep. Williams's protégé, Tyrone Brooks, also won a seat in the legislature after his defeat of incumbent Lottie Watkins for the right to represent the Thirty-Fourth District. Reps. Williams and Brooks were allowed to sit by each other on the floor in the great chamber. By the end of January, the activists-legislators had co-sponsored at least seven pieces of legislation that reflected their core values and experiences with the Black poor. For example, they pressed for passage a bill that allowed temporary compensation for ex-offenders after release from jail to assist them in finding employment and preventing recidivism. Reps. Williams and Brooks also co-sponsored a bill that would permit offenders charged with misdemeanor crimes to be released from the city and county jails on personal recognizance until trial.[49]

Williams knew the challenges of offenders from his own lived experiences with law enforcement; however, he had escaped criminal prosecution for serious traffic-related offenses relatively unscathed until the spring of 1981. He was sentenced to one year in jail and four years on probation after he was convicted on April 24 by a jury in DeKalb County Superior Court for operating a vehicle without a license and leaving the scene of an accident on July 19, 1980. Police alleged that Williams was driving a rented 1979 Buick LeSabre on McAfee Road in DeKalb County when he had an accident with another vehicle in a low-speed head-on collision after trying to make a left turn on Laurel Lane. Witnesses claimed that a "black male who looked like Williams" ran away from the scene on foot. Prosecutors argued during the trial that papers in the vehicle, particularly the rental agreement with the Hertz company, had Williams's name. He insisted that he was not operating the vehicle but never disclosed who was driving the rented car. He was also critical of the *The Atlanta Journal-Constitution*'s coverage of him—publicity that he usually leveraged to his advantage. Shortly after the incident, he blasted the newspaper for being "unfair" and using the story to "persecute and defeat" him ahead of the election. He compared their journalism to "garbage" after printing a story after talking to a "peon" at the county jail. Emphasizing his importance and celebrity status, Williams growled, "I'm not nobody, I'm Hosea Williams!"[50]

Williams's attorneys appealed the case on the grounds that the jury members had been prejudiced against him because of his civil rights activities and that the jury used "insufficient evidence to convict." Williams's attorney, David Botts, also argued in the appeal that the habitual violator law was incorrectly applied to the defendant. Williams also believed that the DeKalb County District Attorney Bob Wilson was using the case as a springboard to a higher office. He believed that Wilson was trying "desperately to use my case to make a name for himself." It is puzzling that Wilson was trying Williams on a traffic charge while junior staff attorneys were simultaneously prosecuting a murder charge. However, an ambitious district attorney trying the case did not modify the facts or the existing evidence in the case. While this case was on appeal, Fulton County Superior Court Judge Osgood Williams revoked Williams's probation, with the warning that he would have to spend one year in jail only if the appellate court ruled against him—allowing him to avoid serving his sentence for the remainder of the year.[51]

Rep. Williams made the best of his time on bail by cashing in some of his political capital with the Reagan administration. Access is the coin of any political realm. Williams and his wife, Juanita, attended a black-tie state dinner on November 19, 1981, honoring Venezuelan President Herrera

Campins. The invitation to a state dinner was yet another example of how Williams felt snubbed during the Carter Administration. Mr. and Mrs. Williams were seated at a table with some of President Reagan's top advisors, including Counselor to the President Edwin Meese; Mrs. David Rockefeller; and Mrs. Michael Deaver, the wife of President Reagan's chief of staff. This was Williams's and his wife's first state dinner. Having the opportunity to "rub shoulders with people that really have the power control" was a memorable experience, he recalled. He was obviously impressed by the ambiance and the spoils of luxury and power. "These tuxedos, these limousines, this food—God intended for man to have it." The dinner was a reaffirmation to him that Black people deserved the same access and the same opportunities as the powerful white men and women who attended the state dinner. Although he enjoyed roasted leg of lamb at the state dinner in DC, he was feeding Atlanta's poor on the following Thursday.[52]

Rep. Williams continued his not-so-subtle flirtation with the Republican Party in 1982 as a way for him to dramatize the plight of the Black poor while also flaunting the access that he had to the highest levels of power—a perk that was no longer extended to Joseph "Broadway Joe" Lowery, Coretta Scott King, and Andrew Young. Always with a flair for the dramatic, Williams joked at a National Black Republican Leadership Council meeting that he was "considering" joining the Grand Old Party. The new chairman of the Council was convinced that the old warhorse of the movement had, indeed, exited the Democratic Party. In recent weeks, Williams recited Republican talking points to various audiences. For example, he proposed that Blacks "get off welfare" and that they "pull themselves up by their own bootstraps" at a meeting where he proposed the creation of a Black Chamber of Commerce during a meeting at the Butler Street YMCA in downtown Atlanta. Although he expressed the efficacy of a free enterprise system, Williams never deviated from policies and initiatives that were designed to improve the financial flexibility of Black people. His proposed Black Chamber of Commerce would not be "anti-white, anti-Jewish, anti-Protestant, Catholic or anti-anything else, but it will certainly be pro-black," he emphasized.[53]

Rep. Williams was using his seat in the Georgia House of Representatives as a Democrat to advance measures to help poor and Black people while simultaneously raising his public profile with the Grand Old Party. He voted for legislative initiatives on the floor of the Georgia House that the Reagan Administration had proposed eliminating at the federal level. Williams voted for a bill to support the Atlanta Legal Aid Society that would add one additional dollar to every court fee that was collected by the DeKalb State Court. The legislation would create an additional revenue stream of twenty-five thousand dollars annually to stop the hemorrhaging caused by the Reagan Administration's cuts to social services. In DeKalb County alone, the amount of Legal Aid clients dropped from twelve hundred cases to eight hundred eighty-eight in 1981. This important program assisted families who had a gross income of less than $474.19 a month to receive free legal aid. Rep. Williams also opposed a measure that would have neutralized gains from the Voting Rights Act of 1965. Georgia Attorney General Mike Bowers had planned a court fight to keep the state's congressional reapportionment plan over the objections of the US Department of Justice. Georgia had to receive preclearance before modifying legislative districts because of its history of gerrymandering that substantially diluted the Black vote. Gov. George Busbee, House Speaker Tom Murphy, and Lt. Gov. Zell Miller supported the Attorney General's decision to fight the federal government on a congressional redistricting plan that would have created a pathway for Fulton County to have a fifty-seven percent Black voting district that would certainly allow for additional Black representation in the US House of Representatives. Black legislators protested the action during a three-hour filibuster. Williams rose from the House floor and denounced the Attorney General's plan, saying that "Blood will flow in the streets of this nation" if this resolution is passed. His pleas were unsuccessful. The House resolution passed 104–62. His outwardly pro-Black positions did not minimize his standing with the Reagan Administration—yet.[54]

Williams had his eyes firmly fixed on a new economic horizon for Blacks. He planned what he referenced as an "international economic development venture" trade mission to Japan. The itinerary consisted of a sixteen-day trip to Japan that included a few days of vacation in Hawaii, which, according to Williams, allowed him "to have fun and see those ladies on the surfboards with their brown bodies." As the initiative was announced during an April 1 news conference on the steps of Atlanta City Hall, some onlookers may have believed that the initiative was an "April Fools" Day joke because Hosea Williams, the bombastic lion of the civil rights movement, was taking a transnational trip for a meeting with the Prime Minister of Japan Zenkō Suzuki for the purpose of creating jobs for Blacks—perhaps he and Abernathy were the first Black citizens to have a private audience with a sitting Japanese prime minister. One critic called the idea of Williams meeting with a head of state "mind-boggling." The fifty-six-thousand-dollar trip had the support of now-Mayor of Atlanta

Andrew Young, Gov. George Busbee, and President Ronald Reagan. In a letter of support, the president wrote that the plans to "aid our national economic revitalization by developing Afro-American/Japanese economic joint ventures are truly innovative ideas. . . . You have my best wishes on a successful journey."[55]

Williams believed that the trip had the potential to build relationships with Japanese investors to create joint ventures with the Black private sector. He thought that partnership, under the auspices of his Afro-American/Japanese International Institute of America, could play a role in addressing the imbalance of trade with Japan and bring some Black businesses closer to the profits and sustainability of some white companies. He addressed the Foreign Correspondents Club of Japan as part of the trade mission trip and broached the idea of a Japanese-Black joint venture, emphasizing the need of more fuel-efficient vehicles. Although he was a longtime patron of General Motors, as evidenced by the fact that he only purchased Cadillacs, Wiliams told the Japanese audience that his recent acquisition was "already falling apart," perhaps a rhetorical ploy to endear him to his audience. Williams and Abernathy also wanted to lay the foundation for a labor exchange program that could send Black workers and entrepreneurs to Japan to learn how to use some of the country's technology in its factories for duplication in the American Southeast. Williams's and Abernathy's pitch apparently resonated with Japanese business leaders, especially after touting Blacks' collective buying power. Toyomitsu Shirasawa, a spokesman for Japan's leading watch manufacturer, Seiko, maintained that the duo forced the company to consider opportunities that it had not conceived of before the visit. Shirasawa admitted that he and his associates had a "clearer understanding of the situation of blacks in America. . . . They made themselves perfectly clear."[56]

Rep. Williams and Rev. Abernathy also discussed a student exchange program between Japanese universities and Black colleges and universities. Williams and Abernathy, both graduates of Black colleges, likely spoke from their own experiences about the challenges and advantages of Black institutions of higher learning. Williams expressed an interest in sending students from Black universities to Japan to understand Japanese business principles for adaptation in America. Williams, a businessman in his own right, envisioned these Black exchange students managing the joint ventures in the future. He was critical of American universities focusing solely on equipping students with skills necessary to function at a major firm and not including small to medium-sized firms in their curricula. The exchange program he maintained, could equip students at Black colleges and universities with a holistic toolkit to lead any business, regardless of its size. He had high aspirations. "The fruits of this mission will first be borne by the Afro-American universities and colleges in the US," Williams said. He declared the trip a success upon arriving at the Hartsfield International Airport. Channeling the spirit of Chinese philosopher, Lao Tzu, he emphasized to the media that the trip was "the first step in a thousand-mile journey."[57]

Williams received some good news from the Georgia Court of Appeals two months after returning from his trade mission trip to Japan: The Court reversed his felony conviction on the grounds that the state representative was no longer a "habitual violator" at the time of the accident in July 1980, overturning Judge Richard Bell's five-year sentence, which included one year in the county jail and four years on probation. Assistant District Attorney Susan Brooks argued that Williams's status as a habitual violator could only be lifted by the Department of Public Safety once the offender secured a valid driver's license, not the ruling of a Superior Court judge who had sentenced him under an earlier statute. The Court agreed with Williams's attorney, David Botts, that the defendant's habitual violator status and the mandatory five-year license revocation period expired in June 1980, one month before the accident. Williams had long declared that the law was unfairly applied to him because the judge in the case had already rendered that Georgia's most famous driver was eligible to apply for a new license under the 1972 iteration of the law rather than the harsher 1975 version of the same statute. Conversely, the second highest court in the state upheld Williams's conviction on leaving the scene of the accident. Williams was ecstatic by the verdict. "Personally I would like to say this is a good news to my ears. . . . I owe that young lawyer David Botts my life," said Williams shortly after the decision." Rep. Williams had every right to be relieved by the news, particularly because he did not have to vacate his seat in the Georgia House of Representatives.[58]

Although the questions swirling around Williams's eligibility to remain as the Fifty-Fourth District's representative were settled for now, he was lambasted by his opponents for his frequent absences that kept him from voting on important legislation. Potential usurpers also attacked the representative supporting Reagan. James Finley, who had been defeated by Williams four consecutive times for the House seat, was the most vocal critic. Williams, he claimed, "has the highest or one of the highest absentee rates of anyone in the House." The absenteeism claims could have had some validity. Rep. Williams only answered eleven times during the roll call during the first thirty days of the legislative session. The body agreed by unanimous consent to forego the roll call thirteen times during the 1982 session. Williams defended his absences by citing his efforts to create jobs for Blacks in the Fifty-Fourth District. Another contender pressed Williams on his support for Reagan. Williams retorted that his endorsement was politically pragmatic, because he believed that not one Black person in America "could have even gone to the White House" were it not for his sharp political instincts. The incumbent believed that neither of his opponents were formidable enough to defeat him in an election on the basis of their ability to bring jobs to the District. In Williamsonian arrogance, he claimed that the biennially vanquished Finley could not stimulate jobs in "40 years." With even less respect and increased indignation, he claimed that it would Amos Moore, another candidate, at least "100 years" to match his legislative productivity.[59]

Rep. Williams was not helping himself stave off criticism from opponents in the middle of a tight reelection campaign. He was arrested again while awaiting DeKalb County Superior Court Judge Richard Bell's decision to reduce his sentence on the leaving the scene of an accident conviction in 1981. He was detained on June 24 for driving under the influence after neighbors contacted the police of a suspicious vehicle around 2:00 AM. Police officers arrived and observed him behind the steering wheel of a white 1981 Cadillac Eldorado near 2219 Rosewood Road in Decatur, a short distance from the Bingo Palace that he managed on McAfee Road. Officers alleged that he registered a 0.12 on a breathalyzer test, which declared him legally drunk as the reading was above 0.10. The arresting officers found $1,119.90 in the form of cash and checks in the vehicle. Rep. Williams was taken to the DeKalb County Police station, where he was administered a "intoximeter" test. He probably sensed that the local police would not render an accurate reading of the in-house alcohol analysis and requested a blood test at the DeKalb General Hospital. Although he admitted to having a drink, Williams was adamant that the DeKalb Police Department unfairly targeted him because of his legendary record as a civil rights activist, citing multiple instances during the previous two weeks when he had been stopped for having a California tag on the front of the vehicle and another encounter when police claimed that the luxury vehicle that he was driving was stolen. The defendant-turned-comedian drew incessant laughter from media and other onlookers who were at the capitol when he challenged the validity of the police report: "What would I be doing slumped behind the steering wheel when I could lean back in a Cadillac?" Perhaps channeling the inner barrister in him, he asked, with a twinkle in his eye and a devious grin, "How could I be drunk driving when the car was in park?"[60]

Judge Bell refused to reduce the state representative's sentence for the 1981 conviction. Williams claimed that the judge was using the case to create publicity for himself while he was running for a seat on the Georgia Supreme Court (it is worth noting that Bell was ranked last in a Georgia Bar Association poll of six potential candidates on their qualifications for the state's highest court). Nevertheless, Williams turned himself to authorities at the DeKalb County jail at 4:00 AM on Friday, June 25, after missing a court appearance the preceding day. Judge Bell's decision to detain the state representative for twelve months created a quandary for Williams and the citizens in the Fifty-Fourth District because his jail sentence deprived his constituents of representation in the Georgia House. Williams petitioned the State Board of Pardons and Paroles for an earlier release. In response to the request, the board chairman emphasized that Williams would not be released "just so he can run for office." Although he was still incarcerated, the fifty-six-year-old inmate was given trusty status, allowing him to perform "general janitorial work," including mopping and sweeping floors. He did receive some good news in jail regarding his eligibility to remain in the race when Georgia Secretary of State David Poythress decided that his conviction, according to state law, did not disqualify him from running for office because the crime did not involve moral turpitude. Public figures, including his old movement comrades, Rev. Ralph Abernathy, Rep. Tyrone Brooks, and Mayor Andrew Young, launched a public relations campaign to have the old warhorse released early from jail to protect his chances at reelection. "Hosea Williams may be guilty of a lot of things, but Hosea Williams does not deserve to be in prison," the mayor said. Williams reported that he had not received any financial contributions in advance of the August 10 Democratic primary. He was forced to rely on his son, Andre, and other supporters to help him run his reelection campaign from his DeKalb County cell. Some of his colleagues kicked the embattled warrior while he was down. During a special session, State Representative Vinson Hall, for example, introduced a failed resolution to prohibit jailed representatives from receiving the living expense of forty-four dollars a day.[61]

Rep. Williams received an unexpected vote of confidence in his reelection campaign (from a DeKalb County jail) from some unlikely allies, despite what others saw as self-inflicted wounds in advance of election day.

He was campaigning from a jail cell while his opponents torpedoed him to his predominately Black, Democratic constituents about his support for President Reagan. Williams's rap sheet made matters worse. Nevertheless, the State Board of Pardons and Paroles granted the four-term legislator some release time to attend the special session to ensure that his district had representation. Equally shocking, his nemesis, *The Atlanta Journal-Constitution*, which he carefully cultivated to his advantage over a thirty-year period, gave him an endorsement five days before the Democratic primary. With an asterisk noting the paper's selection of Williams as the best candidate to represent the Fifty-Fourth District, the writer wrote that "The *Constitution*'s endorsement of Rep. Hosea Williams is based on his effectiveness as a legislator, which is OK, and not his effectiveness as a driver, which is not." Williams defeated James Finley and Amos Moore, despite the continuous assaults on his character and judgment. Although it is impossible to predict the impact of the *Constitution's* endorsement, it is safe to assume that the free publicity came at a time when he was locked up and unable to leverage one of his greatest attributes—his penchant for and masterful manipulation of the media. Williams's defeat of two relatively uncontroversial figures in a local election in the wake of the Reagan endorsement spoke to his popularity and his constituents' belief that he best represented their interests, effectively mitigating any chatter among the small population of Blacks who had labeled the activist-legislator a "sell out."[62]

His standing and "Teflon-like" reputation among the everyday DeKalb citizens was further evidenced by his acquittal of the June 24 DUI charge, which could have ended in a mistrial because of the prejudicial prosecutorial questioning of a witness about Williams's other traffic violations. Williams's defense hinged on a claim that he was in a parked car, whereas the police stated that the vehicle was in gear, effectively challenging the allegation that he was even driving. The activist-legislator claimed that he was "set up" because of his participation in civil rights activities. He asserted that police officers and other law enforcement officers used their authority to arrest and levy trumped-up charges against activists. "Every time police officers saw you behind the wheel they carried you to jail," he said to the jury, which comprised four Black men and two white women. Williams had some influential sympathizers who spoke to the jury as character witnesses on Williams's behalf. For example, Robert Gottlich, a division manager and vice president of Church's Chicken, a company that Williams picketed on behalf of employees seeking equitable treatment, appeared as a character witness for the defendant. Others coming to Williams's defense in the trial included former editor of *The Atlanta Constitution* Hal Gulliver; and Revs. Ralph Abernathy and William Holmes Borders.[63]

Rep. Williams was eligible for release under the Early Release Program as jail trusty but declined to sign the parole papers because of his mistrust of the police. It is clear that he feared being arrested again by police officers who knew that another arrest would extend his prison sentence. He argued that, under the trusty program, he was promised that he was eligible for release after four months without any conditions, specifically being home between the hours of midnight and 6:00 AM and a prohibition from being in the company of known felons. Williams argued that the latter was impossible because of his association with Atlanta's poor as a minister and director of a soup kitchen. Contending that restrictions were too rigorous, he appealed to the Georgia State Supreme Court to no avail. The Court dismissed the lawsuit because it did not have original jurisdiction in the case. Williams, then, appealed to the DeKalb Superior Court. Judge Hinton Fuller, although sympathetic, refused to grant a release. "I personally believe [that] he's served enough time in jail . . . but I do not feel it's my responsibility to modify the sentence," Fuller said from the bench. Williams maintained that he was being held as a "political hostage." His claim had some merit. The judge believed that he had completed enough of the sentence, but he still refused to grant a release from jail and the conditions of the parole that Williams sought to avoid out of fear that he would be arrested on false charges. A federal magistrate freed Williams one day after Fuller's decision to remand him to the DeKalb County jail with one condition: Williams had to remain in the Northern District of Georgia pending a hearing in the federal court. Judge Castellani declared that Williams had raised a "substantial federal issue," as he would complete his sentence before the court could reach a resolution. Upon release, Williams said that his imprisonment was a "conspiracy to send me to prison, get me out of politics and break my spirit."[64]

Rep. Williams likely had a renewed vigor to fight for Georgia citizens who believed that they had been trampled by the iron feet of capitalism upon entering the great chamber on January 10, 1983. His support for the poor and marginalized probably still confounded his colleagues as he remained supportive of a president who had led massive spending cuts to social services that benefited poor and working-class Black and white citizens. Williams supported a bill proposed by Reps. Bill Mangun and Bob Holmes to hold auto manufacturers and car dealers accountable if they sold a "lemon" to unsuspecting customers. The bill would require the seller to provide the customer with a new vehicle or refund one hundred percent of the purchase price within thirty days if the dealer or manufacturer had not addressed the vehicle's deficiencies. Not only did Rep. Williams support the passage of the bill, but he also proposed a constitutional amendment that required industrial and commercial companies to submit the value of their inventory based on the average monthly value for ad valorem tax purposes to supplant the existing law that required dealers to report their inventory on January 1. This anti-business proposal would increase the amount of state taxes that dealers had to pay, as the inventory on January 1 of each year was much smaller because of dealers' special sales and car rebates to reduce inventory during the fourth quarter of each year.[65]

Williams's extended detention in the DeKalb County Jail from June through November 1982 likely strengthened his resolve to propose and pass legislation that assisted inmates who had been exploited by a rigged criminal justice system. He believed that he, too, was a victim of a color-conscious justice system despite his socioeconomic station and celebrity status. He and Rep. Tyrone Brooks introduced legislation designed to provide all people released from Georgia prisons a fifty-dollar weekly stipend for up to six months if the ex-offenders are unable to secure employment. The activist-legislators believed that a one-time payment of twenty-five dollars, a new suit, and a bus ticket were wholly inadequate. The program would benefit more than eight thousand people annually at a price tag of approximately $9.6 million. Rep. Brooks declared that the state would simply have to "shift funds from somewhere else" to pay for the worthy program. The bill's sponsors argued that the state would save money because the proposed law would reduce the costs of reincarcerating the thirty percent of offenders who returned to prison within three years. Williams and Brooks probably surmised that if the state treasury was on the hook for paying this large sum of money, then state officials would gradually divest from the ballooning prison industrial complex that targeted primarily Black and poor people. The bill's detractors believed that the proposal was useless and expensive and that it promoted shiftless citizens. A spokesman from the Department of Revenue claimed that the law would make offenders dependent on the government—a Republican Party talking point that did not dissuade Brooks and Williams. A Georgia citizen responded to the proposed law in an opposing editorial in *The Atlanta Journal-Constitution* by arguing that "Brooks and Williams completely miss the point. . . . This weak-minded proposal is silly and wasteful and circumvents viable solutions for keeping those people out of jail," wrote Charles Loop. Another reader wrote sardonically that "Brooks and Williams show brilliance at every turn" by comparing them to "kids in a candy store with no supervision and a pocket full of money."[66]

Rep. Williams's unbroken streak of making head-scratching headlines during the 1983 legislative session continued when he proposed a law that would give segregationist and former Georgia Governor Lester Maddox a state pension. Maddox had served in statewide office for four years as governor from 1967 to 1971 and four years as the state's lieutenant governor from 1971 to 1975. His eight-year term was well shy of the required eighteen years of governmental service required to qualify for a pension. Conversely, Gov. George Busbee was entitled to an annual pension of fifty-seven thousand dollars because of his combined twenty-six years as a state legislator and two-term chief executive of the state—the source of two lawsuits on the grounds that he was "involuntarily separated" from his job because the state prohibited him from running for a third term. Williams concluded that the governor's racist tirades were blistering to Blacks but that his actions showed that he had a concern for the state's poorest citizens—the latter a record that endeared him to his unlikely advocate. Rep. Williams suggested that Maddox was "the only governor I know who is poorer when he left office" than when he ascended to the governorship. Willams's measure was roundly criticized by Blacks. One reader wrote to the editor of *The Atlanta Voice*, a newspaper that was often sympathetic to Williams, that the "so-called civil rights leader" needed "to lay off that ignorant oil" because he was acting "very, very strange lately."[67]

Perhaps Rep. Williams's advocacy for Gov. Maddox was not strange but, rather, a carefully crafted strategy to align himself to the struggle of the poor white man, whereas the public had only thought of the old civil rights lion as solely wedded to the causes of the Black man. Williams, a combustible combination of a young Tom Watson, Huey Long, and Huey Newton, instinctively understood as an unconventional populist that a Black upper-middle-income governing class dominated Atlanta politics and that he was always in search of a way to distinguish himself from the "downtown power structure" that was buttressed by Jesse Hill, Andrew Young, Maynard Jackson, Michael Lomax, and other influential Black Atlantans. He was an opportunist who saw a clear path to accomplish several objectives: secure free publicity in *The Atlanta Journal-Constitution* that did not involve a vehicle or a driver's license; reinvent his brand while considering a run for political office that required a considerable white constituency to secure an electoral victory at the city or congressional district level; elevate his standing as preacher of the Gospel who embodied forgiveness and love much in the same vein as Jesus Christ or, in his mind, the spirit of Martin Luther King Jr; preserve his standing as a Robin Hood-like figure who continued to remain a champion for the poor, despite his growing entrepreneurial capitalist portfolio as the owner and president of his chemical company and three bingo operations that were run by him or members of the Williams family; and maintain the goodwill of the poor and marginalized who will always outnumber the affluent groups in any city. It is possible that Williams had outflanked and outmaneuvered the elitists in government, which only strengthened his populist appeal.[68]

The businessman-civil rights activist-legislator furthered his populist message of economic uplift against the "downtown power structure" when he shared his vision of a "Sweet Auburn Good-Time Summit Festival" on Black Atlanta's most iconic street. The all-day festival included business development opportunities, gospel, jazz, popular, and country music to heighten the festive spirit. Using his preferred method of communicating with the masses, the press conference, he denounced the Coretta Scott King-led Martin Luther King Jr. Center for Social Change, Mayor Andrew Young, and the Atlanta City Council for being "derelict" in their responsibilities to advance "Sweet Auburn's" revitalization efforts. He claimed that many of the Black organizations and politicians were prostituting Auburn Avenue for selfish gain. Williams also asked for the support of the white business community who, he believed, should only supplement the efforts of Black organizations. The festival was a success in terms of community participation. Police estimated a crowd of more than fifteen thousand. He used the festival to preach his message of economic development. "This means we're opening the door to the revitalization of Auburn Avenue for what it must be: an economic base owned and controlled by black people. Williams said." Financially, the effort, which was organized in less than six weeks, was not successful. Organizers claimed a loss of approximately two thousand dollars. Williams had raised thirteen hundred dollars in donations and pledges. He also committed to underwriting the debts if the other organizers were unable to find the necessary dollars. Commenting nearly a month after the festival, the state representative stated that the daylong fest was "worth every penny to see the street alive again."[69]

The media-savvy state representative attempted to capitalize on the visibility that he garnered around the Sweet Auburn festival. Ten days after the event, he announced that he was "strongly considering" a run for Rep. Wyche Fowler's Fifth Congressional District seat in the US House of

Representatives. Fowler, a white candidate who enjoyed support from the Black and white communities had been elected three times to the seat in a district that had been redrawn to include a majority of Black residents. State Rep. Williams rated himself as "super qualified" to represent Georgia's Fifth Congressional District, regardless of his skin color—a message that he had tacitly and explicitly emphasized since he endorsed Reagan for president in October 1980. Although he was noncommittal as to whether he would seek Fowler's seat, Rep. Williams did announce on January 31, 1984, that he would not seek a sixth term to represent the Fifty-Fourth District in the Georgia House of Representatives. After ten years, "I ought to move on," he said.[70]

Rep. Williams's decision to not seek reelection did not have an impact on his commitment to author and advocate for bills that benefited poor and historically marginalized Georgians. He continued fighting for the little man before pursuing his next tour of public service. Reps. Williams and Brooks jointly proposed bill HB 152, the "Aid to Dependent Children Act." The bill ensured the eligibility for practically any Georgia resident under the age of eighteen years old, regardless of their primary caretaker, to receive financial assistance from the state welfare program. Before the bill's passage, Georgia residents were unable to receive welfare benefits if both parents resided in the same residence. An unemployed father who lost his job for reasons he could not control "had to leave the home if he wants his family fed," Williams said. Reps. Williams and Brooks garnered enough support from liberals and conservatives to pass the statute by a wide margin of one hundred eight to forty-nine. All of Williams's proposed measures did not pass the great chamber. For example, he proposed an amendment to HB 900, a bill that governed the purchasing latitude for the Legislative Services Committee. Rep. Williams offered an amendment to guarantee that at least ten percent of all contracts be awarded to minority entrepreneurs. The amendment failed as a result of one hundred thirty-seven "no" votes whereas only thirty-three voted in favor of the proposal. His voting pattern in the Georgia House of Representatives was incongruous with his support for Reagan. Rep. Williams voted for proposed legislation that was specifically tailored to the wide swath of voters who were harmed by President Reagan's administration federal cuts.[71]

Rep. Williams constantly walked the tightrope between conviction and compromise. This balancing act was evident during the debate in the great House over a bill to recognize Martin Luther King Jr.'s birthday as a state holiday. He was the House's chief advocate for a statewide holiday since he was sworn in 1974. The bill had not made it out of committee to the floor in more than ten years. Eighteen other states had already established a legal holiday in honor of Georgia's most famous native. Worse, in the eyes of some Georgians, the delay was a repudiation of the state's leadership, as President Reagan had already signed a bill honoring King's birthday on the third Monday in January the previous year. The bill that passed both chambers did not honor King on his birthday. Rep. Williams proposed an amendment that would have legalized the state holiday on January 15. His effort was roundly defeated by a margin of twenty-eight in favor and one hundred twenty-six who opposed the amendment. Worse, in Williams's observation, his colleagues were diluting King's legacy by allowing the governor broad discretion to choose as the legal holiday January 19, April 26, or June 3. As an additional insult, the bill called for a Confederate Memorial Day. Rep. Williams opposed the final bill on principle: "I voted against the bill that passed . . . because it was too much of a compromise and fell too far below the dignity of Dr. King," the still-fiery lieutenant said after the historic vote. For once, Williams and King's widow, Coretta, were on the same side of the argument. Although she was grateful that the law had passed, she wanted to "see Georgia observe the holiday when the federal government" honored the slain leader on the third Monday of January. On balance, the legislation had to have the support of the legislators and their constituents, who were diehard segregationists who opposed not simply the causes for which King was killed but King as a man who, in their eyes, did not merit the same honor as the revered Robert E. Lee or others who spent their lives defending the perceived and innate inferiority of Blacks.[72]

Rep. Williams spoke from the floor of the Georgia House of Representatives for the last time as a state legislator on February 29, 1984. His parting address to his colleagues on "Leap Year" was replete with the same expected befuddlement that accompanies the quadrennial calendar occurrence. The graying fifty-eight-year-old civil rights lion said that his ten years in the House was "one of the most gratifying experiences" of his life. He hinted that his departure from the House did not mean that he was exiting politics. He floated ideas about considering a run for lieutenant governor, labor commissioner, or US Representative from the state's Fifth Congressional District. The departing representative indicated that he would make a decision after anonymous members of his "blue ribbon think tank" weighed the advantages and disadvantages of running for each of the aforementioned political offices. He also mentioned his planned fundraiser for former Governor Lester Maddox on March 24 in Atlanta, with the objective of raising one hundred thousand dollars, as one of the last bills he proposed that would give Maddox a one-time payment of ninety-six thousand dollars was defeated in the House. Williams still maintained that his unrelenting support for Maddox was due to the defiant segregationist's cancer diagnosis, his financial hardship, and his ambiguous claims that, while governor, he did more for Blacks than any previous state chief executive in the state's history. Perhaps this was an ingenious ploy to endear him to a large bloc of white voters in the event he ran for an office that required considerable white support to secure an electoral victory.[73]

Williams's peculiar but carefully calculated strategy to engage a diverse electorate did not prohibit him from being honored by one of the state's most revered HBCUs: his alma mater. Morris Brown College conferred upon one of her most distinguished graduates the honorary doctor of laws degree during the institution's 103rd Founders Day on March 23, 1984. President Robert Threatt asserted from the podium that the civil rights lion was being recognized by the institution for his "crucial but unheralded contributions to the advancement of the civil rights struggle of the 1960s." Morris Brown College had given Williams an opportunity to pursue the baccalaureate degree after he was denied admission by Morehouse College and Clark College because of his not having satisfied the colleges' requirements at the time he applied for admission on returning from Europe after World War II. The honorary degree likely offered the honoree a sense of validation and knowing that he made good on a promise to uphold the College's highest ideals.[74]

Hosea Williams announced his intention to seek Georgia's Fifth Congressional District seat one week after he received the honorary degree from Morris Brown College. The three-time white incumbent, Wyche Fowler, had enjoyed support from a mixed coalition of Black and white constituents. Fowler had won more than seventy percent of the Black vote during his two previous electoral victories. This was not the first time Williams and Fowler faced each other in an election contest. Fowler had defeated Williams when the two vied for the presidency of the Atlanta City Council in 1973. Williams pledged in his campaign announcement to an audience of more than two hundred supporters that he would not use race as a central component of his campaign. The state had ten representatives in Congress in 1984. None were white, at a time when Blacks constituted nearly thirty percent of Georgia's population. He did emphasize the need of Black representation in Congress. Other well-known Black challengers had bowed out of the race once Fowler declared that he would seek a fourth term. State Senator Julian Bond, Fulton County Commission Chairperson Michael Lomax, and former Mayor of Atlanta Maynard Jackson did not believe that they could overcome Fowler's likeability and the overall advantage of incumbency. Moreover, one observer believed that Williams was "less than the class of the Atlanta black political field" because of his eccentricity, impatient bluster, and "Williamsonian" brand of populism.[75]

Williams attempted to portray himself as a pro-business candidate who had a deep-seated sympathy for the poor and who could draw support from a diverse network. "I know as the business community goes so goes the city," he said. To the same mostly white, affluent audience of business leaders, he reaffirmed his belief that the poor were still being sacrificed on the altars of middle-class comfort and upward advancement. Despite Williams's inability to maintain message discipline, he secured endorsements from high-profile, mainstream supporters. Mayor Andrew Young wrote a letter that was distributed to more than fifteen thousand potential voters. Young wrote that Williams was "the most qualified black in the race." He also emphasized the confidence that King had in the "bull in a China shop's" leadership. Young wrote that Williams was "personally chosen by the late Dr. Martin Luther King Jr. as his top field general" in the SCLC. A local observer called the endorsement "astonishing," as Young was expected to remain neutral in the race. Joseph Lowery also supported Williams's candidacy, citing his former adversary's maturation as a leader. "I've had my problems with Hosea. But he's grown, he's mellowed," Lowery said. Williams also had the support of Dillard Munford, conservative businessman and owner of the Majik Market convenience store chain. To show his bipartisan appeal, the aspiring congressman won the support of W. R. Richardson, the principal of Richardson and Associates Electronics. Richardson's endorsement was striking because of his role within the state's conservative circles. He was an adviser to Georgia's Young Republicans and served as chairman of the Conservative League of Georgia. Some white Atlantans were not sold on Williams's bid for Congress. One white reader of *The Atlanta Journal-Constitution* wrote that Williams was a "wild man" who "at best was a character and at worst nothing more than a racial agitator and self-promoter."[76]

Williams was ultimately shellacked by Fowler in the election for the Fifth District's Congressional seat, despite his unexpected diverse coalition of supporters. In a field of five candidates, Williams came in second place with nineteen thousand eight hundred thirty-six votes, or thirty percent of the vote, to Fowler's forty-thousand eight hundred seventy-eight votes.

Fowler had comfortably won by 61.8 percentage points. To Williams's credit, none of the remaining three candidates, including Alveda King Beal, Martin Luther King Jr.'s niece, won more than 4.2 percentage points. Although he lost his election, there was still a cause for celebration in the Williams home on election night. His wife, Juanita, won his old seat in the Georgia House of Representatives in a tight election against James Finley. Finley had lost to Williams four times before being defeated by Williams's wife. As for Williams, he performed better than expected. His appeal was a sign for him that he was popular enough and had the record to turn out the vote. He had his eyes on another seat, coincidentally held by James Finley's brother, that he believed he could win the following year.[77]

Hosea Williams did not spend the 1984 holiday season with his family. The US Supreme Court reaffirmed the decision of the 11th US Circuit of Appeals to uphold Williams's prison sentence from his July 18, 1980, collision that led to his being convicted of the misdemeanor charge of leaving the scene of an accident. The Court ruled that he had not been denied his Sixth Amendment right to confront his accusers during the trial. He reported to the DeKalb County Jail on December 19 while carrying *Roget's Thesaurus*, *The American Heritage Dictionary*, and Richard Bach's 1977 book *Illusions: The Adventures of a Reluctant Messiah* to complete the remainder of his forty-one-day sentence. He had already served one hundred thirty-nine days in jail before he was released on an appeal bond in 1982. After professing his innocence, he proclaimed that he was going on a fast during the sentence to cleanse his mind and spirit. District Attorney Bob Wilson was possibly correct when he accused Williams of attempting to gain sympathy by asking for deputies to arrest him on the steps of the State Capitol six days before Christmas when he had until December 28 to ask the Supreme Court to reconsider his case. Perhaps what is most interesting with regard to Williams's decision to report to finish out his sentence was that his church, the Martin Luther King Jr. Poor People's Church of Love, still planned to feed between three thousand and four thousand Atlantans at the Wheat Street Baptist Church. The Black Robin Hood of the poor still made the provisions, with a dedicated team, to provide food for the needy while he was fasting in a cold DeKalb County jail cell.[78]

TEN

"I'm an Opportunist," 1985–2000

Hosea Williams celebrated the beginning of 1985 in a DeKalb County jail cell. He was unable to join his family and enjoy the traditional New Year's Day meal that likely consisted of collard greens, fried chicken, black-eyed peas, and cornbread. Williams was obviously prohibited from raising a glass of champagne in toasting to a prosperous year. However, the former state representative was granted a four-day leave from prison from January 18 to January 22 to participate in a celebration more grandiose than the party he would have thrown at his home at 8 East Drive—Ronald Reagan's presidential inauguration and one of the nine $125-per-ticket inaugural balls. The terms of Williams's temporary reprieve to attend the inauguration called for two conditions: He was prohibited from consuming alcohol and operating a motor vehicle. In a letter to the editor of *The Atlanta Journal-Constitution*, an Atlantan called the law a "farce" for granting the former state representative a "furlough." Apparently, the Presidential Inaugural Committee inadvertently invited Williams to one of the balls. Committee Spokesman Tucker Eskew admitted that Williams was persona non grata. "The thing just slipped through and we regret the error. . . . It would probably be in everyone's best interest if he didn't come," Askew said. With an elevated sense of self-importance, Williams said that "Blacks of my stature" should have access to Reagan for at least "five minutes." Another committee spokesperson called Williams's request to meet with the president during inauguration week "outrageous." Rev. Williams no longer had access to the levers of power with Reagan or his administration likely because of his public encounters with law enforcement and what Reagan probably perceived as disloyalty. Williams withdrew his support for Reagan in 1984 when he endorsed his movement brother, Jesse Jackson, in his failed bid to secure the Democratic Party's nomination for president.[1]

There is only fragmentary evidence about Rev. Williams's experiences and outcomes from his trip to the inauguration; however, he continued flirting with the Republican Party despite his continued self-identification as a vacillating Democrat. He used his consistent inconsistencies to whet the local media's appetite and Atlanta's hunger for stories about him and his political future. He strategically leveraged the free publicity in preparation for his next political move. Records indicate that he returned from Washington DC on January 22 to complete the final two weeks of his jail sentence; however, it is likely that he had rubbed elbows with influential Republicans. During a January 23 jail interview, he shared his inclinations to seek the Republican nomination for Georgia's Fifth Congressional District seat if he secured the "right national support." He predicted "leading masses of Blacks" to the Republican ranks, effectively creating a "two-party-system" in the Deep South. After his release at 8:50 AM on Tuesday, February 5, he garnered publicity through his efforts to recruit more Blacks to the Republican Party. He admonished approximately one hundred Cobb County, Georgia, Republicans at the Marietta City Hall for neglecting Black voters. He outlined his reasons for endorsing Reagan in 1980 during his fifteen-minute speech that solicited "much applause" and a "standing ovation." He told the predominately white audience that the Democratic Party's "white liberal wing" has exploited Black people as "political hostages" and that Republicans needed to look beyond race as a party identifier, because he was not a lone disaffected Black Democrat. He reminded the group that they needed to consider Blacks in their campaign strategy, because it was unlikely that the Republican Party could produce another Reagan-like figure in 1988. Perhaps Williams simplified to the Cobb County GOP his very complex persona that had befuddled Blacks, whites, Democrats, Republicans, his supporters, and his detractors in an honest, un-Sphinx-like declaration: "People ask me, 'Are you a liberal or a conservative?' I'm an opportunist," he said.[2]

Rev. Williams was a con man with convictions. He merged his propensity to exploit an opportunity with logical and pragmatic approaches by using a savvy media relations strategy that directly improved the lives of Black and poor people. He instinctively understood that these two groups were the easiest groups to ignore by elitists and downtown power structures. Williams was always distinguishing and rebranding himself through manufactured but sophisticated and sensationalized schemes to dramatize the plight of the most marginalized communities. He purchased and rode a ten-speed bike when his license was suspended and wrote a press release to that effect to highlight his commitment to his constituents. He arranged to surrender to the sheriff deputies in the most conspicuous places after notifying the news media of the scheduled arrangement when other celebrities hid behind sunglasses and publicists. Publishers and editors could not resist writing stories about the preacher who ran three bingo parlors. Rev. Williams's courting of the Republican Party was consistent with his pattern of seeking publicity to increase the visibility of Black and poor people.

Williams's central argument hinged on the reality that Blacks needed to have the leverage to push either major party toward developing substantive policies that directly benefited their communities. He believed that Blacks were not a monolith simply because they advocated for equal protection under the laws and the protection of the civil rights gains that he played a crucial role in securing during the movement. Williams did not discuss criminal justice reform when speaking to conservative and white Republican audiences. He did not have to: His celebrity status as Martin Luther King Jr.'s field general gave him a degree of authenticity that allowed him to make appeals to Republicans' financial senses. The Republican Party during Reagan's administration, with the exception of supporting the King federal holiday bill, had virtually ignored Blacks in their political calculus. Blacks who embraced conservatism felt neglected and were at a political crossroads. Williams was simply trying to create a winning formula for both Blacks and the Republicans, even if he knew that he would never carry the Grand Old Party banner in an election.[3]

By July 1985, Williams was once again weighing the advantages and disadvantages of running for local office in Atlanta. He considered seeking the presidency of the Atlanta City Council, a seat that was held by Marvin Arrington. Rev. Williams insisted on his call-in show that Arrington was not "sensitive" to the needs of his constituents and had "sold out to the rich, downtown power structure." He also lambasted Fifth District Atlanta City Councilman Morris Finley with the same criticism. Williams had defeated Councilman Finley's brother, James, five consecutive times for the right to represent the Fifty-Fourth District in the Georgia General Assembly. Williams sensed that Councilman Finley was more vulnerable than Arrington and saw an opportunity to exploit the incumbent's weaknesses, particularly his inability to funnel funding to the East Atlanta Library renovation project, as low hanging political campaign fruit. Rev. Williams qualified to run for Councilman Finley's seat on Friday, August 23. Williams used his newspaper, *The Crusader*, to attack Finley with less than several months before the election. He blamed Finley for a woman's death in his district because, in Williams's logic, he had failed to secure the necessary funding for a traffic light near the location where the fatal accident occurred. Williams also used the death of Eddie Kirkland, a Black male resident of Bowen Homes in Atlanta, to get free publicity while also calling for a coroner's inquest. This tragedy presented an easy scenario for him to fire up Black residents in the district by shouting from a bullhorn that "medical examiners have been known to cover up for the police."[4]

Williams campaigned on a platform that promised to deliver more funding to the city's Fifth District. The critics did not believe that the former five-term state representative was a serious candidate. Finley, on the contrary, was a respectable candidate in the eyes of those who attended a September 29 candidate forum. Clint Babom, a Finley supporter, said that the incumbent had "done a fine job." This same voter said that Williams was "nice" but that his "loud" approach to problem solving was a "turn off." Marti Hagan, another Finley supporter who attended the same candidate forum, said that Williams did not have a chance at winning the election, because he "seemed to be a joke" and that his reputation "makes it very difficult to get things done." J. Dennis Jackson, another candidate in the election, accused Williams of drunk driving. Williams refuted the claim and correctly argued that he had never been convicted of driving drunk.[5]

Rev. Williams and Councilman Finley were the top two contestants in the October 8 election. Williams had amassed one thousand six hundred seventy-three votes, whereas official election results showed that Finley had the support of one thousand three hundred eighty-three voters. Williams had won only 49.8 percent of the vote, shy of the fifty percent required to avoid a runoff. Williams was granted a recount after he made a formal request to the Fulton County Board of Registration and Elections because one hundred seventy-one Fifth District voters had submitted blank ballots. Poll watchers attested to voters using pencils instead of the appropriate metal stylus. The recount yielded a net loss of two votes. Finley accused Williams of pursuing the recount solely for publicity. Speaking of himself in the third person, the challenger declared "That's the one thing Hosea Williams does not need." He certainly relished in the free publicity that he leveraged to his advantage and perhaps owed his runoff victory to the media coverage that he received. He won by securing sixty-five percent of the vote in an election where only twelve percent of eligible voters exercised their right to the ballot. Williams's colleague in Bloody Sunday, Atlanta City Councilman John Lewis, declared after the upset victory that "The people have spoken." Williams gave a more colorful populist response: "We beat 'em all. We beat the rich white power structure, we beat the black power structure, we beat the *Journal* and *Constitution*. . . . My smashing victory shows that it's [the neighborhood movement] very much alive," the victorious councilman-elect declared. Williams's victory was the runoff anomaly. Three incumbents retained their seats in other runoffs, including Councilman James Howard and school board members Bob Waymer and D. F. Glover.[6]

Rev. Williams's victory was a mandate of twelve years of district stagnancy. Some perceptive local observers believed that the new councilman was a "cannon loose on the deck" but far from a "crazy man." Even one of his most vocal critics, Jim Minter of *The Atlanta Journal-Constitution*, believed that the newest councilman had the ability to be a positive force because of his "maverick courage." Minter admitted that he, like so many others, was guilty of devoting an inordinate amount of time and attention to focusing on Williams's motor vehicle driver's report. He gave a balanced appraisal of Williams's accomplishments in Atlanta, citing how hiring practices changed at Sears, Mead Packaging, the C&S Bank, Church's Fried Chicken, and Rich's department store because of his incessant protests on behalf of these companies' employees. Minter also believed that the "old one-two punch" of Williams and Mayor Young from their days with the SCLC during the movement could be reignited if the two were willing to work together.[7]

The councilman-elect brought 1985 to a close by continuing the fifteen-year tradition of providing a full course Thanksgiving meal to Atlanta's poor. Atlanta's Black Robin Hood had somehow convinced the Korean Chamber of Commerce to donate seventeen hundred pounds of turkey, twenty cases of ribs, and forty cases of soft drinks to assist the Metro Atlanta chapter of the SCLC and Williams's church, the Martin Luther King Jr. Poor People's Church of Love, when other solicitation efforts had fallen short of expectations. Collecting the food was only one dilemma that he had to address. Williams had to recruit volunteers to prepare the food while he searched for a venue, as three kitchens in the Atlanta University complex were leased by other groups. Worse, one of the stoves at the Wheat Street Baptist Church was malfunctioning. However, Williams's dogged persistence paid off once again to the benefit of those in need. By the end of Thanksgiving night, his efforts led to more than forty-six hundred people receiving a Thanksgiving meal. One homeless person said, while eating a piece of pecan pie: "I think they really care about poor people." When Williams was asked about the success of the meal, he cited the dinner as an example of Jesus's teachings to give to the poor. As one of King's former lieutenants, he was perhaps the one most committed to dwelling among and uplifting the poor. Williams was fully aware of the duration of his continued service to the cause. He said that Martin Luther King Jr would be pleased. "King is probably somewhere saying, 'Ol' Hosea is still carrying on.'"[8]

Councilman-elect Williams ushered in 1986 in the same way as he brought in 1985—in a jail cell. On January 1, he was stopped in Atlanta at approximately 1:45 AM on Boulevard and Glenwood Avenue as he pulled out of an Amoco gas station in his white-topped red Cadillac Eldorado. He exited the gas station after purchasing a Tab soda and some pork skins. Officer W. Prescott Jr. initiated the traffic stop after alleging that Williams had crossed the center line and had changed lanes without signaling. A search of the convertible revealed three full bottles of liquor, including vodka, gin, and scotch. The young officer initiated a sobriety field and multiple breathalyzer tests. His blood alcohol consumption level rendered two separate readings at the scene of the arrest: .12 and .13. He took another breathalyzer at Grady Memorial Hospital that showed a blood alcohol level of .09. According to the law, a reading of .10 established "automatic guilt" of driving under the influence. Conversely, a reading between .05 and 0.9 gives the officer considerable discretion to arrest or release a suspect. Williams believed that he was being punished once again by the Atlanta Police Department for his public attacks on the former white police chief, John Inman, who the old warhorse believed had used his office to target Black Atlantans. Referring to himself in the third person, the defiant and fiery activist-legislator said during a press conference on the steps of Atlanta City Hall that the "rednecks were trying to destroy Hosea Williams." The councilman-elect asserted that he had only consumed three glasses of champagne at a wedding reception. Williams believed that senior officers prodded the young policeman to write a false report in the police department's attempt to blunt the positive momentum behind his recent election victory. It is likely that Williams explored ways as an Atlanta City councilman to mete out retribution on an agency that he believed targeted him for many years.[9]

Councilman-elect Williams was officially sworn in as a member of the Atlanta City Council on January 6, one day after his sixtieth birthday. At Williams's request, and much to the chagrin of Williams's critics, Councilman Marvin Arrington appointed the old civil rights lion to serve on the Public Safety and Legal Administration Committee alongside Councilpersons

John Lewis, Dozier Smith, Archie Byron, Myrtle Davis, Mary Davis, and Ira Jackson. One Atlantan wrote to the editor that this "bone-headed decision" was the worst form of "political deal making" that "insulted the community" because of Councilman Williams's record of traffic offenses. Another frequent patron of *The Atlanta Journal* compared Williams's fitness to serve on the committee as "an indigent from the streets" providing fiscal "advice to the finance committee." Responding to the detractors, Arrington did not see any conflicts assigning the duly elected councilman to a committee that he was passionate about reforming. Arrington had also appointed Williams to serve on the Human Resources Committee, the Committee on Council, and the Executive Committee.[10]

Williams showed that he had a vision for the city as evidenced by his ten-point plan to improve the efficiency of the Council machinery, despite his inexperience with lawmaking and governance at the municipal level as an elected official. His plan was met with some resistance by some of his more subdued Atlanta City Council colleagues. The four most contentious components of his proposed plan included mandatory town hall meetings in the twelve districts, a citizen review committee for each department (he was probably thinking of the Atlanta Police Department), a reorganization of the City Council, and ethics legislation—all measures that some council members believed were presumptions and ill-timed, especially considering his recent DUI arrest and allegations that he sidestepped some election laws during his contest against Morris Finley. One unnamed councilman hinted privately that the newest and most famous member on the Council "may have to be taken to the toolshed" as an exercise in humility. Williams dismissed what he referred to as "individual jealousies," claiming that his effectiveness will only be measured "by the amount of support I [he] can get from the people."[11]

The first federal holiday in commemorating Martin Luther King Jr.'s birthday in Atlanta in 1986 publicly featured some lingering hostilities that deepened the fractures between two members of King's inner circle during the movement and his widow, Coretta, regarding the citywide celebrations and the recently disbanded King Holiday Commission that had been authorized through federal legislation. Neither Williams nor Abernathy were included on the thirty-one-member committee. Seventeen representatives, including eight members of Congress, four members of the federal executive branch, three members from King's family, and two King Center staff were already accounted for. This group, invariably under the direction of Mrs. King, were to choose the remaining fourteen committee members.

Abernathy and Williams felt that they had been purposely overlooked by Mrs. King and other members of the family who, they perceived, were profiting in the form of major financial donations and notoriety. Councilman Williams was also not involved with any of the King Day celebrations. "I felt left out," Williams said. By all accounts, King's closest friend and confidant during the movement, Ralph Abernathy, was more than thirty-five hundred miles away from Atlanta to speak to a wide range of groups in Anchorage, Alaska, to honor the life of Martin Luther King Jr. "I was not invited to participate in the activities in Atlanta," said Abernathy. He continued, "I don't want to be sitting in the back. I want to be participating." A representative from the King Center said that he was not "excluded on purpose," because the Center was intentional about asking the movement veteran to speak in Alaska due to the demand for Alaskans to learn about the civil rights movement. Sending King's closest friend and confidant to Alaska was seen as an exile, even if it was not intentional. Mrs. King was a deft and savvy operative who understood the power of optics. One is challenged to explain this oversight as an innocent one. On the other hand, Williams had been publicly critical of Mrs. King's management of the King estate since the martyr's death in 1968. He constantly accused her of catering to the "corporate executives, scholars, theoreticians and academic people" instead of the rank and file who "would have given their lives for Dr. King."[12]

Councilman Williams was not accustomed to being on the periphery of any initiative since King's death. He was an alpha male who consumed all the publicity from his strategically calibrated efforts to manipulate the media to further his own agenda, even if his motives were somewhat self-serving and partially pure. Shortly after Williams's City Council victory in the previous November, Mayor Andrew Young, who had known Williams since 1961, succinctly summed up his individualistic inclinations: "Hosea is his own man. I can't imagine him listening to me" or the neighborhoods. He campaigned as being "unbossed and unbought," Young said. Williams's pattern bears this out. Dorothy Cotton, the highest ranking woman within the SCLC spoke of his inability to delegate responsibility during the movement, "Hosea wanted total control and that's where the problems came," she said in 1981. Only one person could moderately channel Williams's temperament and insatiable drive to promote himself, and that was Martin Luther King Jr. Williams wanted to be a larger focus of the King Center's programmatic thrust and, arguably, in a paid capacity. He said, "As far as I am concerned, the people that were close to King . . . are missing from the center. . . . And the people that's carrying on the struggle today should be the products of the center, and that's not true." If Coretta had indeed purposely excluded Williams from the major planning efforts, she would have pursued this alternative as a matter of self-preservation. He did not genuflect to anyone, and he certainly would not have deferred to Mrs. King on matters that he believed she was not sufficiently capable of leading due to her gender, and arrest record and beatings, or the lack thereof, during the movement.[13]

Councilman Williams had a resounding victory in his five-hour DUI trial on March 17. Traffic Court Judge Edward Brock declared that the prosecution had not presented enough evidence to convict him of the DUI charge that could have sent him to jail for another twelve months. Williams once again proclaimed his innocence after the trial. "I certainly was not guilty and I was not guilty of DUI," Williams said. His lawyer, David Botts, hired James Woodford, an expert witness, to testify that the breathalyzer results were flawed because of his respiratory rate. Woodford claimed that his natural rate of breathing caused a false breathalyzer reading by eighteen percent, giving an impression that the amount of alcohol in his bloodstream was higher when, in reality, he was below the .10 level that met the standard of being legally drunk. Woodford testified that Williams's blood alcohol level was probably around .07 percent. Another witness, Phillip Hancock, who once served as the director of Georgia's breath alcohol testing unit, declared that, on the basis of the evidence, Williams was probably not intoxicated. Two employees from the Amoco gas station testified under oath that Councilman Williams was not behaving as if he were drunk. This charge and the witness testimony plausibly question the reputation of Williams as a drunk driver and further gives oxygen to the idea that the Atlanta and DeKalb Police Departments conspired to retaliate against the activist-legislator for his role in challenging racism and the ugly underbelly of capitalism.[14]

Councilman Williams's efforts to bring attention to the death of forty-one-year-old Bowen Homes resident Eddie Kirkland during his campaign against Morris Finley paid off in March 1986. The Civilian Review Board, formed in 1984 after police killed a teenager, had determined that Atlanta Police Department officers had used excessive force when they arrested Kirkland the previous August. An autopsy indicated that Kirkland had died from an overdose of acute cocaine poisoning after he consumed a packet of the potent narcotic that burst in his stomach and entered his bloodstream. The findings of the five-member Civilian Review Board ran counter to an internal police probe that exonerated the ten officers of the brutality charges. The Board's charge was to make formal recommendations to the mayor for consideration. This was the first instance in which a citizen's review panel had rendered a decision that fully refuted the police report. Mayor Young had supported the police department's findings, placing him in a precarious cross fire with the department and his movement comrade, who said of the mayor that he "disheartened the Civilian Review Board" by questioning its credibility. Although the police officers were not formally charged in Kirkland's death, Councilman Williams's persistent efforts succeeded in showing that the decedent's life mattered, despite his socioeconomic station and criminal history. Moreover, his reputation as a bombastic, hell-raising activist-legislator fighting for equality and justice on behalf of marginalized communities gave him a theoretical headshield from critics' attacks.[15]

Councilman Williams had also received fulsome praise from neighborhood leaders and his peers on the City Council regarding his responsiveness to community needs after a stumbling start to his tenure representing the Fifth District. His absences from the first council meeting and the four subsequent committee meetings appeared to be behind the embattled legislator. Within the previous six months, he had been cleared of election law violations that allegedly occurred during his campaign and declared innocent in a bench trial in his DUI case. Councilman and future Atlanta mayor Bill Campbell said that the newest councilman "has been effective" and "blending in very well" with the legislative body. Charles Turner, chairman of a neighborhood planning unit, indicated that Williams's personal challenges did not adversely affect his ability to serve the constituents. "We tell him whatever problems we have, and he'll work on them." Turner concluded his appraisal by saying that Williams was a councilman who was "available to the people." The unexpected positive recognition had to allow Williams to experience some vindication, not that he sought it from individuals in the city and on the council, who were drinking from the wells that he and other activists built during the movement. He was acutely aware of the expectations, especially considering that Young had supported Finley in the election: At worst, Williams probably viewed this endorsement as traitorous; from a more benign posture, he may have seen his movement brother's endorsement of Finley as a survival technique to keep him as far away as possible from City Hall while he was mayor. Although the two activists loved each other and shared a bond that was forged in the white-hot fires of the civil rights movement, they were polar opposites who did not concede much on matters of principle—the latter a characteristic that was often incongruous in politics.[16]

Rev. Williams celebrated his 61st birthday on January 5, 1987. He had been agitating for civil and voting rights since 1965, when others had abandoned the cause to pursue more lucrative opportunities. He believed that the respect that he had justly earned was elusive. "At 61 years old, I'm tired of being rejected," he said. "They know I'm good." The "they" he was likely referencing were the intellectuals, theoreticians, and downtown power structures all over America whom he had long repudiated and protested against while simultaneously seeking their validation, something that he craved. In his mind, the intellectuals did not respect his role as the chief defender of the poor—those men and women who had been lost, left behind, and buried under the rubble of an economic system that failed to give them an opportunity to enjoy the blessings of liberty and financial freedom.[17]

Williams was a self-proclaimed "opportunist" who sought to use any available platform to promote himself while highlighting the interests to which he had devoted his entire life as an activist. He was twenty-one years removed from his most tragically triumphant moment on the Edmund Pettus Bridge in Selma, Alabama—a glorious comma in the long, run-on sentence of his career as an activist-legislator and humanitarian. Williams was analogous to a world-class athlete who reached the pinnacle of his sport's success near the beginning of a "hall of fame-esque" career. Critics—for example, the intellectuals, theoreticians, and downtown power structures—doubted his ability for another run without his first ballot hall of fame head coach, Martin Luther King Jr. Then, the gravitational pull of destiny lured him north of Atlanta to Forsyth County, Georgia, in January 1987.[18]

Hosea Williams knew all about South Georgia, but North Georgia was unknown territory. Throughout his busy career, it had been just across the horizon, out of his sight. Even when his eyes were opened he could not believe what he saw. Two decades after the civil rights movement, de facto segregation had permeated life and law in his own backyard.

Forsyth County bordering Gwinnett and Fulton Counties and Lake Lanier, represented the worst of racism, fear, and intimidation. Located approximately thirty miles from Atlanta, it had a population of approximately thirty-eight thousand residents, nearly all of whom were white. It had a remained a world of its own, unnoticed, a white enclave unlike any other in the South. Although Georgia 400, a major state highway, now ran through Forsyth, the county remained isolated and devoid of a significant

Black presence. Blacks had largely abandoned the county after a racial cleansing ensued in the aftermath of several incidents involving white women. Ellen Grice, the wife of a planter, alleged that she was raped by a Black man on September 5, 1912. Five Blacks were arrested. Authorities said that Tony Powell confessed to the assault. Grant Smith, a Black minister, was whipped by a "mob of 300 infuriated white men" because he hinted that Grice may have spread the tale after she was caught having a consensual sexual relationship. According to reports at the time, he was placed in the courthouse vault for his safety. Blacks learned of the beating while at a picnic and began conspiring to burn the town in retaliation. Governor Joseph Mackey Brown declared martial law in a failed attempt to quell the tension. Several days later, Mae Crow, another white woman, was severely beaten on September 9. Crow died of her injuries two weeks later. Shortly after her funeral, domestic white terrorists in town began posting threatening notices on the doors of Black homes, warning them that they had less than forty-eight hours to leave the county. Nearly eleven hundred Black residents, many of them property owners, fled the county and sought sanctuary in neighboring cities. The men connected with the crimes were convicted and hanged publicly.[19]

By the 1980s many Atlantans were unaware of Forsyth County's history despite the signs that had been posted at the county line for many years that read: "NIGGER DON'T LET THE SUN SET ON YOU IN FORSYTH COUNTY." Miguel Marcelli, a Black Atlanta firefighter, and his girlfriend, Shirley Webb, an employee at the Sophisticated Data Research Company, were oblivious to the county's sordid past when they attended the latter's company picnic at Lake Lanier on July 26, 1980. As the young couple left the outing around 6:15 p.m., Marcelli was shot in the neck when a bullet entered his windshield. The car flipped over at least once since Marcelli was unable to regain control of the vehicle after being wounded. Webb, fearing for her and Marcelli's life, sought assistance from some white residents who lived on Athens Park Drive. The residents opened and then closed the doors in the young woman's face. Marcelli survived and eventually recovered from this harrowing incident.[20]

This story received little coverage in Atlanta. Only two articles appeared in the *Atlanta Constitution* during the trial of Melvin Crow, the local white man who was convicted on two counts of aggravated assault with a deadly weapon for shooting Marcelli. Crow, born seventeen years after the racial cleansing in Forsyth, was probably a cousin to the same Mae Crow whose death in 1912 spurred the racially motivated murder spree. C. B. Hackworth, a young reporter who had written for the *Times* in Gainesville, Georgia, from 1979 to 1986 covered the Marcelli story and had published, after intensely lobbying his editors, a three-part series of reports recounting the infamous 1912 rape and subsequent lynching and expulsion of Black residents in the North Georgia town. Hackworth's editors objected to the publication of the articles on the grounds that the material was not worthy of media coverage because Forsyth's reputation as a backward bastion of bigotry was well-known in the northern section of the Peach State. Hackworth left the *Times* in 1986 to report for *Creative Loafing*, a widely distributed free news weekly publication in Atlanta. His first article for "The Loaf," which was printed on November 15, 1986, was titled "The Forsyth Saga: There is a County in Georgia where Black Americans May Not Live." One can argue that Hackworth's article condemning, or, at the very least, retelling the history of Forsyth, played a prominent role in the saga that would play out in less than two months.[21]

Chuck Blackburn, a white karate instructor and resident of Cumming, Georgia, read the *Creative Loafing* article and rejected the conclusions that Forsyth had not changed its racist character. He incorrectly surmised that the county he loved and called home had evolved. When he planned a "brotherhood march" with Black and white participants to commemorate Martin Luther King Jr.'s birthday, the president-elect of the Cumming-Forsyth Chamber of Commerce, Roger Crow, also from the same family as Mae Crow, maintained that a march was unnecessary because the county was not a "racist, lawless anachronism." The fact that Blackburn had received graphic death threats in the days preceding the 2.5-mile unity walk dispelled Crow's notion that the county did not have a racist element. Understandably shaken, he decided against the march and moved his family from the area. A local white pastor, Bruce Flowers, echoed Crow's sentiments: "I hear all of this stuff that it's all-white and racist but I haven't seen any of this." Dean Carter, another martial arts instructor who lived in neighboring Hall County and knew Chuck Blackburn, assumed responsibility for organizing the march, which was reframed from a demonstration of "brotherhood" in Forsyth County to a defiance of racial hate. He had received support from Revs. Lowery and Williams. "We'll see to it that there's a march in Forsyth County if I have to go up there myself," said Williams. He was certainly aware of Forsyth's history when he agreed to participate in the march.[22]

Rev. Williams extended an offer to lead the march on Saturday, January 17, two days before the state and nation observed the King federal holiday. He arrived wearing his trademark blue overalls and red long-sleeved shirt. Williams stepped off of the bus with his favorite weapon of choice, a bullhorn. Unlike in years past, the blustery civil rights lion was wearing black-framed glasses because of his declining sight. Shortly after the ninety-member nonviolent delegation arrived by bus, they were assaulted by four hundred Klansmen and other jeering white counterdemonstrators as they marched. Many of the Klansmen wore white robes and hoods, and others were dressed in military camouflage. The whites who had gathered to intimidate the marchers threw rocks and beer bottles at the faces of the unarmed adults and their children—some as young as ten years old. The seventy-five law enforcement officers from the Georgia Bureau of Investigation (GBI), the Georgia State Patrol, and the local police were outnumbered by the whites who yelled racial slurs and held signs along the parade route that read "Go home, nigger" and "Forsyth Stays White." "We lost control of the crowd," said GBI official, Bonnie Pike. Speaking with greater urgency about the lack of police protection, Williams said that it was "by the grace of God that someone didn't get killed" in what felt like a war zone. With a Gen. Douglas MacArthur-like promise, Williams vowed to return with a much larger army, despite the seething white vitriol. The whites who vowed to preserve Forsyth's all-white composition were led by white supremacist and Ku Kluxer J. B. Stoner. Stoner had a lengthy history of inciting racial disharmony. He had been out of jail for only two months after serving a three-and-a-half-year sentence for bombing the Black Bethel Baptist Church in Birmingham, Alabama, in 1958, avoiding sentencing and imprisonment until 1983. Stoner addressed approximately one thousand Klansmen at the Forsyth County Courthouse after the marchers boarded their bus to return to Atlanta. "The only way you can keep love and peace and tranquility in Forsyth is to keep those black savages out," yelled Stoner.[23]

Eight hours after Williams's march on Forsyth, some of his critics, along with friendly former colleagues, were in formal gowns, tuxedos, and cummerbunds at a ritzy fundraising gala for The Martin Luther King Jr. Center for Nonviolent Social Change at the Marriott Marquis in downtown Atlanta. The protest loomed large at the dinner. The eighteen hundred attendees were shocked and angered by the news footage. Former mayor Maynard Jackson decried the attacks and condemned the KKK as a "terrorist organization" that should be deemed as "anti-American criminals." Gov. Joe Frank Harris said that he was "embarrassed" by the bestial behavior of the "rabble-rousers" in Forsyth. The grand matron of the affair, Coretta

Scott King, said that it was "inconceivable" in 1987 "that such violent acts can be made against such a peaceful and worthy march for brotherhood and sisterhood in this country." Another one of Williams's adversaries, Fulton County Commission Chairman Michael Lomax, told the attendees that it was incumbent upon the state to show "the hate mongers that decent people outnumber indecent people, even in Forsyth." John Lewis, recently elected US Congressman from Georgia's Fifth District, said during an interview after the gala that the protest in Forsyth revealed that "pockets of racism" were still in existence throughout America. Rev. James Orange, a seasoned SCLC and movement alum, strongly encouraged the crowd to remain in Atlanta and support Williams because what happened earlier "today could very easily happen to you."[24]

The crusty warrior, now older, heavier, and grayer, had already begun planning for a return to Forsyth the following Saturday. The battle-readied Williams had quickly returned to movement mode, and he relished the nostalgia of planning for, and leading, a mass demonstration. "The civil rights family has not been together like this since we buried Martin Luther King Jr.," he yelled, at a mass meeting at the West Hunter Street Baptist Church. He held steering committee meetings in his headquarters on Boulevard Drive in Atlanta to discuss the outline of the procession and other march protocols, such as the prohibition of jewelry and the assignment of easily identifiable march marshals as safety precautions. Although the logistics were not as complex as his last big protest, the march from Selma to Montgomery, he realized that he had to coordinate the effort with different groups and individuals to ensure maximum participation. The march's leader held meetings with Coretta Scott King, the SCLC, and the NAACP to determine "who marches where," a sensitive topic because the movement veterans typically vied to march at the front of the line to maintain order and to ensure television and newspaper coverage—especially the publicity-conscious Williams. In a surprise decision, the old warriors opted not to march on the front row, reserving the frontline for some of the protesters who participated in the January 17 march. Williams and the committee also had to grapple with the budgetary component of the march that had ballooned to forty thousand dollars. Costs included rental fees for one hundred MARTA buses, portable toilets, and other march necessities. Don King, the boxing promoter, had donated five thousand dollars to the effort. The group had also raised money at a pep rally at Ebenezer Baptist Church.[25]

Hosea Williams and the other march organizers had predicted a large crowd but were not expecting an international media coterie to cover the largest civil rights march since 1965. Approximately twenty thousand protesters descended on Forsyth to participate in the Brotherhood March, drastically outnumbering the one thousand angry white counterdemonstrators. Approximately ten thousand marchers arrived to board a Forsyth shuttle around dawn near Martin Luther King Jr.'s crypt at The King Center on Auburn Avenue. The one-hundred-plus MARTA buses that the organizers rented at a price of twenty-two thousand dollars for four hours did not depart from the Center until 10:50 AM, nearly 1.5 hours after the scheduled departure. Buses did not arrive until 1:45 PM because of the traffic. Even the air space was so congested that the Federal Aviation Administration had to redirect other planes and helicopters from flying through Forsyth. A large American media delegation, including ABC, CBS, and NBC, were in Forsyth to cover the march for their viewers. International media outlets in Canada and Sweden were also represented. Perhaps there was an element of irony in a West Germany network, ARD, covering the march to include in footage in a documentary about the US Constitution that was going to be aired later in the year. The news media, invariably anticipating episodes of violence against the nonviolent marchers, were unable to capture the nonexistent violent clashes between white and Black attendees because of the heavy presence of law enforcement. Law enforcement was prepared for the crowd, as evidenced by the presence of nearly three thousand state and local police, including the National Guard, who were dispatched to deter white counterdemonstrators from attacking the protesters.[26]

The one thousand angry, recalcitrant, white demonstrators, including mothers and young children, spewed invective at the peaceful marchers and proudly waved signs denouncing Williams for bringing the negative publicity on this rural county. One man, twenty-six-year-old Paul Stetar, said that he was not at the march to cause trouble, "but to demand that the white people have the same rights as the niggers." With a more subdued tone and, in his mind, being a semiprogressive, construction worker Ray Jenkins said that "Cumming will let the blacks come through to work and eat. But Hosea Williams wants to force them on us." Edward Fields, the editor of a racist tabloid, *The Thunderbolt*, accused the leader of the march for disturbing the peace. There was a "peaceful Ku Klux Klan, and then Hosea Williams comes up here with a busload of niggers and demand that they be dumped in front of our rally," said Fields. Not all counterdemonstrators walked along the parade route. A paraplegic, Jerry Brown, proudly waved the American and Confederate flags and stated that "We believe in equal rights, but the niggers want it all. . . . Thank God for James Earl Ray."

Some counterdemonstrators were silent but equal in their vitriolic response to Black protesters. An unnamed woman in the crowd who chose not to proofread her anti-Black propaganda held a sign that read "GO HOME NIGER."[27]

The marchers sang several movement anthems, including "We Shall Overcome" and "Ain't Gonna Let Nobody Turn Me 'Round" as they walked toward the trek's final destination, the Forsyth County Courthouse. That afternoon, the protesters arrived at 2:45 PM—much later than the planned 1:30 PM starting time. In addition to Williams, notable speakers also included Mayor Andrew Young. The mayor reflected on the differences between the marches of the 1960s and the march on Forsyth. He said that times had changed in that they were not marching against state-sanctioned racism in Cumming, as they had the protection of the governor and the support of Georgia's two US Senators, Wyche Fowler and Sam Nunn. Joseph Lowery told the crowd that "We did not come to scare you to death," but to show that Blacks and whites can live better lives together. Congressman John Lewis, once again reunited with his Bloody Sunday brethren, told the crowd that racism is not acceptable in Forsyth or "anywhere in this country." Don King did not speak but also attended the march that he helped to underwrite. There was also a large population of everyday citizens. Members of a Greek Orthodox church drove from California to attend the march. Students from Duke University and several HBCUs, including Tuskegee University and the schools within the Atlanta University Consortium, listened to the speeches on the steps of the Courthouse that ended around 4:30 PM.[28]

Hosea Williams had returned to the spotlight and was credited with dramatizing how the tentacles of racism touched every aspect of an unusual community, but he also quickly followed up with remedies in the form of a clearly articulated six-point plan to begin the racial reconciliation in Forsyth County. He called for a biracial committee, the Coalition to End Fear and Intimidation, to consist of leaders from the civic and business communities to serve alongside Forsyth county residents and representatives from several civil rights organizations. They were collectively charged with considering economic development and equitable housing programs that benefited Blacks who desired to live in the embattled area that included the county engaging the federal government to monitor compliance with employment and housing laws relative to Blacks. Williams and other proponents of the plan asked that land "unlawfully seized" from Blacks seventy-five years earlier be returned to them or their heirs or that they receive compensation for the property losses. Forsyth County and Cumming officials unanimously agreed to, at the least, form a biracial committee on February 2.[29]

Williams also attended a church service as a way to keep the pressure and spotlight on the county. He likely predicted that the news coverage could not resist a large delegation of Blacks attending a church in the county for the first time in seventy-five years. Rev. Williams maintained that he and the other Blacks were not visiting the churches to start demonstrations but to "worship" and show a "moral commitment" with the religious leaders and congregants in at least sixteen churches. He vowed to attend a smaller church where he would not create a chaotic scene. He wanted to avoid a large house of worship, because, uncharacteristically, he did not want the press to accompany him on this worship experience. His reasoning is unlikely, as he told reporters of his plans to integrate a church with "at least 500 Blacks" in advance of the Sunday service. He and approximately seventy people, predominately Black, left Atlanta in a motorcade on February 1. He chose to worship at the First Baptist Church of Cumming. Other members of his delegation chose to attend six other churches in the county forty miles north of Atlanta. The pastor preached a sermon on tolerance and the importance of valuing the ideas of others with diverging opinions. After the service, Williams said that the church service helped to change his attitude toward the county.[30]

Ever the savvy media provocateur, Williams had learned that Oprah Winfrey was filming her daily syndicated talk show from Forsyth to listen to approximately one hundred twenty-five Whites about the recent events and the county's culture. One resident claimed that "We have a right to have a white community." Winfrey did not allow the marches' leader to appear on the show, likely because she could not predict the outcome of the dialogue between Williams and the whites in the audience. Nonetheless, Williams arrived at the Dinner Deck restaurant, the site of the taping, to "protest our black sister Oprah Winfrey's schemery to exclude all blacks from her show." He also accused the talk show host of minimizing the very active Klan presence in Cumming. Williams and his delegation were ordered by police to return to their vehicles. They refused. "Arrest me, arrest me," screamed the veteran jail inmate in front of news cameras. Williams and seven others, including his second oldest daughter, Elizabeth, were arrested for trespassing. Coretta Scott King and Lowery held a joint news conference condemning the detention of Williams and other members of his group. They were "outraged" by what they believed was an "unlawful" arrest. Williams declared that he would protest the "illegal" arrest, vowing to not "eat another mouthful of food until justice prevails or until I die," he said in a statement. His successor as executive director of the SCLC and fellow movement comrade, Rev. C. T. Vivian, also supported Williams. "He has broken no law, he will pay no fine, he will make the time," said Vivian. Winfrey was interviewed after the television taping. She was asked about her feelings about spending a night in the county. Oprah's response was: I am not "comfortable at all. I am leaving." She also apologized that the old warhorse was detained. "I have nothing but respect for Rev. Hosea Williams," said Oprah.[31]

Despite the positive momentum, Williams was roundly criticized by observers who believed that he was engaging in shameless self-promotion. One contributor to *The Atlanta Journal-Constitution* wrote that he projected himself as a "ridiculous" example of a civil rights activist during his "cruelly brief burst of forgotten glory." Frederick Allen pointed to Williams's behavior after he was arrested as evidence. Williams did admonish the press for "unfair" media coverage and pledged to punish the news media by "going into hiding" immediately before giving a public speech of support and answering questions at a press conference. Allen did not understand Williams or his masterful manipulation of the media, nor did he comprehend that he was a helpless pawn in the infamous newsmaker's plot and ploy. Every time Williams was mentioned in the media, his causes of liberty, justice, and equality remained in conversations around dinner tables, in the board rooms of companies that were not treating Black employees equitably, legislative chambers, and the municipal offices throughout the State of Georgia and elsewhere. There would be many treks to Forsyth as part of a long-term campaign to eliminate the vestiges that haunted after January 1987. The outcome of the march also yielded mixed results. C. T. Vivian summed up what Allen and other detractors did not fully appreciate: "No matter what anybody says, Hosea created a new movement. He willed Forsyth on the American psyche." "He did it by himself," Vivian continued, "If Hosea had not moved, we'd still be rolling alone," unaware of the simmering turmoil and the peculiar discriminatory culture in Forsyth.[32]

Councilman Williams was active in the city of Atlanta, especially when police-officer-involved incidents culminated with the death of an unarmed Black man in one of the city's public housing projects. On September 10, 1987, Atlanta police officer M. L. Long fatally shot Eddie Lee Callahan six times during a brief scuffle in Carver Homes. The thirty-seven-year-old Callahan was shot five times in the back and once in his side. The officer and investigators reported that Callahan allegedly attempted to dislodge Officer R. A. Watson's service revolver from his holster. Eyewitnesses countered this narrative by indicating that Callahan was handcuffed and on his back when he was shot. Williams and Joseph Lowery demanded the termination of both officers within twenty-four hours of the fatal shooting. Approximately one hundred Carver Homes residents attended the City Council meeting on September 14, demanding immediate action against the two police officers. The City Council's Public Safety Committee, of which Councilman Williams was a member, unanimously voted to pass a resolution that he introduced, condemning the officers and demanding accountability. The officers were suspended without pay after they were initially placed on desk duty pending an investigation. Councilman Williams attended a rally near Carver Homes at the Emanuel Baptist Church. As he stirred up the crowd, Williams told the two hundred protesters that the same police officers were under investigation for allegedly beating another Black man named Ronald Jones. Jones had a broken jaw and lost several teeth. Williams compared Jones's beating to "the whooping of a slave."[33]

The tensions heightened between Councilman Williams and Mayor Young after the officers' pay was reinstated within days of the decision to suspend them without compensation. The associate medical examiner, Dr. Saleh Zaki, did not find any evidence that Callahan was handcuffed; hence, the city officials could not necessarily justify the suspension. Negotiations between city officials and the attorneys led to a crooked bargain, according to Williams. Walking back the decision to pay the officers equated to a "compromise with evil," he said. Williams suggested that Young was permitting a more ruinous culture of corruption that supplanted the days of white mayors and white police chiefs. Young countered at a rally by saying that he was responsible for keeping Williams and Lowery alive during the very dangerous episodes during the movement. According to the mayor, who assumed an adult-like posture while slapping the proverbial hands of the childlike, immature, and hot-blooded dissenters, Lowery and Williams, "Hosea Williams, Joe Lowery and I were on opposite sides of every issue during the civil rights days . . . that's what's kept them alive." The Callahan investigation and Williams's instigation of the matter, challenged Young's trademark diplomacy and calmness under pressure. Williams claimed that Mayor Andrew Young challenged him to a fist fight over the former's insistence of another grand jury to investigate another police-involved killing of a Black man: "The mayor became very, very upset. He invited me to a fist fight." Young's chief of communications, Sandra Walker, was cornered by a reporter with regard to Williams's revelations. She said that Young had "no comment."[34]

Officer Long was tried and acquitted by a jury of nine whites and three Blacks of involuntary manslaughter and the lesser charge of using excessive force. While leaving the courtroom, Long reaffirmed his desire to return to his job in the Zone Three area as quickly as possible. He also expressed confidence in the jury's decision and the judicial system. The jury "knew it was a good shooting," said the acquitted officer. Long's attorney denounced Williams as a "loudmouthed politician" who had participated in "rumor mongering" to solicit unnecessary attention to the case. Long's acquittal did not shock many of the Carver Homes residents. Blacks were accustomed to whites, especially police officers, escaping the grips of justice when they were accused of killing non-whites.[35]

The year 1988 was another year that proved to be filled with head-scratching reprieves and indictments. Williams sued Grand Dragons David Holland and Daniel Carver of two KKK units in the aftermath of the first Brotherhood March on Forsyth for 1.5 million dollars for disrupting the march and injuring peaceful protesters. Ed Stephens and other KKK members were also named as defendants in the civil suit. Stephens's attorney, Sam Dickson, argued that the GBI was at fault for permitting the protesters' bus to "disgorge in front of people with opposite views." Williams's attorney, Morris Dees, had recently won a hefty seven-million-dollar decision against the United Klans of America for the lynching of a nineteen-year-old Black man in Mobile, Alabama. Williams asked the judge to drop the suit because he could not square the thought of bankrupting the defendants "who have nothing but their cars and their paychecks" with his conscience. He emphasized that he was led to this decision because, as a follower of Christ, "redemption" and "forgiving" one's enemies would certainly meet with the approval of Jesus and Martin Luther King Jr. US District Judge Charles A. Moye Jr. dismissed the six jurors, which included one Black individual, without notifying them of the reason for Williams's request.[36]

Williams's decision provoked a lot of discussion among the advocates who praised his choice and the detractors who suggested that he had made an ill-informed decision. John Lewis endorsed Williams, saying that he was "building a sense of community." One of Williams's perennial critics, Lewis Grizzard, the humorist and frequent contributor to *The Atlanta Journal*, wrote that it "took a big man" to forgive the Klansmen. Tom Teepen, an editor for the *Atlanta Constitution*, wrote that the old warrior had a "root decency" about him that many never noticed. Others were not so complimentary. One person said that Williams hit a "new low with black people" and was now a "disgrace" to the race." Ralph Abernathy and Joseph Lowery respected Williams's decision but emphasized that forgiving the Klan without their repenting was not reconcilable with the teachings of Jesus Christ or Martin Luther King Jr. Even Williams's closest friend and protégé, Tyrone Brooks, believed that his reputation across the state may be "tarnished" as a result of his choice to offer an olive branch to the Klan.[37]

The truth is that Williams knew that he would likely never see a dime from the blue-collar Klansmen. They had very little in liquid cash and assets. As a result, he briefly rebranded himself as an altruistic, Christ-loving man who espoused the tenets of forgiveness over financial gain. The self-avowed "opportunist" once again took control of the situation. The only thing that Williams gained by dropping the civil suit moments before the verdict was to be read in federal court was the gushing publicity that he craved.[38]

Councilman Williams thought that he had identified another potential opportunity to find the public spotlight when he vacated his seat on the Atlanta City Council to run for mayor against Maynard Jackson in 1988. Councilman and future Atlanta mayor, Bill Campbell, was right when he said that Williams had a "cult following" who would support him for any political office, regardless of the stakes. A recent poll in *The Atlanta Journal-Constitution* showed that the old warhorse was viewed favorably by forty-four percent of potential voters, compared with a seventy-eight percent favorability rating for the former mayor. Jackson, who had served as the city's first Black mayor from 1974 to 1982, was seeking a third term in office. Jackson carried himself like a confident incumbent when asked about his high-profile competition. "I know Hosea so well there's no way in the world of saying why he's doing this," said Jackson. In other words, the former mayor believed that Williams's decision to run against him would only end in defeat for the challenger. The populist Williams decided to run against Jackson because he believed the former mayor is wedded to "a small black clique, and elite clique and the rich power structure." Williams was keenly aware of the enormous odds against him. He compared himself to a "sheep" volunteering to jump into the "lion's den." Once again, he was masterfully playing the role of the outmatched underdog against a well-funded machine run by the Black governing class to appeal to what one writer called "the lowest level of his constituency."[39]

This time, the lion won. The former mayor trounced Williams by a margin of 4–1, capturing seventy-nine percent of the vote. Despite his obvious wealth and prestige, he overwhelmingly won the vote of the working class Atlantan. Williams acknowledged that he operated with a significant deficit, particularly regarding his reputation with the "downtown power structure" and the lack of money to finance his campaign. Jackson fought with a $1.5 million war chest that was financed by wealthy Black and white donors. Most of Williams's campaign contributions came from family, friends, and the members of his devoted cult following. To facilitate a municipal peaceful transfer of power, Mayor Andrew Young transported Williams to the mayor-elect's victory party at the Marriott Marquis hotel in downtown Atlanta. This gesture was a positive sign that Young and Williams had moved past their fierce disagreement over the issues surrounding police brutality and the murder of Black men during the outgoing mayor's administration.[40]

Hosea Williams ended the decade without a constituency to represent at the state or the city level for the first time since 1975. One of Williams's critics, State Representative Billy McKinney, suggested that the charismatic "bull in a china closet" had lost his mystique. Atlanta City Council President Marvin Arrington suggested that it was time for the aging activist to "pass the baton" to a newer generation with more acceptable, mainstream approaches to facilitate the equitable treatment of Blacks. The old warhorse, now sixty-four years old, believed that he could still operate at peak performance. "I am more popular in this city now than I have ever been," he said in February 1990. Fulton County Commission Chairman Michael Lomax, who, Williams believed, belonged to the "downtown power structure," said that it was "premature" to consign the activist-legislator to the dustbin of history. He said that Williams may have one more "international event left in him." Lomax used Williams's past civil rights glory as a barometer of the great fighter's future. After all, Hosea Williams was chiefly responsible for the two largest demonstrations of international proportions for civil and voting rights in the past twenty-five years, in two different states, and in two different decades.[41]

Hosea Williams could not continue defying father time. Although strong, he no longer had the strength and stamina of the barrel-chested bull of the early 1960s. The wear and tear on his body was evident. He had gained weight despite his frequent fasts. Williams was also wearing large-framed bifocals, a sign that his sight had deteriorated. It is likely that some of his citations for traffic infractions could have been alleviated if he had sought the expertise of an optometrist much earlier. Congressman John Lewis noticed that Williams had not taken advantage of the world-class medical care at some of Atlanta's hospitals. Even Hosea Williams "gets weary," said Lewis. "Hosea, as a nonviolent warrior, physically has not taken care of himself. At times he should be looking out for his own well-being." His dizzying schedule at sixty-four years old had not slowed down. He should have been preparing for retirement, but he continued to host his weekly television show as well as spearhead the massive Feed the Hungry initiative. He also continued to manage the three bingo halls.

Perhaps he became more attuned to his own mortality on April 17, 1990, when Rev. Ralph D. Abernathy died from cardiac arrest at Atlanta's Crawford Long Hospital. Abernathy had a series of serious health challenges between 1983 through 1986, including two strokes and a bypass operation to repair a blocked artery. Williams and Abernathy were not on good terms when Abernathy took his last breath, despite Williams's claims that he attempted to see Abernathy at least three times during his last hospital stay. Abernathy was plausibly disturbed by Williams's public repudiation of him in the local media. In January, Williams asserted that Abernathy was "the loneliest man in the world." Abernathy was also aware that his old friend had branded him the "Judas of the movement" for committing what Rev. Otis Moss Jr. referred to as the "second assassination" of the martyred leader. Williams still attempted to show his affection for someone he loved as a friend and brother. Rev. Williams claimed that he attempted to visit and pray with Abernathy in his hospital room six days before he died but was restrained by Ralph Abernathy III and prevented from doing so. Williams would also suffer a ruptured blood vessel in his left arm, perhaps as a result of the encounter. The old warhorse was confined to a hospital room for eleven days.[42]

Williams recovered in time to qualify for his last run for political office, commissioner of DeKalb County's Third District. South DeKalb County was one of the most affluent Black counties in the country. Williams paid the requisite fee and completed the paperwork the day he was discharged from the hospital. Williams was an early favorite in the crowded field of opponents who were attempting to unseat the incumbent and Gov. Joe Frank Harris appointee, Nathaniel Mosby. Most of his opponents did not anticipate that Williams would join the race by the filing deadline. One candidate, Republican Rita Bass, believed that her chances of winning were drastically minimized since the "big gun" had entered the contest. The former state legislator and city councilman believed that he had a prohibitive advantage over Mosby. The incumbent did not have the record, nor had he run a political campaign. Moreover, Williams did not think that Mosby had comparable experience in economic development.[43]

The aspiring county commissioner garnered publicity by ignoring the incumbent and challenging the DeKalb County chief executive officer at the opening of his campaign headquarters on Candler Road and Interstate 20. He charged that Manuel Maloof had only appointed seven percent of Blacks to the county's two hundred eighty-seven appointable positions. Williams asserted that disproportionate representation of Blacks from government positions in South DeKalb County was unfair and restricting this group from reaping the due financial benefits. "We want to share in the fruits of this rich county," Williams said to the approximately twenty-five supporters who came to the official campaign launch.[44]

Williams ran a quality campaign that culminated with a landslide victory over the challengers. Commissioner-elect Williams won eighty-two percent of the vote over his closest challenger, Republican Rita Bass. Williams was back. He had a guaranteed political constituency again and a cause for which to fight: economic development that benefited Blacks in South DeKalb County. He maintained that the overwhelming vote in his favor was evidence that he was elected because the people sought new leadership that only he could bring to the commission. With this electoral victory, Williams had been officially elected to three levels of government: the Georgia House of Representatives, the Atlanta City Council, and now, the DeKalb County Commission. He represented areas that typically yielded very low voter turnout. Perhaps Williamsonian populism appealed to Black, blue-collar workers as well as the voters who were underemployed. This deep-seated faith in his abilities to make their futures brighter compelled them to campaign and vote for one who, they believed, vigorously fought the establishment politicians on their behalf. His message of hope and fierce defense of poor people resonated with his constituents at every level. Although he often claimed that he was financially broke, his businesses were modestly successful. He had the latitude to infuse funds into his campaigns that he believed he could win. He was not owned by any coterie or oligarchy of businesses. He added another company to his growing financial portfolio when he opened the Apollo South Restaurant and Lounge on Campbellton Road in southwest Atlanta shortly after his electoral victory. Because of his financial independence, he could claim that he was "unbossed and unbought."[45]

Hosea Williams was sworn in as the commissioner for DeKalb County's Third District on January 8, 1991. Similar to his desire as a newly elected

Atlanta City councilman, he had already expressed an interest in pursuing a leadership role before he attended a single meeting. He believed that his previous experience in higher-profiled elected positions conferred upon him the right to lead. He had his eyes on the position of presiding officer. The ceremonial designee conducted commission meetings in the absence of the county's chief executive officer. He decided to defer to commissioners with more seniority. The seven-member commission elected Republican Commissioner Robert Morris to the position. Williams's colleagues chose him to serve as deputy presiding officer.[46]

The DeKalb County Commission commemorated Martin Luther King Jr.'s sixty-second birthday with a ninety-minute program in the Manuel J. Maloof Building. Approximately seven hundred fifty DeKalb County employees listened intently to Commissioner Williams's movement heroics as a lieutenant to the martyred dreamer. He had discarded his conservative dark suit for his blue movement overalls. Williams embraced these opportunities, which allowed him to relive some of his most glorious triumphs during the civil rights movement. He likely discussed campaigns in St. Augustine, Birmingham, Selma, Grenada, and Chicago. Williams shared with the audience how King's transformative leadership strengthened his faith in a higher power. "Martin Luther King Jr. was not my God," he said. "But he was my leader and through him I found God." According to reports, Williams's colorful stories incited uncontrollable laughter and tears because of his ability to move an audience—any audience. A spokesman declared that this event had been the largest and best attended King program since the county began honoring the Atlanta native in the 1970s. This was not a surprising fact. Williams was a celebrity, and he was aware of his status and effectively leveraged it to suit multiple purposes.[47]

The camaraderie and goodwill were soon challenged after Commissioner Williams received twenty thousand dollars from the county for the Small Business Economic Development Corporation that he founded. County policy prevented commissioners for voting on measures that benefited entities that were connected to family members. Williams claims that he was no longer involved with the nonprofit operation that was solely operated by his daughter Elizabeth. Williams had not disclosed his connection to the organization before he and five other commissioners voted in favor of the grant award. Some of the commissioners asked for a new vote on the measure after the revelations of Williams's ties to the company. Further investigations revealed that Williams's company Southeastern Chemical Manufacturing and Distribution, operated by his wife, Juanita, had a supply contract for sixteen thousand dollars. The latter was awarded before Williams's election to the commission. Williams requested for the county's new ethics board to examine his actions; he was confident that he was free of any impropriety when he successfully lobbied for the twenty thousand dollars. The DeKalb County Board of Ethics cleared Williams of wrongdoing and voted without dissent to drop the probe. However, the board issued a strong caveat to Williams to abstain from voting on funding requests that were tied to family members. The Commission eventually voted 4–3 in December 1991 to deny the funding.[48]

The Atlanta Journal-Constitution published its report on Williams's complex web of business enterprises that included nonprofit and for-profit entities. He had thirteen nonprofit operations under the same address, 1959 Boulevard Drive. Williams also listed four for-profit companies, including A-1 Chemicals and Supplies, the Kingwell Chemical Corporation, Terry Enterprises, and Southeastern Chemical Manufacturing and Distribution. The bulk of the generated revenues resulted from bingo licenses and operations under the auspices of the Metro Atlanta SCLC, the Kirkwood Community Center, and the Martin Luther King Jr. Poor People's Church of Love. The Metro Atlanta SCLC leased a building on Memorial Drive, in close proximity to one of the county police precincts. In return, Williams's church and the Kirkwood Community Center contracted with the SCLC branch to utilize the building and bingo equipment. This arrangement permitted Williams to operate six nights a week, as he had acquired three different state licenses—effectively allowing him to remain in compliance with the Georgia law that permitted a bingo operation to operate only twice per week. The entangled business arrangement resembled a Mafialike underworld operation. There is no existing hard evidence beyond Williams's own testimony that the Mafia had asked him to run bingo operations throughout the country. However, he was surprisingly able to secure the state licenses to run the most profitable bingo enterprise in Georgia. Williams's companies annually collected between four hundred thousand and five hundred thousand dollars. The GBI frequently audited the operations and did not identify any irregularities that required sanctions.[49]

The Martin Luther King Jr. Poor People's Church of Love was, in reality, a front for a bingo operation. Williams had publicly lambasted Coretta Scott King and others for years for what he believed was identical to "prostituting" the name of Martin Luther King Jr. to promote interests that were not related to King's cause of uplifting the poor. Williams had violated the Internal Revenue Service's stipulations that bingo could only serve as an "insubstantial" component of the church. The church did not have a sanctuary and rarely hosted services, but it oversaw the largest bingo operation in Georgia.[50]

Williams was a staunch defender of the poor, but he was not a pauper himself, despite his earlier declarations that he was broke. His family's operations had received a substantial amount of city and state dollars during his tenure in elected office. The four for-profit business operations had received $1.6 million dollars between 1986 and 1991 from the city of Atlanta and the DeKalb and Fulton County coffers. Williams's wife, Juanita, owned Terry Enterprises. The operation was operated by their son, Hosea Williams Jr. Terry Enterprises had received $1.4 million between 1986 and 1990. He began backpedaling on his previous assertions of his pauperism. "I don't want anybody to get the concept I am poor. I work with the poor," said Williams in 1991. Although Williams's web of entangled operations may have appeared illegal, he had not broken any laws that prompted legal action by the federal, state, or county governments. Any signs of illegal activity would have triggered investigations, trials, and a jail sentence for alleged white-collar crimes.[51]

Williams's notoriety in the local media because of his financial operations led him to declare that he was the "most popular human being in Atlanta." *The Atlanta Journal-Constitution*'s report, he believed, was part of a conspiracy to destroy him, despite his claims that his hands were "clean." The paper had covered Williams with the same verve and vigor since the early 1970s, after the publishers realized that his charisma, colorful antics, and quotes were good for circulation and advertisers. He claimed that he received more coverage in the paper than his famous leader. "I can't believe that I got more coverage in the *Atlanta Constitution* than Martin Luther King Jr. ever even did," said Williams. He continued to play the role of the little man who was bullied by the mighty media that was controlled by the downtown power structure. The coverage of his finances was likely the one topic that he did not want aired in the media, because it distracted from his public persona of a poor man helping other people, despite the reality that he was one of the most financially secure civil rights activists of considerable stature. He likely feared that his ability to drum up attention for the causes that benefit the poor would be jeopardized by the unwanted attention. Nevertheless, his commitment to the poor through the Feed the Hungry and Homeless program was never in question. On the contrary, it insulated him from criticism. After being accused of another hit-and-run violation a few days before the article was published, Chris Dickinson, a Dunwoody resident, berated *The Atlanta Journal-Constitution* in a column: "After all, what about the Thanksgiving turkey drives he does for the hungry? People should spend less time criticizing Mr. Williams and spend more time praising him," said the metropolitan Atlanta citizen. He had wealth but chose to dwell among the poor. His constituency of those sympathetic to the plight refused to convict him the influential court of public opinion.[52]

Williams's first and only term on the DeKalb County Commission was marked by frequent tardiness and absenteeism. Now sixty-five years old with deteriorating health and an expanding business portfolio, he was no longer physically able to effectively serve. He missed key votes because of lingering health conditions. During his first year, he attributed his absences and tardiness to wounds that he sustained during World War II. He had been diagnosed with kidney failure, which also played a role in his lack of attendance. One of the fellow commissioners and critics, John Fletcher, claimed that Williams's disregard for county business was akin to "dereliction of duty." Other commissioners complained that Williams was incognito and refused to return telephone calls. It was painfully clear that he was simply unable to fully meet the needs of his Third District constituents. He admitted in early 1992 that his Feed the Hungry and Homeless initiative had depleted his energy—a revelation that he had never made in public. "I need 30 days of rest. After feeding the hungry on Christmas and on Martin Luther King Day, I am so tired. I need the rest."[53]

The beleaguered warrior would have his thirty-day rest—in a DeKalb County jail cell. He received a lenient one-month sentence after he plead guilty to a hit-and-run charge that stemmed from an incident when he rear-ended Frederick Lamar Johnson on July 19, 1991. The felony charge was reduced to a misdemeanor, allowing Williams to avoid a maximum seven-year prison sentence and losing his seat on the county commission. Williams claimed that he left the scene because the driver was "belligerent," and he felt threatened. Judge Robert Mallis required Williams to surrender his license for two years, pay a one-thousand-dollar fine, and $1,463.13 in restitution to Johnson as part of the plea. Williams was also required to enter into an alcohol rehabilitation facility for treatment. Hosea Williams Jr., defending his father's character, said that "Rev. Williams did not have a drinking problem." DeKalb County Chief Executive Officer Manuel Maloof was hopeful that Williams would finally pursue a treatment plan. Williams claimed in a jail interview after sentencing that he only had less than six drinks per week. He vowed to refrain from consuming alcohol upon his release. "It's causing too many problems for me and too much pain to others. . . . That's one thing they won't have to browbeat me with" any longer, he said. Despite his many traffic citations and jail sentences, he was a celebrity among the other inmates. When eating with the other prisoners, they chanted in unison "Ho-zay-uh, Ho-zay-uh!"[54]

Councilman Williams was released from the DeKalb County Jail and entered the Psychiatric Institute of Atlanta's alcohol rehabilitation program. He was in the hospital for a few days before being admitted to Emory Hospital for a burst blood vessel. This was his second hospital stay in two years to treat a vascular problem. Because of Williams's age, doctors wanted to take the necessary precautions to prevent other issues from causing additional medical emergencies. He had completed his hospital stay and sentencing requirements on May 4. The seventy-day confinement, he said, "was the best thing that ever happened to me . . . it gave me time to rest and to think."[55]

Williams's health challenges continued in 1993 and 1994. He underwent major back surgery at Emory Hospital in February 1993 because of lingering neurological problems related to injuries sustained in World War II that could have been exacerbated by the countless beatings he received during the civil rights movement. Lee Jenkins, a spokesperson for the hospital, expected the sixty-seven-year-old firebrand to be immobilized for an extended period of time because of his age and other underlying health conditions. The timing of the surgery conflicted with his responsibilities as chair of the DeKalb County Commission Budget Review Committee. The proposed budget of two hundred seventy-four million dollars by new Chief Executive Officer Liane Levetan required intense debate because of the committee's task to reconcile a gap of twenty-three million dollars. Doctors expected the councilman to return to normalcy within sixty days. However, he still had not returned to the commission by May 25 because of several unexplained setbacks after the surgery. He was still grappling with the neurological issues in 1994. Williams had to undergo a second surgery on his back on March 16, 1994, because of spinal cord issues and progressive arthritis.[56]

Councilman Williams's health and a tight reelection campaign compelled him to announcement his retirement from politics on June 23, 1994. Williams claimed that his failing health did not play a factor in his retirement at age sixty-eight. When he was cornered about his mounting health challenges, Williams refuted any doctors' statements to the contrary. "Unhealthy . . . don't you see how good I look?" Although the confident councilman was optimistic about his chances at reelection, he faced an uphill battle, because his district was redrawn after the census of 1990. The Third District was no longer predominately Black. Its boundaries included the predominately white areas of Tucker, portions of Stone Mountain; the majority Black area of Scottdale, and the lily-white city of Avondale Estates. The retiring councilman expressed regret that he was leaving the "prestigious suite of elected politics" to return to where he was most needed—the poverty pockets of metropolitan Atlanta. Williams had also committed to penning two books, an autobiography and a "true history" on the life of Martin Luther King Jr.[57]

Soon, however, Williams was forced to grapple with an enemy scarier than any foe he encountered during the civil rights campaign: prostate cancer. Doctors informed the seventy-one-year-old of the cancer diagnosis in the summer of 1998. Williams had vehemently opposed the removal of his prostate because he stood an increased chance of losing his ability to actively engage in sexual intercourse. He had elected to monitor the cancer through the oncological approach known as "watchful waiting," as research had proven that this form of cancer grew slowly and rarely spread throughout the body. Williams said about his prognosis, "I enjoy life and I still enjoy sex, and I'd rather be dead than impotent and wearing a diaper."[58]

Williams's sense of humor could not shield him from the gut-wrenching loss of his son and namesake in September 1998. Hosea L. Williams Jr. died on September 21, 1998, at Duke University Hospital in Durham, North Carolina. The official cause of death was complications from a bone marrow transplant. He had been diagnosed with leukemia in 1997. Councilman Williams's top aide and friend to "Junior," Terrie Randolph, said that he was recuperating from the surgery without much difficulty. His prognosis was so good that he had been released from the hospital earlier than expected. By all accounts, the father and son shared a close bond. He often accompanied his father on civil rights marches. He also followed his dad in the chemical products business, serving as president of one of the family's firms before branching out on his own. The younger Williams was a graduate of Morehouse College and the University of Georgia Law School. Junior left behind a wife, four children, two brothers, and four sisters. The senior Williams was debilitatingly crushed.[59]

Councilman Williams's personal life continued to take a downward spiral exactly one year after he buried his oldest son. He was diagnosed with kidney cancer in September 1999. He underwent surgery to remove the cancerous right kidney at Piedmont Hospital in Atlanta within days of the diagnosis. The ninety-minute surgery was successful. However, Williams's surgeon, Dr. James Bennett, had to extract surrounding tissue to determine whether the cancer had spread to other parts of Williams's seventy-three-year-old body. The Atlanta community doubted whether the annual Feed the Hungry and Homeless program would continue, because its founder was in no shape to lead the massive humanitarian effort. Even from his hospital bed, Williams was coordinating plans for the twenty-ninth Thanksgiving dinner. The dinner proceeded as planned at Turner Field, the home of the Atlanta Braves. Nearly thirty-five thousand hungry Atlantans were fed by hundreds of volunteers, including Georgia Governor Roy Barnes and his wife, First Lady Marie Barnes.[60]

On August 10, 2000, the city of Atlanta sponsored a fitting ceremony to recognize Williams's contributions for his herculean humanitarian efforts and his decades' long commitment to civil and voting rights. The city of Atlanta officially renamed a 3.3-mile portion of Boulevard Drive to Hosea L. Williams Drive. This segment of the street wound between Moreland Avenue and Candler Road in the area of southeast Atlanta that bordered south DeKalb County. Atlanta Mayor Bill Campbell, who once served on the Atlanta City Council with Williams, unveiled the green street sign before an estimated crowd of 500 supporters. Sensing that Williams was in grave condition, Campbell told the crowd that "We planned this to make sure that a grateful city honors a great man while he is still around to appreciate it." One of Williams's sons, Torrey, said ominously that "We are happy that the people and the city has recognized my father while he is still living." Prominent state officials and civil rights activists including Gov. Roy Barnes, Lt. Gov. Mark Taylor, Rev. C. T. Vivian, Rev. Joseph Lowery and SCLC President Martin Luther King III also attended this prelude to what seemed to be Williams's final farewell. Martin Luther King Jr.'s son reiterated what Williams and those who marched with the old warhorse of the movement had known all along: "Martin Luther King Jr. could not have done what did if he didn't have Hosea Williams." The honoree was too weak to attend—a development that was not announced until the day of the ceremony. [61]

Hosea Williams's health continued to decline. He entered the Piedmont Hospital for the final time on October 20, 2000. He had been undergoing intensive chemotherapy treatment since his kidney was removed. He was placed on a respirator on October 31 because of complications from an infection. His cancer had spread to other organs. He died at 3:26 PM on November 17, eight days before the thirtieth Thanksgiving mass meal for

Atlanta hungry and homeless populations. While he was ill, his daughter, Elizabeth Williams Omilami, had been named interim director of the Feed the Homeless and Hungry program.[62]

On November 21, 2000, thousands of people marched into Ebenezer Baptist Church on Auburn Avenue in Atlanta, Georgia, to the tune of "This Little Light of Mine" to pay their final respects to the Rev. Hosea Lorenzo Williams. He was laid to rest in a bronze casket, draped with an American flag, that had been drawn to the church by two mules. He was wearing his trademark blue denim overalls, red shirt, and red Converse sneakers. As a tribute to Williams, many of those in attendance wore the same outfit; overalls had come to be the unofficial uniform of the modern civil rights movement. The thousands of mourners, including the high and the humble, gathered together at the historic house of worship that was co-pastored by Rev. Dr. Martin Luther King Jr. from 1960 until he was assassinated in April 1968. They braved the bitter cold temperatures to honor the man that many knew simply as "Uncle Hosie." The mourners included Executive Cabinet-level secretaries; a former ambassador to the United Nations; a governor of a state in the Deep South; and a mayor of, arguably, the most robust city in the South. Rodney Slater, the US Secretary of Labor in the Clinton Administration, said that Williams fought "to bring into the fold . . . those without a voice, the poor." Dr. King's widow, Coretta Scott King, praised the old warhorse as a "man of God." In a playful tribute, Williams's good friend and confidant, Alley Pat, suggested that previous speakers were giving "highfalutin" tributes that were somewhat devoid of honesty. "I used to hang out with him after midnight. . . . Hosea always said that he was unbossed and unbought but he could be rented or leased," joked Pat. Georgia Governor Roy Barnes recalled that "Hosea was in your face, but he was always compassionate and caring." Barnes left the audience with a pointed observation: "Long after Hosea Williams has been dead, the results of his efforts, his struggles, his compassion, and his love for human beings will be remembered."[63] The bull had made his final exit from the china shop. Martin Luther King's general had left the field. More than two decades after his death, as the nation continues to be roiled by unrest and headlines remind us of the unfinished business of the civil rights movement, restoring to our collective memory the activist legacy of Hosea Williams and the battles he championed is more important than ever.

HOSEA WILLIAMS'S FAMILY TREE

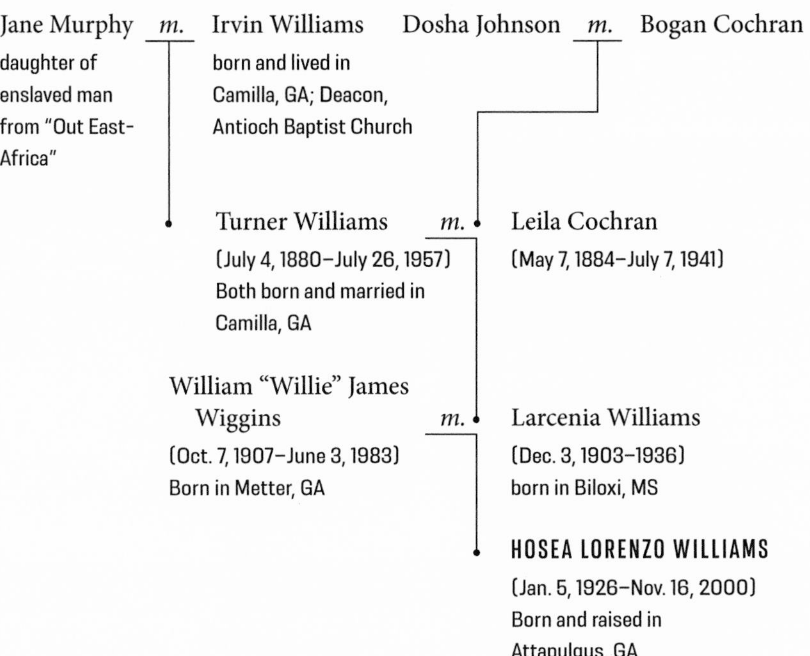

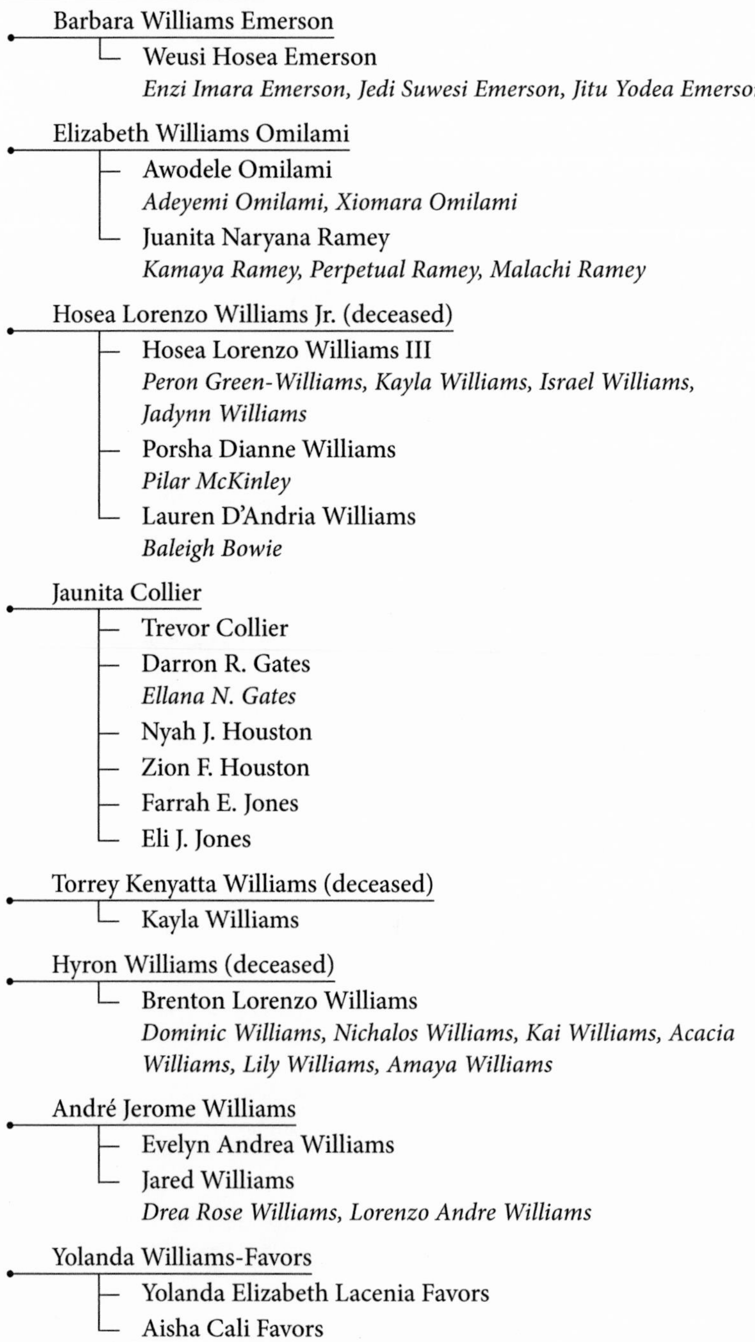

HOSEA LORENZO WILLIAMS

- Barbara Williams Emerson
  - Weusi Hosea Emerson
    Enzi Imara Emerson, Jedi Suwesi Emerson, Jitu Yodea Emerson
- Elizabeth Williams Omilami
  - Awodele Omilami
    Adeyemi Omilami, Xiomara Omilami
  - Juanita Naryana Ramey
    Kamaya Ramey, Perpetual Ramey, Malachi Ramey
- Hosea Lorenzo Williams Jr. (deceased)
  - Hosea Lorenzo Williams III
    Peron Green-Williams, Kayla Williams, Israel Williams, Jadynn Williams
  - Porsha Dianne Williams
    Pilar McKinley
  - Lauren D'Andria Williams
    Baleigh Bowie
- Jaunita Collier
  - Trevor Collier
  - Darron R. Gates
    Ellana N. Gates
  - Nyah J. Houston
  - Zion F. Houston
  - Farrah E. Jones
  - Eli J. Jones
- Torrey Kenyatta Williams (deceased)
  - Kayla Williams
- Hyron Williams (deceased)
  - Brenton Lorenzo Williams
    Dominic Williams, Nichalos Williams, Kai Williams, Acacia Williams, Lily Williams, Amaya Williams
- André Jerome Williams
  - Evelyn Andrea Williams
  - Jared Williams
    Drea Rose Williams, Lorenzo Andre Williams
- Yolanda Williams-Favors
  - Yolanda Elizabeth Lacenia Favors
  - Aisha Cali Favors

NOTES

INTRODUCTION

1. Hosea L. Williams, interview by Taylor Branch, October 29, 1991, Hosea L. Williams Papers, Archives Division, Auburn Avenue Research Library on African American Culture and History, Atlanta-Fulton Public Library System; Hosea L. Williams, interview by Barbara Taggert and Lake Lambert, n.d., Atlanta, Georgia, Hosea L. Williams Papers; Andrew Young, interview by Callie Crossley, October 1, 1985, for *Eyes on the Prize: America's Civil Rights Years (1954–1965)*. Washington University Libraries, Film and Media Archive, Henry Hampton Collection.
2. "Bull in a China Shop' s Retiring," *Atlanta Journal-Constitution*, June 24, 1994; Andrew Young, interview; Stoney Cooks, interview by Thomas C. Dent, May 28, 1981, Box 139, Item 15, Side 1, Tom Dent Collection, Amistad Research Center at Tulane University, New Orleans, Louisiana.
3. Williams, interview by Branch.
4. Hosea L. Williams, interview by Barbara Taggert and Lake Lambert; John Lewis, "Rep. John Lewis: An Oral History of Selma and the Struggle for the Voting Rights Act," *Time*, December 25, 2014. Accessed March 12, 2021. https://time.com/3647070/selma-john-lewis-voting-rights-act/; "Civil Rights Leader Will Seek Sanction of Court for March," *Selma Times Journal*, March 8, 1965.
5. Williams, interview by Branch.
6. Gary Pomerantz, "Hosea's Truth Is Marching On: Veteran Civil Rights Warrior Waits on the Sideline for the Next Cause," *Atlanta Journal-Constitution*, February 4, 1990.
7. Dorothy Cotton, interview by Tom Dent, July 27, 1981, Audiocassette, mono. 16-bit Box 140, Item 15, Side 1, Tom Dent Collection, Amistad Research Center at Tulane University, New Orleans, Louisiana.
8. Hosea L. Williams, interview by Moorland-Spingarn Research Center, March 19, 1996, Transcript, Hosea L. Williams Papers.
9. "The Sorry Condition of Hosea Williams Inc.," *Atlanta Constitution*, July 23, 1991.
10. "The Sorry Condition of Hosea Williams"; Pomerantz, "Hosea's Truth," *Atlanta Journal.*
11. "The Sorry Condition of Hosea Williams," *Atlanta Journal*; for a fuller examination of "respectability politics," see Evelyn Brooks Higginbotham, *Righteous Discontent: The Women's Movement in the Black Baptist Church, 1880–1920* (Cambridge, MA: Harvard University Press, 1993).
12. George Bush, "George W. Bush Speaks at John Lewis' Funeral," YouTube video, 6:17, July 30, 2020, https://www.youtube.com/watch?v=Rwvvt_mzV_Q.
13. Bill Clinton, "Bill Clinton Speaks at John Lewis' Funeral," YouTube video, 17:33, July 30, 2020, https://www.youtube.com/watch?v=P4LlvCsKw-o.
14. Barack Obama, "Barack Obama Speaks at John Lewis Funeral," YouTube video, 39:34, July 30, 2020, https://www.youtube.com/watch?v=V1pKoCq1bno&t=640s.

15. Ibid.
16. Lyndon B. Johnson, "Special Message to the Congress: The American Promise [on the Voting Rights Act], 3/15/65. MP506," YouTube video, June 24, 2013, https://www.youtube.com/watch?v=5NvPhiuGZ6I&t=199s.
17. Ernie Suggs, "He Never Let Things Get in His Way," *Atlanta Journal-Constitution*, November 17, 2000.
18. "Hosea Williams / Civil Rights Activist / 1926-2000 'His Actions Helped Liberate All of Us' Lieutenant to Martin Luther King, Jr. Succumbs," *Savannah Morning News*, November 17, 2000.
19. "Thousands Pay Respects to Civil Rights Leader. The Rev. Jesse Jackson Is among Those Paying Their Respects to Hosea Williams," *Savannah Morning News*, November 21, 2000.
20. Peniel E. Joseph, *Waiting 'Til The Midnight Hour: A Narrative History of Black Power in America* (New York: Henry Holt and Co., 2006), xvii.
21. See, for example, Katherine Mellen Charron, *Freedom's Teacher: The Life of Septima Clark* (Chapel Hill: University of North Carolina Press, 2009); Barbara Ransby, *Ella Baker & the Black Freedom Movement: A Radical Democratic Vision* (Chapel Hill: University of North Carolina Press, 2003).
22. Ernie Suggs, "Farewell to a True Hero, a True Warrior: Advocate for Poor Helped Ignite Nation," *Atlanta Journal-Constitution*, November 21, 2000.
23. Ken Willis, "Williams Charges SCLC With Courting 'Elitists,'" *Atlanta Journal-Constitution*, April 3, 1979; Rolundus Rice, "Willie Bolden, graveside tribute to commemorate the life of Hosea Williams" (home movie), November 16, 2013, Lincoln Cemetery, Atlanta, Georgia, Apple iPhone 5, 34:58 long (contact Rolundus R. Rice at rolundusrice@gmail.com to access the movie); See George Lipsitz, *A Life in the Struggle: Ivory Perry and the Culture of Opposition* (Philadelphia: Temple University Press, 1988) for a fuller analysis of Antonio Gramsci's idea of the "organic intellectual."
24. See Doris Kearns Goodwin, *Team of Rivals: The Political Genius of Abraham Lincoln* (New York: Simon & Schuster, 2005).

CHAPTER 1: "LITTLE TURNER," WORLD WAR II, AND ATLANTA

1. For a still-influential analysis on the Democratic Party in Georgia and throughout the South, see VOKey Jr., *Southern Politics in State and Nation* (New York: Alfred A. Knopf, 1949).
2. Key, *Southern Politics*, 106, 108; William Anderson, *The Wild Man from Sugar Creek: The Political Career of Eugene Talmadge* (Baton Rouge: Louisiana State University Press, 1975), vii, 21–22.
3. Decatur County Historical Society, *Decatur County Georgia: Past and Present, 1823–1991* (Roswell, GA: W. H. Wolfe Associates, 1991), 31.
4. Hosea Williams's parents were both blind. He did not meet his father until he was twenty-eight years old.
5. Hosea L. Williams, interview with unnamed interviewer, n.d., Hosea L. Williams Papers. The author reviewed several primary source documents in the Hosea Williams Papers. There were some documents that showed that Williams was born in "Vilence" Florida. However, there is not a city in Florida with this name.

The author suspected that perhaps the author of the document meant "Valencia" Florida. Another "Biographical Sketch" listed Attapulgus, Georgia, as his birthplace, but there was a line drawn through the name "Attapulgus," and the word "Vilets" was handwritten next to "Attapulgus." A birth certificate lists "Attapulgus" as his official birthplace.

6. Williams, interview by Taylor Branch; Barbara Emerson, email message to author, November 7, 2013. Emerson, born on March 3, 1948, is the eldest daughter of Hosea and Carrie Mae Pugh. She states that her paternal grandparents met at the Macon School for the Colored Blind.
7. George B. Tindall, *The Emergence of the New South, 1913–1945* (Baton Rouge: Louisiana State University Press, 1967), 111; James C. Cobb, *Georgia Odyssey: A Short History of the State* (Athens: University of Georgia Press, 2008), 51.
8. National Emergency Council, *Report on Economic Conditions of the South* (Washington, DC: US Government Printing Office, 1938).
9. Friends of Attapulgus High School, "Attapulgus" (Attapulgus, GA: Highway Marker, 2006), Location: North Main Street, Attapulgus, GA; K. Rödelsperger, B. Brückel, J. Manke, H. J. Woitowitz, and F. Pott, "Potential Health Risks from the Use of Fibrous Mineral Absorption Granulates," *British Journal of Industrial Medicine* 44, no. 5 (May 1987), 337–43.
10. Historic Chattahoochee Commission, Decatur County Commission and the Decatur County Historical Society, "Amsterdam, Georgia" (Attapulgus, GA: Highway Marker, 1986), Location: US 27 median at Amsterdam, SE of Bainbridge; Scott E. Buchanan, *Some of the People Who Ate My Barbeque Didn't Vote for Me: The Life of Georgia Governor Marvin Griffin* (Nashville, TN: Vanderbilt University Press, 2011), 8; E. H. Griffin, "Bainbridge Tobacco Warehouse Opening Sales Amount to 42,174 Pounds Which Average $21.02," *Post-Search Light*, August 5, 1926.
11. Arlene Montgomery, telephone interview by author, Bainbridge, GA, April 2, 2014. Arlene Montgomery is the daughter of Ethel Jackson, the fifth child of Turner and Leila Williams. Montgomery holds a PhD and is a professor at Hampton University in Hampton, Virginia. She is also a retired nurse with the US Army. The author has observed Hosea Williams's maternal grandmother's name spelled different ways. Williams, himself, does not mention her by name in the records. He simply refers to her as "Mama." Interviews with some surviving family members revealed that she is referred to as "Lelar." Her tombstone at Bethel AME Church in Attapulgus has her name spelled as "Leilar." She is referred to throughout this work as "Leila."
12. Barbara Williams Emerson, emailed personal picture to author, March 15, 2014; Leopold Wise, in-person interview by author, Attapulgus, GA, March 31, 2014. Wise resides in Attapulgus and is Turner William's nephew.
13. Ibid.; Year: *1910*; Census Place: *Beat 5, Harrison, Mississippi*; Roll: *T624_741*; Page: *3B*; Enumeration District: *0051*; FHL microfilm: *1374754*. Ancestry.com. *1910 United States Federal Census* [database online]. Provo, UT: Ancestry.com Operations Inc., 2006.
14. Year: *1910*; Census Place: *Beat 5, Harrison, Mississippi*; Roll: *T624_741*; Page: *3B*; Enumeration District: *0051*; FHL microfilm: *1374754*. Ancestry.com. *1910 United*

States Federal Census [database online]. Provo, UT: Ancestry.com Operations Inc., 2006; Mayo Livingston, Jr., *The Story of Decatur County's Carpet of Green and Gold: Turpentining, 1889–1968* (Bainbridge, GA: Post Printing, 1996), 2–3.

15. Year: *1930*; Census Place: *Attapulgus, Decatur, Georgia*; Roll: *350*; Page: *2A*; Enumeration District: *0006*; Image: *720.0*; FHL microfilm: *2340085;* Arlene Montgomery, telephone interview by author, Bainbridge, GA, April 2, 2014.
16. Year: *1930*; Census Place: *Attapulgus, Decatur, Georgia*; Roll: *350*; Page: *2A*; Enumeration District: *0006*; Image: *720.0*; FHL microfilm: *2340085*. Ancestry.com. *1930 United States Federal Census* [database online]. Provo, UT: Ancestry.com Operations Inc., 2002; Hosea L. Williams, unpublished fragmented manuscript transcript, Hosea L. Williams Papers.
17. "Klan Helps Revival," *Post-Search Light*, April 22, 1926; "Educational Meeting of the Ku Klux Klan," *Post-Search Light*, February 20, 1930; Decatur County Historical Society, *Decatur County Georgia: Past and Present, 1823–1991* (Roswell, GA: W. H. Wolfe Associates, 1991), 36; Nancy MacLean, *Behind the Mask of Chivalry: The Making of the Second Ku Klux Klan* (New York: Oxford University Press, 1994), 3.
18. "Children Must Be in School," *Post-Search Light*, January 16, 1930.
19. James D. Anderson, *The Education of Blacks in the South, 1860-1935* (Chapel Hill: University of North Carolina Press, 1988), 1; Decatur County Historical Society, *Decatur County Georgia: Past and Present,* 73; Hosea L. Williams, resume, n.d., Hosea L. Williams Papers.
20. Arlene Montgomery, email message to author, April 4, 2014.
21. Leopold Wise, in-person interview by author, Attapulgus, GA, March 31, 2014; Annie Rae Washington, in-person interview by author, Attapulgus, GA, April 1, 2014. Annie Rae Washington was a contemporary of Azzie and Ethel Williams, Little Turner's aunts. Washington met the Williams family in 1948 when she lodged with them for one week before she started teaching in the Decatur County School System.
22. Anderson, *The Wild Man from Sugar Creek*, 230; Hosea L. Williams, unpublished fragmented manuscript transcript, n.d., Hosea L. Williams Papers.
23. Year: *1930*; Census Place: *Attapulgus, Decatur, Georgia*; Roll: *350*; Page: *2A*; Enumeration District: *0006*; Image: *720.0*; FHL microfilm: *2340085*. Ancestry.com. *1930 United States Federal Census* [database on-line]. Provo, UT: Ancestry.com Operations Inc, 2002; Hosea L. Williams, unpublished fragmented transcript, n.d., Hosea L. Williams Papers. His account fails to mention the exact year when they became intimate, but one can infer that the two began a sexual relationship before he reached his sixteenth birthday, because he was forced to leave town shortly after his grandmother's passing as a result of the illicit association.
24. Hosea L. Williams, unpublished fragmented transcript, n.d., Hosea L. Williams Papers.
25. Ibid.
26. Ibid.
27. Ibid.
28. Ibid.; Leopold Wise, in-person interview, Attapulgus, GA, March 31, 2014. Williams stated that he was around thirteen years old around the time he fled

Attapulgus, GA, for Tallahassee, FL. Family members also argue that he was around twelve years of age. However, in his own words, he is adamant that his grandmother was already deceased. Solid evidence proves that she died in 1941, which would have made Williams at least fifteen years of age when he left for Florida.

29. "Cullman Men See Mob Burn Georgia Negro," *Cullman Democrat*, May 27, 1937; Paul Kwilecki, *One Place and Four Decades of Photographs from Decatur County, Georgia* (Chapel Hill: University of North Carolina Press, 2013), 238.
30. W. Fitzhugh Brundage, *Lynching in the New South: Georgia and Virginia, 1880–1930* (Champaign: University of Illinois Press, 1993), 50, 53, 107.
31. Hosea L. Williams, unpublished fragmented manuscript transcript, Hosea L. Williams Papers; Gilbert C. Fite, *Richard B. Russell: Senator from Georgia* (Chapel Hill: University of North Carolina Press, 1991), 61; Although it is difficult to identify records that document whether the State Department paved the driveway as a favor to Turner, a newspaper article from 1935 does indicate that the Department presented a check for one hundred thousand dollars to the Board of Commissions of Roads and Revenues of Decatur County to "pay the balance of said contract when the balance of State Road No. 1 from Bainbridge South to Tallahassee, Florida is graded, graveled, and paved." The streets mentioned in this article do pass by the one hundred thirty-one acres that Turner Williams owned. See "Pictured Below is the Check for $100,000 Received From the State Highway Dept," *Post-Search Light*, February 7, 1935.
32. Ibid.
33. Glenda Alice Rabby, *The Pain and the Promise: The Struggle for Civil Rights in Tallahassee, Florida* (Athens: The University of Georgia Press, 1999) 1, 2–4.
34. Hosea L. Williams, unpublished fragmented manuscript transcript, Hosea L. Williams Papers.
35. Ibid.
36. David Kennedy, *Freedom from Fear: The American People in Depression and War, 1929–1945* (New York: Oxford University Press, 1999), 518, 522; John J. Stephan, *Hawaii Under the Rising Sun: Japan's Plans for Conquest after Pearl Harbor* (Honolulu: University of Hawaii Press, 1996), 17.
37. Philip McGuire, "Desegregation of the Armed Forces: Black Leadership, Protest and World War II," *Journal of Negro History* 68, no. 2 (Spring 1983), 147; Lee Finkle, "The Conservative Aims of Militant Rhetoric: Black Protest During World War II," *Journal of American History* 6, no. 3 (December 1973), 692.
38. John Hope Franklin and Alfred A. Moss Jr., *From Slavery to Freedom: A History of African Americans,* 8th ed. (New York: McGraw-Hill, 2000), 481.
39. Williams, interview by Branch.
40. Ibid.
41. US Army, Enlisted Record and Report of Separation No. 10816675, n.d., The Personal Papers of Barbara Williams Emerson, Stone Mountain, GA; Williams, interview by Branch.
42. Ibid.
43. Ibid.; David S. Morrison, "The Pro and Con of Hosea Williams," *Atlanta Weekly*, May 24, 1981. The author, attempting to secure additional service records from

the National Personnel Records Center, was informed in a letter dated August 6, 2014, that "The record needed to answer your inquiry was in the area that suffered the most damage in the July 1973 fire at the National Personnel Records Center," Lindsay Schuller to Rolundus Rice, August 6, 2014, letter in author's possession.

44. In the 1991 interview with Taylor Branch, assuming it is transcribed accurately, Hosea Williams indicated he had served "in infantry, 41st infantry." That unit, however, appears to have served in the Pacific Theater of Operations. Williams's Report of Separation paperwork indicates that he was assigned to the 4257th Quartermaster Trucking Company, likely an all–African American unit charged with providing transportation for troops and cargo during the Allied Occupation. However, Report of Separation documents show the last unit a soldier was assigned to at the time of discharge, and often servicemen leaving the Army might be briefly assigned to other units while awaiting return from the European Theater.
45. Although no Purple Heart is referenced on this notice of separation, there are examples of World War II veterans receiving the decoration and not having it included on their "Report of Separation." The qualifications of the Purple Heart do allow for its being awarded as the result of wounds received from "friendly fire," but the context for the injury must include engagement with "enemies" or "opposing armed forces."
46. See Notice of Personal Action, July 11, 1960, Hosea L. Williams Papers. In a letter from the Veterans Administration Regional Office in Atlanta, dated August 7, 1961, Williams was notified that his records had been certified by the Veterans Administration and that he was justly entitled to receive "disability compensation on account of his service-connected disability." See Letter, Elbert B. Anderson to Hosea L. Williams, August 7, 1961, Hosea L. Williams Papers.
47. Kimberly Phillips, *War! What is it Good For? Black Freedom Struggles and the U.S. Military from World War II to Iraq* (Chapel Hill: The University of North Carolina Press, 2014), 16, 26, 62.
48. US Army, Enlisted Record and Report of Separation No. 10816675, n.d., Barbara Williams Emerson Papers; Williams, interview by Branch; Hosea L. Williams, interview by George King, Southern Regional Council, "Will the Circle Be Unbroken?" n.d., Program Files, Manuscript, Archives, and Rare Book Library, Emory University.
49. Williams, interview by Branch; Williams, interview by King.
50. Williams, interview by Branch; Williams, interview by King.
51. Hosea L. Williams, interview by Ralph McGill, September 15, 1986, Ralph McGill Papers, 1853–1971, Manuscript, Archives, and Rare Book Library, Emory University, Atlanta, GA; Decatur County Historical Society, *Decatur County Georgia*, 73; Anderson, *The Education of Blacks in the South*, 1.
52. Barbara Williams Emerson, interview by author, September 2, 2014, Stone Mountain, GA; Obituary of Carrie Mae Smith, February 21, 1995, Hosea L. Williams Papers.
53. Williams, interview by King; Tyrone Brooks, interview by author, Atlanta, GA, April 17, 2014; Morrison, "The Pro and Con of Hosea Williams."

54. Williams, interview by King.
55. Hosea L. Williams, one-page autobiographical blurb, 1959, Barbara Williams Emerson Papers; Williams, interview by Branch; Emmogene Williams, telephone interview by author, Lithonia, GA, September 14, 2014; Victoria Jenkins, telephone interview by author, Lithonia, GA, September 14, 2014.
56. Williams, interview by Branch; Emmogene Williams, interview.
57. Williams, interview by King; John Wesley Dobbs's obituary, September 2, 1961, The Martin Luther King Jr. Center for Nonviolent Social Change, Atlanta, GA.
58. Obituary for Juanita Terry Williams, August 28, 2000, C. T. and Octavia Vivian Papers, Manuscript, Archives, and Rare Book Library, Emory University, Atlanta, GA; Morrison, "The Pro and Con of Hosea Williams."; Hosea L. Williams's bachelor of science diploma from Morris Brown College, June 6, 1951, Barbara Williams Emerson Papers.
59. Barry King, "Williams: A Man of Many Roles and Vocations," *Atlanta Constitution*, March 3, 1979; Hosea L. Williams, one-page autobiographical blurb, 1959, Barbara Williams Emerson Papers; Brooks, interview; Morrison, "The Pro and Con of Hosea Williams."

CHAPTER 2: "THE DEFIANT HEAD HOUSE NIGGER"

1. Williams, interview by Branch, transcription, Series 2, Box 3, Folder 1, Reverend Hosea L. Williams Papers, Archives Division, Auburn Avenue Research Library on African-American Culture and History, Atlanta-Fulton Public Library System; Hosea L. Williams, interview by Lake Lambert and Barbara Taggert, Atlanta, GA, n.d., Series 2, Subseries C, Box 4, Folder 2, Auburn Avenue Research Library; Willie Bolden, graveside tribute to commemorate the life of Hosea Williams, Lincoln Cemetery, November 16, 2013.
2. Williams, interview by Branch.
3. Martin Luther King Jr., quoted in Stephen Tuck, *Beyond Atlanta: The Struggle for Racial Equality in Georgia, 1940–1980* (Athens: University of Georgia Press, 2001), 127.
4. Phinizy Spaulding, "Oglethorpe and the Founding of Georgia," in *A History of Georgia*, ed. Kenneth Coleman (Athens: University of Georgia Press, 1991), 16, 19; "An Early Description of Georgia: From the Gentleman's Magazine, January 1756, Volume 26," *The Georgia Historical Quarterly* 2, no. 1 (March 1918), 37, 39.
5. Spaulding, "Oglethorpe and the Founding of Georgia," 19.
6. C. Vann Woodward, *Origins of the New South, 1877–1913* (Baton Rouge: Louisiana State University Press, 1951), 211–12; Howard N. Rabinowitz, "From Exclusion to Segregation: Southern Race Relations, 1865–1890," *The Journal of American History* 63, no. 2 (September, 1976), 326; August Meier and Elliot Rudwick, "The Boycott Movement Against Jim Crow Streetcars, 1900–1906," *The Journal of American History* 55, no. 4 (March 1969), 756; William F. Holmes, "Civil Rights, 1890–1940," in *A History of Georgia,* ed. Kenneth Coleman (Athens: University of Georgia Press, 1991), 277.
7. "100-year-old Former Teacher, Schools Improving-Veteran Educator," *Savannah Morning News*, May 1, 1974; Holmes, *Civil Rights, 1890-1940*, 277–78; Meier and Rudwick, "The Boycott Movement Against Jim Crow Streetcars, 1900-1906," 757;

John Dittmer, *Black Progressives in Georgia, 1900–1920* (Chicago: University of Illinois Press, 1980) 17–18; Howard O. Robinson, "W. W. Law and The Savannah Branch of the National Association for the Advancement of Colored People" draft of unpublished manuscript, 18.

8. Robinson, "W. W. Law"; Patricia Sullivan, *Lift Every Voice: The NAACP and the Making of the Civil Rights Movement* (New York: The New Press, 2009), 41; *Savannah Tribune*, March 10, 1917.
9. Robinson, "W. W. Law," 5; Sullivan, *Lift Every Voice*, p. 62.
10. The National Association for the Advancement of Colored People, "Fifteenth Annual Report of The National Association for the Advancement of Colored People" (New York: NAACP National Office, 1922), 29; Brundage, *Lynching in the New South*, 232.
11. Letter, Ralph Mark Gilbert to E. Frederick Morrow, March 7, 1942, Selected Branch Files, 1940–1955. Branch Department Files, Geographical File, Savannah, Georgia, 1942–1955 (Bethesda, MD: University Publications of America, 1999), Group II, Box C-40; The First African Baptist Church was organized in 1778 by George Leisle (variously spelled), a Black slave. Various historians have debated the authenticity of the claim that First African Baptist was the first independent Black church in America. See W. E. B. Du Bois, *The Negro Church* (Atlanta: Atlanta University Press, 1903), p10; Gayraud S. Wilmore, *Black Religion and Black Radicalism* (Garden City, NY: Doubleday Anchor, 1973), 110; Carter G. Woodson, *History of the Negro Church* (Washington, DC: Associated Publishers, 1921), 87–89.
12. Ralph Mark Gilbert, letter to the editor, *Crisis*, January 22, 1943, Selected Branch Files, 1940–1955.
13. Letter, W. W. Law to Lucille Black, April 2, 1953, Selected Branch Files, 1940–1955.
14. See chapter 1 for discussion of Williams's service during the World War II and subsequent classification as a disabled veteran.
15. Williams, interview by Branch; Williams, interview by Lambert and Taggert.
16. Williams, interview by Branch; Hosea Williams, job description, n.d., Hosea L. Williams Papers; James Bryant Conant, *Theodore William Richards: January 31, 1868–April 2, 1928* (Washington, DC: National Academy of Sciences, 1974), 257.
17. Hosea L. Williams, interview by Branch; Williams, interview by Lambert and Taggert.
18. Williams, interview by Branch; Hosea Williams's Book Tape, no. 3, recording, December 10, 1973, Hosea L. Williams Papers; "Hosea Williams, Former Chemist Speaks Out," *Chemical & Engineering News Archive*, from the *Journal of the American Chemical Society*, June 17, 1968, 46, no. 26, 21.
19. Williams, interview by Lambert and Taggert.
20. Williams's Book Tape, no. 3; Ralph Lane Polk, *Polk's City of Savannah Directory* (Detroit, MI: R. L. Polk & Co., 1952), 343.
21. Williams's Book Tape, no. 3.
22. Williams's Book Tape, no. 3.
23. Ibid.; Robinson, "W. W. Law," 175–76, 190, 276.
24. Williams, interview by Branch; Barbara Emerson, email message to author, November 7, 2013; Obituary of William James Wiggins, Hosea L. Williams Papers.

25. "NAACP Drive Gets Going," *Savannah Tribune*, March 31, 1955; Letter, Lucille Black to W. W. Law, January 20, 1955, Selected Branch Files, 1940–1955, Branch Department Files Geographical File Savannah, Georgia, 1942–1955, Auburn University Archives, Auburn, Alabama; Letter, Martin Luther King Sr. to Charles E. Batten, March 5, 1948, Morehouse College Martin Luther King Jr. Collection, 1944–1968, Robert W. Woodruff Library of the Atlanta University Center; Letter, Lucille Black to Hosea Williams, May 24, 1955, Branch Department Files, Reel 6, Auburn University Archives; Letter, Lucille Black to Hosea Williams, November 30, 1955, Branch Department Files, Reel 6 (Pt27, Series A), Auburn University Archives.
26. "Chicago Boy Who Was Lynched in Mississippi," *Savannah Tribune*, September 8, 1955; Hosea L. Williams, unpublished fragmented manuscript transcript, n.d., Hosea L. Williams Papers.
27. Taylor Branch, *Parting the Waters*, 146; *Montgomery Improvement Association Newsletter*, ed. Jo Ann Robinson, July 26, 1956, 1, no. 3; Papers of Arthur DShores, Birmingham Civil Rights Institute Archives, Birmingham, AL; Robert S. Graetz, telephone interview by author, Montgomery, AL, July 8, 2011. Graetz was the only white minister who actively participated in the Montgomery Bus Boycott, driving Blacks to home and work using his personal vehicle. As a result of his courage during the three hundred eighty-one-day boycott, his home was bombed, and he and his family were constantly threatened by whites in the city who viewed the minister as a traitor to the race.
28. Williams, interview by Lambert and Taggert; Hosea L. Williams, video interview with unnamed interviewer, n.d., Hosea L. Williams Papers.
29. Samuel L. Brown, "Local Man Selected as President of State NAACP Conference," *Savannah Tribune*, December 8, 1956.
30. Madison Boyd's Biography, William M. Boyd Collection, Archives Division, Auburn Avenue Research Library on African American Culture and History, Atlanta-Fulton Public Library System; Brown, "Local Man Selected as President," *Savannah Tribune*, December 8, 1956.
31. Williams, interview by Branch. The author could not understand why Hosea Williams, and not Turner's son, Turner Williams Jr., was known as "Little Turner." The confusion was settled after the author spoke with Arlene Montgomery. Montgomery suggested that whereas Turner Jr. was much "softer" and "easy-going," Hosea Williams was a "go-getter" and was rebellious just like Turner Sr. Arlene Montgomery, telephone interview by author, Bainbridge, GA, April 2, 2014.
32. Letter, Ralph Mark Gilbert to H. W. Stillwell, November 1, 1942, selected branch files, 1940–1955; Branch department files geographical file, Savannah, GA 1942–1955, Reel 6, Auburn University Archives; Letter, Ralph Mark Gilbert to H. W. Stillwell, November 23, 1942, selected branch files, branch department files 1942–1955, Reel 6, Auburn University Archives; Letter, H. W. Stillwell to Ralph Mark Gilbert, November 26, 1942, selected branch files, branch department files, 1942–1955, Reel 6, Auburn University Archives.
33. Letter, Ralph Mark Gilbert to H. W. Stillwell, November 23, 1942, selected branch files, branch department files, 1942–1955, Reel 6, Auburn University Archives.

34. Williams's Book Tape, no. 3; Williams, interview by Branch; Robinson, "W. W. Law," 196; Constance B. Motley, *Equal Justice Under Law: An Autobiography* (New York: Farrar, Straus and Giroux, 1998), 253, 258; *Cohen v. Public Housing Administration*, 257, F.2d 73 (5th Cir. (Ga.) 1958); *Cohen v. Public Housing Administration,* 358 US 928, 79 S.Ct 315, 3 L,ED.2d 302 (1959). For a detailed examination of "White flight," see Kevin Kruse, *White Flight: Atlanta and the Making of Modern Conservatism* (Princeton, NJ: Princeton University Press, 2005).
35. Williams, interview by Branch; Letter, G. V. Wells to Hosea Williams, November 7, 1958, Hosea L. Williams Papers.
36. Ibid.
37. Williams, interview by Branch.
38. "Registration Council Formed to Help Get More Voters," *Savannah Tribune*, February 28, 1959.
39. William Chafe, *Civilities and Civil Rights: Greensboro, North Carolina and the Struggle for Black Freedom* (Oxford, England: Oxford University Press, 1979), 71–72, 85–86; Aldon Morris, "Black Southern Student Sit-In Movement: An Analysis of Internal Organization," *American Sociological Review* 46, no. 6 (December 1981), 744; Ransby, *Ella Baker*, 237.
40. Harry Murphy, "Three Negro Students Arrested for Sit-Down," *Savannah Morning News*, March 17, 1960; "The Need for the Hour: Responsibility," *Savannah Evening Press*, March 18, 1960; Robinson, "W. W. Law," 259.
41. "Local Lunch Counter Sit Downs Continue," *Savannah Tribune*, March 26, 1960; "NAACP Sunday Mass Meeting Attracts Overflow Audience," *Savannah Tribune*, April 2, 1960; "NAACP Slaps Easter Bunny at Mass Meeting," *Savannah Herald*, April 2, 1960; Tuck, *Beyond Atlanta*, 128, 134.
42. "Mayor's Bi-Racial Committee Denounced by NAACP, *Savannah Tribune*, April 2, 1960; "Hartsfield Balks at Bi-Racial Panel," *Atlanta Constitution*, April 6, 1960.
43. Standard Form (SF-50), Notice of Personal Action, Reassignment, July 11, 1960, Hosea L. Williams Papers; Andrew Young, *An Easy Burden: The Civil Rights Movement and the Transformation of America* (New York: HarperCollins, 1996), 259; Tuck, *Beyond Atlanta*, 280.
44. Williams's Book Tape, no. 3.
45. Ibid.

CHAPTER 3: SAVANNAH'S REBELLIOUS "NEGRO CHIEFTAIN"

1. "NAACP Launches 'Crusades for Votes,'" *Savannah Tribune*, April 9, 1960; Patrick Kelly, "Negro Vote Drives Open," *Savannah Morning News*, April 3, 1960.
2. "Free Shelter from MrJones," *Savannah Herald*, June 11, 1960.
3. "$500 Check Answers Prayer of CV," *Savannah Tribune*, May 23, 1960; Williams's Book Tape, no. 3.
4. Adam Fairclough, *To Redeem the Soul of America: The Southern Christian Leadership Conference and Martin Luther King Jr.* (Athens: University of Georgia Press, 1987), 94; "$500 Check Answers Prayer of CV," *Savannah Tribune*, May 23, 1960; "Get-Out-The-Vote Diagram, Reverend Hosea L. Williams Papers, Auburn Avenue Research Library; Sample Literacy Test Used by the Chatham County Crusade for Voters, Hosea L. Williams Papers.

5. "Negroes Controlled Savannah Election, *Pittsburgh Courier*, October 1, 1960; Tuck, *Beyond Atlanta*, 129; "Mayor's Bi-Racial Committee Denounced by NAACP, *Savannah Tribune*, April 2, 1960; "Voters' Registration Increased," *Savannah Tribune*, June 25, 1960; "Negro Vote In Chatham Heavy One," *Savannah Morning News*, September 15, 1960.
6. "Rep. Preston Concedes: Businessman-Farmer Wins on Recount in Georgia," *New York Times*, September 21, 1960; William F. Holmes, "Populism and Progressivism, 1890–1920" in *A History of Georgia*, 295; Fairclough, *To Redeem the Soul of America*, 94.
7. Highlander Folk School was founded in 1932 by Myles Horton. Horton was a graduate of New York University who had studied under famed theologian, Reinhold Niebuhr. See Myles Horton, Judith Kohl, and Herbert Kohl, *The Long Haul: An Autobiography* (New York: Teacher's College Press of Columbia University, 1998); Katherine Mellen Charron, *Freedom's Teacher: The Life of Septima Poinsette Clark* (Chapel Hill: The University of North Carolina Press, 2009), 5, 275–76.
8. Williams's Book Tape, no. 3.
9. Ibid.
10. Press release, "Savannah NAACP Marks Year-Long Withholding of Patronage Campaign," March 19, 1961, Selected Branch Files, 1940–1955 Branch Department Files Geographical File Savannah, GA, 1942–1955, Reel 6 (Pt27, Series A), Auburn University Archives, Auburn, AL.
11. "Savannah Negroes Boycott Schools," *Atlanta Journal*, March 23, 1961.
12. "A Shameful Situation," *Savannah Morning News*, March 23, 1961; "Clash with NAACP: Negro Leaders Attack Boycott," *Savannah Morning News*, March 24, 1961; "School Boycott Apparently at End Here Today, *Savannah Evening Press*, March 29, 1961.
13. "Negroes Seek to Get Into Library Here," *Savannah Evening News*, May 23, 1960; "Mayor Says Library Open to all Races." *Savannah Morning News*, June 21, 1961; "Negro-Driven City Buses are Planned," *Savannah News*, June 15, 1961; "Negro Bus Driver Hired," *Savannah Evening Press*, June 16, 1961; "First Negro Bus Driver on Duty," *Savannah Herald*, July 1, 1961.
14. "15-Month Battle for Dignity: Savannah Boycott Smashes Lunchroom Bias in Stores," *Pittsburgh Courier*, July 22, 1961; "Savannah Market Bows to Boycott," *Pittsburgh Courier*, August 22, 1961; "Grocer's Hiring Plan Accepted," *Savannah Evening News*, August 10, 1961; "These Tactics Defensible," *Savannah Morning News*, August 11, 1961.
15. Williams's Book Tape, no. 3. According to Williams, singing played an integral part during the boycott. He mentioned one song that they sang while picketing: "Take My Charge Card and Throw It in the Trash Can." The lyrics were "Yea, gonna take my charge card, throw it in the trash can throw it in the trash can. Gonna take my charge card, throw it in the trash can and get in debt no more."
16. Numan V. Bartley, *The Rise of Massive Resistance: Race and Politics in the South During the 1950's* (Baton Rouge: Louisiana State University Press, 1969), 68; Harry Murphy, "Seek Integration: Negroes File School Suit," *Savannah Morning News*, June 19, 1962; "Appeals Court Orders to Desegregate Public Schools," *Savannah Morning News*, May 25, 1963.

17. James Lawson, telephone interview by author, Lithonia, GA, May 7, 2014 (Rev. James Lawson met Martin Luther King Jr. in 1957. The former was an expert in Gandhian nonviolence and helped to organize the student sit-in campaign in Nashville, TN, in 1960.); Yvonne Ryan, *Roy Wilkins: The Quiet Revolutionary and the NAACP* (Lexington: University Press of Kentucky, 2014), 56, 75.
18. Ryan, *Roy Wilkins*, 75.
19. Young, *An Easy Burden*, 141, 144, 258; "History of the Southern Christian Leadership Conference produced by the SCLC's Department of Information, Southern Christian Leadership Conference Records, Manuscript, Archives, and Rare Book Library, Emory University; Williams, interview by Branch.
20. Williams's Book Tape, no. 3; "HL. Williams Loyalty to NAACP Questioned," *Herald*, July 14, 1962; "Hosea Williams to Withdraw Nomination to National NAACP," *Herald*, July 14, 1962.
21. Williams's Book Tape, no. 3; Williams, interview by Branch.
22. Fairclough, *To Redeem the Soul of America*, 95; "Crusade for Voters to Expand," *Savannah Evening Press,* March 7, 1963.
23. Anthony Lewis, "The Right to Have a Coke," *New York Times*, October 23, 1977; Benjamin Van Clark, "The Destiny of Black Folks: The Savannah Story," Reverend Hosea L. Williams Papers, Archives Division, Auburn Avenue Research Library.
24. Willie Bolden, telephone interview by author, Lithonia, GA, May 8, 2014. Bolden worked with Williams and the Chatham County Crusade for Voters in Savannah. He was fired from his job at the Manger Hotel for being sympathetic to the protests. He left Savannah with and began working on Williams's staff with the SCLC. Bolden eventually attended Harvard University and returned to work as the head of personnel in the Atlanta Public School System; Clark, "The Destiny of Black Folks," Reverend Hosea L. Williams Papers; "40 Negroes Arrested at Savannah," *Atlanta Constitution*, June 8, 1963; Young, *An Easy Burden*, 260; Garrow, *Bearing the Cross*, 234–35.
25. "Hosea Williams: The Untold Story," DVD, Dorothy Daniels, producer (Atlanta: ABC, 2010); "Night Marches Opposed," *Savannah Morning News*, June 24, 1963; Tuck, *Beyond Atlanta*, 135; Willie Bolden, "Fireside Chat with the Williams Family and Civil Rights Activists," Panel discussion, Atlanta City Council, Atlanta, GA, February 17, 2014.
26. "Savannah Negroes March: State Sends 52 Patrolmen," *Atlanta Constitution*, June 18, 1963.
27. Kathy Palmer, "To End Night Marches: Mayor Calls for Meeting," *Savannah Evening Press*, June 20, 1963; Young, *An Easy Burden*, 260; Williams's Book Tape, no. 3; "Tear Gas Used to Scatter Negro Mobs; 274 Arrested," *Savannah Morning News*, June 20, 1963.
28. "Negroes Assemble Near County Jail, *Savannah Morning News*, July 5, 1963; "Negro Leader Here is Jailed on Warrant," *Savannah Evening Press*, July 9, 1963; "Hearing Slated for Negro Leader," *Savannah Evening Press*, July 10, 1963; "Savannah Jails Negro Chieftain: Marches Disturb Peace, Woman Says," *Atlanta Journal*, July 10, 1963; "Clarke Out; Williams In: Charge Marches Cause "Lost Sleep," *Crusader* 1, no. 1, July 12, 1963.

29. "900 Negroes Gather Downtown," *Savannah Morning News*, July 10, 1963; "Savannah Negro Runs as Clerk Candidate," *Atlanta Daily World*, July 15, 1961; "Clerk Race Interest High," *Savannah Morning News*, July 24, 1961; "Integration Leader's Bond Now $30,000," *Savannah Morning News*, July 12, 1963.
30. "Negro Leader Says Protests May Resume Here, *Savannah Evening Press*, August 1, 1963; Meeting Minutes of the Committee of 100, August 1, 1963, A. Pratt Adams Jr. Papers, MS 2165, Georgia Historical Society, Savannah, Georgia; Letter, Joseph M. Oliver to A. Pratt Adams, July 31, 1963, A. Pratt Adams Jr. Papers.
31. "Race Panel Sees Savannah Peace," *Atlanta Constitution*, August 3, 1963; "Hosea Williams Out on $15,500 Bond," *Savannah Evening Press*, August 10, 1963. Andrew Young asserted that Williams's bond at one point during his imprisonment reached fifty-five thousand dollars. Evidence to the contrary suggests that the bond never exceeded thirty thousand dollars. Also, Williams posited that he spent sixty-six days in jail during the protests in 1963. However, the newspaper chronicles his arrest and release within a thirty-day period.
32. Tuck, *Beyond Atlanta*, 127; "Mayor Speaks at Crusaders Meeting," *Savannah Herald*, July 3, 1960; "Candidates Quizzed by Negroes," *Savannah Morning News*, August 24, 1962; Williams's Book Tape, no. 3.
33. Hosea Williams: The Untold Story," DVD, Dorothy Daniels, producer (Atlanta: ABC, 2010).
34. Ibid.
35. Young, *An Easy Burden*, 281; Hosea L. Williams's resume, The Papers of Reverend Hosea L. Williams, Auburn Avenue Research Library.

CHAPTER 4: "KING'S KAMIKAZE"

1. Fred Shuttlesworth, interview by David Colburn, n.d., Gainesville, FL, Civil Rights Library of St. Augustine; Andrew Young, interview by Tom Dent, July 8, 1980, audiocassette, mono. 16-bit, Box 138, Item 13, Side 1, Tom Dent collection, Amistad Research Center at Tulane University, New Orleans, LA.
2. Steven F. Lawson, *Black Ballots: Voting Rights in the South, 1944–1969* (New York: Columbia University Press, 1976), 251; Garrow, *Bearing the Cross*, 151; Ted Sorensen, *Counselor: A Life at the Edge of History* (New York: HarperCollins, 2008), 271, 282–83; Godfrey Hodgson, *America in Our Time: From World War II to Nixon—What Happened and Why* (Garden City, NY: Doubleday and Co., 1976), 105.
3. Williams, interview by King; Williams, interview by Branch. There is no independent evidence that supports Williams's claims that the attorney general lobbied the secretary of agriculture to grant his request.
4. "Savannah, Georgia," *Southern Christian Leadership Conference Newsletter* 2, no. 4 (January 1964), 10, Martin Luther King Jr. Papers; "Negroes Press Registration," *Atlanta Journal*, January 2, 1964; Lawson, *Black Ballots*, 284.
5. "1435 New Voters Register in Savannah During January," *Southern Christian Leadership Conference Newsletter* 2, no. 5 (February 1964), 1.
6. "On the Front Line: A Conversation with Andrew Young," *Atlanta Journal-Constitution*, October 13, 1996; "Motorists Complaints are Denied," *Savannah Morning News*, March 19, 1964; "Integration Leader Faces Traffic Cases," *Atlanta Constitution*, March 19, 1964.

7. Alan Taylor, *American Colonies,* 77; Southern Christian Leadership Conference, "St. Augustine, Florida: 400 Years of Bigotry and Hate,"1964, 4, 6, Civil Rights Library of St. Augustine, FL; "Staff Report on St. Augustine," US Commission on Civil Rights, May 18, 1964, Lyndon Baines Johnson Papers, The Lyndon Baines Johnson Library, Austin, TX.
8. Leo C. Jones, Richard O. Russell, William Owens, George Stallings, and C. W. Young, "Racial and Civil Disorder in St. Augustine: Report of the Legislative Investigation Committee," February 1965, 29–30, Civil Rights Library of St. Augustine, FL; "President Kennedy Urged to Deny Funds for St. Augustine Quadricentennial," *Florida Star*, May 11, 1963; St. Augustine Foot Soldiers Remembrance Project, *The Heroic Stories of the St. Augustine Foot Soldiers*, 4, Civil Rights Library of St. Augustine, FL; Young, *An Easy Burden,* 289.
9. "Youths Moved from St. John's Jail Sent to Mariana and Ocala Homes," *Florida Star*, August 17, 1963; St. Augustine Foot Soldiers Remembrance Project, *The Heroic Stories*, 4., Civil Rights Library of St. Augustine, FL; Jones, Russell, Owens, Stallings, Young, "Racial and Civil Disorder in St. Augustine," 29–30.
10. Ibid., 31.
11. Ibid., 32–33.
12. Ibid., 34; Garrow, *Bearing The Cross*, 323; Hester Campbell, "Our Trip to St. Augustine," Civil Rights Library of St. Augustine, FL; "Staff Report on St. Augustine," United States Commission on Civil Rights, May 18, 1964, Lyndon Baines Johnson Papers.
13. David Colburn, *Racial Change and Community Crisis: St. Augustine, Florida, 1877–1980* (New York: Columbia University Press, 1985), ix, 31; Martin Luther King Jr., "1964 Annual Report," Martin Luther King Jr. Papers; Williams, interview by Branch; C. T. Vivian, interview by author, May 14, 2014; Young, *An Easy Burden*, 290; "Mobilize Community," *Southern Christian Leadership Conference Newsletter* 2, no. 7 (June 1964), 3, Martin Luther King Jr. Papers.
14. Robert Hayling, interview by Andrew Young, St. Augustine, FL, n.d., Civil Rights Library of St. Augustine, FL; Jones, Russell, Owens, Stallings, and Young, "Racial and Civil Disorder in St. Augustine," 29; Williams, interview by Branch; Campbell, "Our Trip to St. Augustine".
15. Hodgson, *America in Our Time*, 156, 171; "Dr. King Speaks Here: Negroes May Bring Pressure for Rights," *Savannah Morning News*, January 17, 1964; Nick Kotz, *Judgment Days: Lyndon Baines Johnson, Martin Luther King, Jr. and The Laws* (New York: Houghton Mifflin Company, 2005), 126.
16. Gardner H. Shattuck, *Episcopalians and Race: Civil War to Civil Rights* (Lexington: University Press of Kentucky, 2000), 138; Mary Peabody, "Journal of Trip to St. Augustine," n.d., Civil Rights Library of St. Augustine, FL.
17. Campbell, "Our Trip to St. Augustine"; Peabody, "Journal of Trip to St. Augustine"; Shattuck, *Episcopalians and Race,* 138.
18. Campbell, "Our Trip to St. Augustine."
19. Ibid.; "Mother of Massachusetts Governor Jailed in Florida," *New York Times*, April 1, 1964; Peabody, "Journal of Trip to St. Augustine"; Kotz, *Judgment Days*, 127; Jones, Russell, Owens, Stallings, and Young, "Racial and Civil Disorder in St. Augustine," 35; Garrow, *Bearing the Cross*, 318.

20. "300 Youths in March," *New York Times*, April 1, 1964; Garrow, *Bearing the Cross*, 318.
21. Jones, Russell, Owens, Stallings, and Young, "Racial and Civil Disorder in St. Augustine," 9.
22. Shuttlesworth, interview; C. T. Vivian, interview; Young, *An Easy Burden*, 295; Jones, Russell, Owens, Stallings, Young, "Racial and Civil Disorder in St. Augustine," 9; Colburn, *Racial Change and Community Crisis*, 3.
23. Williams, interview by Branch; Young, *An Easy Burden*, 291–93.
24. Federal Bureau of Investigation Internal Memo, Agent 105-83 to JEdgar Hoover, June 16, 1964, Civil Rights Library of St. Augustine, FL; "In St. Augustine: Jackie Robinson Urges Action," *Daytona Beach News Journal*, June 16, 1964.
25. John Herbers, "16 Rabbis Arrested as Pool Dive-In Sets Off St. Augustine Rights Clash," *New York Times*, June 19, 1964; Federal Bureau of Investigation, "Racial Situation: St. Johns County, Florida, June 19, 1964, Civil Rights Library of St. Augustine, Florida; Leo C. Jones, "Report of the Legislative Investigation Committee," 16.
26. Herbers, "16 Rabbis Seized," *New York Times*, June 19, 1964; Federal Bureau of Investigation, "Racial Situation."
27. Jones, Russell, Owens, Stallings, Young, "Racial and Civil Disorder in St. Augustine," 20–22; Shuttlesworth, interview; Williams, interview by Branch; Garrow, *Bearing the Cross*, 334.
28. "Business Slump Hits St. Augustine," *Southern Christian Leadership Conference Newsletter* 2, no. 7 (June 1964), 1; Jones, Russell, Owens, Stallings, and Young, "Racial and Civil Disorder in St. Augustine,"1.
29. Jones, Russell, Owens, Stallings, Young, "Racial and Civil Disorder in St. Augustine," 44–45; Garrow, *Bearing the Cross*, 336–37; Holstead "Hoss" Manucy was a rabid segregationist whose brutality was comparable to that of a celebrated villain of the modern Black freedom struggle. According to Williams, "Manucy was terrible. Hoss had the mentality of Sherriff Jim Clark in Selma, Alabama." Selma would be the site of the SCLC's next major campaign the following year. See Williams, interview by Branch.
30. Allen Matusow, *The Unraveling of America: A History of Liberalism in the 1960s* (Athens: University of Georgia Press, 1984), 95; Steven F. Lawson and Charles Payne, *Debating the Civil Rights Movement, 1945–1968* (New York: Rowan and Littlefield, 2006), 3, 29; Gavin Wright, *Sharing the Prize: The Economics of the Civil Rights Revolution in the South* (Cambridge, MA: Harvard University Press, 2013), 22.
31. Wright, *Sharing the Prize*, 23; Robert A. Caro, *Master of the Senate: The Years of Lyndon Johnson* (New York: Random House, 2002), xvi; Young, *An Easy Burden*, 297.
32. "Civil Rights Leader Arrested," *Savannah Evening News*, August 10, 1964.
33. "King Will Talk Here Thursday," *Savannah Morning News*, September 29, 1964; Eighth Annual Southern Christian Leadership Program Booklet, Martin Luther King Jr. Papers; Martin Luther King Jr., "Annual Report to the Southern Christian Leadership Convention," n.d., Martin Luther King Jr. Papers; Fairclough, *To Redeem the Soul of America*, 165.

34. "Named King Aide," *Baltimore African American*, December 19, 1964; Williams, interview by Branch.
35. Garrow, *Bearing the Cross*, 358–59; Williams, interview by Branch.
36. Hosea L. Williams, "The Department of Voter Registration and Political Education Proposed Budget: January 1, 1965–June 30, 1965," Hosea L. Williams Papers; Young, *An Easy Burden*, 338.

CHAPTER 5: SELMA AND THE VOTING RIGHTS ACT

1. John Lewis, *Walking with the Wind: A Memoir of the Movement* (New York: Harcourt, Brace & Co., 1998), 312.
2. Fairclough, *To Redeem the Soul of America*, 228; Williams, interview by Branch.
3. Williams, "The Department of Voter Registration."
4. Ibid.
5. V. O. Key, *Southern Politics*, 11; Numan V. Bartley, "Social Change and Sectional Identity," *The Journal of Southern History* 61, no. 1 (February 1995): 4.
6. Wayne Flynt, *Alabama in the Twentieth Century* (Tuscaloosa: University of Alabama Press, 2004), 3; Malcolm C. McMillan, *Constitutional Development in Alabama, 1798–1901: A Study in Politics, The Negro, and Sectionalism* (Chapel Hill: University of North Carolina Press, 1955), 268.
7. Flynt, *Alabama in the Twentieth Century*, 14.
8. Lawson, *Black Ballots*, 89; Lewis, *Walking with the Wind*, 312; Hasan Kwame Jeffries, *Bloody Lowndes: Civil Rights and Black Power in Alabama's Black Belt* (New York: New York University Press, 2009), 1–2; Young, *An Easy Burden*, 337.
9. Garrow, *Bearing the Cross*, 359–360; Fairclough, *To Redeem the Soul of America*, 167; Williams, interview by Lambert and Taggert.
10. Fairclough, *To Redeem the Soul of America*, 229; Garrow, *Bearing the Cross*, 371; Williams, interview by Lambert and Taggert.
11. Lewis, *Walking with the Wind*, 329; Helen L. Bevel, *James Bevel and the Nonviolent Right to Vote Movement* (Chicago: The Institute for the Study and Advancement of Nonviolence, 2009), 102; Young, *An Easy Burden*, 45. Ralph Abernathy, King's closest associate, was a minister but did not have any seminary training. Abernathy and Williams were particularly close after King's assassination.
12. Young, *An Easy Burden*, 399; Taylor Branch, *At Canaan's Edge: America in the King Years, 1965–1968* (New York: Simon and Schuster, 2006), 45; Williams, interview by Branch.
13. Young, *An Easy Burden*, 285, 298; Andrew Young, interview by Jovita Moore, "Hosea Williams: The Untold Story," DVD, Dorothy Daniels, producer (Atlanta: ABC, 2010); Tom Houck, interview, "Hosea Williams: The Untold Story," DVD, Dorothy Daniels, producer (Atlanta: ABC, 2010); Dorothy Cotton, interview by Joseph Mosnier, July 25, 2011, in Ithaca, New York, video recording, Southern Oral History Program, University of North Carolina, Chapel Hill.
14. John Lewis, interview by Jovita Moore, "Hosea Williams: The Untold Story," DVD, Dorothy Daniels, producer (Atlanta: ABC, 2010); Williams, interview by Branch.
15. John Lewis, interview by Jack Bass and Walter Devries, Transcript, November 20, 1973, Interview A-0073 Southern Oral History Program Collection (#4007) in

the Southern Oral History Program Collection, Southern Historical Collection, Wilson Library, University of North Carolina, Chapel Hill; Williams, interview by Branch.

16. "71 Arrested in Selma Alabama Voter Drive," *Chicago Defender*, January 20, 1965; Garrow, *Bearing the Cross*, 379; Williams, interview by Lambert and Taggert.
17. Hosea L. Williams, "Chronology of Events in Selma," n.d., Hosea L. Williams Papers; Garrow, *Bearing the Cross*, 382; Williams, interview by Lambert and Taggert; Young, *An Easy Burden*, 337.
18. Dan Carter, The *Politics of Rage: George Wallace, The Origins of the New Conservatism and the Transformation of American Politics* (Baton Rouge: Louisiana State University Press, 2000), 243–46; Williams, interview by Lambert and Taggert; Hosea L. Williams, "Chronology of Events in Selma," n.d., Hosea L. Williams Papers; Garrow, *Bearing the Cross*, 391, 394; Lewis, *Walking with the Wind*, 328; "Man, 26, Injured by Ala. Troopers, Dies of Wounds," *Atlanta Daily World*, February 27, 1965; James Bevel, interview by James A. DeVinney, November 13, 1985, for *Eyes on the Prize: America's Civil Rights Years (1954-1965)*, Washington University Libraries, Film and Media Archive, Henry Hampton Collection; William Dinkins, interview by Blackside, Inc., September 17, 1979, for *Eyes on the Prize: America's Civil Rights Years (1954–1965)*, Washington University Libraries, Film and Media Archive, Henry Hampton Collection.
19. Ralph David Abernathy, *And the Walls Came Tumbling Down: An Autobiography* (New York: Harper and Row, 1989), 325–26.
20. Carter, *Politics of Rage*, 246–249; Abernathy, *And the Walls Came Tumbling Down* (New York: Harper and Row, 1989), 325–26.
21. Williams, interview by Branch; Williams, interview by Lambert and Taggert (There are different versions regarding postponing the march until the following day. Garrow suggested in *Bearing the Cross* that Williams and Bevel wanted to proceed with the march. Williams was silent on whether Bevel advocated to reschedule until Monday. Williams argued that he appealed to Bevel to lobby on his behalf to King via telephone. Bevel told Williams after the call that King had permitted the march to proceed. Williams learned that Bevel had not conveyed King's decision, as evidenced by the response he received from Andrew Young after chartering a plane to Montgomery); Charles Varner, telephone interview by author, Lithonia, GA, June 15, 2014. The MIA office, along with over four hundred business, churches, schools, and Black residents, were displaced as a result of the City of Montgomery's demolition of the neighborhood to construct the Interstate 65 corridor, primarily because of the area's role in facilitating civil rights protests.
22. Williams, interview by Branch.
23. Abernathy's account is not consistent with either Williams's account or Young's account. If King had agreed to proceed with the protest, Young would not have been dispatched on a chartered plane that morning to stop the march. See Abernathy, *And the Walls Came Tumbling Down*, 325, 327–29.
24. Ibid.; Williams, interview by Lambert and Taggert; Young, *An Easy Burden*, 354–55; Lewis, *Walking with the Wind*, 336; Branch, *At Canaan's Edge*, 44.
25. Lewis, *Walking with the Wind*, 336; Young, *An Easy Burden*, 355; Williams, interview by Lambert and Taggert; Williams, interview by Branch.

26. Lewis, *Walking with the Wind*, 336; Young, *An Easy Burden*, 355; Williams, interview by Lambert and Taggert; Williams, interview by Branch.
27. Lewis, *Walking with the Wind*, 337, 340; Roy Reed, "Alabama Police Use Gas and Clubs to Rout Negroes," *New York Times*, March 8, 1965; "Use Bullwhips, Tear Gas: Beat Negroes at Selma," *Chicago Defender*, March 8, 1965; Lewis, interview by Moore; Hosea L. Williams, "My Account of Selma," Hosea L. Williams Papers.
28. Young, *An Easy Burden*, 357–58; Reed, "Alabama Police Use Gas"; Lewis, *Walking with the Wind*, 343–44; Nicholas Katzenbach, interview by Blackside, Inc., December 10, 1985, for *Eyes on the Prize: America's Civil Rights Years (1954–1965)*, Washington University Libraries, Film and Media Archive, Henry Hampton Collection.
29. Williams, "My Account of Selma"; Lewis, interview by Moore; Young, *An Easy Burden*, 358–59; John Lewis and Amelia Boynton were Hosea's co-plaintiffs. See *Williams v. Wallace*, 240 F.Supp. 100 (1965), US District Court M. D. Alabama, N.D., March 17, 1965.
30. Betty Washington, "The Men Behind Martin Luther King: Subject: Hosea Williams," *Chicago Daily Defender*, May 26, 1965; Williams, "My Account of Selma"; Young, *An Easy Burden*, 359; Jack Bass, *Taming the Storm: The Life and Times of Judge Frank M. Johnson Jr. and the South's Fight Over Civil Rights* (New York: Doubleday, 1992), 35; Young, *An Easy Burden*, 358; Nicholas Katzenbach, interview by Blackside, Inc., December 10, 1985, for *Eyes on the Prize: America's Civil Rights Years (1954–1965)*, Washington University Libraries, Henry Hampton Collection.
31. Williams, "My Account of Selma"; John Herbers, "Clergyman Dies of Selma Beating," *New York Times*, March 11, 1965; Young, *An Easy Burden*, 361–62.
32. Young, *An Easy Burden*, 358; *Williams v. Wallace*, 240 F.Supp. 100 (1965), United States District Court M. D. Alabama, N.D., March 17, 1965.
33. *Williams v. Wallace*, 240 F.Supp. 100 (1965), US District Court M. D. Alabama, N.D., March 17, 1965.
34. Ibid.; "President Accuses Wallace of Shirking," *Atlanta Journal*, March 20, 1965; Williams, "My Account of Selma"; Alvin Spivak, "President Requested to Supply Guards for Montgomery March," *United Press International*, March 20, 1965.
35. Williams, "My Account of Selma"; Alexander Aldrich, Personal Journal of Selma-to-Montgomery March, April 7, 1965, Rev. Hosea L. Williams Papers; Roy Reed, "Freedom March Begins at Selma," *New York Times*, March 22, 1965.
36. Aldrich, "Personal Journal"; Roy Reed, "Hundreds Pour into Selma for March to Montgomery," *New York Times*, March 21, 1965; Williams, "My Account of Selma." John Lewis posited that seven hundred mattresses were purchased at $1.45 each; seven hundred blankets were donated by churches and schools; and four carnival-size tents were rented at four hundred thirty dollars each, along with seventeen thousand square feet of polyethylene for ground cloth, costing one hundred eighty-seven dollars; seven hundred rain ponchos; two twenty-five-hundred-watt generators; and two thousand feet of electrical wiring. See Lewis, *Walking with the Wind*, 356.
37. Al Kuttener, "Troops Line Road, Ring Campsite," *United Press International*, March 22, 1965; Williams, "My Account of Selma"; Aldrich, "Personal Journal."

38. Rex Thomas, "300 Marchers Camps in Mud 20 Miles from Goal," *Atlanta Journal*, March 24, 1965; Williams, "My Account of Selma."
39. *Williams v. Wallace*, 240 F.Supp. 100 (1965), US District Court M. D. Alabama, N.D., March 17, 1965; Williams, "My Account of Selma"; Aldrich, "Personal Journal"; Lewis, *Walking with the Wind*, 359.
40. Young, *An Easy Burden*, 366; "How Long Will It Be: Not Long," *Chicago Defender*, March 27, 1965; Aldrich, "Personal Journal"; Lawson, *Black Ballots*, 321; James R. Wargo, "Montgomery March is Costing $50,000 King tells Cleveland," *United Press International*, March 24, 1965; "Selma March Cost Pentagon $510,000," *Atlanta Daily World*, May 9, 1965.
41. Lewis, interview by Moore; Lewis, *Walking with the Wind*, 361.
42. Ross Hagen, "Jefferson Men Arrested in Lowndesboro Slaying," *Selma Times Journal*, March 26, 1965.

CHAPTER 6: SCOPE, SNCC, AND BLACK POWER

1. Young, *An Easy Burden*, 372; Garrow, *Bearing the Cross*, 415–16; Williams, interview by unknown person, Atlanta, GA, 1965 Southern Regional Council, "Will the Circle be Unbroken," program files, Manuscript, Archives, and Rare Book Library, Emory University, Atlanta, Georgia.
2. Garrow, *Bearing the Cross*, 416, 426–429; James Bevel, interview by James A. DeVinney, November 13, 1985, for *Eyes on the Prize: America's Civil Rights Years (1954–1965)*, Washington University Libraries, Film and Media Archive, Henry Hampton Collection; Fairclough, *To Redeem the Soul of America*, 259.
3. "King Aide Here for March," *Chicago Defender*, April 17, 1965; Sarah Lyall, "B. C. Willis, 86; Led Chicago Schools for Thirteen Years," *New York Times*, August 31, 1988; Williams, "The Department of Voter Registration."
4. Ted Simmons, "500 Collegians Start Seminar Here," *Atlanta Constitution*, June 15, 1965.
5. Ted Simmons, "Rights, Labor Merger Vital, King Tells Students Here," *Atlanta Constitution*, June 16, 1965.
6. "28 U.S. Colleges Join SCLC's SCOPE Project," *Chicago Defender*, June 22, 1965; Hosea Williams, quoted in Young, *An Easy Burden*, 374.
7. "The SCOPE of Freedom July Incident Report," The Papers of Rev. Hosea Williams, Auburn Avenue Research Library.
8. The SCOPE of Freedom August Incident Report," The Papers of RevHosea Williams, Auburn Avenue Research Library; "Atlanta Scope Workers Beaten," *Atlanta Constitution*, August 3, 1965.
9. Fairclough, *To Redeem the Soul of America*, 263; Hosea L. Williams, interview by Branch.
10. "The SCOPE of Freedom August Incident Report," The Papers of Rev. Hosea Williams, Auburn Avenue Research Library; "$202,545 SCLC Theft Laid to Workers," *Atlanta Constitution*, September 1, 1965.
11. Williams, interview by Branch.
12. James R. Ralph Jr., *Northern Protest: Martin Luther King Jr., Chicago, and the Civil Rights Movement* (Cambridge, MA: Harvard University Press, 1993), 37–39; Young, interview by Dent.

13. Young, *An Easy Burden*, 381–83; Hosea L. Williams, interview by Steve Estes, Atlanta, GA, February 9, 1996, Hosea L. Williams Papers, Auburn Avenue Research Library; Garrow, *Bearing the Cross*, 440–44.
14. "Negro Voter Registration Drive Renewed," *Chicago Defender*, January 4, 1966; "Dr. King to Lead Vote Drive in Birmingham," *Chicago Defender*, January 6, 1966.
15. Glenn T. Eskew, *But for Birmingham: The Local and National Movements in the Civil Rights Struggle* (Chapel Hill: University of North Carolina Press, 1997), 15, 83.
16. "100 Negroes Stage a March in Birmingham, Alabama," *New York Times*, January 5, 1966.
17. Gene Roberts, "Alabama Police Combat Disorder," *New York Times*, January 12, 1966.
18. Peniel Joseph, *Stokely: A Life* (New York: Basic Civitas Books, 2014), ix; Jeffries, *Bloody Lowndes*, 58–59, 147; Edward M. Rudd, "New Political Group in Lowndes to Name Own Negro Candidates," *Southern Courier* II, no. 1, January 1–2, 1966.
19. John Klein, "Civil Rights Leaders Disagree on Using Votes in the Black Belt," *Southern Courier* II, no. 4, January 22–23, 1966; Jeffries, *Bloody Lowndes*, 152; Williams was extremely busy and continuously driving long distances. He was found guilty of reckless driving on January 24, 1966. He was fined one hundred dollars and given a thirty-day suspended sentence. See "Williams Fined," *Southern Courier* II, no. 5, January 29–30, 1966.
20. John Klein, "Civil Rights Leaders Disagree on Using Votes in the Black Belt," *Southern Courier* II, no. 4, January 22–23, 1966; Jeffries, *Bloody Lowndes*, 152.
21. Klein, "Civil Rights Leaders Disagree"; Jeffries, *Bloody Lowndes*, 152.
22. Susan Youngblood Ashmore, *Carry It On: The War on Poverty and the Civil Rights Movement in Alabama, 1964–1972* (Athens: University of Georgia Press, 2008), 154; Jeffries, *Bloody Lowndes*, 167–68; Joe L. Reed, interview by author, tape recording, Montgomery, AL, March 8, 2011.
23. John Klein, "Leaders in Fifteen Counties Meet to Plan Bloc Vote," *Southern Courier* II, no. 2, March 12–13, 1966.
24. "Confederation of Alabama Political Organizations," *Southern Christian Leadership Conference Newsletter* 3, no. 2 (March–April 1966), 1, The Morehouse College Martin Luther King Jr. Collection at the Robert W. Woodruff Library of the Atlanta University Center; "Rights Workers Disagree: SCLC Raps SNCC on Alabama Vote Drive," *Chicago Daily Defender*, April 25, 1966; Martin Luther King, quoted in Jeffries, *Bloody Lowndes*, 168–69.
25. "Confederation of Alabama Political Organizations," *Southern Christian Leadership Conference Newsletter* 3, no. 2 (March–April 1966), 3, The Morehouse College Martin Luther King Jr. Collection.
26. For more on A. G. Gaston, see Suzanne Smith, *To Serve the Living: Funeral Directors and the African American Way of Death* (Cambridge, MA: Harvard University Press, 2010); "Birmingham Vote Drive Nets 20,000," *Chicago Daily Defender*, March 3, 1966; "Gaston Runs off at Mouth: King Aide," *Chicago Daily Defender*, January 18, 1966; "Civil Rights Roundup," *Chicago Daily Defender*, February 12, 1966; AGGaston, interview by Production Team C, November 1, 1985, for *Eyes on the Prize: America's Civil Rights Years (1954–1965)*, Washington University Libraries, Film and Media Archive, Henry Hampton Collection.

27. Ibid.; "58,000 Negroes Still Unregistered in B'ham," *Chicago Daily Defender*, February 8, 1966; Hosea L. Williams, "Report to the Board of Directors, 1966," Southern Christian Leadership Conference records, Manuscript, Archives, and Rare Book Library, Emory University, Atlanta, GA.
28. Gene Roberts, "Alabama Negroes and G.O.P. Jolted," *New York Times*, May 5, 1966; Jeffries, *Bloody Lowndes*, 176.
29. Young, *An Easy Burden*, 395; David Carter, *The Music Has Gone Out of the Movement: Civil Rights and the Johnson Administration, 1965–1968* (Chapel Hill: University of North Carolina Press, 2009), 104–5; John Dittmer, *Local People: The Struggle for Civil Rights in Mississippi* (Chicago: The University of Illinois Press, 1994), 389; Garrow, *Bearing the Cross*, 475; Fairclough, *To Redeem the Soul of America*, 310; Aram Goudsouzian, *Down the Crossroads: Civil Rights Black Power and the Meredith March Against Fear* (New York: Farrar, Straus and Giroux, 2014), 39.
30. Young, *An Easy Burden*, 394; Williams's Book Tape, no. 3; Fairclough, *To Redeem the Soul of America*, 310; Garrow, *Bearing the Cross*, 475; Goudsouzian, *Down the Crossroads*, 42, 44; Michael S. Lottman, "Leaders Join for MissMarch: Bigger than Selma They Say," *Southern Courier* II, no. 24, June 11–12, 1966.
31. Carter, *The Music Has Gone out of the Movement*, 104; Robert Lee Long, "Long Journey to Justice: Residents Recall Day King Came to Town," *DeSoto Times-Tribune*, January 17, 2012; Garrow, *Bearing the Cross*, 476.
32. Stokely Carmichael, interview by Judy Richardson, November 7, 1988, for *Eyes on the Prize: America's Civil Rights Years (1954–1965)*, Washington University Libraries, Film and Media Archive; Joseph, *Waiting 'Til the Midnight Hour*, 135. Joseph wrote that only King and Bernard Lee represented SCLC in this meeting.
33. Goudsouzian, *Down the Crossroads*, 48–49; Williams, interview by Branch.
34. Young, *An Easy Burden*, 395–396; Williams, interview by Branch.
35. Goudsouzian, *Down the Crossroads*, 67.
36. David Underhill, "March Doubles Vote Registration Along Route Mississippi," *Southern Courier* II, no. 25, June 18–19, 1966; Williams, interview by Branch.
37. Williams interview by Branch; Joseph, *Waiting 'Til the Midnight Hour*, 140–41.
38. Joseph, *Waiting 'Til the Midnight Hour*, 141–42; David Underhill, "The Cry Changes to Black Power," *Southern Courier* II, no. 26, June 25–26, 1966; Charles Payne, *I've Got the Light of Freedom: The Organizing Tradition of the Mississippi Freedom Struggle* (Los Angeles: University of California Press, 1995), 376–77; Williams, interview by Branch.
39. David Underhill, "The Cry Changes to Black Power," Southern Courier, No. II, No. 26, June 25–26, 1966; Joseph, *Waiting 'Til the Midnight Hour*, 143; Gene Roberts, "Marchers Stage Mississippi Rally," *New York Times*, June 18, 1966.
40. Hosea L. Williams, Tape 12, "Hosea's Philosophy," Transcription, n.d., Hosea L. Williams Papers.
41. Ibid.
42. David R. Underhill, "Civil Rights Groups to Push Through in Areas March Passed Through," *Southern Courier* 11, no. 27, July 2–3, 1966; Goudsouzian, *Down the Crossroads*, 290; Gene Roberts, "12,000 End Rights March to Jackson: Meredith Hailed at Rally at Mississippi Capitol," *New York Times*, June 27, 1966.

43. "Dr. King's Group Plans Solo Drive, *New York Times*, June 29, 1966; Goudsouzian, *Down the Crossroads,* 277; Al Kuettner, "SCLC in Decision to Go it Alone," *Chicago Daily Defender*, June 30, 1966.
44. Goudsouzian, *Down the Crossroads,* 289; Payne, *I've Got the Light of Freedom*, 378; Richard Bone, "A Black Man's Quarrel With the Christian God," *New York Times Book Review*, September 11, 1966.
45. Dittmer, *Local People*, 403; "Grenada Rescinds Open Door Policy," *Baltimore Afro-American*, July 16, 1966; Gene Roberts, "Dr. King Declares Rights Movement is Close to a Split," *New York Times*, July 9, 1966.
46. Dittmer, *Local People*, 404.
47. Roy Reed, "At 101 Degrees, Protest Becomes Swim In: Negroes at Grenada, Miss., Splash Instead of March," *New York Times*, July 13, 1966.
48. "SNCC Head Barred from SCLC Rally: Carmichael Told No on 'No March' Message," *Chicago Defender*, July 13, 1966.
49. Martin Luther King Jr., "Statement on Violence in Grenada, Mississippi," June 9, 1966, Southern Christian Leadership Conference records, Manuscript, Archives, and Rare Book Library, Emory University; "Negroes Attacked in Mississippi Civil Rights Protest: 350 Battered by Bricks, Bottles in Racial Clash," *Chicago Daily Defender*, August 11, 1966.
50. Dittmer, *Local People*, 404–405; "Tough Miss U.S. Judge Warns Grenada Cops He Means Business: Attack on 33 Children Amazes Him," *Baltimore Afro-American*, September 24, 1966; Gail Falk, "Trouble in Grenada: Court Orders Protection for Negro Pupils," *Southern Courier* II, no. 39, September 24–25, 1966.
51. Dittmer, *Local People*, 406; Edward C. Burks, "Dr. King Arrives in Grenada, Miss.: He Tells 1,000 at Meeting We're Going to Remain," *New York Times*, September 20, 1966.
52. Gail Falk, "New Freedom Movement Fights for an Open City," *Southern Courier* II, no. 39, September 24–25, 1966.
53. Charles McLaurin, interview for Duke University Oral History Project on SNCC, July 2016.
54. Gail Falk, "New Freedom Movement Fights for an Open City," *Southern Courier* II, no. 39, September 24–25, 1966.
55. Hosea L. Williams, "Biographical Sketch," Hosea L. Williams Papers.

CHAPTER 7: CHICAGO, KENTUCKY DERBY, AND POOR PEOPLE'S CAMPAIGN

1. James R. Ralph Jr. and Martin Luther King Jr., *Chicago and the Civil Rights Movement* (Cambridge, MA: Harvard University Press, 1993), 33, 42–43.
2. Ralph, *Chicago and the Civil Rights Movement*, 7, 13–14, 16.
3. Martin Luther King Jr., "Statement on Chicago Freedom Movement," December 2, 1966, Southern Christian Leadership Conference records, Manuscript, Archives, and Rare Book Library, Emory University; Williams, interview by Branch.
4. John McDermott, interview by Shelia C. Bernard, October 25, 1988, for *Eyes on the Prize: America's Civil Rights Years (1954–1965)*, Washington University Libraries, Film and Media Archive, Henry Hampton Collection; Harvard Sitkoff, *King: Pilgrimage to the Mountaintop* (New York: Hill and Wang, 2007), 166; Young, *An Easy Burden*, 381, 406.

5. "Rev. Williams Named Leader of SCLC Voter Campaign," *Chicago Defender*, December 3, 1966.
6. Alan B. Anderson and George Pickering, *Confronting the Color Line: The Broken Promise of the Civil Rights Movement in Chicago* (Athens: University of Georgia Press, 1986), 306.
7. Williams, interview by Branch.
8. "'Vote-A-Baloo' Set: Registration Drive to Involve Youths," *Chicago Daily Defender*, January 13, 1967.
9. Donald Janson, "Dr. King Plagued by Apathy and Resistance in Chicago Slums: Rights Leaders Cite Some Gains, but Find Problems of Northern Ghetto Tougher than Those in the South," *New York Times*, January 16, 1967.
10. Ibid (for more on the Mennonites' participation in the Chicago campaign, please see Todd Miller Shearer, *Daily Demonstrators: The Civil Rights Movement in Mennonite Homes and Sanctuaries* [Baltimore: Johns Hopkins University Press, 2010]; Garrow, *Bearing the Cross*, 544.
11. Williams, interview by Branch; Young, *An Easy Burden*, 418; Garrow, *Bearing the Cross*, 536.
12. "Democrats Blasted: Back Independents Sais SCLC Aide," *Chicago Defender*, February 28, 1967; Young, *An Easy Burden*, 419.
13. Ralph, *Chicago and the Civil Rights Movement*, 224–25.
14. Ralph, *Chicago and the Civil Rights Movement*, 99, 100, 103.
15. Tracy E. K'Meyer, *Civil Rights in the Gateway of the South: Louisville, Kentucky, 1945–1980* (Lexington: University Press of Kentucky, 2009), 113, 117; Louisville Metropolitan Human Relations Commission, "Facts for Action," Hosea L. Williams Papers.
16. K'Meyer, *Civil Rights in the Gateway of the South*, 124; John A. Kleber, ed., *The Encyclopedia of Louisville* (Lexington: University Press of Kentucky, 2001), 789.
17. Memorandum, Hosea Williams to Martin Luther King Jr., Re: SCLC, March 8, 1967, The Morehouse College Martin Luther King Jr. Collection at the Robert W. Woodruff Library of the Atlanta University Center.
18. Ibid.
19. Ibid.; Garrow, *Bearing the Cross*, 548; Williams, interview by Branch.
20. Southern Christian Leadership Conference, "Southern Christian Leadership Conference Staff News," March 1967, The Morehouse College Martin Luther King Jr. Collection at the Robert W. Woodruff Library of the Atlanta University Center; K'Meyer, *Civil Rights in the Gateway of the South*, 124.
21. Hosea L. Williams, "Proposed Plan for Louisville Open Housing Project," March 14, 1967, Hosea L. Williams Papers.
22. David Hill, "Two Horses, Two Races: The Civil Rights Movement Goes to the Kentucky Derby," *The Awl*, May 5, 2011.
23. Ben A. Franklin, "Rights Forces Gather for Louisville Housing Drive," *New York Times*, April 17, 1967; K'Meyer, *Civil Rights in the Gateway of the South*, 129.
24. Douglas Robinson, "Louisville Aides Seek Derby Peace: But Rights Leader Remain Adamant on Housing Law," *New York Times*, April 29, 1967; K'Meyer, *Civil Rights in the Gateway of the South*, 136.

25. Douglas Robinson, "Protest at Derby is Reportedly: Rights Leaders Said to Have Ruled Out Demonstrations," *New York Times*, May 6, 1967; K'Meyer, *Civil Rights in the Gateway of the South*, 136.
26. K'Meyer, *Civil Rights in the Gateway of the South*, 139; Letter, Georgia Davis to Vernon Jordan, July 15, 1967, Hosea L. Williams Papers On November 7, 1967, Georgia Davis was elected as the first woman and African American to the Kentucky State Senate.
27. "Election Results in Louisville Race Still Unclear," *New York Times*, November 18, 1967; Press release, "Civil Rights Drive by SCLC And Other Groups Wins Open Housing Victory in Louisville," December 30, 1967.
28. Letter, Hosea Williams to Martin Luther King Jr., December 13, 1967, Martin Luther King Jr. Papers, The Martin Luther King Jr. Center for Nonviolent Social Change, Atlanta, GA.
29. William Rutherford, interview by Production Team X, November 22, 1988, for *Eyes on the Prize: America's Civil Rights Years (1954–1965)*. Washington University Libraries, Film and Media Archive, Henry Hampton Collection; Williams interview by Branch; Garrow, *Bearing the Cross*, 581.
30. Williams, interview by Branch.
31. Memorandum, William Rutherford and Bernard LaFayette to All SCLC Staff Members Re: Special Staff Retreat January 14–16, 1968, January 4, 1968, Southern Christian Leadership Conference records, Manuscript, Archives, and Rare Book Library, Emory University; Memorandum, Hosea L. Williams to Martin Luther King Jr., Steering Committee, Executive Staff Committee and Field Staff Members Re: SCLC's Special Staff Retreat on the Washington Poor People's Campaign, January 10, 1968, Southern Christian Leadership Conference records, Manuscript, Archives, and Rare Book Library, Emory University.
32. Martin Luther King Jr., "See You in Washington Remarks at Ebenezer Baptist Church," January 17, 1968, Southern Christian Leadership Conference records, Manuscript, Archives, and Rare Book Library, Emory University; Williams, interview by Branch.
33. Martin Luther King Jr., "See You in Washington Remarks at Ebenezer Baptist Church," January 17, 1968, Southern Christian Leadership Conference records, Manuscript, Archives, and Rare Book Library, Emory University.
34. Memorandum, Hosea L. Williams to Bernard LaFayette Re: Washington Poor People's Campaign, February 11, 1968, Southern Christian Leadership Conference records, Manuscript, Archives, and Rare Book Library, Emory University; Memorandum, Andrew Young to All SCLC Field Staff Re: Executive Staff Assignments for Washington DC Campaign, February 12, 1968, Southern Christian Leadership Conference records, Manuscript, Archives, and Rare Book Library, Emory University.
35. Memorandum, Hosea L. Williams to Bernard LaFayette Re: Washington Poor People's Campaign, February 11, 1968, Southern Christian Leadership Conference records, Manuscript, Archives, and Rare Book Library, Emory University.
36. "Action Committee Meeting Minutes," February 11, 1968, Southern Christian Leadership Conference records, Manuscript, Archives, and Rare Book Library, Emory University.

37. V. English, B. Wilcox, and B. Labaree, "'Things Are Not Right in This Country'—King," *Southern Courier* IV, no. 8, February 24–25, 1968.
38. Gerald D. McKnight, *The Last Crusade: Martin Luther King Jr., the FBI and the Poor People's Campaign* (Boulder, CO: Westview Press, 1998), 27.
39. Memorandum, Hosea L. Williams to All Project Leaders and Field Staff Involved in the Mobilization of Field Troops for the Washington Poor People's Campaign, March 5, 1968, Southern Christian Leadership Conference records, Manuscript, Archives, and Rare Book Library, Emory University.
40. Memorandum, Hosea L. Williams to Staff of the Southern Christian Leadership Conference Re: Weekly Report and Dr. King's People to People Tour, March 8, 1968, Southern Christian Leadership Conference records, Manuscript, Archives, and Rare Book Library, Emory University.
41. Ibid.
42. Ibid.
43. "Hosea Williams Arrested on Speeding Charge, *Atlanta Daily World*, March 14, 1968.
44. Sylvie Laurent, *King and the Other America: The Poor People's Campaign and the Quest for Economic Equality* (Oakland: University of California Press, 2018), 176–77; Michael K. Honey, *To the Promised Land: Martin Luther King Jr. and the Fight for Economic Justice* (New York: W. W. Norton & Co., 2018), 136.
45. Laurent, *King and the Other America*, 176–77.
46. Laurent, *King and the Other America*, 138.
47. "Labor and Rights: Race Enters a Garbage Dispute," *New York Times*, March 24, 1968; Young, *An Easy Burden*, 449–50; Walter Rugaber, "A Negro is Killed in Memphis March: Violence Erupts on Route of Protest Led by Dr. King," *New York Times*, March 29, 1968.
48. Garrow, *Bearing the Cross*, 621.
49. Young, *An Easy Burden*, 458; Hosea L. Williams, interview by Branch.
50. Michael K. Honey, *Going Down Jericho Road: The Memphis Strike, Martin Luther King's Last Campaign* (New York: W. W. Norton and Co., 2007), 428–29; Garrow, *Bearing the Cross*, 622.
51. William F. Pepper, *Orders to Kill: The Truth Behind the Murder of Martin Luther King Jr.* (New York: Warner Books, 1995), 26–29; Hosea Williams, interview by unnamed interviewer, April 4, 1968, YouTube Video Clip; Federal Bureau of Investigation, "Lorraine Motel Room Assignments," April 3–4, 1968, The National Civil Rights Museum, Memphis, Tennessee; Young, *An Easy Burden*, 464.
52. Pepper, *Orders to Kill*, 30–31; Betty Washington, "Rights Leader Based Here Recalls Slaying Aftermath," *Chicago Daily Defender* (Daily Edition), April 15, 1968; Young, *An Easy Burden*, 469.
53. Hosea L. Williams, "Tape 12," 1973, Hosea L. Williams Papers.
54. Ibid.
55. Anthony Ripley, "50,000 Expected for Funeral of Dr. King in Atlanta Today," *New York Times*, April 9, 1968; Anthony Lucas, "Atlanta is Peaceful During the Funeral, Police Officials Praise Calm of the Crowd," *New York Times*, April 10, 1968; Brooks, interview; Benjamin E. Mays, *Born to Rebel: An Autobiography* (Athens: University of Georgia Press, 1971), 358; Homer Bigart, "Leaders at Rites: High

and Lowly Join in Last Tribute to Rights Champion," *New York Times*, April 10, 1968.

56. Southern Christian Leadership Conference, "Minutes of the Board of Directors," Southern Christian Leadership Conference records, Manuscript, Archives, and Rare Book Library, Emory University.
57. Carter, *The Music Has Gone Out of the Movement*, 238.
58. Fairclough, *To Redeem the Soul of America*, 385; Bob Hunter, "Williams Denies Split Among SCLC Policymakers," *Chicago Daily Defender*, April 24, 1968; "King's Followers Divided on Policy of Non-Violence," *Ukiah Daily Journal*, April 23, 1968.
59. "Poor People's March Is Big Challenge for Abernathy," *Chicago Daily Defender*, April 27, 2014; Fairclough, *To Redeem the Soul of America*, 386; Ethel L. Payne, "Jesse Jackson's Exit Seen as Sign of Power Battle, *Chicago Daily Defender*, June 5, 1968; Earl Caldwell, "New Chief Named to Spur Campaign of Poor in Capital," *New York Times*, June 1, 1968.
60. Earl Caldwell, "More Militant Poor People's Campaign Is Pledged," *New York Times*, June 3, 1968.
61. See Dan T. Carter, *The Politics of Rage: George Wallace, the Origins of the New Conservatism and the Transformation of American Politics* (New York: Simon and Schuster, 1995), 468.
62. "Rustin Threatens to Quit as Chief of Poor March," *Chicago Daily Defender*, June 8, 1968; Ethel L. Payne, "Jesse Jackson's Exit Seen as Sign of Power Battle," *Chicago Daily Defender*, June 5, 1968; Ethel L. Payne, "Inner Strife Threatens to End Poor Campaign," *Chicago Daily Defender*, June 25, 1968; Fairclough, *To Redeem the Soul of America*, 387; Carter, *The Music Has Gone Out of the Movement*, 197–233.
63. Fairclough, *To Redeem the Soul of America*, 388.

CHAPTER 8: THE MOVEMENT CONTINUES

1. Mark Kurlansky, *1968: The Year that Rocked the World* (New York: Ballantine Books, 2004), 10; William Chafe, *The Unfinished Journey: America since World War II* (New York: Oxford University Press, 2003), 11; Hodgson, *America in our Time*, 67–70.
2. Williams, interview by Estes; Barbara Williams Emerson, interview by Jovita Moore, "Hosea Williams: The Untold Story," DVD, Dorothy Daniels, producer (Atlanta: ABC, 2010).
3. Abernathy, *And the Walls Came Tumbling Down*, 3–4; Williams, interview by Branch.
4. Abernathy, *And the Walls Came Tumbling Down*, 34, 55, 62, 93–94; Hosea L. Williams, "The Reverend Doctor Hosea Williams' Biographical Sketch," Hosea L. Williams Papers; Williams, interview by Branch.
5. Leon Fink and Brian Greenberg. *Upheaval in the Quiet Zone: A History of Hospital Workers' Union, Local 1199* (Urbana: University of Illinois Press, 1989), 130.
6. Southern Christian Leadership Conference, *Soul Force* 2, no. 1, April 4, 1969, The Martin Luther King Jr. Center for Nonviolent Social Change, Atlanta, GA; "SCLC Sets Poor Drive in Alabama," *Afro-American*, April 19, 1969; Abernathy, *And the Walls Came Tumbling Down*, 557–58; Williams, interview by Estes.

7. Abernathy, *And the Walls Came Tumbling Down*, 560–561, 568; Williams, interview by Estes; Memorandum, Charles Fennessey, to All Medical College Employees, June 24, 1969, Catherwood Library Kheel Center at Cornell University, Ithaca, NY.
8. James Lee Kauffman, *Selling Outer Space: Kennedy, the Media, and Funding for Project Apollo, 1961–1963* (Tuscaloosa: The University of Alabama Press, 1994), 2; "Poor Heading for Apollo Site: Plan to Protest U.S. Priorities," *The Toledo Blade*, July 14, 1969; William Greider, "Protesters, VIPs Flood Cape Area," *The Washington Post*, July 15, 1969; Hosea L. Williams, "Annual Report to the Board of Directors Meeting during SCLC's 12th Annual Convention, August 13–16, 1969, The Papers of Rev. Hosea L. Williams, The Auburn Avenue Research Library.
9. Southern Christian Leadership Conference, *Soul Force* 3, no. 3, August 13, 1969, The Martin Luther King Jr. Center for Nonviolent Social Change, Atlanta, GA; Williams, "Annual Report."
10. Ibid.
11. Martin Waldron, "Alabama Blacks Seek County Rule in Special Vote," *New York Times*, July 27, 1969; Williams, "Annual Report."
12. Irvin H. Phillips, "Crowds Turned Out to watch Power Change Hands," *Afro-American*, August 23, 1969; Waldron, "Alabama Blacks Seek County Rule." *New York Times*; Williams, "Annual Report."
13. "SCLC Battered, Fatigued by '60s, Plans Rejuvenation by '71," *The Baltimore African American*, January 10, 1970.
14. "Williams Keynotes NACD Convention," *Baltimore Afro-American*, April 25, 1970.
15. "SCLC Goes to Resort Town to End Poverty," *Baltimore Afro-American*, January 23, 1970.
16. "Civil Rights Group Leaders Disrupt Church Service," *Spartanburg Herald-Journal* 99, no. 29, April 4, 1971.
17. "Negroes Threaten Columbus Boycott, *Atlanta Constitution*, June 20, 1971; "Columbus Puts Police on Alert, *Atlanta Constitution*, June 21, 1971.
18. "Williams Calls Carter a Racist," *Atlanta Constitution*, June 5, 1971; "Macon Rally Called: Williams and Carter Clash," *Atlanta Constitution*, June 12, 1971; WSB-TV newsfilm clip of Governor Jimmy Carter condemning Hosea Williams for creating racial unrest in Columbus, GA, June 21, 1971, WSB-TV newsfilm collection, reel 1598, 9:09/10:08, Walter J. Brown Media Archives and Peabody Awards Collection, The University of Georgia Libraries, Athens, GA, as presented in the Digital Library of Georgia; Charles Wheeler and Harmon Perry, "Oreos' Aren't Cookies to the Negroes in Columbus," *Atlanta Constitution*, June 27, 1971.
19. Ibid.
20. Letter, Ralph D. Abernathy to friend, December 7, 1971, Hosea L. Williams Papers; "Hosea Williams to Preach Trial Sermon," *Atlanta Daily World*, December 12, 1971.
21. Letter, Terrie Randolph to Dr. Donald J. Wilson, January 31, 1972; Letter, Terrie Randolph to Rev. Leo Lester, January 13, 1972; Hosea Williams, engagement agreement, January 25, 1972; Letter, Terrie Randolph to Louise Land, March 8,

1972; Hosea Williams, speaking itinerary, February 7–10, 1972, Hosea L. Williams Papers.

22. Thomas A. Johnson, "Blacks Look to South for Political Future," *New York Times*, August 30, 1970; David Campbell and Joe Feagin, "Black Politics in the South: A Descriptive Analysis," *The Journal of Politics* (February 1975), 129–62.
23. Hosea L. Williams, interview by Tom Chaffin, October 19, 1997, Sam Nunn Oral History Collection, Manuscript, Archives, and Rare Book Library, Emory University, Atlanta, GA.
24. "VEP Vote Power Survey Finds: Georgia Far Behind Region in Number of Blacks Elected, *Atlanta Voice*, February 26, 1972.
25. Joseph Lowery, Statement on the Separation of Jesse Jackson, December 15, 1971, Southern Christian Leadership Conference records, Manuscript, Archives, and Rare Book Library, Emory University, Atlanta, GA; Hosea L. Williams, Book Tape E—Jesse and Abernathy, March 17, 1974, Hosea L. Williams Papers, series 2, box 2, folder 6; Edgar Smith, "Young Wins in Fifth," *Atlanta Voice*, August 12, 1972.
26. Williams, interview by King; "Four Rights Leaders Begin Fast at Holy Family," *Atlanta Voice*, April 29, 1972; Marvin S. Arrington, Sr., *Making My Mark: The Story of a Man Who Wouldn't Stay in His Place* (Macon, GA: Mercer University Press, 2008), 104; "Atlanta Holy Name Hospital Employees Win After Strike; Administrator is Ousted," *Jet*, June 29, 1972, 17.
27. Boyd Lewis, "On Leave? Fired? Hosea Williams Unsure of Status with SCLC," *Atlanta Voice*, July 1, 1972.
28. "Williams Gets Endorsement," *Atlanta Daily World*, August 6, 1972; "Vice Mayor Jackson Endorses Hosea Williams, *Atlanta Voice*, August 5, 1972.
29. Edgar Smith, "Workers Defy Court: 'Williams Go to Jail,'" *Atlanta Voice*, September 2, 1972; John L. Davis, "Courts Involved in Case: Mead Corporation Workers try to Settle Problems," *Atlanta Daily World*, September 3, 1972.
30. Norwood Chaney, "Hosea Still on the Firing Line: 'Police Force Will Not Stop Us,'" *Atlanta Voice*, September 23, 1972.
31. "Mead Employees Reject Company Offer, *Atlanta Voice*, September 30, 1972; Bob Allison, SCLC Signs Covenant, *Atlanta Voice*, October 14, 1972; "SCLC Signs Covenant," *Atlanta Voice*, October 14, 1972.
32. "SCLC and Sears Sign Revolutionary Covenant," *Atlanta Voice*, November 1, 1972.
33. "SCLC Free Food House," *Atlanta Voice*, November 25, 1972; Brooks, interview.
34. Ira Johnson, "Poor People's Union," *Atlanta Voice*, December 9, 1972; "SCLC Launches Union to Help Poor People, *Baltimore Afro-American*, December 23, 1972.
35. "A Word of Thanks from Atlanta/Dekalb SCLC," *Atlanta Voice*, December 30, 1972.
36. Hosea L. Williams, Book Tape #F, March 27, 1974, Hosea L. Williams Papers.
37. "SCLC President Clashes with Mrs. King Over Money Crisis," *Atlanta Daily World*, January 17, 1973; B. Norwood Chaney, "Whose Dream Is Being Fulfilled?" *Atlanta Voice*, January 20, 1973; Williams, interview by Branch (In 1977, MrsKing was able to lead the efforts in building her husband's permanent crypt, a large reflecting pool—an idea she got after her visit to the Taj Mahal—and a chapel

on a twenty-three-acre site on Auburn Avenue that included her husband's birth home and the Ebenezer Baptist Church where her husband co-pastored from 1960 to 1968); Edythe Scott Bagley, *Desert Rose: The Life and Legacy of Coretta Scott King* (Tuscaloosa: The University of Alabama Press, 2012), 264–65.

38. B. Norwood Chaney, "Launching Spring Offensive: Black Workers on Strike at Rich's Department Store," *Atlanta Voice*, April 7, 1973; Williams, interview by King.
39. Bill Cutler, "Rich's Strike Continues," *Atlanta Voice*, April 21, 1973.
40. Ibid.; Glenda Elaine Brown, interview by author, Decatur, GA, April 4, 2014. Glenda Elaine Brown and Hosea Williams engaged in an inappropriate intimate relationship shortly after they met in 1973. The long affair resulted in the birth of Hyron Lorenzo Williams on December 5, 1985. Their son passed away at Atlanta Medical Center on February 14, 2004, after spending nearly a month recovering in the hospital after a car accident. Hyron Williams was eighteen years old; Williams, interview by King.
41. B. Norwood Chaney, "Hosea Sues Rich's for $6 Million," *Atlanta Voice*, April 28, 1973; "Rev. Williams Files Suit: Restraining Order Issued Against Rich's Picketers," *Atlanta Daily World*, April 26, 1973; Morrison, "The Pro and Con of Hosea Williams." *Atlanta Journal.*
42. "Picketing Believed to be Nearing End," *Atlanta Daily World*, May 24, 1973; Arnold Fitzgerald, "Tentative Agreement Reached in Rich's Dispute," *Atlanta Voice*, May 26, 1973.
43. Bill Cutler, "Hosea Williams: Why I'm Running," *Atlanta Voice*, September 15, 1973; Morrison, "The Pro and Con of Hosea Williams." *Atlanta Journal* Williams also led a prolonged demonstration against Sears Roebuck and Company that resulted in the company's agreement to implement several affirmative action concessions. Sears agreed to maintain a daily balance of four hundred thousand dollars in Black-owned banks and purchase advertisements in Black-owned newspapers. The company also agreed to increase its subcontracting with Black businesses. Last, Sears agreed to revisit its hiring policy to strongly consider hiring candidates who were previously convicted of a crime but had since paid all debts to society.
44. John H. Calhoun, "An Analysis of Last Week's 1973 City Election Voting," *Atlanta Daily World*, October 11, 1973; Bill Cutler, "Atlanta Voters Reject 'Scary Whitey' Tactics," *Atlanta Voice*, October 20, 1973.
45. John H. Calhoun, "An Analysis of Atlanta's October 16 Runoff Election," *Atlanta Daily World*, October 26, 1973; Jon Nordheimer, "Atlanta Elects a Black Mayor, but Hosea Williams Is Defeated," *New York Times*, October 17, 1973; Tom Linthicum, "Stand Together: Jackson Rejects Calls for Rejection of Fear Mongering," *Atlanta Constitution*, October 9, 1973.
46. "Williams Outlines New SCLC Plan," *Baltimore Afro-American*, December 1, 1973; Jim Merriner, "Hosea Williams: A Stormy Career, *Atlanta Constitution*, October 15, 1973.
47. "Police Probe Incident Allegedly Involving Rev. Hosea Williams: Officer Also Investigated," *Atlanta Daily World*, January 11, 1974; "Policeman Suspended for Not Citing Williams," *Atlanta Daily World*, January 13, 1974.

48. "Expected from Reapportionment: More Black Legislators," *Atlanta Daily World*, February 16, 1974.
49. "Rev. Williams to Stand Trial on Weapons Charges," *Atlanta Daily World*, March 12, 1974.
50. Gregg Mathis, "Rev. Williams Pleads for Atlanta's Salvation," *Atlanta Voice*, July 6, 1974; Wolfgang Saxon, "M. W. Chenault, 44, Gunman Who Killed Mother of Dr. King," *New York Times*, August 22, 1995; "Protesters Hit With Fines; Williams' Hearing Tuesday: Smith Urges Hosea To Apologize to Ministers," *Atlanta Daily World*, June 30, 1974; "Mrs. M. L. King Sr., Deacon Are Fatally Shot In Church," *Atlanta Daily World*, July 2, 1974; Frederick Allen, *Atlanta Rising: The Intervention of an International City* (Atlanta: Longstreet Press, 1996), 216.
51. "Burglars Hit SCLC for $10,000," *Atlanta Constitution*, October 3, 1974; Hosea L. Williams, SAVE SCLC solicitation letter, October 21, 1974, Hosea L. Williams Papers.
52. "Many Seek Posts in Tuesday's Election," *Atlanta Daily World*, November 3, 1974.
53. Claudia Townsend, "Votes, Seats: Hosea tells Dekalb Goals," *Atlanta Constitution*, August 23, 1974.
54. Gregg Mathis, "Hosea Says Trial is Political Repression," *Atlanta Voice*, October 26, 1974; Douglass Wells, "Rev. Williams Bound Over on All Charges," *Atlanta Daily World*, September 22, 1972; Fred Steeple, "Williams Faces Two Trials," *Atlanta Daily World*, November 1, 1974.
55. Gregg Mathis, "State Fails Try: Hosea Acquitted," *Atlanta Voice*, November 9, 1974.
56. "Resounding Victories at the Polls Scored by Busbee, Miller and Young," *Atlanta Daily World*, November 7, 1974.

CHAPTER 9: POLITICS, PROSECUTION, AND PERSECUTION

1. "Civil Rights Leader to Lead Dr. King Memorial Service," *Daily Register*, January 9, 1975; Georgia General Assembly, House of Representatives, *Journal of the House of Representatives of the State of Georgia at the regular session.* Atlanta, State of Georgia, Clerk's Office, House of Representatives, 1975, 13; Jim Galloway, "Advocate for Atlanta: Tom Murphy: 1924–2007: Stalwart of the Statehouse," *Atlanta Journal-Constitution*, December 19, 2007.
2. Celestine Sibley, "Verbal Storms Only Thunder as House Opens," *Atlanta Constitution*, January 14, 1975.
3. Georgia General Assembly, House of Representatives, *Journal of the House of Representatives of the State of Georgia at the regular session.* Atlanta, State of Georgia, Clerk's Office, House of Representatives, 1975, 41–42, 45.
4. Hosea L. Williams, "From the Desk of Rep. Hosea Williams," *Atlanta Voice*, February 1, 1975.
5. "Atlanta Critic Williams Says Mayor Should Fight for Poor," *Baltimore Afro-American*, November 8, 1975.
6. "Quotables," *Atlanta Constitution*, January 17, 1975; Bob Waymer, "Rep. Hosea Williams Gets His First Bill Passed," *Atlanta Voice*, March 8, 1975.
7. "Public Safety Suspends Hosea Williams' License," *Atlanta Constitution*, May 21, 1975.

8. "Jay Lawrence, "Hosea Williams Loses License," *Atlanta Constitution*, May 28, 1975.
9. Ibid.
10. Hosea L. Williams, "Dr. King's Aide Still Fighting Press Release," Johnson Publishing Company Clipping Files Collection, Archives Research Center of the Atlanta University Center at the Robert W. Woodruff Library, June 7, 1975.
11. Frederick Allen, "Chemical Firm: Hosea's in a New Business," *Atlanta Constitution*, August 7, 1975; Hosea L. Williams to Bob Johnson, August 7, 1975, Johnson Publishing Company Clipping Files Collection, Archives Research Center of the Atlanta University Center at the Robert W. Woodruff Library.
12. Frederick Allen, "Williams Indicted on Driving Charges," *Atlanta Constitution*, September 20, 1975; Frederick Allen, "Williams Turns Himself In," *Atlanta Constitution*, September 26, 1975.
13. Jim Gray, "He Believed Him: Officer Explains Why He Didn't Hold Williams," *Atlanta Constitution*, October 22, 1975; Gary Hendricks, "Police: Hosea Driving," *Atlanta Constitution*," November 21, 1975.
14. Frederick Allen, "Williams Turns Himself In," *Atlanta Constitution*, September 26, 1975; "Williams Arraigned After 100th Arrest," *Baltimore Afro-American*, November 8, 1975; "Afro-American League Supports Williams," *Atlanta Voice*, November 8, 1975.
15. "City SCLC Broke, Closing," *Atlanta Constitution*, January 25, 1976; Margaret Shannon, "The Widow's Might," *Atlanta Constitution*, February 1, 1976; "Hosea Files for Bankruptcy," *Atlanta Constitution*, September 15, 1976.
16. "Taxi Drivers to Unite, Take Demands to Mayor," *Atlanta Constitution*, February 17, 1976; "Taxi Drivers Threaten a Peachtree 'Cruise-In,'" *Atlanta Constitution*, February 18, 1976.
17. "Sit-Ins Threatened: Blacks Demand 'a Piece' of Russel Building Pie," *Atlanta Constitution*, February 18, 1976; Fay S. Joyce, "Building Contracts: Blacks May Get Slice of Russel Work Pie," *Atlanta Constitution*, March 5, 1976.
18. "House Incumbents Take Lead," *Atlanta Constitution*, August 11, 1976; Gary Hendricks, "Traffic Charge: Williams Case Goes to Jury," *Atlanta Constitution*, November 18, 1976; Gary Hendricks, "In Traffic Case: Rep. Williams Wins Acquittal," *Atlanta Constitution*, November 20, 1976.
19. Sharon Bailey, "Grievances Aired: MARTA Draws Williams' Ire," *Atlanta Constitution* November 6, 1976; Sharon Bailey, "Clash Disrupts MARTA Meeting," *Atlanta Constitution*, December 14, 1976; "Non-Violent Action: Rep. Williams Warns MARTA," *Atlanta Constitution*, December 23, 1976.
20. "Guidelines for MARTA: Joint Venture Variance Found," *Atlanta Constitution*, February 8, 1977; Sharon Bailey, "MARTOC Gets Blacks' Gripes," *Atlanta Constitution*, February 16, 1975.
21. Dorothy Carr, "Back to the Streets? SCLC Election May Reveal Split in the Ranks," *Atlanta Journal-Constitution*, August 14, 1977.
22. Steven A. Holmes, "Jackson Asks for Unity," *Atlanta Constitution*, August 18, 1977; Steven A. Holmes, "Lowery and Williams Get Top SCLC Jobs," *Atlanta Constitution*, August 19, 1977; "Rights Group Acts to Heal Moderate-Militant Rift," *New York Times*, August 19, 1977.

23. Jay Lawrence, "Finley Faces a Williams Challenge," *Atlanta Constitution*, September 21, 1977; "District 5 Election Results," *Atlanta Constitution*, October 5, 1977.
24. Hosea Williams, "As Century's True Militant," *Atlanta Journal*, January 14, 1978.
25. Staff meeting minutes, January 23, 1978, Box 14, Southern Christian Leadership Conference records, Stuart A. Rose Manuscript, Archives, and Rare Book Library, Emory University; Staff meeting minutes, April 24, 1978, Box 14, Southern Christian Leadership Conference records; Staff meeting minutes, May 8, 1978, Box 14, Southern Christian Leadership Conference; Hosea Williams to Fred Taylor, April 14, 1978, Box 14, Southern Christian Leadership Conference.
26. Terrie Randolph, email to author, March 6, 2021; Willie Bolden, graveside tribute to commemorate the life of Hosea Williams, Lincoln Cemetery, November 16, 2013.
27. Hosea Williams to Mattie Brooks, December 28, 1977, Box 14, Southern Christian Leadership Conference records, Stuart A. Rose Manuscript, Archives, and Rare Book Library, Emory University; Mattie Brooks to Hosea Williams, December 29, 1977, Box 14, Southern Christian Leadership records; Tyrone Brooks to Hosea Williams, March 21, 1978, Southern Christian Leadership Conference records, Stuart A. Rose Manuscript, Archives, and Rare Book Library, Emory University.
28. Henry Eason, "House Passes Bill Closing Bingo Loopholes," *Atlanta Constitution*, February 17, 1978; "Quotable," *Atlanta Constitution*, February 17, 1978; Staff meeting minutes, May 17, 1978, Box 14, Southern Christian Leadership Conference records, Stuart A. Rose Manuscript, Archives, and Rare Book Library, Emory University; "The Sorry Condition of Hosea Williams *Atlanta Constitution*."
29. "SCLC to Open Bingo Parlor," *Atlanta Journal-Constitution*, December 1, 1978; Dorothy Carr, "Strife, Lack of Public Support Are Crippling Civil Rights Groups," *Atlanta Journal-Constitution*, December 31, 1978.
30. Sam Hopkins, "SCLC Runs Short of Food, Funds, Toys to Cheer Holidays for Poor, Youngsters," *Atlanta Constitution*, December 22, 1978.
31. Carr, "Strife." *Atlanta Journal.*
32. Sharon Bailey, "MARTA Attacked in Dispute," *Atlanta Constitution*, January 23, 1979.
33. Beau Cutts and Sam Hopkins, "GA House Defeats King Holiday Bill," *Atlanta Constitution*, February 24, 1979; Georgia General Assembly, House of Representatives, *Journal of the House of Representatives of the State of Georgia at the regular session*, Atlanta, State of Georgia, Clerk's Office, House of Representatives, 1978, 22, 29, 82
34. Leslie Henderson, "Williams' Arrest Sparks Concerns," *Atlanta Constitution*, March 2, 1979; George Rodrigue, "Hosea Williams Is Indicted on Habitual Offender Charge, *Atlanta Constitution*, May 2, 1979; George Rodrigue, "Williams Pleads Guilty: Fined for Driving Without a License," *Atlanta Constitution*, July 13, 1979.
35. Tina McElroy Ansa, "National Job at Stake: Williams Losing SCLC Directorship," *Atlanta Constitution*, March 27, 1979; "Hosea Refused to Quit Other Jobs as Requested, SCLC's Lowery Says," *Atlanta Journal-Constitution*, April 1, 1979.
36. Ibid.; "Notes on People: Southern Leadership Conference Ousts Williams," *New York Times*, March 30, 1979.

37. Ken Willis, "'Save SCLC' Group Plans Session," *Atlanta Journal-Constitution*, March 31, 1979; Ken Willis, "Williams Charges SCLC With Courting 'Elitists,'" *Atlanta Journal-Constitution*, April 3, 1979.
38. Tina McElroy Ansa, "SCLC Execs Reject Hosea Williams' Firing," *Atlanta Journal-Constitution*, April 11, 1979; "SCLC Fires Tyrone Brooks for 'Unbecoming' Conduct," *Atlanta Journal-Constitution*, April 13, 1979; Barry King, "SCLC Internal Dispute Leads to Atlanta Scuffle," *Atlanta Journal-Constitution*, April 14, 1979; Charles Smith, "SCLC Seeking Writ to Evict Williams," *Atlanta Journal-Constitution*, May 18, 1979.
39. "Peace is Tough for Fighter Like Williams," *Atlanta Journal-Constitution*, April 17, 1979; Bob Waymer, "Hosea is Giving a Test," *Atlanta Journal-Constitution*, April 19, 1979.
40. Bill Krueger, "Reidsville: A Hellhole, Or A Better Prison," *Atlanta Journal-Constitution,* August 3, 1979; Milovan Dijas, *Of Prisons and Ideas* (New York: Harcourt, 1986), 2
41. Jingle Davis, "Prison Foes Will March," *Atlanta Journal-Constitution*, August 6, 1979; Sara Hansard, "Youth Drowns During Break a River on Protest March to Riot-Torn Prison, *The Washington Post*, August 9, 1979; Raleigh Bryans, "Judge Forbids Reidsville Rally: Protesters Arrested, Vow to Return," *Atlanta Journal-Constitution*, August 13, 1979; Steve Johnson and Howard Moll, "Reidsville Protesters Stay in Jail, *Atlanta Journal-Constitution*, August 13, 1979
42. "Prison Protest," *Atlanta Journal-Constitution*, August 9, 1979.
43. John Barber, "Who Is Hosea Williams," Box 2, Folder 13, April 1974, Reverend Hosea L. Williams Papers, Archives Division, Auburn Avenue Research Library; "Hosea Williams Takes Trip to Libya," *Atlanta Journal-Constitution*, September 8, 1979; Frederick Allen, "Andrew Young Resignation, PLO Overtures Open a Chasm of Black-Jewish Resentment," *Atlanta Journal-Constitution*, October 4, 1979.
44. Gene Tharpe, "Appeasement 1979 Style," *Atlanta Journal-Constitution*, September 25, 1979.
45. Douglas E. Kneeland, "Reagan is Endorsed by 2 Black Leaders: Backing of Williams and Abernathy 'Overwhelms' G.O.P. Nominee," *New York Times*, October 17, 1980; Carol Ashkinaze, "Williams Calls Carter Non-Responsive," *Atlanta Journal-Constitution*, October 18, 1980.
46. Williams, interview by Chaffin; Ashkinaze, "Williams Calls Carter."*Atlanta Journal.*
47. "Abernathy, Williams Meet Reagan," *Atlanta Constitution*, November 7, 1980; Bob Harrell, "Black Group to Have White House Access," *Atlanta Constitution*, December 11, 1980; George Rodrigue, "Williams Calls for 'Black Agenda,'" *Atlanta Constitution*, November 27, 1980
48. "Quotable," *Atlanta Journal-Constitution*, December 16, 1977.
49. "Tyrone Brooks, *Atlanta Voice*, January 24–31, 1981.
50. Suzanne Dolezal, "Rep. Hosea Williams Charged in Wreck," *Atlanta Journal*, July 20, 1980; George Rodrigue and Laura Lippman, "Hosea Williams May Face Hearings in 2 Counties," *Atlanta Journal-Constitution*, July 22, 1980.
51. David B. Hilder, "Hosea Williams Says He's Confident He'll Win on Appeal,"

Atlanta Journal-Constitution, April 26, 1981; Barry King, "Judge Revokes Probation on Williams," *Atlanta Journal-Constitution*, May 6, 1981; "RevHosea Williams Sentenced to Six Years," *Atlanta Voice*, May 9, 1981; C. P. Williams-Shucker, "Hosea Williams Asks for New Trial," *Atlanta Journal-Constitution*, July 18, 1981.

52. "Hosea Williams Comments on D.C. Trip," *Atlanta Voice*, December 12, 1981; Lewis Grizzard, 'Let 'em All Eat Caviar,'" *Atlanta Journal-Constitution*, November 22, 1981.
53. John Brady, "Black Chamber of Commerce is Proposed," *Atlanta Journal-Constitution*, December 17, 1981; Ann Woolner, "Hosea Considers Joining the GOP," *Atlanta Journal-Constitution*, January 31, 1982.
54. Cathy Schoppenhorst, "Elliot Sponsors Bill to Help Legal Aid, *Atlanta Journal-Constitution*, February 25, 1982; Fran Hesser and Jerry Schwartz, "Senate, House Back Bowers on Remap Suit," *Atlanta Journal-Constitution*, March 9, 1982; Hal Gulliver, "Reagan's Guys Invade Japan," *Atlanta Journal-Constitution*, March 30, 1982.
55. Bob Dart and Tracy Thompson, "Williams, Abernathy Plan Trade Mission to Japan," *Atlanta Journal-Constitution*, March 28, 1982; T. L. Wells, "Hosea Williams Talks About Trip," *Atlanta Journal-Constitution*, April 1, 1982.
56. Martha Davidson, "Seeing Light in Japan's Success," *Atlanta Journal-Constitution*, April 8, 1982; Martha Davidson, "Black Leaders Whet Japanese Interest," *Atlanta Journal-Constitution*, April 11, 1982.
57. Martha Davidson, "U.S.-Japan Exchange Program Predicted, *Atlanta Journal-Constitution*, April 21, 1982; Sharon Bailey, "Japan Trip is 'First Step,' Williams Says Upon Return," *Atlanta Journal-Constitution*, April 22, 1982.
58. Linda Horton, "Hosea Williams Wins 1, Loses 1 In Appeals Court," *Atlanta Journal-Constitution*, May 27, 1982.
59. John Braun, "Williams Fighting Absenteeism Charges," *Atlanta Journal-Constitution*, June 24, 1982.
60. G. G. Rigsby and T. L. Wells, "Hosea Williams Faces New Arrest Warrant," *Atlanta Journal-Constitution*, June 25, 1982.
61. G. G. Rigsby and T. L. Wells, "Williams is Jailed; Could Be Off Ballot," *Atlanta Journal-Constitution*, June 26, 1982; G. G. Rigsby and Dick Parker, "'No Way' Hosea Williams' Term Will be Reduced, Says Official," *Atlanta Journal-Constitution*, June 29, 1982; G. G. Rigsby, "Rep. Williams Allowed to Run for House Seat," *Atlanta Journal-Constitution*, July 1, 1982; Mark Platte and John Vardeman, "Three Black Leaders Urge Release of Williams," *Atlanta Journal-Constitution*, July 7, 1982; Jim Walls, "Candidates Report Meager Contributions," *Atlanta Journal-Constitution*, July 15, 1982; Greg Witcher, "Young Says Hosea Williams Doesn't Deserve to be in Jail," *Atlanta Journal-Constitution*, July 22, 1982; Pamela Fine, "Trusty Status Given to Hosea Williams," *Atlanta Journal-Constitution*, July 30, 1982; Tom Crawford and John Vardeman, "Hosea Williams Not Forgotten a Session Opens Without Him," *Atlanta Journal-Constitution*, August 4, 1982; Susan Wells, "2 Judges Rated Low by Bar Got Most Primary Votes," *Atlanta Journal-Constitution*, August 12, 1982.
62. "Dekalb Legislative Contests," *Atlanta Journal-Constitution*, August 5, 1982;

Prentice Palmer and G. G. Rigsby, "Hosea Williams Will Leave Jail to Attend Legislative Sessions," *Atlanta Journal-Constitution*, August 5, 1982.

63. Pamela Fine and Tracy Thompson, "Williams Acquitted in DUI Trial," *Atlanta Journal-Constitution*, October 24, 1982.
64. Beverly German, "Parole Issue Stalls Release of Williams," *Atlanta Journal-Constitution*, October 25, 1982; Susan Wells, "Williams Claims He is Being Kept Hostage in Jail," *Atlanta Journal-Constitution*, October 26, 1982; "High Court Dismisses Rep. Williams' Lawsuit," *Atlanta Journal-Constitution*, October 28, 1982; David Corvette, "Judge Sympathetic but Refuses to Free Hosea Williams," *Atlanta Journal-Constitution,* November 10, 1982; Tracy Thompson and John Verdeman, "Rep. Hosea Williams Released on Bond," *Atlanta Journal-Constitution*, November 11, 1982.
65. Beau Cutts, "Proposed Law Would Put Squeeze on 'Lemon' Autos," *Atlanta Journal-Constitution*, January 14, 1983.
66. Cathy Schoppenhorst, "Williams, Brooks Want $50-a-Week Pay for Ex-Convicts," *Atlanta Journal-Constitution*, January 18, 1983; Charles Loop, "Makes No Difference, *Atlanta Journal-Constitution*, January 28, 1983; William R. Hurst, "Kids in a Candy Store," *Atlanta Journal-Constitution*, February 4, 1983. Williams also announced a legal defense organization to represent poor and young people who had been "wrongfully convicted." See "Hosea Williams Announces Legal Fund," *Atlanta Journal-Constitution*," June 11, 1983.
67. Prentice Palmer, "Hosea: Give Maddox a Pension," *Atlanta Journal-Constitution*, March 23, 1983; "Maddox Deserves a Pension, Too," *Atlanta Journal-Constitution*, March 24, 1983; H. McDuffie, "Pension for Ex-Governor Maddox is a No! No!" *Atlanta Voice*, April 2, 1983.
68. Pamela Fine, "GBI's Bingo Beat: Big Business, Little Glory," *Atlanta Journal-Constitution*, September 10, 1983.
69. Nathan McCall, "'Sweet Auburn' Fest Set for November," *Atlanta Journal-Constitution*, October 1, 1983; Steve Harvey, "15,000 fill Auburn Avenue for Festival," *Atlanta Journal-Constitution*, November 13, 1983; Michael Szymanski, "Auburn Festival a Hit with the Crowds, but Stays a 'Miss' in the Ledger Books," *Atlanta Journal-Constitution,* December 8, 1983.
70. Michael Szymanski, "Hosea Williams Considering Running for 5th District Seat," *Atlanta Journal-Constitution*, November 22, 1983; Gayle White, "Williams Serving Last House Term," *Atlanta Journal-Constitution*, February 1, 1984.
71. Georgia General Assembly, House of Representatives, *Journal of the House of Representatives of the State of Georgia at the regular session.* Atlanta, State of Georgia, Clerk's Office, House of Representatives, 1984, 466–67, 915–17; Hal Straus, "House Backs Two-Parent Aid," *Atlanta Journal-Constitution*, February 1, 1984.
72. Georgia General Assembly, House of Representatives, *Journal of the House of Representatives of the State of Georgia at the regular session*, Atlanta, State of Georgia, Clerk's Office, House of Representatives, 1984, 952–954; Steve Harvey, "Georgia House OK's Day in King's Honor," *Atlanta Journal-Constitution*, February 2, 1984.
73. Steve Harvey, "Hosea Williams leaves Legislature, not politics," *Atlanta Journal-Constitution*, March 1, 1984.

74. "Hosea Williams Honored," *Atlanta Journal-Constitution*, March 23, 1984.
75. Beverly Barnes, "Williams Reveals Bid for Congress, *Atlanta Journal-Constitution*, March 30, 1984; Tom Teepen, "5th's Fowler Is in for a Fight," *Atlanta Journal-Constitution*, April 3, 1984.
76. Cheryl Lauer, "Vote for Me Because I'm the Best Man, Williams Says," *Atlanta Journal-Constitution*, May 17, 1984; Ann Woolner, "Young Signs Letter Endorsing Williams," *Atlanta Journal-Constitution*, July 6, 1984; "5th District Bedfellows," *Atlanta Journal-Constitution,* July 8, 1984; David K. Secrest, "Munford and a Mixed Bag of Whites Endorse Williams for Congress," *Atlanta Journal-Constitution*, July 21, 1984; "Whites Wary of Williams," *Atlanta Journal-Constitution*, August 14, 1984.
77. "Statewide Races," *Atlanta Journal-Constitution,* August 15, 1984.
78. Tracy Thompson, "U.S. Court Reinstates Conviction of Hosea Williams in '80 Wreck," *Atlanta Journal and Constitution*, June 8, 1984; David Corvette, "Williams Reports to Jail Term," *Atlanta Journal-Constitution*, December 20, 1984; "Hosea, the Scribe," December 24, 1984; Susan Howard, "4,000 Expected for Free Christmas Dinner," *Atlanta Journal-Constitution*, December 23, 1984.

CHAPTER 10: "I'M AN OPPORTUNIST"

1. Sam Hopkins, "Williams Gets Jail Furlough for Inaugural," *Atlanta Journal-Constitution*, January 11, 1985; ARHooks, "Hosea and Justice," *Atlanta Journal-Constitution*, January 28, 1985; "Williams Abandons Support for Reagan," *Atlanta Journal-Constitution*," February 10, 1984; Jim Auchmutey, "Williams Hasn't Purchased Tickets; Isn't Expected to Attend Inaugural," *Atlanta Journal-Constitution,* January 13, 1985; Rob Levin, "Williams' Bid to Meet Reagan Rebuffed," *Atlanta Journal-Constitution,* January 18, 1985.
2. "Hosea Williams Leaves Jail," *Atlanta Journal-Constitution*, February 6, 1985; "Williams Hints He'll Run as a Republican," *Atlanta Journal-Constitution*, January 24, 1985; "Williams Tells Cobb Republicans to Draw Blacks into Party Ranks," *Atlanta Journal-Constitution*, July 10, 1985.
3. Tom Teepen, "GOP Misses Boat on Blacks," *Atlanta Journal-Constitution*, July 11, 1985.
4. Robert Anderson, "Williams Ponders Race for Council Helm," *Atlanta Journal-Constitution*, July 25, 1985; "Hosea Williams Urged to Run," *Atlanta Journal-Constitution*, August 22, 1985; Frederick Allen, "Williams Goes the Hate Route," *Atlanta Journal-Constitution*, August 25, 1985; "Give Police Room on Killings Probe," *Atlanta Journal-Constitution*, August 19, 1985.
5. Nathan McCall, "Candidates Outnumber Forum Audience," *Atlanta Journal-Constitution*, September 30, 1985; Frederick Allen, "5th District Race Anything But Boring," *Atlanta Journal-Constitution*, October 1, 1985.
6. Nathan McCall, "2 on Council Are Forced into Runoff," *Atlanta Journal-Constitution*, October 9, 1985; Katheryn Hayes, "Hosea Williams Demands Recount," *Atlanta Journal-Constitution*, October 10, 1985; Katheryn Hayes, "Election Board Agrees to Recount Williams-Finley Council Race Ballots," *Atlanta Journal-Constitution*, October 17, 1985; Katheryn Hayes, "Williams Loses Votes in Recount: Incomplete Tally Gives Him 2 Fewer," *Atlanta Journal-Constitution*, October 19,

1985; Katheryn Hayes, "Finley, Williams Go Through the Mill to Get to 5th District Runoff," *Atlanta Journal-Constitution*, October 25, 1985; Katheryn Hayes and Nathan McCall, "Hosea Williams Ousts Councilman Finley: Incumbents Hold Seats in Other 3 City Runoffs," *Atlanta Journal-Constitution*, October 30, 1985.

7. Jim Minter, "Hosea Williams Might Be What City Hall Needs," *Atlanta Journal-Constitution*, November 3, 1985.
8. Gary White, "City's Poor to Enjoy Thanksgiving Feasts: Groups Sponsor Traditional Turkey Day Dinners for the Needy," *Atlanta Journal-Constitution*, November 26, 1985; Debbie Newby and Connie Green, "Giving Thanks: 'It's a Blessing to Have a Place Like This,'" November 29, 1985.
9. Jane O. Hansen, "Hosea Williams Charged with DUI in Atlanta," *Atlanta Journal-Constitution*, January 2, 1986; John Lancaster, "Hosea Williams Says Officer Lied in His Report," *Atlanta Journal-Constitution*, January 3, 1986.
10. "City Council Committees Set," *Atlanta Voice*, January 11, 1986; Nathan McCall, "Williams is Named to Police Committee," January 9, 1986; Bob Moore, "An Insult to Community," *Atlanta Journal-Constitution*, January 16, 1986; W. M. Sellars, "Arrington's Balancing Act," *Atlanta Journal-Constitution*, January 17, 1986.
11. Nathan McCall, "Williams' Plan May Get Cool Reception," *Atlanta Journal-Constitution*, January 5, 1986.
12. "Trying to Satisfy the Dream," *Atlanta Journal-Constitution*, January 17, 1986; Connie Green, "2 King Aides Visibly Absent from Activities: Abernathy, Williams Say They Feel Left Out," *Atlanta Journal-Constitution*, January 19, 1986; Cotton, interview by Dent.
13. Bill Montgomery and Katheryn Hayes, "It's a Happy Hosea Williams: 'We Beat 'em All,'" *Atlanta Journal-Constitution*, October 31, 1985; Connie Green, "2 King Aides Visibly Absent from Activities: Abernathy, Williams Say They Feel Left Out," *Atlanta Journal-Constitution*, January 19, 1986.
14. John Brady, "Williams Found Innocent in DUI Case," *Atlanta Journal-Constitution*, March 18, 1986.
15. Larry Copeland, "Civilian Review Board Unsure of Next Step After Contradictory Police Investigation," *Atlanta Journal-Constitution*, March 21, 1986.
16. Nathan McCall, "After Rocky Start, Williams Appears on Track: Freshman City Councilman is Given High Marks by Community Leaders," *Atlanta Journal-Constitution*, June 10, 1986.
17. Jim Nesbitt, "Hosea Williams Says He's Tired of Rejection," *News and Observer*, March 8, 1987.
18. "Williams Tells Cobb Republicans to Draw Blacks into Party Ranks," *Atlanta Journal-Constitution*, July 10, 1985.
19. Harvey Craig, "State Troopers Rescue Negroes at Cumming, GA: Six Blacks Threatened with Lynching Are Taken to Marietta," *Atlanta Constitution*, September 8, 1912; "Georgia in Terror of Night Riders: Farmers Appeal to Governor for Troops to Suppress Crusade Against Negroes," *New York Times*, December 26, 1912.
20. C. B. Hackworth, "The Forsyth Saga: There is a County in Georgia where Black Americans May Not Live," *Creative Loafing*, Volume 15, Issue 25, November 25, 1986; "Assault Case Goes to Forsyth Jurors," *Atlanta Constitution*, November 20, 1980.

21. "Forsyth Man Found Guilty of Shooting Black Atlanta Fireman, *Atlanta Constitution,* November 21, 1980; C. B. Hackworth, text message to author, June 23, 2021.
22. John Brady, "Forsyth Doesn't Deserve 'Lawless, Racist' Image, County Officials Say," *Atlanta Journal-Constitution,* January 16, 1987; John Brady, "Security Beefed Up for March, Klan Demonstration in Forsyth," *Atlanta Journal-Constitution,* January 17, 1987.
23. John Brady and John Earle, "Violent Protesters Disrupt Forsyth March: Klansmen Throw Bottles and Rocks at Demonstrators," *Atlanta Journal-Constitution,* January 18, 1987; Ron Taylor, "Civil Rights Enemies Square Off: Williams, Stoner Have '60s-like Confrontation," *Atlanta Journal-Constitution*, January 18, 1986.
24. Priscilla Painton, "Forsyth Events Sober Celebrants: King Dinner Speakers Deplore Racial Incident," *Atlanta Journal-Constitution*, January 18, 1987.
25. Priscilla Painton, "Unity of Civil Rights Veterans Simplifies Issue of Protocol," *Atlanta Journal-Constitution*, January 24, 1987.
26. Mike Christensen, "20,000 March on Forsyth County: 60 Arrests Mark Day of Tension; 1,000 Turn Out in Counterprotest," *Atlanta Journal-Constitution*, January 25, 1987; Bert Roughton Jr. and Katherine Gibney, "Bus Convoys Stretched Miles as 10,000 Show Up to Ride," *Atlanta Journal-Constitution,* January 25, 1987; Monte Plott, "Media Give an Eyeful of Events: Droves of Reporters Include Foreign Teams," *Atlanta Journal-Constitution*, January 25 1987.
27. Bill Montgomery, "Huge Size of 'Army' Stuns Foes," *Atlanta Journal-Constitution*, January 25, 1987.
28. W. Stevens Ricks, "Officers Keep Lid on Tight: Massive Presence Heads off Trouble," *Atlanta Journal-Constitution*, January 25, 1987; Nathan McCall, "Civil Rights Veterans Note How Times Have Changed," *Atlanta Journal-Constitution*, January 25, 1987; Mike Christensen, "20,000 March on Forsyth County: 60 Arrests Mark Day of Tension; 1,000 Turn Out in Counterprotest," *Atlanta Journal-Constitution*, January 25, 1987; "Rekindling of New Revolution and Dream," *Atlanta Voice*, January 31, 1987; Herbert Denmark Jr., "Will Forsyth County March Unity Last?" *Atlanta Voice*, January 31, 1987.
29. Bill Montgomery, "Activists Carry Demands to Forsyth County: Hosea Williams Leads Delegation Calling for a Biracial Committee, *Atlanta Journal-Constitution*, January 30, 1987.
30. Bill Montgomery, "Williams Says 500 May Visit Churches in Forsyth County," *Atlanta Journal-Constitution*, February 1, 1987; Bill Montgomery, "Blacks Go to Church in Forsyth: Group of 70 Met With Warm Words," *Atlanta Journal-Constitution,* February 2, 1987.
31. Bill Montgomery, "Williams Vows to Remain in Forsyth Jail: Councilman Arrested Trying to Picket 'Oprah' Broadcast," *Atlanta Journal-Constitution*, February 10, 1987; Robert Byrd, "Oprah Winfrey Brings Her Show to Forsyth County," *The Associated Press*, February 9, 1987.
32. Frederick Allen, "Hosea Making Himself Look Ridiculous Again," *Atlanta Journal-Constitution*, February 12, 1987; Jim Nesbitt, "Hosea Williams Says He's Tired of Rejection," *The News and Observer*, March 8, 1987.
33. Larry Copeland, "2 Policemen Suspended in Fatal Shooting: Move Follows

Carver Homes Tenants' Angry Protest Before Council Panel," *Atlanta Journal-Constitution*, September 15, 1987; Adam Gelb, "Protest Set Over Killing by Officer: Citizens Draw Up List of Demands for Mayor," *Atlanta Journal-Constitution*, September 14, 1987.

34. Larry Copeland and Jim Galloway, "2 Suspended Officers Will Stay on Payroll: Medical Examiner Doubts Man Shot at Carver Homes Was Handcuffed," *Atlanta Journal-Constitution*, September 17, 1987; Larry Copeland, "200 March, Decry Callahan's Death," *Atlanta Journal-Constitution*, September 20, 1987; Larry Copeland, "Williams: Mayor Wanted to Scuffle Over Call for Probe," *Atlanta Journal-Constitution*, October 22, 1987; Maurice J. Hobson, *The Legend of the Black Mecca: Politics and Class in the Making of Modern Atlanta* (Chapel Hill: University of North Carolina Press, 2017), 152.
35. Steven Ricks, "Long Cleared in Slaying of Callahan: Courtroom Erupts as Officer Gets Acquittal on Misdemeanor Charge," *Atlanta Journal-Constitution,* November 20, 1987.
36. Bill Montgomery, "Lawyer Blames Klan Leaders for Disrupting Forsyth County March, *Atlanta Journal-Constitution*, September 21, 1988; Bill Montgomery, "Judge Seals Klan Verdict After Williams Seeks to Drop Suit," *Atlanta Journal-Constitution*, October 6, 1988.
37. Lewis Grizzard, "Hosea Proved He's a Better Man Than His Enemies," *Atlanta Journal-Constitution*, October 16, 1988; Tom Teepen, "Hosea Did the Christian Thing, but Court Did Justice's Good Work," *Atlanta Journal-Constitution*, October 27, 1988; Courtlen Burke, "Hosea Has Hit a New Low," *Atlanta Journal-Constitution*, October 26, 1988; Bill Montgomery, "Judge Seals Klan Verdict After Williams Seeks to Drop Suit," *Atlanta Journal-Constitution*, October 6, 1988.
38. Jim Newton and Amy Wallace, "Woman Duped by Williams, Warrant Says: Nightclub Owner Alleges Deception in Loan Deal," *Atlanta Journal-Constitution*, November 23, 1988.
39. Kevin Sack and Larry Copeland, "Williams Steps in to Liven up Mayor's Race," *Atlanta Journal-Constitution,* August 17, 1989.
40. Larry Copeland and Bert Roughton, "4-to-1 Margin Awards Him a Mandate," *Atlanta Journal-Constitution*, October 4, 1989; Hobson, *The Legend of the Black Mecca*, 180.
41. Pomerantz, "Hosea's Truth." *Atlanta Journal.*
42. Gary Pomerantz, "Three Pages in a Book Soured His Last Months and His Link to the Movement," *Atlanta Journal-Constitution,* April 18, 1990; Gary Pomerantz, "Scuffle is Reason Williams Missed Abernathy's Funeral," *Atlanta Journal-Constitution*, April 25, 1990.
43. Douglas A. Blackmon, "Hosea Williams Surprises Dekalb Field, enters Commission Race," *Atlanta Journal-Constitution*, April 27, 1990.
44. Douglas A. Blackmon, "Williams Lashes Maloof: Charges SDekalb Has Been Neglected," *Atlanta Journal-Constitution*, June 15, 1990.
45. Ken Foskett, "Williams Wins Big in Dekalb: Activist Beats Bass, Gets 82% of the Vote," *Atlanta Journal-Constitution*, November 7, 1990; "And Into Nightlife," *Atlanta Journal-Constitution*, December 12, 1990.

46. Mara Rose Williams, "Hot Contest Possible in Dekalb: Board Will Choose Presiding Officer," *Atlanta Journal-Constitution*, January 8, 1991; "Dekalb Commission Elects Officers," *Atlanta Journal-Constitution*, January 9, 1991.
47. Mara Rose Williams, "Williams Recalls Campaigns with King," *Atlanta Journal-Constitution*, January 24, 1991; "Working in Harmony," *Atlanta Journal-Constitution*, January 17, 1991.
48. Douglas A. Blackmon, "Dekalb OK'd Funds to Agency Later Linked to Hosea Williams," *Atlanta Journal-Constitution*, March 7, 1991; Douglas A. Blackmon, "Williams Flap Now May Target Family Firm: Ethics Issue Cited in Dekalb Contract," *Atlanta Journal-Constitution,* March 12, 1991; Douglas A. Blackmon, "Dekalb Handing Williams Case to New Ethics Board," *Atlanta Journal-Constitution*, March 13, 1991; Douglas A. Blackmon, "Ethics Board Drops Probe of Williams," *Atlanta Journal-Constitution*, May 15, 1991; "Dekalb: Commissioners Deny Funding," *Atlanta Journal-Constitution*, December 18, 1991.
49. Douglas A. Blackmon, "Three Bingo Permits Keep Bingo Hall Hopping," *Atlanta Journal-Constitution*, July 21, 1991.
50. Douglas A. Blackmon, "Hosea Williams's Church: Moving in Mysterious Ways," *Atlanta Journal-Constitution*, July 21, 1991.
51. Douglas A. Blackmon, "City, County Contracts Give Family Firms a Boost," *Atlanta Journal-Constitution*, July 12, 1991.
52. Douglas A. Blackmon, "Hosea Williams: 'My Hands are Clean,'" *Atlanta Journal-Constitution*, July 24, 1991; Ken Foskett, "Williams Says Prosecutor is Out to Ruin Him," *Atlanta Journal-Constitution*, August 20, 1991; Chris Dickson, "Williams is Persecuted," *Atlanta Journal-Constitution*, August 4, 1991.
53. Norma Wagner, "Williams Misses Second Meeting, Accused of 'Dereliction of Duty,'" *Atlanta Journal-Constitution*, August 14, 1991; Hosea L. Williams, "Say It Again," *Atlanta Journal-Constitution*, February 20, 1992.
54. Beverly Shepard and Norma Wagner, "Williams Gets 30 Days for Hit-and-Run: Plea Agreement Ensures He Can Stay on Commission," *Atlanta Journal-Constitution*, February 12, 1992; Beverly Shepard, "Resting Up in Jail, Williams Vows to Stay Out of Bars," *Atlanta Journal-Constitution*, February 22, 1992.
55. Beverly Shepard, "Hosea Williams Back in the Swing after Hospital Stay: Says Alcohol Rehab Was Beneficial," *Atlanta Journal-Constitution*, May 5, 1992.
56. Shelley Emling, "Hosea Williams Due for Surgery Today," *Atlanta Journal-Constitution*, February 10, 1993; Shelley Emling, "Williams's Absence Causes Cause Some Concern," *Atlanta Journal-Constitution*, May 26, 1993; "Atlanta: Hosea Williams Stable After Back Surgery," *Atlanta Journal-Constitution*, March 17, 1994.
57. Susan Lacceti, "Civil Rights Leader Says He's Retiring from Politics," *Atlanta Journal-Constitution*, June 24, 1994.
58. Bill Hendrick, untitled article, *Atlanta Journal-Constitution*, September 7, 1997.
59. Kay Powell, "Hosea L. Williams II, 43, Eldest Son of Civil Rights Leader," *Atlanta Journal-Constitution*, September 22, 1998.
60. Gita M. Smith, "Williams Faces Cancer Surgery Today," *Atlanta Journal-Constitution*, October 1, 1999; Gita M. Smith, "Hosea Williams Rests after Cancer

Surgery: Dinner Served: Activist on His Back, but Feed the Hungry Up and Running," *Atlanta Journal-Constitution*, October 2, 1999; Ernie Suggs, "Hungry, Homeless, Get Respite for a Day; Hosea Williams' Group Moves on, Despite His Absence, to Feed 35,000 at Turner Field," *Atlanta Journal-Constitution*, November 26, 1999.

61. Ernie Suggs, "Street Name to Honor Ill Civil Rights Crusader," *Atlanta Constitution*, August 10, 2000.
62. Ernie Suggs, "Hosea Williams, Still Critical, Off Respirator," *Atlanta Journal-Constitution*, November 7, 2000; Ernie Suggs, "Fight is Over for Civil Rights Giant," November 17, 2000.
63. Obituary of Rev. Hosea L. Williams, C. T., and Octavia Vivian Papers, Manuscript, Archives, and Rare Book Library, Emory University, Atlanta, GA; Ernie Suggs, "Farewell to a True Hero, a True Warrior: Advocate for Poor Helped Ignite Nation," *Atlanta Journal-Constitution*, November 21, 2000.

BIBLIOGRAPHY

ARCHIVAL COLLECTIONS

Adams, A. Pratt Jr. Papers. Georgia Historical Society, Savannah, GA.

Boyd, William M. Papers. Archives Division. Auburn Avenue Research Library on African American Culture and History, Atlanta-Fulton Public Library System, Atlanta.

Civil Rights Library of St. Augustine, in Collaboration with Flagler College. St. Augustine, FL.

Johnson, Lyndon Baines. Presidential and Vice-Presidential Papers. Lyndon Baines Johnson Presidential Library, Austin, TX.

Martin Luther King Jr. Center for Nonviolent Social Change. King Library and Archives, Atlanta.

McGill, Ralph. Papers. Manuscript, Archives, and Rare Book Library. Emory University, Atlanta.

National Association for the Advancement of Colored People. Selected Branch Files, 1940–1955. Branch Department Files Geographical File, Savannah, Georgia 1942–1955 (Bethesda, MD: University Publications of America, 1999), Group II, Box C-40.

National Civil Rights Museum. Memphis, TN.

Shores, Arthur D. Papers. Birmingham Civil Rights Institute Archives. Birmingham, AL.

Southern Christian Leadership Conference Records. Manuscript, Archives, and Rare Book Library, Emory University, Atlanta.

Southern Regional Council Program Files. Manuscript, Archives, and Rare Book Library. Emory University.

Williams Emerson, Barbara. Papers. Stone Mountain, GA.

Williams, Hosea L. Papers. Archives Division. Auburn Avenue Research Library on African-American Culture and History, Atlanta-Fulton Public Library System, Atlanta.

Vivian, C. T., and Octavia. Papers. Commercial microfilm. Manuscript, Archives, and Rare Book Library, Emory University, Atlanta.

ORAL HISTORIES

Bevel, James. Interview by James A. DeVinney for Eyes on the *Prize: America's Civil Rights Years (1954–1965)*, Washington University Libraries, Film and Media Archive, Henry Hampton Collection, November 13, 1985.

Bolden, Willie. "Fireside Chat with the Williams Family and Civil Rights Activists," Panel discussion, Atlanta City Council, February 17, 2014.

Brooks, Tyrone. Interviews by author, Atlanta, April 17, 2014.

Carmichael, Stokely. Interview by Judy Richardson for *Eyes on the Prize: America's Civil Rights Years (1954–1965)*, Washington University Libraries, Film and Media Archives. Henry Hampton Collection, November 7, 1988.

Dinkins, William. Interview by Blackside, Inc., for *Eyes on the Prize: America's Civil Rights Years (1954–1965)*, Washington University Libraries, Film and Media Archive, Henry Hampton Collection, September 17, 1979.

Graetz, Robert S. Telephone interview by author, Montgomery, AL, July 8, 2011.

Hayling, Robert. Interview by Andrew Young, Civil Rights Library of St. Augustine, Gainesville, FL, n.d.

Jenkins, Victoria. Telephone interview by author, Lithonia, GA, September 14, 2014.

Lawson, James. Telephone interview by author, Lithonia, GA, May 7, 2014.

Shuttlesworth, Fred. Interview by David Colburn, Civil Rights Library of St. Augustine, Gainesville, FL, n.d.

Vivian, C. T. Telephone interview by author, Lithonia, GA, May 14, 2014.

Washington, Annie Rae. In-person interview by author, Attapulgus, GA, April 1, 2014.

Williams, Hosea L. Interview by Taylor Branch, Atlanta. Transcript. Hosea L. Williams Papers. Archives Division. Auburn Avenue Research Library on African-American Culture and History, Atlanta-Fulton Public Library System. Atlanta, October 29, 1991.

Williams, Emmogene. Telephone interview by the author, Lithonia, GA, September 14, 2014.

Wise, Leopold. In-person interview by author, Attapulgus, GA, March 31, 2014.

PUBLISHED SOURCES

Abernathy, Ralph D. *And the Walls Came Tumbling Down*. New York: Harper and Row, 1989.

Anderson, Alan B., and George Pickering. *Confronting the Color Line: The Broken Promise of the Civil Rights Movement in Chicago*. Athens: University of Georgia Press, 1986.

Anderson, James D. *The Education of Blacks in the South, 1860–1935*. Chapel Hill: University of North Carolina Press, 1988.

Anderson, William. *The Wild Man from Sugar Creek: The Political Career of Eugene Talmadge*. Baton Rouge: Louisiana State University Press, 1975.

Ashmore, Susan Youngblood. *Carry It On: The War on Poverty and the Civil Rights Movement in Alabama, 1964–1972*. Athens: University of Georgia Press, 2008.

Bartley, Numan V. *The Rise of Massive Resistance: Race and Politics in the South During the 1950s*. Baton Rouge: Louisiana State University Press, 1969.

———. "Social Change and Sectional Identity," *The Journal of Southern History* 61, no. 1 (February 1995): 3–16.

Bass, Jack. *Taming the Storm: The Life and Times of Judge Frank M. Johnson Jr. and the South's Fight Over Civil Rights*. New York: Doubleday, 1992.

Bevel, Helen L. *James Bevel and the Nonviolent Right to Vote Movement*. Chicago: The Institute for the Study and Advancement of Nonviolence, 2009.

Branch, Taylor. *Parting the Waters: America in the King Years, 1954–1963*. New York: Simon & Schuster, 1988.

———. *At Canaan's Edge: America in the King Years, 1965–1968*. New York: Simon and Schuster, 2006.

Brundage, W. Fitzhugh. *Lynching in the New South: Georgia and Virginia, 1880–1930*. Champaign: University of Illinois Press, 1993.

Buchanan, Scott E. *Some of the People Who Ate My Barbeque Didn't Vote for Me: The Life of Georgia Governor Marvin Griffin*. Nashville, TN: Vanderbilt University Press, 2011.

Caro, Robert A. *Master of the Senate: The Years of Lyndon Johnson*. New York: Random House, 2002.

Carter, Dan T. *The Politics of Rage: George Wallace, the Origins of the New Conservatism and the Transformation of American Politics*. New York: Simon and Schuster, 1995.

Carter, David C. *The Music Has Gone Out of the Movement: Civil Rights and the Johnson Administration, 1965–1968*. Chapel Hill: University of North Carolina Press, 2009.

Chafe, William. *Civilities and Civil Rights: Greensboro, North Carolina and the Struggle for Black Freedom*. Oxford, England: Oxford University Press, 1979.

Colburn, David. *Racial Change and Community Crisis: St. Augustine, Florida, 1877–1980*. New York: Columbia University Press, 1985.

Conant, James Bryant. *Theodore William Richards: January 31, 1868–April 2, 1928*. Washington, DC: National Academy of Sciences, 1974.

Decatur County Historical Society. *Decatur County Georgia: Past and Present, 1823–1991*. Roswell, GA: W. H. Wolfe Associates, 1991.

Dittmer, John. *Black Progressives in Georgia, 1900–1920*. Chicago: University of Illinois Press, 1980.

———. *Local People: The Struggle for Civil Rights in Mississippi*. Chicago: University of Illinois Press, 1994.

Du Bois, William Edward Burkhardt. *The Negro Church*. Atlanta: Atlanta University Press, 1903.

Eskew, Glenn T. *But for Birmingham: The Local and National Movements in the Civil Rights Struggle*. Chapel Hill: University of North Carolina Press, 1997.

Fairclough, Adam. *To Redeem the Soul of America: The Southern Christian Leadership Conference and Martin Luther King Jr.* Athens: University of Georgia Press, 1987.

Finkle, Lee. "The Conservative Aims of Militant Rhetoric: Black Protest During World War II." *The Journal of American History* 6, no. 3 (Dec. 1973): 692–713.

Fite, Gilbert C. *Richard B. Russell: Senator from Georgia*. Chapel Hill: University of North Carolina Press, 1991.

Flynt, Wayne. *Alabama in the Twentieth Century*. Tuscaloosa: University of Alabama Press, 2004.

Franklin, John Hope, and Alfred A. Moss Jr. *From Slavery to Freedom: A History of African Americans*, 8th ed. New York: McGraw-Hill, 2000.

Frazier, E. Franklin. *Black Bourgeoisie*. New York: Free Press Paperbacks, 1957.

Garrow, David J. *Bearing the Cross: Martin Luther King, Jr. and the Southern Christian Leadership Conference*. New York: HarperCollins, 1999.

Goudsouzian, Aram. *Down the Crossroads: Civil Rights Black Power and the Meredith March Against Fear*. New York: Farrar, Straus and Giroux, 2014.

Hodgson, Godfrey. *America in Our Time*. Garden City, NY: Doubleday and Co., 1976.

Honey, Michael K. *Going Down Jericho Road: The Memphis Strike, Martin Luther King's Last Campaign*. New York: W. W. Norton and Co., 2007.

———. *To the Promised Land: Martin Luther King and the Fight for Economic Justice.* New York: W. W. Norton, 2018.

Holmes, William F. "Civil Rights, 1890–1940," in *A History of Georgia*, ed. Kenneth Coleman, 277–294. Athens: University of Georgia Press, 1991.

Horton, Myles, Herbert Kohl, and Judith Kohl. *The Long Haul: An Autobiography.* New York: Teacher's College Press of Columbia University, 1998.

Jeffries, Hasan. *Bloody Lowndes: Civil Rights and Black Power in Alabama's Black Belt.* New York: New York University Press, 2009.

Joseph, Peniel. *Waiting 'Til the Midnight Hour: A Narrative History of Black Power in America.* New York: Henry Holt and Co., 2006.

———. *Stokely: A Life.* New York: Basic Civitas Books, 2014.

K'Meyer, Tracy E. *Civil Rights in the Gateway of the South: Louisville, Kentucky, 1945–1980.* Lexington: University Press of Kentucky, 2009.

Key, V. O. Jr. *Southern Politics in State and Nation.* New York: Alfred A. Knopf, 1949.

Kennedy, David. *Freedom from Fear: The American People in Depression and War, 1929–1945.* New York: Oxford University Press, 1999.

Kotz, Nick. *Judgment Days: Lyndon Baines Johnson, Martin Luther King, Jr. and The Laws.* New York: Houghton-Mifflin, 2005.

Kwilecki, Paul. *One Place and Four Decades of Photographs from Decatur County, Georgia.* Chapel Hill: University of North Carolina Press, 2013.

Kruse, Kevin. *White Flight: Atlanta and the Making of Modern Conservatism.* Princeton, NJ: Princeton University Press, 2005.

Laurent, Sylvie. *King and the Other America: The Poor People's Campaign and the Quest for Economic Equality.* Oakland: University of California Press, 2018.

Lawson, Steven F. *Black Ballots: Voting Rights in the South, 1944–1969.* New York: Columbia University Press, 1976.

Lawson, Steven F. and Charles Payne. *Debating the Civil Rights Movement, 1945–1968.* New York: Rowan and Littlefield, 2006.

Lewis, John. *Walking with the Wind: A Memoir of the Movement.* New York: Harcourt, Brace & Co., 1998.

Livingston, Mayo Jr. *The Story of Decatur County's Carpet of Green and Gold: Turpentining, 1889–1968.* Bainbridge, GA: Post Printing, 1996.

Maclean, Nancy. *Behind the Mask of Chivalry: The Making of the Second Ku Klux Klan.* New York: Oxford University Press, 1994.

Matusow, Allen. *The Unraveling of America: A History of Liberalism in the 1960s.* Athens: University of Georgia Press, 1984.

Mays, Benjamin E. *Born to Rebel: An Autobiography.* Athens: University of Georgia Press, 1971.

McGuire, Philip. "Desegregation of the Armed Forces: Black Leadership, Protest and World War II." *The Journal of Negro History* 68, no. 2 (Spring 1983): 2–35.

McMillan, Malcolm C. *Constitutional Development in Alabama, 1798–1901: A Study in Politics, The Negro, and Sectionalism.* Chapel Hill: University of North Carolina Press, 1955.

McKnight, Gerald D. *The Last Crusade: Martin Luther King, Jr., the FBI, and the Poor People's Campaign.* Boulder, CO: Westview Press, 1998.

Meier, August and Elliot Rudwick. "The Boycott Movement Against Jim Crow

Streetcars, 1900–1906." *The Journal of American History* 55, no. 4 (March 1969): 756–775.

Morris, Aldon. "Black Southern Student Sit-In Movement: An Analysis of Internal Organization." *American Sociological Review* 46, no. 6 (December 1981): 744–767.

Motley, Constance B. *Equal Justice Under Law: An Autobiography*. New York: Farrar, Straus and Giroux, 1998.

National Emergency Council. *Report on Economic Conditions of the South*. Washington, DC: US Government Printing Office, 1938.

Payne, Charles. *I've Got the Light of Freedom: The Organizing Tradition of the Mississippi Freedom Struggle*. Los Angeles: University of California Press, 1995.

Pepper, William F. *Orders to Kill: The Truth Behind the Murder of Martin Luther King Jr.* New York: Warner Books, 1995.

Polk, Ralph Lane. *Polk's City of Savannah Directory*. Detroit, MI: R.L. Polk & Co., 1952.

Rabby, Glenda Alice. *The Pain and the Promise: The Struggle for Civil Rights in Tallahassee, Florida*. Athens: The University of Georgia Press, 1999.

Rabinowitz, Howard N. "From Exclusion to Segregation: Southern Race Relations, 1865–1890." *The Journal of American History*, 63, no. 2 (September 1976): 325–350.

Ralph, James R. Jr. *Northern Protest: Martin Luther King Jr., Chicago, and the Civil Rights Movement*. Cambridge, MA: Harvard University Press, 1993.

Ransby, Barbara. *Ella Baker and the Black Freedom Movement: A Radical Democratic Vision*. Chapel Hill: University of North Carolina Press, 2003.

Robinson, Jo Ann, ed. *Montgomery Improvement Association Newsletter*. July 26, 1956, Vol. 1, no. 3.

Rödelsperger, K., B. Brückel, J. Manke, H. J. Woitowitz, and F. Pott. "Potential Health Risks from the Use of Fibrous Mineral Absorption Granulates," *British Journal of Industrial Medicine*, 44, no. 5 (May 1987): 337–343.

Ryan, Yvonne. *Roy Wilkins: The Quiet Revolutionary and the NAACP*. Lexington: University Press of Kentucky, 2014.

Shattuck, Gardner H. *Episcopalians and Race: Civil War to Civil Rights*. Lexington: University Press of Kentucky, 2000.

Shearer, Todd Miller. *Daily Demonstrators: The Civil Rights Movement in Mennonite Homes and Sanctuaries*. Baltimore: Johns Hopkins University Press, 2010.

Sitkoff, Harvard. *King: Pilgrimage to the Mountaintop*. New York: Hill and Wang, 2007.

Smith, Suzanne. *To Serve the Living: Funeral Directors and the African American Way of Death*. Cambridge, MA: Harvard University Press, 2010.

Sorensen, Ted. *Counselor: A Life at the Edge of History*. New York: HarperCollins, 2008.

Spaulding, Phinizy. "Oglethorpe and the Founding of Georgia," in *A History of Georgia*, ed. Kenneth Coleman, 16–24. Athens: University of Georgia Press, 1991.

Stephan, John J. *Hawaii Under the Rising Sun: Japan's Plans for Conquest after Pearl Harbor*. Honolulu: University of Hawaii Press, 1996.

Sullivan, Patricia. *Lift Every Voice: The NAACP and the Making of the Civil Rights Movement*. New York: The New Press, 2009.

Taylor, Alan. *American Colonies: The Settlement of North America*. New York: Penguin Books, 2001.

Tindall, George B. *The Emergence of the New South, 1913-1945*. Baton Rouge: Louisiana State University Press, 1967.

Tuck, Stephen G. N. *Beyond Atlanta: The Struggle for Racial Equality in Georgia, 1940–1980*. Athens: University of Georgia Press, 2001.

Wilmore, Gayraud S. *Black Religion and Black Radicalism*. Garden City, NY: Doubleday Anchor, 1973.

Woodson, Carter G. *History of the Negro Church*. Washington, DC: Associated Publishers, 1921.

Woodward, C. Vann. *Origins of the New South, 1877–1913*. Baton Rouge: Louisiana State University Press, 1951.

———. *Sharing the Prize: The Economics of the Civil Rights Revolution in the South*. Cambridge, MA: Harvard University Press, 2013.

Wynes, Charles E. "Postwar Economic Development," in *A History of Georgia*, ed. Kenneth Coleman, 225–237. Athens: University of Georgia Press, 1991.

Young, Andrew. *An Easy Burden: The Civil Rights Movement and the Transformation of America*. New York: HarperCollins Publishers, 1996.

PERIODICALS AND SERIALS

Atlanta Constitution
Atlanta Daily World
Atlanta Journal
Atlanta Journal–Constitution
Atlanta Weekly
Baltimore African American
Chicago Daily Defender
Chicago Defender
Crusader
Cullman Democrat
Daytona Beach News Journal
Desoto Times Tribune
Florida Star
Gentleman's Magazine
Herald
New York Times
Pittsburgh Courier
Post-Search Light
Savannah Evening News
Savannah Herald
Savannah Morning News
Savannah Tribune
Southern Courier
Ukiah Daily Journal
United Press International

INDEX

Please note that *italicized* page numbers in this index refer to illustrations.